MY
CORNER
OF
THE SKY!

My Corner Of The Sky!

Though I never expected life to be quite like this!

By KERRI DYER-KEEN

iUniverse, Inc.
New York Bloomington

My Corner of the Sky
Though I never expected life to be quite like this!

iUniverse books may be ordered through booksellers or by contacting:

iUniverse
1663 Liberty Drive
Bloomington, IN 47403
www.iuniverse.com
1-800-Authors (1-800-288-4677)

ISBN: 978-1-4502-2664-6 (sc)
ISBN: 978-1-4502-2665-3 (ebook)

Printed in the United States of America

iUniverse rev. date: 5/28/2010

DISCLAIMER

I WAS TOLD THAT I SHOULD SAY THAT SOME OF THE NAMES IN THIS STORY HAVE BEEN CHANGED TO PROTECT THE GUILTY.

NOT TRUE - NO ONE IS REALLY GUILTY OF ANYTHING!

WHAT HAPPENED – HAPPENED!

SOME OF THE NAMES ARE GENUINE, *(especially the showbiz names. Showbiz people like seeing nice things being said about them in print!)*

BUT EVEN THOUGH NAMES HAVE BEEN CHANGED, THE ACTUAL THINGS DONE OR SAID MAY NOT HAVE BEEN.

NO SENSE OF BLAME OR RECRIMINATION IS FELT TOWARDS ANY BODY IN THE STORY – NOT ANYMORE, ANYWAY!

EVERYBODY, INCLUDING ME MYSELF, DID THE BEST THAT THE CIRCUMSTANCES OF THE TIME ALLOWED FOR.

LIFE IS JUST TOO WONDERFUL, AND PRECIOUS FOR ME TO WASTE EVEN ONE MINUTE OF IT IN RECRIMINATION. OR REGRET!

Please - JUST ENJOY BEING ALIVE

IN YOUR OWN SPECIAL CORNER OF THE SKY!!!

KERRI DYER-KEEN

FOREWORD

The Australian Ladies Variety Association was formed at the Inaugural Banquet in 1979 by a group of fifty charter members being of the NSW Australia variety entertainment industry. Toni Stevens and Harriet Littlesmith based this association on the British one, also asking Dame Vera Lynn to be our first Patron.

The aim of our association was to unite the females of the industry, female variety artists and the wives of male artists to form a charity to assist the sick and elderly within the theatrical industry.

A.L.V.A. was formed, by laws written and Government permission given to our charity status.

Kerri Dyer was a charter member and we started our first year with luncheons, meetings and our first fundraiser was a Mississippi costumed Paddle Wheeler event in May 1979 on the Lane Cove River complete with jazz band.

Kerri was a wonderful talent. She had been singing in clubs and was regularly appearing on variety shows on television. The 'Star' factor was there ahead of her.

Then in July of that year Kerri had a horrific car accident. A.L.V.A. went into action to help where we could. Toni Stevens, our first president, brought all of her wonderful skills to the fore and assisted Kerri like no other.

A.L.V.A. has continued to help over the last thirty years in many ways – from accommodation, paying medical bills, buying medical equipment, helping people stay in their own homes with homecare and generally paying bills when our people are in need.

In the last ten years alone A.L.V.A. has helped in these small ways to the tune of three hundred and fifty six thousand dollars. Our girls have worked very hard, holding functions, balls, race days, running Art Unions for years selling tickets in shopping centres to raise money to help in our community.

When Kerri received her settlement she gave a generous donation to A.L.V.A. and on an occasion last year 2009, when she was in Australia, she was our guest speaker and entertained us at one of our luncheons by singing and telling newer members her story. Once again helping us to raise money to help those less fortunate.

Seeing Kerri after her accident in 1979 one would never have believed that what we see before us today would ever have been be possible.

Kerri's determination and courage makes us all look forward to reading her story.

Pat Scroope A.L.V.A. Inc. Benevolent Treasurer Susie Smithers- 2009/10 Queen Bee

www.alva.org.au

FIRST OF ALL THIS HERE BOOK SHOULD POSSIBLY COME WITH A BIT OF A HEALTH WARNING!

Just as it has been said that Kerri Dyer-Keen was a bit of a hard work girlfriend, wife, and mother,

some have also said that this is unfortunately a bit of a hard work book as well.

And why is that you ask? Well, let's see if that is true shall we!

Kerri has written the whole book by herself, even though the powers that be – doctors and things, told her - "You won't be able to do that".

But Kerri being Kerri, said she that could, would, and did!

Although she has not really adhered to any of the 'old world' rules about how to write a book the 'correct' way, she has done it, never the less!

She hopes that you won't be put off by her pigheadedness, and will find it an interesting, if not mad story of her life.

But most of all she hopes that you find it – a good giggle, and a 'jolly good read'!

Even though life has chosen not to treat her according to any sane rules, her life has, all the angst aside been not too bad at all!

She hopes you enjoy your trip through 'My Corner of the Sky'!

Kerri also says - *(a bit mouthy, isn't she?)* "My innate love of music and entertainment formed the basis of what some might call, my 'different' personality, and I ask you to take life by the throat, just as I did the flea ridden monkey you will read about later, and enjoy both life, and this book to the full!

At 15 a school opera, Hansel and Gretel came along.

"Nibble, nibble, mousekin, who's nibbling at my housekin?!

Aha! My first nibble at success!

When I left school at 16 a differently -normal state existed for a year or two - and then it was - 'Hello showbiz'!

Nearly ten 'different' years of youthful fun and treading the boards followed with the 'speculation' made during those years definitely looking as though it was just about ready to accumulate, when something unexpected and horrible happened.

Having been unconscious for four and a half months, I horrendously found myself

no longer needing to learn the complicated dance steps I had just been learning.

I then needed to learn how to live – that's all! All over again!

I was no better than a 29 year old baby!

But re-learn how to live – I definitely eventually did!

Nowadays I have a new husband - a new country - and have had a baby girl that a disabled 38 year old wasn't supposed to be able to have"! I have actually watched her grow up, to her present 21 years of age!

Now at nearly 60 years of age myself, I still hanker after what I used to be and have. I know that it can never be, but it has inevitably become for me,

a continuing true story of triumph over adversity!

As the papers said at the time of the accident -
"Read all about it"!

So how about you do just that?

I say with a big smile on my face-

please -

"ENJOY YOUR TRIP THROUGH **MY CORNER OF THE SKY**"!

When I was very young, I wished for a different life - Ha!
That should teach me to be careful what I wish for!

"And just why do you say that", do I hear you ask?

Well how about I let you know.

This is my book, about myself and what I feel are my three lives!

I may be someone you don't yet know,
but someone that I hope you will learn to like, and laugh with.

This book is written as I speak and as I related all these, what I consider 'normal' incidents, to my morning coffee girl friends here in Ashford, Kent, England.

I am just a 'normal' lady, with a bit of a different story to tell!
I hope that in some small way it may help any of you who struggle, even apparently against all odds!

I have to admit that this book may seem childlike at times from a woman of almost sixty, but I feel that:-

"That exact quality of childish wonderment at my own
Corner of the Sky of life, makes the book and myself,
just that little bit 'DIFFERENT'"!!!

Me doing my job, just a week before the accident
that changed my life!

Kerri Dyer was an entertainer who was in a car accident in Australia in 1979. She was unconscious for four and a half months, and according to medical evidence was supposed to die. Which she probably actually did!

An out of body experience apparently firstly sent her to 'the gate', but she honestly feels that nearly 30 years ago she was 'sent back' for some reason,

Only God, knows WHY!

You might see words in this book that appear to be incorrectly spelled.

She though, is Australian/British, and each country spells its own way!

So using the spell checker, set for the relevant country, the words are right!

Kerri says that at almost 60, she realises the old need for conformity,

but says that she is now part of a new century.

The age of individuality!

And Kerri is (unfortunately?) a true 'individual'!

This book shows us that!

"Shouldn't I be free to wander at will in my own garden?", is what she has been asking since she was a child!

But after her accident, she now asks -

"Am I now not allowed to share my own individual, yet absolute love of life?"

No one else has written any of this book for her!

("That is probably why it has taken me 29 years odd"!)

For that reason you will also find some 'made up' words to fit the circumstances at the time, as Kerri cheekily believes that;

"Even as with the great painters, everyone paints/writes in their own individual styles"!

Oh don't Panic!. She doesn't feel that she is at all comparable to great painters, but she does write in her own individual style, just as she performed 'pretty successfully', in her own inimitable way when she took to a stage to sing, in Australia and the East, all those years ago!

The made up words, and some of the spellings in this book may seem a bit odd,

and again Kerri says "sorry", but trusts that you will forgive, ignore, and asks you again to sit back, relax, and enjoy your trip through -

'MY CORNER OF THE SKY'!!

"Hello there big boy"!

"My first thanks must go to Toni Stevens/McClean, the original
founder of ALVA,
Susie Smithers the 2008/9/10 president, the past and future
presidents,
Pat Scroope the benevolent treasurer, Faye Warnock,

Margaret Flanagan, oh – and just all of the other lovely ladies of The Australian Ladies Variety Association Inc."

An extract from a 1980 ALVA Buzz
"The first A.L.V.A. HONOURS Award was presented to Kerri Dyer in 1980 for her bravery and determination following her accident."

Without ALVA's help and encouragement from my 'almost death' in 1979, my post accident time and beyond would have been far less productive than it has actually turned out to be!

Having devoted nearly ten years to singing,

I was amazed when I couldn't talk or sing at all after the accident!

I am still finding it really difficult to sing all that well.

But as you will read,

I am determined, even at nearly 60, to sing properly again!

Why? I can't really say!

I know my voice will never be as it once was of course - I have lost that!

But when I think about it now, I would have to say that I have still been a very fortunate unfortunate lady. How so?

Well! Fortunate firstly because of the result of my court case,

even though it was over 30 years ago, and pre recession.

Secondly, I have been very fortunate in my friends, my family, and the events of my third life

A lot of good things have happened along side of the bad things, and ALVA was always there for me when I lived in Australia. Alright, maybe not always physically now, but they have been there from the very start in a variety of ways, and have always played a big part in the new found happiness of my life!

I guess that you could genuinely say that - ALVA, REALLY IS THE AUSTRALIAN LADIES <u>VARIETY</u> ASSOCIATION!

Another ALVA Buzz extract:-

"Our first combined endeavour for a member in acute distress was to help our colleague,

Kerri Dyer, who was badly hurt in a terrible car accident in July 1979.

Kerri needed ongoing care, but when finally she arrived home from hospital, ALVA members and others, were on hand to help clean her house, sort out her affairs, and look after her basic needs. We were also on hand to help her move when the time came for her to relocate to a disabled home. Happily, Kerri defied all notions of "never being able to do many things again", (including) talking so that we could understand what she was trying to say; walking more normally; having a child; and driving a car. In 1999 she settled in England with her new husband and daughter, and is doing well!"

"ALVA will always have my utmost thanks!"

Before I really get stuck into the story though, my effusive thanks must also go to Ali and Lynne, two ladies who have put up with my ramblings since I moved to England 20 years ago. They have shared three hundred or so fried egg breakfasts and panini afternoon teas with me so far. They and the iUniverse team have also done a big part of the necessary editing needed before printing, and I hope that you will, and they have all thoroughly enjoyed reading about the madness of my former life!

Ali

Lynne

Oh – yeah, that's right! Almost forgot!

(Which unfortunately I still do a lot of.)

I mustn't forget my long suffering, patient and understanding husband, Edmund Keen - Definitely mustn't forget him! He has been my absolute rock, a solid arm to lean on and has been absolutely phenomenal!!

Without everyone's patience and encouragement over the last 30 years,

I don't think that I would ever have got to this point -

My gratitude will be eternal, and then some!!!!!!!!!!!!!!!!!!!!!!

If you are fortunate, as I guess I was,

you live a fairly 'normal' and yet different kind of childhood.

I then found myself catapulted slowly *(that's if you **can** catapult slowly),* into the exciting world of Showbiz.

For nigh on ten years I thoroughly enjoyed my chosen life path as an entertainer.

From behind the curtains this voice would begin singing -

"Rivers belong where they can ramble -etc.------ and then on the word SKY"-

out I would come!

Very popular it was too, even if I do say so myself!

'The Dyer had arrived', you might say!

Just as I was about to grab the ultimate ring of success, a catastrophic,

life changing accident came at me from out of the blue!

Stardom', which had once been so close, was no longer attainable.

"In the split second that it takes for a set of lights to change, I suddenly found

myself grappling, believe it or not - no longer for that ring of success -

but for - **SURVIVAL"**!

FROM THE AUTHOR!

Almost ready to go, and as much as I hate to start on a 'downer',
I have a confession to make! As I said, I have never written a book
before.

I was a singer, singing words that somebody else wrote!

I was 'good with the chat' maybe, but never have been that creative
with words, me!

Oh, and also this can't be a fully true autobiography. I would
probably be sued –

or else lose some really good friends!!

And anyway, I was asleep for most of the doings of the first chapter,
and even for some of the second.

'Out of it' you might say!

"So I have had to surmise some conversations from what I have been
told happened! I have also tried to make what I do remember of what
must have been an horrendous time for everyone, into more of an
interesting story - so you might say that this is a semi- biographical
story based on 'a true tale of triumph over adversity'"!

(What a mouthful!)

But please don't let that put you off ! All the growing up bits, and the
showbiz parts, are *shamefully(?)* 100% true. But I have had to guess,
or emphasise some things about the 'in hospital time', and yes, I
have to admit it - even enlarge a few other little things along the way,
purely to add a touch of humour or drama in to the true story of what
has certainly been an interesting, and very unusual life!

Entertainment is in my blood, and I believe that even books should
be an entertaining read. This one, I think and hope, is!

All that aside though – the hospital time was still the most harrowing
time of my life. Believe you me! And although I must always have
been looking for that something different in my life, my *last, and
luckily, forever something different* has proven to be far more than even
I had ever previously bargained for. It has been positively delightful!

At least I think so! My life is now beautiful most of the time, but it is still perpetually different with my Ed.

My own name, and a few other names which are used with permission, and for the sake of verifiable honesty, are the genuine ones, and although some of the names in this book are fictional, *(often to make life more pleasant for those actually involved)* the people that those fictional names represent, however, may not be.

Unfortunately, nor is what they did, or didn't get up to!

(Here we go!)

(On our way!)

Those of you who will have known of Kerri Dyer, and were around in Australia at the time in 1979, *(which by the way would probably be a minuscule number in the scheme of things after all this time)*, might think that you can probably guess the correct names of the people involved.

All I want to say to you all, after all this time is that this book was not written to intentionally, harm or demonise anyone. It has mainly been a work of therapeutic value for a brain damaged me, and is my way of hopefully leaving a continuing legacy to my much loved show biz's ALVA!

The circumstances of the accident were to be honest, not always nice!,

But I want you all to know that *everybody did the best they could at the time.*

To tell the truth it has even taken *me* all this time to deal with it!

And yes, believe it or not, even those that may appear to be 'villains of the piece', also did the best they could at the time! Sometimes just writing the facts as they happened can create a damning impression of blame.

But take it from me though, and I was after all, there;

No criticism is intended, implied or for that matter felt;

Not any more, anyway!

Of course, I hope that you will agree with me,

the Doctors and Nurses did a FANTASTIC job!

(We'll get there soon – Promise!!)

They had kept me alive, and eventually sent me home in a wheelchair
-*(just in case, mind you! Didn't want me falling down straight away, and
undoing all their good work now did they?)*

The staff had diligently taught me to 'walk'(?) kind of and were
moderately pleased with their success. They were thrilled to see me
leave as well as I was at that time *(which probably wasn't all that well;
not compared to 2009; thirty years on)*, but they all blew me kisses and
wished me a good and happy life!

*(Of course, if they hadn't done such a good job, I wouldn't be here
today to write this book - would I)?* So all I can say — is **well done** to
everyone who was involved!

(If you read this book, then you'll know who you were!)

Even though I have been told by some, that some of the names were
changed to protect the guilty, I actually changed a lot of the names
and places in order to protect the true identity of some of the main
players. *(Not the Showbiz stars though! They love seeing their name and
photos in 'nice' things. It comes with the territory!)* And besides, I no
longer feel that anyone is really 'guilty' of much at all! Life is Life!

In nearly 60 years I have learned that life 'don't always go as you
would like'!

I would have to say though, that having been lucky enough to have
come through all the strife, happy and now confident and well loved,
I wanted to try and offer encouragement to anyone else who might
find themselves in a similar yet 'different', situation. Thus this book!

All things are possible, even those things that sometimes seem jolly
unlikely!

Judgments about a time, or of things that occur can only be made in
conjunction with actual happenings, can't they?

And all I can say now, from the comfort of my lovely home, with
my husband supposedly watching athletics on the TV but snoring
his head off on the couch; with my twenty one year old daughter on
a break from Uni, and busy in the kitchen; and me typing on the
computer keyboard,

is that I am ecstatically happy that I feel that we all must have made the correct judgments back in 79-88 – eventually.

(Here - we definitely go this time!!! Hooray!)

"WHERE AM I"?

This chapter is what I have been told went on, and the conversations are based on what I was told me by some of the nursing staff, and also what I thought I heard!
I guess that I wasn't actually there! But my body was!

"I hate to say it Dr. Andrews, but if there is no obvious sign of improvement either today or tomorrow, then I am afraid that, for her quality of life, we'll need to talk to her next of kin about the desirability or not, of disconnecting her life support machine. After all, it has been about *(he paused and looked at the charts)* three months with absolutely nothing happening", said Dr. Davies.

"There have been no signs of any improvement. Unfortunately none at all, and not wanting to seem crass, we have a busy case load coming up, and could do with the intensive care bed"! An oppressive air of depression, stealthily wafted through the small, busy ward.

The patient in the bed had been admitted under emergency situations about three months before, and although the body had no blatantly obvious injuries, the 28yr old, now plugged into the life support machine, had been just lying there. For three long months, apart from the time that the medical staff had been moving her about busy trying to save her life, she had just lain there deathly still, majestically doing a big fat nothing! Not even the unannounced, unwanted, arrival of a mosquito, into that meticulously sterile ward had caused so much as a twitch to be evidenced. The patient, Mrs O, had apparently not heard, or seen anything at all. For the mosquito though, I guess it was a bit like 'meals on the wing'. *(Well, after all - they don't have wheels, now do they?)* She had even moved hospitals without knowing that the workers were there.

Patients, unconscious as she was, are normally continually monitored by medical instruments, so the machine attached to her body throughout the whole procedure, went on with it's regular, usual be-ep! - be-ep! - be-ep! Then - all of a sudden the machine squeaked very loudly, and in a totally different mood! - it just about screamed at the ward!

Bee-eep! -- Bee-eep! -- bee-eep!

That extended noise definitely heralded change!

The staff had been anxiously waiting for signs of improvement for three long months, so the excitement around the bed was positively palpable. They had all been so worried that the body in the bed might not come round at all. They had done their best, which had been masterful to be sure, and doctors and nurses hated to lose patients under any circumstances!

According to their assessment of the situation, the body in the bed, had not been even remotely aware of anything that was going on at the time

(Is that so? I wonder! - Aw, I am so sorry! I am told that I shouldn't really put my own two cents worth in, but I can't help it! This is after all my story, and I have always been a bit of a nosy biddy. I do like to help out if I can. People can't possibly know what it was really like unless I do interrupt occasionally. Well alright, I will be honest, will I? More than occasionally then!)

Maybe I had heard them saying they were thinking of ringing Andy and my parents, and discussing with them, the practicality or not, of 'pulling the plug', and just letting me drift away. I know that I must have thought *(if what I was doing at that stage could be classed as thinking!)*, "am I in a bath"? It didn't feel like it, it wasn't wet, and what is more, there was definitely no breeze! *(How could I 'just drift away', and what did they mean by 'plug'?*

I promise you in advance of this next bit, that I am *not* some sort of 'nutter', and that it has taken me, myself quite a while to mentally accept what did actually happen, and is not just a figment of my imagination! It was an extremely believable dream that I had, apparently just prior to

2

coming too. I believed at the time leading up to the accident, that you lived, hopefully being thoughtful to others, yet also hopefully having a good time while you were alive. Then you died! Finito! Kapput!

Oh sure - I had believed in a God, and eternal life after death. But only if "you were a good girl". I had though decided by the time of the accident that He wouldn't want to have had anything much to do with the likes of me. I mean, after all I had severely failed on the few attempts that I had previously made at it, *(being part of his select club, I mean)*. I had been a 'Sally' *(in the Salvation Army)*, but I had left when I took up showbiz, and after that I don't think that it could even remotely be said that I was ever a model candidate for His 'elite' club membership.

(Again - you'll read why, if you continue reading.)

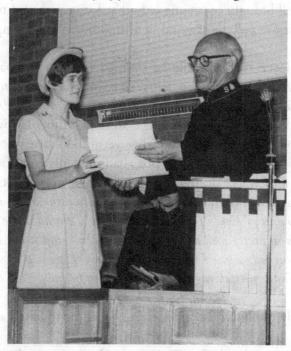

About 1966 enrolement in Salvation army, Summer Uniform.

When I sit quietly, and force myself to remember, *(which is still not always a nice thing to do)*, I can actually feel and sense myself rising ethereally from the bed. I come to a gentle stop, facing two great big gates. They are clear glass gates, that for some reason I couldn't see through in order to get a look at the world behind them *(They may as well have been solid metal, for all that they were about to let me see!)*

What they were the gates to, as I said, I couldn't really see! I timidly walked towards them, and an old gentleman matter of factly boomed out at me, - "name"?

He was glancing sideways, and looking totally disinterested in it all. His long, white, almost translucent hair, hung limply over his shoulders as he impatiently tapped his foot. *("Now I ask you", I must have said to myself - "Hasn't he ever learned the word please"?)*

I was taught to at least say please, and thank you! Just where had this 'thing' been brought *(or dragged)* up? His colourless, voice matched his pallid entity. At first I felt a bit put out, but not really knowing what I was doing there, or how I got there in the first place and in an effort to be the well brought up young lady that I was supposed to be *(note, I said supposed to be!)*, I answered in a timorous voice, saying,-- "Kerri Dyer."

Utter silence ensued while he shuffled through the pages of his book! *(And I am hear to tell you, that for some reason, that silence was very, very unsettling, and upsetting. Almost ominous, you might say!)*

Yet, back in the ward, in amongst all the kafuffle that would have been going on, a familiar friendly, caring, yet authoritative voice, unheard by anyone but 'the woman in the bed', had suddenly and unexpectedly come from somewhere deep down inside her memory banks. It issued an order that just couldn't be ignored! *(Come to think of it - it was a bit of a 'bossy so and so' kind of voice if you ask me! Reminded me of someone I thought knew pretty well at the time. But who could it be? And then I must have laughed, 'cause I had been told before that I was a bit of a bossy so and so! Was it me, talking to myself then? Ho ho ho!!)*

Suddenly though, it became serious! Nothing to laugh at really !

"Suck in - expand the diaphragm. One - two - deep breath — breathe!", the voice continued. No questions were asked by me as to what a diaphragm was. Just a seemingly natural, and instinctive reaction to an instruction that I had somehow, somewhere been given many many times before.

"Do you really think she's back?", I thought I had heard one of the nurses ask excitedly, through the mental haze that surrounded my being!

"Looks like it!", said the head doctor, afraid to make a more positively affirmative statement than that at that time. But then, on seeing their slightly disappointed looking faces, he must have relented a little, and said to them all - "I will say this though - She does look as though she is giving it a jolly good try to wake up. Good show you lot!

You have all done a 'super' job!" - "Well done everyone!", and smiling at the doctor's recognition of everyone's hard work over the last three months, the matron carefully disconnected the now unnecessary life support machine It appeared to the team that the lungs that had been apparently 'just resting' and letting the machine do the work for so long, had now decided that their vacation was over, and had said to all the medical staff, *(that is of course if lungs talk!)* - "We will do our own breathing from here on, thank you!"

But - it still appeared that breathing for myself was going to be about the full extent of any visible improvement at that time.

Back at the gate though, the man *(you remember the one with the long translucent hair and beard)* just stood there, looked me up and down with a most disquieting demeanour. He was jabbing his long, pointy, bony looking index finger at one of the lists in what appeared to me to be a gigantic big book that he had in his arms. Asking again in his strident, booming, disbelieving voice, he said

"Now, I will ask again! What did you say your name was"?

(I am pretty sure that I must definitely have been feeling very disgruntled by this time, and I no doubt began impatiently tapping my own foot!)

Where in the heck *was* I, and *why* would he want to know my name?

I didn't know him - did I? I didn't think I did anyway, and although I had never paid any attention to this piece of good advice before, I suddenly remembered my step-mum telling me a million times, "always be a bit wary of men asking too many questions". So, here I was, finally taking that piece of advice to heart!

"About bloody time", my stepmother Peg would probably have said! *(Sorry about the language - just quoting from what I remember of her habit of being forthright about things! She sometimes had a bit of a mouth on her, she did!* She would have agreed that I had no doubt left it a bit late to listen, but I was definitely being wary now, and as I'd only just recently been married to *(what I thought of at the time as)*, the 'love of my life', I most definitely wouldn't have been out on the 'lookout'.

(Oh yeah! - To be sure - I may always have liked them mature, but now when I think of it, the bearded gentleman looked like he would've been just a trifle old, even for me! He would have been just a tad too 'ripe' so to speak. Also he looked as though he had been around for quite a long, long time, didn't he?)

But thinking that maybe he was a bit deaf because of his obvious age, and that he hadn't heard me properly, I sang back in my loudest most melodious, well projected sing song voice. "My name is Kerri Dyer"! *(Funny how I was still able to sing back then? I wonder what happened on the way back?)*

He shuffled backwards to get away from the sound *(must have had a strong voice me!),* but then I went on, singing a little more quietly. "Oh hang on" I mumbled in a sotto voce voice, blushing at my own stupidity.

"I Just remembered", and full of joy, and getting a little louder I sang - *(key change?)* - "Only recently married, didn't I? My name has changed"!

Having run out of melody ideas, I quietly and sheepishly added, speaking in my little girl voice, "maybe that's the name you should be trying to find. Silly me"! Then for some obscure reason I fumbled in my handbag, and handed him my driver's license. Now, just why I would have had that, or my bag with me for that matter, I can't begin to imagine, except that I knew that I had only gotten around to having the license changed into my new married name a few weeks before, and I was still so proud to be able to officially use my new married name! *(The novelty hadn't yet had time to wear off!)*

I guess that having been so slack about getting it under way, I had been carrying it with me ever since. The spectre looked me up and down shrugging it's shoulders!

(Do they even have shoulders to shrug? Well anyway, it looked like a shrug to me !)

After another yell of *'name'* he had seemed to enjoy leaving me standing there impatiently tapping my foot. And then I hear, after waiting for what seemed like hours - *(just you wait until you hear this!).* He was muttering under his breath to himself, and turning pages while chucking away bits of paper before he said in a most disgusted voice, waving his arms and gesticulating with a most annoyed looking face, "Well now;-I must say that that was a complete and utter waste of my valuable time, wasn't it? You are not even supposed to be here yet." And then he belligerently said looking most disgusted again *(was it with me?),* "Oh for heaven's sake. "Get out of here, and stop wasting my precious time. Come back when we are ready for you. There is still work for you to do! Get back there! Go ,Go, go"!

(I probably just stood there, wondering what on earth was going on. But of course, come to think of it now, we were no longer on earth then, were we?)

Upon my continued silence, he then dared to add in an exasperated, and very annoying way - "Didn't you hear me? Go on" he said, "get going - Bye Bye, see you later"!

(Talk about a feeling of rejection!) Well I mean, really? How do you think you would you feel? And from what I can work out from the dates and things, I guess that I woke up some time the next morning.

Ooh, I am *so* sorry about that!

But out of body experiences are just so-o-o enthralling though aren't they?

Even more so when they are truly for real, as this one was!

I guess that I got so involved in the almost unbelievable, but definitely truthful memory, that I got a bit side tracked!

I do tend to do that I suppose! Back to the story though, eh?

Now where was I? Oh yeah, that's right! The doctors and nurses hated to lose patients! But they weren't going to lose that one, not the Dyer, as

I had been lovingly(?) known among my friends in the entertainment world. Although the nurse had set all the alarm bells ringing, and had brought the whole team running, with a lot of movement going on around me, what do you think I did? Typical of me, I just lay there, looking 'not alive' for a further month and a half. But again, 'not to panic'!

The Dyer was 'alive' alright, but I guess though that I had never been in the mood for making life easy for anyone. Not for me, nor for anyone else, some would say!

There I was, completely devoid of almost any movement. Apparently lifeless; Not even open eyes *(just flutters;.* None of your normal awakening mumbles even. I guess that you could say though, that I was, in a way, the perfect patient. No apparent trouble whatsoever! A worrying, perfect patient!

Yeah, I guess that's what I would have been!

I never complained, me, *(well I couldn't have, even if I had wanted too, could I?)* and I had apparently created not one jot of trouble. Although, they had had to lift me about to give me bed baths and things, and wipe my bum. Must keep her clean and smelling nice", they probably would have said. But you know what, that must have been a true sight to be seen! *(Come to think of it - no I don't suppose that it would have been)!* The thought of that *(my big fat bum being wiped I mean)* is obnoxiously horrible.

(Mind you it probably wasn't so big or so fat back then.
Almost, but not quite! Still an obnoxious thought though!!!!)
And it surely would still have been extremely embarrassing!
Come to think of it though, does one 'poo' when unconscious?
Luckily, I can't remember those kinds of details!

The hospital staff would of course, have been kept very busy just trying to keep me, not only clean, but alive as well! My first husband and I had evidently been in a 'bit of an accident, and as I was unconscious, I had obviously felt nothing since arriving firstly at Lewisham Hospital amid frantic emergency situations, and then shortly after, at Prince Henry Hospital. They do tell me though, that there had evidently been mass rushing about, getting this and that when I had first been brought in, but that they suddenly needed more advanced equipment to give the newly arrived coma patient the best chance I think. So they moved me by ambulance again from Lewisham Hospital, to Prince Henry Hospital. After a few, to be expected, *(I suppose)* initial dramas, things had then turned into a time of quietude, and a worrying silence was heard for three long months *(can silence be heard?)*. Visitors came and went. My first husband evidently came in diligently most days for the first month or two, only to find an apparently almost dead wife! He evidently even lost his job partly because of it!

I had, so they had told me once I was properly awake, and later confirmed by my friend Toni Stevens, been an entertainer. And, not to toot my own trumpet or anything, evidently, according to some, I had been a pretty good one at that! It turns out that the poor audience of regulars at the Mandarin Club, which was where we were supposed to have been going when the accident happened, had really missed out on my 'talent' that evening! I'd like to think that they would have been devastated if they had known why my show had been cancelled, but in reality, I doubt it!!

Poor them for missing out on my undoubted *(so they tell me, and evidenced by Video tapes!)* talent though, but even poorer me, for being unable to perform any more for them! I was evidently in my element when performing.

(On stage, that is; but then come to think of it, it might be said that I just liked acting up! Would that be same thing, do you think?)

Remembering the Mandarin Club's crowd of old though, they probably wouldn't have actually given my absence a second thought anyway. As long as they could get a drink, and see a show of some kind, they would have been happy enough! The management would have been able to get a replacement pretty easily. The 'Mando's', as it was called in the business, was a pretty popular 'gig'! An 'act' could be sure of being 'seen' there! All the big wigs dropped in eventually, as well as some of the not so 'big wigs'! The more you worked there, the better your chances of being 'discovered', and most 'acts' continually dreamed of being discovered! Me especially, even though it was getting a bit late for me for 'fame' to fall on my lap! *(They unfortunately didn't have things*

9

quite like Fame Academy, or X Factor, with their life changing prizes, to help with the discovery of a person's talent in those days.) The audience and my replacement probably had no idea that the girl who was supposed to have been entertaining them was in fact in hospital, doing a totally 'different' kind of show.

The Greatest Show on Earth! She was fighting for her life!

They also didn't know that I would stay there, on and off, for many, many more Sunday nights, and what is more, they probably wouldn't have cared very much either!

During the very early part of my 'in hospital' time, of which I have only a 'blotchy' memory, I was evidently very well cared for, and it was sort of an OK time for me. Not so though for my family. I guess that my real mum was flabbergasted, when the police first contacted her after the accident! I hadn't really seen all that much of them since the wedding *(that you'll read about a bit later)*, and I had seen very little of them during the previous years. My dad wasn't on the phone at the time, so he definitely would've wondered what the police car that arrived wanted with him! Knowing my darling daddy, a little bit of knee trembling probably went on at the sight of 'the old bill'!

I think the younger family members, at my real mum's place were probably as upset as teenagers who hadn't really known their sister very well could be, but they were about to be very very good to their older sister later on, and they still are, nearly 30 years later!

Mum and the kids, who aren't kids any more.
They have kids of their own!

You see, my mum and dad were divorced when I was a toddler, and because of various reasons, that you'll also read about a bit later, I grew up with dad and my step-mum, Peggy. My real mother and I hadn't actually spoken for long periods *(a lot of years)* before my wedding to Andy. I was a bit cheeky I suppose. I got in touch with them to ask my sister to be my chief bridesmaid, *(well I mean that's what sisters do isn't it? Be brides maids for each other!),* and as a truly great bonus, my brothers had *(begrudgingly at their young ages I should imagine)* also acted as ushers at that wedding.

My biological mum and my then husband were the first people to actually see me in the hospital, and my step-mum and dad came to the hospital a bit later because they didn't have transport, wouldn't have had the money for a cab, and would have had to cadge a lift. *(probably with the police?)* At first Peggy *(my step-mum),* very shamefully, evidently wasn't allowed to go in to see me. Visiting must have been limited to husband and parents only, and the hospital rightly said that as my mother had already been, and that as there was no record of there being a second Mrs Dyer, Peg was not allowed in.

(You see, Peggy and Charlie had never actually got around to getting married had they? She had been my mother for over 20 years, but she still wasn't allowed to come in, because she didn't have a particular, stupid piece of paper!)

They did tell me that Peg's brother nearly threw Andy down the stairs when he realised that Andy had maybe had something to do with Peg not being allowed in.

Luckily though, my real Mother sorted it all out, and Peggy got in to see me.

She saw *me*, but I very unfortunately didn't get to see *her*, although remembering how much of a softy Peg could be though, she would probably have been totally engulfed in tears, so it was maybe a good thing I didn't see her! But then, you never know, if I *had* seen her, maybe I would be able to cry now?

I possibly would have got some practice in, crying with her.

Unfortunately, Peggy, actually died while I was still in the coma, because of both her size *(he was a big lady, about 20 stones when she died.)* and grief, and I don't suppose that her not having been allowed in to see me at first, had helped the situation much either. My being as if dead, had probably hastened my daddy's death a few days after I came out of the coma as well. But then he evidently did have a 'dicky ticker' anyway, not helped by the other complaint that they say he suffered from. *(Most definitely unbeknown to me at the time. Tell you about that a bit later too).* He had at least managed to live long enough to actually see me, speak to me, and know that I had survived. It must have been an absolutely traumatic, and horrendous time for them all though! The trauma of *my own* dual loss, only fully hit me about two years after I had 'come too'. Poor Peg though would have had to cope, not only with the possible loss of a daughter that she adored, but also with the terrible illness, and eventual death of her much loved for 25 years, as good as husband!

To tell the truth, at first I was as devastated as any brain damaged person could be about daddy's death *(which I unfortunately have to admit, was not all that devastated at the time)*, but once the reality of the situation had woven it's way properly into my battered brain, I must confess that I was a bit of a write off for a while. How could I have been so cruelly rude to my weird, but loving *(in his own way)* daddy when

I first woke up? *(I hadn't known that I was being rude though, had I?)* But then, and although the following is no real excuse I know, I was unknowingly *so* rude to everybody when I did eventually wake up. My darling daddy, and my husband *(whom I don't think I even recognised at first!)* were both victims of my not really being 'with it'!

He actually had to remind me of who he was! I never even got a chance to say how sorry I was to dad. So sorry for leaving him before time, and for my being so 'not there' the last time that I had seen him before he died. I think that he died the day after his seeing me! I can't really be too sure of much of what happened at that time. Just too busy coping with still being alive I suppose! Also, with my not having really known that he had been getting progressively so ill, I hadn't been able to maybe help out in some way, even if I could have done.

I don't know! My whole life, unbeknown to me, seems to have been one drama after another. Mores the pity! I guess that you could say that I must have been granted at least one of my early age wishes anyway. Both my childhood wish, as well as my typically unthinking teenage wish, had been for a 'different' life! And although it has been what you might call a 'not normal' life, everything 'sus' aside, it has turned out to be not a bad life after all! I would have to accept that even though it *has* been most 'un-nice' at times, it has also most definitely been 'different'! There were no two ways about it though now that I was awake, even though the hospital team were still blissfully unaware of that fact, 'blissful, or quiet' was definitely not destined to be on the agenda for any of us from then on! The hospital ward that had up to that time been just 'ticking' away with normal, unheard by me, night and early morning activity sounds, seemed to me now that I was supposedly awake, to be suddenly awash with bustling, activity noises. Noises that, I must say, all seemed decidedly strange, and from what memory I do have of the time, which is understandably not a lot, were unbearably loud to me! I was, almost immediately on actually waking up, even before I opened my eyes, soon to start clearly hearing meaningful sounds. The noises that I could hear, seemed inexplicably, like definite hospital sounds! "Why was I in a hospital", I thought?

Noises that were tantalisingly familiar from the TV shows that I had seen, and yet unfamiliar to me personally, bombarded me in the most intolerable ways. There was no one directly near my bed, but the affronting of my senses was earth shattering.

From what I could hear, it seemed to me, that the people scurrying around the wards outside my private room, were like busy little worker 'ants', or 'beavers'. 'Beavers', in that they were trying to dam up a broken body, and 'ants' in that they were positively everywhere! Each of them seemed to me to have only the one purpose in mind. Moving the bits and pieces of all that they needed to patch up the patient! They were all marching purposefully about, getting on with 'it', and the 'it' seemed to have been centred around my, and the few other patients in the nearby ward's, requirements and needs.

What a scene!!!!!

The nursing staffs, in both hospitals, had all been following the same palliative care process since I had been admitted amid frantic emergency situations. That had been about five in the afternoon, some four and a half months before, on the 28th July, 1979. Over the last months at Prince Henry, the nurse had come to know me, my movements, and non reactions very well. But the grunts and groans she could now hear were somehow different. What with her being a typically efficient, well trained nurse, she took a gamble and had made a quick, and efficient decision! She had immediately reached out and set those alarm bells going for the second time.

At the end of the bed, two of the doctors who had come running in answer to the blast of the klaxon, were looking at the charts hung there on the bed. Hurriedly, and in lowered tones, they discussed the case with the head nurse, and were looking more than a little concerned. "Is this going to be just another false alarm", I think one said?

"She just doesn't seem to be doing anything really concrete yet", said another.

"But then" *(said yet another)*, "the nurse does say that she was humming!"

"Mmm Humming - I wonder?", he added.

"You're right", I must have thought! The nurse that thought she had heard me humming excitedly broke into the conversation, and added.

"It sounded as though it could have been her opening lines of Corner of the Sky. We have seen video's of her performing as an entertainer, and her husband said that she used to sing 'from behind the stage curtains' as she got ready to make her entrance. The sound may have been very muffled but as I told the other doctor, although it was most definitely out of tune, it had the same attempted rhythm and modulation as her opening song. So as I guessed that that was what she seemed to be trying to emulate, I got so excited, that I just instinctively immediately reached out, and hit the buzzer", she said. I know that we nurses are not really supposed to get overexcited about our patients' doings, but Kerri has apparently been been trying so hard. "Over the last two days in particular, she has shown signs of definitely being a bit of a fighter you know! I guess that once you have been a singer as well known as she evidently was in Sydney; one that was in and out of newspaper articles so often; and if you have been in the spotlight as she was, then I suppose that it's bound to be always a singer"! She sheepishly added, "Entertainers are a breed unto themselves. Just as we are, ourselves, Dr Davey"!

"The daily business of the ward has only just eased off a little", continued the nurse that had heard what she had thought was humming, "and I was just about to wash her eyes again, as I have been doing on a regular basis. I was about to update those files when as I have said, I heard her definitely attempting to hum what sounded more than usually like a song. Again, as I have probably also already said, it was so out of tune that if you hadn't known that she was a singer, then you probably wouldn't even have recognised it as a song, but it was definitely one never the less; so 'smack my fingers' if you choose to, but I excitedly set the sirens going again".

In a different, but still full of excitement kind of voice, she continued on.

"Ooh! Mr O will definitely be 'chuffed' when he gets in this lunchtime! He still tries to come in most days you know. I think that he even lost his job because of all the time he was having off. After having already spent a lot of time at the bedside, the doctors must have decided that because Mrs O wasn't really showing any more signs of doing anything interesting, they had best leave her side for now, and go on to some of the other patients. The nurse was finishing up what she was doing, and the doctors had just got out of sight of the bed, when there was the slightest, now unseen by anyone, movement in it. The previously still body, quietly, and silently struggled to take a deep solid intake of breath. *(And boy did I struggle!)*

From what I could decipher of the notes I managed to save from the chaos that overtook my life from that day on, I am pretty sure that the nurse told me that as the doctors left, she had been trying to clear up and crossly talking as if to herself, and as she finally left for the staff room and then on to another ward full of patients that needed nursing, she smiled a bit of worried smile to herself!

No one was about anymore, and I was evidently coughing and spluttering, trying to roll from side to side, and I was desperately willing my eyes to open. Why I didn't really know! I guess that I didn't even know that I was doing it. But having done as I had originally been told by that little voice from somewhere deep inside, I had 'sucked in, taken two short breaths, one longer one, and finally, after much huffing and puffing, out had come the lung rattling inhalation/exhalation, that signalled my 'grand entrance'.

That mysterious internal voice then told me to open my eyes, and for the first time in my life, surprise, surprise, I had tried to do as I was told! *(miracle of miracles, as those who had known Kerri Dyer before might say!)* I must admit that I did find it difficult to do! *(not only to do what I was told, which was a rarity in itself, but also to open my eyes I mean).* This time though, it definitely wasn't my fault! I wasn't being cantankerous, honest! I just couldn't open those eyes, no matter how hard I tried! And I am here to tell you now, that I did try.

(If for no other reason than that I had always been a bit of a nosey so and so, and I wanted to see what was going on around me! To this very day, my daughter says that I am 'nosey'). At that time though I couldn't really have been classed as nosey, couldI? How was I to know that technically, I was supposed to have been dead, and 'not there' at all!!!!

I will say this though, with each hint of success, those there eyeballs were re-bombarded with a shot of 'far too bright', 'far too white' light, causing the eyes, for their own protection to very quickly, and very securely shut again. As if in defiance, and determination not to let

16

me win, but with apparently childlike teasing, the lights around me continued to filter, tantalisingly through the slits in those eyelids. And on what were becoming the ever more frequent moments when the eyes did try opening, they'd be quickly 'dazzled' shut again. But for some reason, unknown to me, it turned out that I was just as instinctively determined as were those there lights, and as 'I had never liked to lose', I continued trying to open my eyes. I guess that my first husband's assessment of my own character had been correct. I was a bit of a stubborn bugger! A silent war was now definitely in progress!

Me versus the lights!

As well as those *(nasty?)* aggressive instructions that I was still continually being given by that inner voice, there were horrible, antiseptic, pungent, nose curling, odours suddenly, and violently attacking senses that had been 'not there' for ever so long. The bustling noises around me also impinged on ears that had been, to the most part, dead to the extraneous sounds of the world.

I must confess though, that at that time, I didn't really understand any of what I thought I had heard them talking about. But I was, without a doubt, soon to find out! My apparently battered, and 'strange feeling' brain began, ever so slowly, trying to piece everything together.

I had thought that I had heard the doctors saying that "things looked bad"! "What things looked bad", I must have thought?

"They can't be talking about me! Can they? Don't tell me one of their other patients is dying"? I had seen a lot of worried faces rushing about! But I knew for sure, that they hadn't been talking about me when I had heard them say - "none of her senses seem to be alive".

At least from that statement on, I had thought that I definitely knew that they couldn't possibly have been talking about me. After all, I could sense and feel a whole lot of things. My senses definitely felt alive, too alive, and from what I can remember, which may not be a lot at this time, it was definitely not a nice feeling. *(A comment said in the politest of ways, of course.)* The pain that I was suddenly feeling was very needle like, and extremely 'un-nice'. And suddenly that same little voice that came from somewhere in the depths of my thoughts quietly shouted at me again.

"Alright you" the voice said.

"Yes, it's me again, and just to make sure that you remember the routine, here we go again. One, two, three. Suck in, expand that ribcage. Breathe". Zsssh-sh!

My chest must have instinctively expanded and deflated!

"Well done", said the voice, "and now, take a another deep breath, come on.

"Bi - g breath! Expand the diaphragm. Go on! Good girl!"

I must have automatically done it , and then I must have thought.

"Hey, hang on there! Where had I learned that procedure?

Oh, not just the breathing bit we all know how to do that from just after birth I think, but all that 'sucking in and expanding the diaphragm thing"?

"And anyway", I asked, "what the heck is a diaphragm"?

Slowly and painfully I turned my woozy head. I lay there, flat on my back, trying, and trying to lift my head. I looked left, and right up as far as the glass windows that formed the top of the wall opposite the end of my bed. I could just make out shadows of the apparent bustle on the other side of the glass pane. "What on earth was going on over there? What in heavens name was I doing over here, and where in the plan of things *was* 'over here, or even 'over there' for that matter"?

That inner voice said almost pedantically "Right - That's enough thinking, and questioning! You have far more interesting things to do. It's sit up time for you young lady! Ready"! Now. One, Two, Three, UP"!, and having just got my limp feeling body half sat up, it went *flop*! But that voice wasn't about to let me just lie there. Oh no, not on your Nellie!! It shouted at me once more. "Alright, again. Come on you, I said UP."

I must have just sat there, because then I heard - "Did you hear me, or did you not?
I said UP"!

That there voice was having an absolute field day! SO bossy. (*Again - A bit like I can be sometimes? Funny about that!)* "But why did it hurt so much", I thought to myself, and "why is just sitting up such a hard thing to do"? I gave up momentarily. "Groan" I went, and I fell back on the bed again. *But* the voice wasn't about to let me give up, was it? "Push!

Make that audience cheer!" said that ghostly, fast becoming obnoxious voice. "Go on keep trying", it commanded again.

"Oh *shut up voice*", says me, in what to me seemed like a strident yell, but which must have been, in reality, just a muffled grunt. The voice though blithely replied as though it hadn't heard me. *(probably chose not to).*

"Come on Kerri! Show us what you're made of. Try! **UP!**"

"One, two, three -ee, Push! Yeah! That a girl'"!

"I did it! I did it!" I excitedly squealed to what was now an empty ward. My gruff excuse for a voice probably sounded more like an animal in pain than words.

"I knew you could", said that once bossy, now kindly, inner voice.

Success!!!! Although no sensible inner voice would do so, it seemed as though that voice was excitedly screaming along with me! 'Cause there I was sitting up! No drums, no lights, no fanfares, no nothing! But I was, although exultant, also a little despondent. "All that effort, and there had been absolutely no one to know, or see!

(The inherent showbiz genes maybe?)

Where was everybody" I must have thought?

(But come to think of it, there wasn't really any reason why there should be anyone there, was there?)

I have to admit now though that I must have been feeling more than just a little bit disappointed!

But why disappointed?

Well I have to admit that I will probably always be a bit of a showy at heart, and to have had no-one there, not even one person to witness my re-emergence into the land of the living! It must have been almost more than I could have borne then, and I guess that it would be even now! Oh sure, I had done as I had been told, and I had sat up alright, but what on earth had I sat up to? I am sure that I must have thought again, "Where in the heck am I"?

But there I kind of half sat, half slumped, with my arms desperately trying to keep my body upright. And my cheeks? Well they were a deep mottled scarlet from all the effort that I had expended, weren't they? My eyes were nearly popping out of their sockets due to all the unexpected exertion! I guess that I just drank in the sterile, strange, complicated surroundings about me, saying to myself again, "where in bloody hell am I? What's happening to me?" I could see for sure that I was in a hospital, but what in heaven's name was going on? From my 'throne' *(was it a bed?)*, there was a drop, of what seemed to me, to be some twenty feet to the floor. *(There's no way in reality that it could have been of course, but it sure as heck looked like it was).*

I have to have a giggle now though! How strange it must have looked to anyone else looking on. There was this 'limp-ish' looking body, kind of sitting up at a very wonky angle, with it's head looking very bewildered, wobbling from side to side. Knowing what I was like, a bit of a handful at the best of times, I would have howled in my indecipherable voice at the time, looking over the edge of the bed, trying to say things like -"And just what do they think I am anyway? A bloody twenty foot giant?" My fuzzy brain 'kind of' worked a bit, but it took me quite a while before I could get the thoughts out via my mouth, if at all! For some strange reason, and contrary to my normal state, my thoughts had become a bit course, with those there thoughts taking the most devious route before they made any sense to me, let alone anyone else. It was as if they had taken the wrong path, had come up against a brick wall, and were desperately trying to bash through to make themselves understood!! But understood by whom? Suddenly I realised again, as if it was a fact that had again only just hit me for the first time, and from somewhere out of the blue, there *was* no one else there! I was all alone! I may have managed to sit up alright, but was I meant to be wobbly like this?

Because I was sat up though, I now had a completely different view of the world that was around me. Where as before I could only see sideways, now I could see not just to them but right through the windows beyond the glass pane at the end of my bed.

"The sun is trying to get higher in the sky," I thought, "so it must be early morning". "But surely", I vaguely remembered, "it had been late afternoon, early evening even when I thought that I had been talking about going home to get dressed for something. Hadn't I"?

Then I must have thought. Hey, this definitely is not my bed, and my home is definitely not a hospital, or it wasn't last time I looked. I have got to get out of here"!

I was completely lost! Instinctively I made to get out of the strange bed, but I couldn't move! I just sat there! Stunned, and wondering why I couldn't. "What's happening?" I thought, totally confused by it all. I guess that it must have been a little like those old time black and white movies. You know the ones? Charlie Chaplin, or Jacques T'artee. Everything was in slow motion! You know, when you could see that they were supposed to be running, but they didn't appear to be going anywhere! Well I felt a bit like that. I couldn't even wiggle along the bed, and panicking again, I flicked my eyes from side to side and I thought to myself - "Alright, the fun's over, I don't think that I like this game anymore! I don't wanna play no more", I howled! I tried to pull my leg out from under the covers, and swing it off the bed, but no joy! I couldn't do even that, could I?! "But why in the hell not"?, I must have thought.

A sense of all consuming traumatic panic hit me again! Why had my just sitting up been, most uncharacteristically, an Herculean feat, and why did I feel like I didn't have any legs? I didn't understand it! I had to have legs. Didn't I?

Still there was no apparent attention getting device to ask anyone what was going on! I could see the legs were there under the blankets, but I couldn't *feel* them. "What on earth was happening? Had I gone mad or something"? My whole world had taken an earth shattering 'tumble'. "All those ever so obvious to me, oddities had to be the result of something, but the result of what", I thought ? I felt as though I was about to burst into tears, but the tears wouldn't come. I dejectedly slumped back, only half sitting/half lying now, and I crossly began to ponder again, trying to remember what I thought I had heard them say!

Hadn't they said that I had been a singer"?

"Had?; I was sure that they had said had; but why had", I thought? I can still sing, can't I? I tried, but 'nothing' except pain in my throat, and as was becoming normal for me that day, I panicked big time all over again! Then I thought - "they had definitely said that I'd been determined! But if I had been determined, what on earth had I been determined to do? I am determined to sing and move along the bed now, so why can't I"? Oh how I wished I could make some sense out of what I had been hearing! Then that inner voice chipped in again. "Stop looking back you silly girl! Forget the past. Now. Do me a favour will you?" "Concentrate on the present!". "You definitely have something to be determined about now, they had been talking about turning off your life support machine for heavens sake! Remember!"

It was as if a bolt of lightning had hit me. I must have decided that that voice was right after all. *I most definitely did have something to be determined about now!*

I didn't want to die! Well, I didn't – did I?

"Aw - why can't I feel my legs? Why in hell can't I cry"?

I bawled a tearless cry to myself, just like a baby that wanted something, and no one would give it them!! I couldn't even move my upper body, nor bend across to make the arms and hands lash out at the mounds! I just sat there looking around, totally amazed at what I most unexpectedly saw. *A Hospital!*

"Right - now think Kerri", I must have thought.

1. - "you are definitely in a hospital"?

"But how can that be"? I asked myself again. "Hospitals are for 'sick' people aren't they? Am I sick? I don't feel particularly sick, not really"!

Panic stricken again, *(goodness, I do seem to have spent a whole lot of time panicking don't I? Still I guess that it was understandable, or was I just a wimp?)* I looked around anew for some way to attract someone's attention. I just had to find out, but I couldn't see anything to use, nor anyone to summon. So I very belligerently thought to myself, "alright then"

2. "There's no one about, so I'll just have to find my own way out of this bed"! Well I couldn't just sit there now could I? Although, as it turned out, I guess that I should have! I tried to loosen the bed clothes, which were neatly folded over and tucked in. Tucked in in the way that only hospital beds can be tucked in, and again noticing the absence of people, I repeated a question that I had asked myself earlier , "Where in the heck is anybody, and why have they put me in what must be a private ward?

Am I contagious or something"?

And then it was a bit like one of those lightning flash things had illuminated my thoughts. "Oh", I thought, with the reality of the situation suddenly hitting me like a huge sledge hammer. "That must be what has happened! I have caught measles or chickenpox, or maybe something worse, and they don't want to run the risk of my giving it to anyone else. Yeah! That must be what it is"? There was no doubt about it though - I definitely needed to ask someone! Anyone! I most certainly had to know! No thought of it maybe being considered nosey, was there? Still with no one there to be seen, I looked around the area directly about me, all the time desperately hoping that some kind of explanation would come walking around the corner, smiling broadly, full of bon vivant, and ready to give me some answers! I painfully tugged two normal 'looking' legs (*maybe a tad puffy, but pretty normal looking*) out from under the sheets, and put them very awkwardly almost on top of the bedding. They were half in, half out! And yet again I hopefully looked around - Still, the ward was empty of anyone who could help! No panic this time though, (*I had probably panicked myself out by then do ya reckon?*). Just steely determination! As much as I didn't really want to believe it - that inner voice had been right! I did, now, have something very important to be determined about!

I had to let someone know that I was there, and that I was actually awake!

SORTING OUT THE CHAOS
THAT REIGNED!

But how was I to do that? Luck must have been on my side for a change, and luckily the nurse decided to come 'goose stepping' back for some reason, and when she finally turned up it was to find me in a state of total distress. But why were there still no tears? I was feeling most dejected and bewildered, and wanting to cry over the fact that I couldn't work out where anyone was, nor why I was even there? What had brought about the sense of massive chaos in my mind? And most of all, why no tears?

I had normally been a bit of a cry baby!!

Gradually as I pieced together snippets of information obtained from the staff, friends and family, and as my own memory of my past came flooding back in its 'own good time', a few of my many questions were answered. I came to realise that, in reality my whole life so far had probably just been a case of nothing much more than twenty eight odd years of 'chaos reigning'. With the emphasis being on the 'odd'.

In 2011 I will be 60 years odd, with the emphasis again, being on the *odd!*

Why? Why odd? Well let's have a look, shall we!

A lot of you who have embarked on reading this book would probably, and justifiably be asking yourselves by now - who is or was this Kerri Dyer anyway? Well, I'll try to tell you if you don't already know, and come to think of it, there's no real reason why any of you should I suppose. I wrote this book a long time after I was well known. I hadn't fully achieved the fame that I had so desperately craved while strutting my stuff on the stages around Sydney, Australia, and overseas. But still, I do think that even after all this time, I have a 'kind of' story to tell. A story that will hopefully provide enjoyable reading and reassurance to the readers so that they too can face there own changed life with confidence, and also maybe, the book will offer encouragement to some of them to get out there, and give life – pardon the language, *(I am about to be a bit rude, and to use a good Australian saying)* – 'a bloody good go'!

Also, if this book is a success and sells, then it will be able to help out some of the people who go out of their ways to cheer us all up, boost our self esteem, and entertain us when we are down!!

The story may be a bit disjointed because as a sufferer of brain stem damage, with ataxia, I still do tend to get my thoughts muddled a bit. Even this long after the accident I have to confess that much to my chagrin, my poor brain doesn't always get things into a logical and fully coherent order. I think I get it right in my head, then say it, and then it turns out to be the wrong thing said at the wrong time!

Also life doesn't always occur in a logical order. At least, not mine anyway! This is also my first attempt at writing a book, and I hope that you agree with me, as well as with those that read it as I wrote, that my tendency to be a bit scatty sometimes goes along way to making this story more human and as though we are actually sat down over a cup of tea or coffee, with me relating all the crazy happenings just to you, personally, as they happened!

There is also a not very thorough précis that sort of makes up the next chapter.

At least if you read that much, those who aren't grabbed enough by any aspect to read on further, then at least you will have hopefully gotten the basic gist of the bulk of my story. But if you *do* read on,*(and I sincerely hope that you do)* then I can guarantee that you will get some explanation and expansion of the facts, in the following chapters.

Basically though, I sincerely hope that you will find it the story of encouragement that I mean it to be, as well as the mad tale of a life that was, in reality, 'bit of a giggle, and a bit 'different'! A 'bit of a giggle' with my usual, or as some would say, 'unusual' touch of humour.

I, Kerri Dyer (now Kerri Keen for the last 20 years) was convinced, as are most young people when they start out on the treadmill of the show business world, that I was a fantastic singer. I probably would have been one of those super egotistical X Factor auditionees that you are glad to see the back of. I am though, pretty positive (*also as those that entertain should be)* that I would have stunned everybody with my singing and performing, and now when I look back on my past, I guess that I must have done so, kinda!! *(I guess that's why I don't allow myself to get too upset when some of the X Factor contestants get a bit carried away! Some of them do turn out to be brilliant - don't they?)* But, let's do as the song that forms the original basis of my own vocal rejuvenation says, "Let's start at the very beginning - a very good place to start".

And as is the case with all babies, I was born! *(Is that 'beginning' enough for you do you reckon?)* When I *was* born, I had a mum, and I had a dad, *(fairly normal so far, but buckle up, I think that we may be in for a bit of bumpy ride!)* They stayed together till I was about 3, maybe 2 and a bit, I can't really be sure. *(But I was little, I do know that, and they did separate, I also know that for sure!)* They separated in preparation for a divorce. Now that was definitely not at all normal at the time! *(I mean, people hadn't gotten into the regular habit of discarding each other at that time in the 50's! Almost, but not quite!)* I had lived with mum at first, which was also pretty normal, but after a while, mum had decided, for reasons that you will read about a little later on, that it would be better, well better, for her at the time anyway, if I lived with my dad. So off I went.

But every six weeks or so, Peg *(my step-mum, you'll get to know more about her too, as we go along too!)*, and my dad Charlie would scrub me up. I'd be hair brushed, teeth cleaned, and dressed in the best of my not 'real nice' dresses, to be sent off to visit my real mum for the weekend or for a few weeks during school holiday times. My real mum would generally have a dress and a 'cardie' *(cardigan)* waiting for me to wear to 'meetings', which is what the Brethren church services on the Sunday morning were called. I think that my step-mum, after the initial period of dressing me in my best so as to prove that I was no worse off living with them, and possibly thinking that she was being a bit clever and devious, purposely dressed me in 'not too good clothes. She was under the mistaken assumption that my real mum was then supposed to feel I think, - "Well she can't possibly wear those clothes for the meeting", and would hopefully buy me something new to bring home. You see, Peg didn't really like us being poor. She had high aspirations for the future, especially where the little girl was concerned, and those aspirations would cost. But they didn't have any money!

Peg was always hopeful that my real mum, who was a bit better off, would, if only purely for the sake of the little girl of course, get some new clothes for me, and that maybe she would let me bring them home to Peg and Charlie's house. What Peggy didn't realise at first, but discovered after a while, was that mum already had a small selection of new clothes kept aside at her place for me to wear to the meetings and social functions, so she wasn't really fooled by Peg's tactics. Being the lovely person she is most of the time though, mum would occasionally, whenever the clothes that she had put aside for me, got a little bit older, or I began growing out of them, let me take one or two of them back to Peg and Charlie's place! So everyone was happy! Peggy's deviousness may not have been quite as fruitful as she wanted, but the clothes I took home, got a lot of wear over the following year or two. Even when I *had* finally grown out of them. Peggy saw to that, and no longer just on Sundays either! Peggy had me squashing myself into them, sometimes like meat into sausage skins, with the same 'about to burst' look of just about ready to cook bangers. She wanted me to get as much wear as I could out of the clothes. I would even get roused on for growing too quickly. So whenever I went to mum's, I had to see if there were any more of what Peg called in her most 'posh, gracious voice' *(which wasn't really posh and gracious at all)*, 'Mummy discards'.

They were often clothes that Peggy would never be able to afford for me herself, so I would be told in no uncertain terms, to see what I could do! *(No pressure then!)*

I used to think that all the "I don't understand why I can't take it home", and "can I please" did actually eventually wear mum down, but I guess, when I look back now, that mum would have been far too clever to have been fooled by all that! Occasionally though, it appeared to the little person that I was, that it had, indeed, worked, and I would go home doubly happy. I had had a wonderful time, as I generally always did have at mum's, *and* I had some 'new' clothes as well. Wow! Was I ever a happy little bunny?!

Whenever I did see my real mum, I also got to see my elder half brother as well. So what's unusual about that then, I hear you ask? - Nothing really I suppose, except that *he* got to live with mum *(and didn't I resent that)!* I think that my brother had been the result of mum's first relationship, well before dad was on the scene, so dad had no claim on him. And as much as it grieves me to have to admit it *(because even though he has been dead for years, and I still love my daddy, warts and all),* one of the reasons I think that mum let dad have me with little or no real objection, was possibly because dad could be a bit vicious when he was crossed. *(Come to think of it – I guess that that too, would have to be one of the understatements of the year)!* At such a young age as mum was, about 23 – 24, I think she probably didn't really want to have to face his temper, and definitely didn't want to risk possibly making matters any worse than they probably already were. Even then, he must have had at that time, his undisclosed 'fondness' for little boys, and men - if you know what I mean. A fondness that absolutely, and some would say, justifiably disgusted mum! I must admit that I don't personally, know of any instances when mum was made truly aware of dad's peculiarity. In those days it was all under covers, and behind closed doors, but from what I have picked up in conversations with the main players in what has been a truly horrific waste of a life, he must have made what would have been considered, at the time, *(or any time for that matter really)* some potentially, grossly 'un-nice' moves on my poor elder brother. My brother had been still too small to really know what was really going on, and mum would definitely not have accepted that kind of activity even being hinted at when she found out the possibility of them. My brother, who was not biologically dad's, had thus unintentionally provided potential fodder for dad's evidently 'no longer invisible' sexual preferences. I am pretty sure that nothing came of my daddy's ambitions where my brother was concerned, but mum understandably found the whole peadophilia thing sickening, and was understandably very concerned for his safety.

(My brother's that is, not my Dad's!)

My dad's sexual inclination, was deeply frowned upon, considered disgusting and was definitely illegal at that time, and in reality, dad should have been given some medical help. Mind you, I am pretty sure that it probably wouldn't have done all that much good. Surely someone has to acknowledge that they even have a problem to fix, before it can be solved! To my dad – well he didn't think that he had a problem, did he? It was all very 'normal' to him! Everyone else had the problem, and of course, the boy was far too well protected for anything other than insinuative gestures to have been made! My mum and nana would have seen to that!

Once my mum and dad had split up though, I think that the ownership of the little girl, me, possibly slowed up the finalisation of the divorce, if it was slowed at all. I can't really be too sure, but what with my being a mere child, my mum finding it too distressing to talk about, and me not wishing to cause her discomfort this far into her life, I haven't really asked her. So I am afraid that you'll just have to take the summation of a pretty bewildered grown up as to the reality of the situation. That summation maybe a bit one sided though, because my impressions are garnered from some of the the things that I remember of what my dad told me! And I don't suppose that his feelings could possibly be biased, now could they? I do remember my daddy telling me when I was about 9 or 10, that he had figured that I was his, and as far as he was concerned - 'That was that'!

Just what he was doing telling me things like that at 10 I am not too sure now, but he must just have become drunk and maudlin, and felt that unloading of his woes on me, would make him feel better, and hopefully make me love him more! Understandably under the circumstances, I think that mum and my nana, whose house we lived in - again, I think, must have decided that the best way for everybody to cope with the situation, was for Charlie to leave. So obviously it was 'goodbye Charlie'! I guess that even back in those days there must have been some kind of Woman Power and all, but that decision about his leaving hadn't really appealed to my daddy, and there was probably quite a bit of noisy argument about it! He no doubt threatened mum, nana, and sometimes even the policemen when they were called. *(I do remember him having a bit of a loud, 'foul mouth')* That of course didn't go down too well, with anyone, but from what Charlie had told me himself a few years before he died – when he was having another one of his drunken reminiscing sessions, he definitely wasn't about to leave *his* little girl with *her*, and *her* mother, in *their* house!

(A touch of old fashioned 'macho', do you think?)

29

I don't think that my daddy had the foggiest idea why he couldn't have me as opposed to mum, nor of the problems that his actually having me might cause him, his way of life, and just about everybody else for that matter. All he knew, was that he had a child! Someone to whom he could pass his genes, of which he was very proud *(justifiably so or not)*. My dad, in reality was a bit of a child himself, and wasn't about to give up his own flesh and blood too easily! So I have to assume that mum and dad separated begrudgingly on his part, in preparation for the divorce!

He believed that they couldn't take his daughter away from him if he made it clear that he wanted me. After all, in his world, man was supreme! To him, and his macho way of thinking, women were just second class, but he definitely wanted his little girl, even though, according to his own philosophy, she would eventually grow into a second class citizen. He was super determined though, that no matter what, and under whatever circumstances prevailed, I was going to be *his* second class citizen! *(I maybe I have him to thank for my own determination? Who knows?)* I was of course, too young to understand any of that at the time! I guess that I loved them both. I can't really know, having been that young. To me they were just mummy and daddy. They had evidently ceased loving each other enough, so as to make their staying together, an impossibility. *(If of course they had ever really done so. Loved each other enough that is!)*

I guess that having had the relationship start off basically pleasantly enough, with a child and all, that mum probably felt, that the suddenly obvious, and unexpected peadophilia was just a problem too far, to try and overcome. The marriage vows may have been in 'sickness and in health', and to do justice to my mum, she would probably have coped with most things, but I guess that dad wouldn't have considered himself as coming under the heading of having been even a little bit 'sick', and mum probably just didn't have the necessary amount of 'health' to cope with his suddenly apparent 'sickness'. Besides, she also had her much loved little boy to protect. According to photos, my darling daddy had been a good enough looking man, but his motives for marriage with my mum, *(hidden at first, if in fact he even had hidden motives)*, apparently turned out to be a little less than 'normal' let us say!

I think that at first, I lived with mum, and just visited dad. Can't really remember that far back! *(I am afraid that I have enough trouble remembering what day it is these days!)* No-one ever asked me. But then, with my being so young and everything - why would they? After all, we are not really overly eloquent when we take our first steps on the pathway of life, are we? Dad probably figured that he was being victimised, so it would have been perfectly natural for him to take whatever he considered the appropriate action! *(I can just imagine, him sat in a smoke filled bar with a few beers under his belt, and with a few of his mates consoling him, and egging him on.)* Unfortunately - the appropriate action in his mind, turned out to be not really all that appropriate in the general scheme of things!

"It's just not right Charlie", dad's friends would probably have said. They would also have said, grinning from drunken cheek to drunken cheek, things like -

"A man has to stick up for what is his",and it must have been reassuring for dad to have his own liquor induced thoughts corroborated. I do remember him telling me that, on more than a few occasions, after his own thinking having been boosted by alcoholic confirmation from his mates, he was actually discovered 'stealing' me from mum's place during non allotted visiting times. No doubt 'half pissed', and consequently noisily, plodding around, trying very hard to be invisible and quiet! *(A thing he wasn't very successful at, even at the best of times, and definitely not when he was intoxicated! Ever seen a drunk desperately 'shooshing' the neighbourhood cat, or the world around him, when it is he himself who is making all the noise? Well – ha ha ha ha, that would probably have been my dad!)*

His carefully laid out plans would be temporarily foiled by his being caught, but did he care? No bl....y fear! He could, would and did, always try again, almost getting himself arrested on a few occasions! But being the dare devilish, sometimes foolish kind of man that I remember him being, he was evidently, according to him - just drunk enough to find it all a bit of an enjoyable challenge!

(Really daddy!)

A lot of loud, very vocal and abusive talking and shouting would definitely have ensued. I either didn't see, or understandably can't remember any of the actual ruckus, but it was going on all around me all right. *(Or so daddy told me!)* He would have said to me, if he had taken the time to involve me at all, that I just had to do as I was told, or risk being clouted. And even in those days, if it was anything like a bit later on, my dad must have clouted pretty hard! From what I remember of dad though, he wouldn't really have wasted any time explaining much to a kid! Kids, to him, didn't really warrant explanations. Not even *his own* child. I don't remember mum ever being the clouting type though! She would just have had a typically severe mother's tongue to beat me with on the occasions that I needed it, and use it she did when necessary! I think that maybe I am glad in a way, as well as lucky, that she wasn't really about when I got a little older. Her tongue would probably have been the fittest in the country, with all the exercise it would have been given. I have a feeling that some of my antics would possibly have astounded her! But then, come to think of it - probably not! Even though she definitely wouldn't have liked some of them – she also knew that I had been brought up in a very 'different' world to her own!

Again, dad was reminiscing with me one day, after one of my jobs *(tell you about them too, later on)* when I was about 20, and he told me that the police had tried warning him again and again. But typical of my dad - he would just ignore the warnings, and then, after having been a good boy, *(in his own assessment, at least)* and having taken me back safely enough, under duress a few times I might add, he would sneak about, and blithely snuffle me away again a day/week or two later. He said that he just couldn't see that he didn't really have the right, and I don't suppose that he would ever have thought that he was running the risk of going to jail! Said in the nicest way of course - "daddy was what you might call as 'thick as a brick' sometimes"!

But then, as I have always said, a lovable brick, nevertheless!

He told me that inevitably, the police would have to again, come get me, and take me back to mum. I am pretty sure that they, even though they were generally more patient in those days *(weren't they?)*, were probably getting more than a little fed up with this all too frequent waste of their time, and they would no doubt have informed dad of what could happen, if he persisted. Mum's and nana's nerves must also have been almost at breaking point, but dad being a bit of a chameleon, who although lovable at times, was also a bit of a vicious, loud, and 'foul mouthed' person, probably wouldn't have made the situation easy for anyone.

Knowing how obnoxious my daddy could sometimes be, I can imagine that some of the language he would have used, would have been totally unacceptable in any neighbourhood, and would no doubt have caused some blushes on the faces of those who lived in the 'poshish' street where my mum had lived. I was told by a shamefaced, but grinning dad, that those who did live nearby were understandably beginning to complain about the police presence and the bad language from dad. The verbal threats made to mum and nana, and even to some of the police, were evidently horrendous, and so they understandably and I suppose, maybe kind of regrettably, decided that something a little more positive just had to be done. Nana and mum probably decided that it was better to just give in, and that it would be better for everyone concerned, them and me most of all, if they just let dad have me. They did try for a good while at first, to keep an eye on me as much as they could though. But they just weren't ready to have a perpetually constant, fisticuffs situation on their hands. So unfortunately, again, bad behaviour had won out! Only for the sake of peace, you understand!

(You know? Peace has a lot to answer for does Peace!) Typical of dad though, his belligerence knew no bounds, and as he said to me a few years before he went and died on me - "I just couldn't see, myself, why they all carried on about it as they did". - And he would say to me, -"you were after all *my* daughter!" *(Oh well!)*

I loathe to say it, but for all of his advanced years I'm not too sure that my dad had ever really grown up!

Hey! - Just thought! Maybe that's catchy as well! Maybe that's why I still feel like a bit of a kid at almost 60! My own daughter often asks me, in an anguished tone of voice -"And just how old did you say you were, again mum?!" So again, maybe bits of my daddy do live on, in my own inherited ways!! I think , and yes, hope that they probably do!

I must admit that I too sometimes have done some rather irrational things, as you will read if you do choose to read on! I had spent most of my youth singing around the house, driving Peggy and Charlie positively mad with my singing and antics. I sang on box crates in the street, with the local kids, for charity, and I did my first TV show at about 9, I think it was, and for nearly ten years from 18 and a bit, I 'trod the boards' in the showbiz world *(more about those things later too if you read on though).*

I did my fair share of school and bank work, and also a lot of gallivanting about once I was actually on the 'club circuit'. I continually tried to work out what 'went down' the best with the audience, and I guess that I had never thought that a person from Greenacre would stand a chance of really 'getting on' in show business. But I kept right on in there - giving it a go!

A lot of things happened over the next, nearly ten years, both good and bad! I had joyfully, as well as ploddingly, striven hard in the belief that one day I would make it big .

As the words of the song say - "I'm - the greatest *star!* – but no-one knows it"!

And then I used to add - *yet!*

But to tell the truth, which again as I said before; I am told I should do - I just couldn't wait for stardom to strike! After nearly 10 years of entertaining, and enjoying the showbiz whirl, and just when I was ready to have my name flashing brightly before everyone's eyes, fate intervened again, obviously having plans of it's own for me.

Funny? I was sure that I was destined to have my name in all the broadsheets, and have the name of **KERRI DYER** up there, where it counted. *(Where, by the way I must have thought it belonged.)*

But I am definitely sure that the headlines that appeared on the front pages of the local and national papers, were not exactly what I had had in mind prior to the accident.

READ ALL ABOUT IT! they read!
'EVITA HOPE SINGER IN CAR SMASH'.

EVITA HOPE SINGER IN CAR SMASH

SINGER Kerri Dyer is in a serious condition in a Sydney hospital after being involved in a car smash.

Kerri, tipped as a contender for the lucrative lead in the musical Evita, suffered serious head and chest injuries in the crash.

Kerri was first taken to Lewisham Hospital but was later transferred to the intensive care unit at the RPA.

The 28-year-old singer from Kingsford has been hailed as one of the brightest and most promising performers in the country.

Entertainment industry colleagues believed this would be "Kerri Dyer's year to make it right to the top."

But today, with her immediate career now in doubt, Kerri is in the intensive care ward "in a serious but stable condition."

Kerri has appeared on most national television shows and at the last Mo Awards night came close to toppling eventual winner, Julie Anthony.

Veteran American chart-topper, Frankie Laine, described Kerri recently as a girl with a perfect voice and booked her to record his favourite song, Pretty Things.

Kerri is married.

Family friends said today a special team of doctors and surgeons was standing by in case her condition deteriorated.

Kerri Dyer

July 30ᵗʰ 1979

BEDSIDE VIGIL FOR SINGER

SINGER Kerri Dyer has been in a coma for three weeks but her husband, keeping a bedside vigil, says she knows he is there.

"She responds to me. I believe she will pull through," Alec O'Hare, 29, said today.

"My place is with her and that is part of the reason for her wanting to fight."

Kerri, 28, and Alec were married for only seven months when a car smash left Kerri unconscious.

This week Kerri's condition improved. She was taken off the criti-cal list at Royal Prince Alfred Hospital.

Alec says her singing helped her a lot because she understood about breathing.

"I would say to her 'Kerri do your breathing exercises' and slowly she would begin to," he said.

"But it is going to be a long road. In that ward two or three months months isn't a long time," he said.

Kerri Dyer

KERRI'S WINNING THE FIGHT

SINGER Kerri Dyer has battled her way out of the deep coma she entered after a car accident in July and is now talking to her husband Alec.

The conversations are brief, but doctors at Royal Prince Alfred Hospital are hopeful the return of her speech is a sign Kerri is on the way to a full recovery.

Kerri, 28, of Kingsford, was considered a likely choice for the lead in the musical Evita after almost topping Julie Anthony in the last "Mo" variety artists awards.

Her blossoming career on the club circuit and television came to an abrupt halt on July 27 with serious head and chest injuries in the car crash.

She was in the RPA intensive care unit for several weeks and started coming out of a coma only two weeks ago.

"It was touch and go there for a while, but I knew Kerri had the will to battle her way through," said Alec.

Kerry D... her car ac... valid.

17th Aug 1979 & 1 Nov. 1979

HALF FULL GLASS!

The next bit kind of sums up, for better or for worse, what has become my outlook on life these days. I am always telling my newer friends what you are about to read - so much so that I wouldn't be overly surprised if some of my more established friends told me, especially if they read the book - "yeah yeah , you've told us all that before.
Change the record will you"!

But I will tell you any way, because you are basically, hopefully, a new audience, and with me being a bit of a 'showy' at heart, I guess that I have always loved a new audience! -
I was told at the hospital, when I had got to the stage where I was ready for them to 'chuck me out', "you should try not to drink from the half empty glass of life".
On my better days I try to think about my life as the substantial remains of a half *full* glass, and I would, as politely as is possible, advise others to do so, as well. I have learnt through the years, that you mustn't waste time moaning about what you 'can't' do. I have done my fair share of that, and I have found that it honestly achieves nothing! Also, we shouldn't always be looking for the snag or 'catch' in a thing. The medical team's final words as I left the Hospital were - "you have to make your life, and that of those around you, better in some way, no matter how small or large a way it might be"!
And "every single day too" they resoundingly added!
I suppose that it is just as well that I have taken it as my credo for life these days. I may have sometimes failed, miserably so, on many

occasions, with frustration and self disgust being the result, but for the last 20 years, with the help of my wonderful husband and daughter, I have begun to look on life with a more positive attitude. Oh sure - I still have my down days, when I forget, but after over nearly 30 years of spasmodic application to the various problems associated with my disability, I am now, again as determined as ever *(well almost, anyway!)*, and as I said on the Steve Raymond show, back in 1989 - *WATCH OUT WORLD!*

Now, 30 odd years after that fateful day in July 1979, this story is written, hopefully not necessarily from a 'poor me' angle. It definitely isn't meant to be that, anyway. *("Poor me", I mean)*. But come to think of it - alright - if I am honest, I suppose that it could be - just a teensy weensy bit. I may no longer be what you would really call poor, but the 'feel sorry for yourself' monster still manages to get in occasionally. This story though, is written with a renewed love of life, and hopefully as encouragement. Encouragement to anyone else who may have worked diligently hard for years, and then when they finally think that they have their 'world on a plate', *(so to speak)*, they find that the excitingly interesting 'meal' that they had worked so hard for, is unceremoniously snatched from their grasp. The 'plate' they are left with may seem at first to be a very unpalatable alternative, but is it when you really look at it?

Life is only what you make of it, after all! *(or that is what they keep on telling us, anyway!)* But then, I suppose that it is true - only *you* can alter your life to be as near as possible to what you would like it to be. My mum would probably say that you can pray, but I say that God still needs application from you, to work his miracles. My present husband, along with a lot of other people, doesn't really believe in miracles, and he tells me that it requires direction. "Alright prayer, if you must he says, "but definitely lots of hard work. You also need lots of determination, but most of all, when you are talking about singing or performing - practice! "That's all then", says me to him! *(Ha! It has never really changed then!)* You will need a big portion of determination to make the most out of a life, that in reality you may have been jolly lucky to have survived with at all. That life may bare no similarity to the life that you had planned out for yourself before, but life is still life, and I now think that you would probably prefer it, even with it's difficulties, to no life at all. Just think, if you were unlucky enough to prematurely die - you would never know what happened next in your favourite serial! *(In my case - Neighbours! Yes - it is still running in England in 2009, although it has not too long ago changed channel and format.)*

I guess though, that I am just relieved that my new plate has turned out to be not quite as 'un-tasty' as it had originally looked, and let me tell you - for a long time after the accident, it definitely looked very 'un-nice'. But I have had a wonderful husband for almost over 20 years, who took on a still very 'wounded soldier', in a monstrously encouraging way. I have a great daughter, who is - a typical teenager *(well alright, just 21).* - She can be a bit of a monster at times, but a nice one, I guess! *(I'm sure that some of you know what I mean!)* At present, in 2010 I am enjoying a relatively comfortable life, with some good friends, as well as the prospect of a fulfilling and interesting future *(unless this world wide credit crunch chews us up, and spits us out!),* with a new *(old [about 150 years], but refurbished)* house.

It's like a mews terrace! Almost very Soho, about 30 miles out of London!!

Lovely!!!

We should all be determined to make the most out of our lives, and yet whilst doing so, spread some good cheer and encouragement around the neighbourhood!

For me – the same determination that I had needed to succeed as a singer, now has had to be put to another, believe it or not, even more productive use - that of optimal survival in a very new, and very 'different' environment.

My daddy used to tell me that there is no point in being a 'misery guts', and yet sometimes he was the biggest one in the world! He used to 'why me'? - a lot - but I have found that you can only carry on doing so for a very limited amount of time. Your audience of understanding listeners, and well wishers is bound to very quickly disappear. Each one of us, has their own problems to deal with, and people can't really, and shouldn't be expected, to take yours on as well!

This next bit was told to me by a very intoxicated, apoplectic-ally, apologetic over something he had done, dad, when I, myself was about 19 or 20, I think it was. Whenever dad got a bit 'pissed' *(which as I have already shamefully admitted, was fairly frequently)*, he would apologise for just about anything, and when I was younger, *(I am also a bit ashamed to admit this)*, I used that trait of his to get some of the things I wanted! *(Oh I was a bad girl I was! But I think that we all did it if the opportunity arose, didn't we?)*

He apologised to me over the fact that he and my real mum had initially split up. He told me that at first he was very, very 'miffed', and that he was out to make someone, anyone, pay for the social indignity of it all. All of his friends had been telling him that 'it was totally unfair'. *(Well friends would wouldn't they?)*

Daddy would 'oh so' conveniently 'forget' to take me back *(smirk, smirk)*, and he used to tell me, "you dearest daughter, you would of course, just gurgle and giggle at all the coming and going, and yelling".

Daddy holding me as a baby

"For you, at your tender age", he said, "it was obviously a bit of a game", but he also said that he honestly couldn't see why there was a problem in the first place anyway! "You were after all, my little girl!", and he reckoned that I belonged with him.

My mum would have had to get a court order to have me returned, after dad had 'borrowed' me. The police would probably have grumbled, and disgustedly grinned at the shenanigans going on, 'once again' and then 'once again', again! Once more the police would return me to mum, only to find that a few days or a fortnight later, I would quietly be 'snuffled 'away again. They 'was not at all pleased'!

Or then there would be those times when dad would supposedly innocently, return me, but not quite on time! *(Generally a few days late!)* I guess that I must have been a bit like a much read library book! *(What's a few days, among friends he would say to me, when he was telling me about his too-ing and fro-ing.)* Yeah! That's what it must have been. I guess that I had somehow become his favourite library book! *(It's just a pity though, that I had never seen him reading anything other than the latest racing form papers)!*

My nana must have disbelievingly watched the whole situation unfold, and she probably regretted, having been mixed up with my dad and mum meeting in the first place, if indeed she had been. I can imagine that back then, she had probably just seen my dad as a great looking, eligible young man of about 28 or 30 at the time that he and my mum first met. She had probably rubbed her hands with glee, and happily bundled them off together. He must have seemed a good catch, for what nan possibly considered her now single daughter, with a son. He was, according to photos, a bit of a 'looker' when they first met. *(My dad that is, not the son! Although the son was probably a cute little thing. Most toddlers are! But then it was maybe a bit dangerous in the implied situation that eventually was!)* So I think that my nan , who has been gone many years now, played a big, almost predominant part in their actually getting married. Again, I think! Can't really know for sure! We are talking about over 60 years ago here, and the moral structures were very different to what they are now!

To be fair to everyone concerned though, a lot of what you have just read, are basically my own deductions of the situation, and are garnered from what dad had told me before he died, so those assessments are only one sided, really.

But – regardless of the truth of the emotions of the circumstances, now most of those concerned are either dead, or if still living, as are my siblings and my mum, they have productive, energetic lives, with the past well and truly in the past!! Dad is no longer around, and this book is partly my way of remembering the nice things, and exorcising the nastiness of that time from my own life!

Looking back on it all though, and before you read the next bit, I guess that I need to be a little fair to my lovely daddy. He is dead now, and he can't defend himself, but I reckon that maybe somehow in his war years, he had probably developed his 'oddity' for liking young men and boys, through no real fault of his own, I might add! He was in charge of a Prisoner of war camp, *(or so I was told. Whether it's true or not, because dad never discussed that part of his life with me, I have no real way of knowing for sure!)* I do know though, that there would have been men and boys of all ages *(some of the intake on both sides, had lied, and were only about 13 and they would have been totally unaware of what they were maybe getting into).* They would have found themselves, after even small misdemeanour's of some kind, stuck in barracks, with no women, and no way of relieving the sexual tensions that they were bound to have experienced in bucket loads full, at any age. They had no doubt been up to all kinds of what society would call 'bad things', but they were still normal healthy men, with normal healthy urges, and those urges had to be satisfied somehow! I hesitate to imagine how, but a lot of the 'behind the hand' chat and inferences I heard when I was 'treading the boards', graphically pointed out that those little boys must have proved very useful indeed! The kinds of adventures into sexual expression that dad supposedly got into, have been around since the early Roman days, and still abound in some European cities today. Those kinds of activity were, of course, very seriously frowned upon in the late forties, early fifties, in England and Australia, and that unfortunately was where my father was at. It was either very unwise, or very expensive and illegal, as well as super foolish to find sexual pleasure outside of socially acceptable, 'normal' boundaries, such as those found in marriage. Even heterosexual couples just living together was a definite no, no in those days!

I must say though, that although I personally never saw anything 'funny' in that 'sus' way about my dad *(I did see a lot of it in showbiz)*, there have been too many illusions to it for me not to believe that it was so. My mum and dad had stayed together long enough though for me to have become a 'little girl', so I don't think, and I hope for mum's sake that it wasn't too bad. Dad was evidently what he was, and couldn't really see that what he was doing was anything too wrong. Mum and dad went their separate ways, and even though dad then had custody of me when they actually parted, supposedly for the time being, mum decided that she would keep a very stringent eye on both of us, and intervene whenever/if ever if it became necessary.

Now - I am afraid that, as I think I said, most of my information about that side of my daddy's character comes from other people, and occasionally memories that I do have of suspiciously 'different' behaviour from him, but I do vaguely remember him not looking too well occasionally towards the end. The trouble was, I was just too busy with my own hectic life, to stop and take the time to try and work out why. Probably if I hadn't been so, ashamedly, busy with my own career, I might have noticed something weird. On those occasions when he had really started getting very sick, he just appeared to me to have 'hung one on' a few times too many, and although he was getting thinner, I guess that I put it down to his age, and his having had too many 'liquid' meals!

Funny *(or sick, depending on your attitude)*, it is now considered almost 'fashionable' to be gay. After all, some of the leading stars are - aren't they? Unfortunately a lot of them are dropping dead with AIDS. But it is even considered an 'in' thing to be, maybe! Knowing my mum as I think I do though, I can only assume that if his intentions towards mum's precious 'little boy', had been as suspicious as was intimated, then it would certainly have been a case of - 'grab the kid and run'. Justifiably concerned, mum would have taken off with her son tucked under her arm, back to her own mum. *(figuratively speaking of course!)* That is after all what mothers are supposed to be for, isn't it? *(Mums protect their offspring, at all costs! I think that probably, I might even commit murder, to save my daughter from being harmed. Again though - I think!)*

Please remember though that as with some of the previous bits, the the following is purely *my* figuring, probably with big gaps of personal things about which I know nothing, and if I am honest, I don't think that I really want to know anything more about any more anyway. I do though reckon with definite certainty that my real mum and dad did at least get married. *(I've seen the marriage certificate, and I know how 'must have it all proper' was my nana, and my mum is the same now!)* Happiness at first was probably a reality? *(It normally is with newly weds, isn't it?! After all - they haven't had time to get to know each other properly yet.)* Mum had me, so I have to assume that it mustn't have been all that bad, although one can never really tell. You know - the old "close your eyes and think of England", sort of thing.

43

As far as I can remember, I was a relatively happy child, with a fairly 'normal' kind of upbringing, dad's gambling escapades aside. *(Mind you, most kid's, having no comparisons, assume that their upbringing could be described as 'normal', don't they?)*

Fortunately for everyone concerned though, it was never really necessary for mum to intervene too much, if at all, once I was actually living with dad and Peggy. In fact, there were often long periods, *(even years)* when mum chose not to be in my life at all. I remember wondering at the time what I had done wrong to create such rejection! I didn't know whether it was her choice, or the prevailing circumstances at the time, but that is really irrelevant now. She loved me as much as she was able then, and I have since found out that she always kept quiet lookout, but never really intervened when I was young. I had some great visits with her while I was actually doing the visits, and then when I grew older, because she knew how determined to do things my own way I had become,she decided not to have any contact. Also - she had secured a very happy home life with her husband and children, and I doubt that she would have wanted daddy dearest polluting her world again.

There were of course, those odd occasions when I was a bit younger, and living with dad and Peggy, when mum would quietly intervene, and see to it that I had anything important that I needed. Like when she found out that Chas (dad) had plans to take me out of school without any qualifications. Mum had quietly stomped in *(if that is at all possible - stomping quietly I mean)*, making sure that I at least stayed on, and sat my final fourth year exams at school. My delightful, but not particularly wanting a smart cookie for a daughter daddy, let my poor long suffering mum, pay for a whole year of my school tuition, plus the extras. You see - dad would have had me leave at 15, with *no* qualifications at all. But mum, even though she wasn't particularly affluent herself at that time, had other ideas. *(My own husband sometimes says that it's a pity I don't appear to have inherited more of my mother's 'better sense' genes. Not that he wants me to be more like mum, he says, but sometimes I could do to be a bit more sensible, that's all. - Oh well"!)*

Poor mum though! I have no doubts that I would have posed a very troublesome, and unduly costly problem for her. The money involved, would probably have been sorely needed for her own new family. At that time I think that mum had Iain, Andrew *(the eldest of my younger siblings)*, and her much loved, diabetic, new husband to look after. My sister, Miriam, and brother Daniel the youngest, were probably just twinkles in their eyes at that time, and the extra expense involved, for her to intervene with me and have me finish school, must have created more than a few hardships and problems for them all! Even though, to a thirteen year old, the contrary seemed to have been the case - she must have loved me loads,'cause mum wasn't about to have me suffer too much! Thank heavens! I may not have always been a 'prize' child, but I had, at least , I'm not really sure how, done well at school, ending up with 5 A's and a B for my final exams. I also won an Alliance Francáis Prize for excellence in French speaking.

Peg and Charlie showed all the natural parental joy at my good results, having got out of it, money wise, pretty lightly. Mum's extra intervention with expenses seemed to have paid off though. *(I of course, hadn't known anything about mum paying for anything at that time!)* It had turned out though, that I was a good little French speaker, I was! *(Pity it didn't last! It would definitely have come in handy with me living so close to France now.)* I don't suppose that my dad had ever looked like having the small amount of money needed to keep me at school, even though the education itself was free. The horses or dogs generally got whatever spare or unknown about, 'borrowed' money that he did have. It wasn't much at the best of times, and I don't suppose that for him my school years would really have been classed as 'the best of times' anyway! He just wanted me out there earning, and bringing home money, a.s.a.p. He was probably pretty sure that he wouldn't have a lot of trouble getting some of it out of me, to bolster his gambling pot!

Mum must have been a bit disappointed that I didn't want to continue on with school past year 4, but my Grades on leaving school were more than good enough to assure a good Banking career at least. *(for a while, anyway!)* That would probably have compensated mum a little, and did also make Peg and Charlie happy as well.

Charlie was forever reminding me about the joys to be had if I were to bring some of my work home occasionally!

(O goodness!, I have just realised what he meant! Bad daddy!)

Come to think of it though - there would have been no 'goodness' about such a fulfilled request - would there?!

But anyway, as it turned out, I must have been born with 'restless gremlins', because they always seem to have been around, and after a while, with me trying to 'fit in' at the bank, they *(the gremlins?)* must have made their presence felt, and they decided for me, that bank work was a 'truly no go option'!

I mean, after all - having done Hansel and Gretel at school - and having performed on the boxes for charity - they *(the gremlins, I must have always had them)* kept whispering *(and rather loudly, I might add!)*, - "You just want to SING, don't you"?!!

(Shoot! I haven't told you about Hansel and Gretel, or the box stages yet, have I? I will!) I won't forget- promise!

PEGGY!

Going back a bit though - dad had told me that he had realised that for him to actually have me living with him he would need someone to help him bring up his little girl. He really knew very little about girls, and the sorts of things they might need, being a bit of a 'man's man', as he undoubtedly was! *(Hadn't thought of that, had he?)*

He figured correctly that he wasn't going to be allowed, nor able, to bring me up alone, and that he probably wouldn't have enjoyed it too much anyway. 'Pooey' nappies, and baby puke, weren't really his idea of fun! They were what he called - 'women's work'! He questioned himself - "who was going to look after the baby when he had to go to work"? - "Nannies are too expensive, and too difficult for me to find. I know - simple, - I won't go to work", he must have jubilantly thought!

(Typical dad - I can just see him twirling his imaginary moustache, saying to himself - "see Charlie, - no problems! Sorted!"). I have to suppose that he has always been technically, a bit of a 'bludger' *(a good Aussie word - meaning a 'do as little as possible' no hoper)* at heart.

"Some illness with a weeks isolation period, that's what I need", he would have thought. So out came this medical book that he had found at the bottom of a 'job lot' of books that he had bought at some jumble sale or other, and he looked for the right communicable disease. Having found it, he then found a call box, scrounged the penny for the call, and phoned in sick with some sort of illness that would legitimately keep him off work for a week and a bit. A bit more time, to clear his head was what he needed, and then maybe he would be able to make it permanent he reckoned - *(or so he told me one rainy afternoon, on one of our get 'together's' when I was working the club circuit, and when he had been drinking at home!).* He'd find some way or other to get the money that he would inevitably need! Being optimistic, as he always was most of the time, he figured that he would get away with it. That of course, was partly because his doctor mate had said that he would give him a sick note verifying any bona fide medical complaint, as long as it was a real complaint! They seem to have gotten away with murder in those days! But then, come to think of it - there are people getting away with murder, even today! Oh well! He must have just been full of the joys of life, and thought right from the very beginning - "fatherhood here I come". Dad had a habit of always looking on the bright side of life! *(so maybe I have also inherited his ability to always do just that! I know that I got it from somewhere!)*

But as it turned out, 'fatherhood' was not really the best career choice for my daddy. He had obviously had NO experience of bringing up a female toddler. So that option soon lost it's appeal! He did tell me once, a long time ago, that it took only two days of changing nappies for him to wonder what on earth he had done. Although I wasn't 'technically' still in nappies as such, I was still in them at night time, and because of the new surroundings, I was prone to still be in need of them during the days sometimes too. He had to wipe up sick, *(of which there were bucket loads of due to the strangeness of my new daily routine, and because of some of the 'sus' food he was evidently feeding me),* and he had to find some way to entertain *(or at least try to),* a small, out of her normal environment child. From what memory I do have of that time, *(which obviously isn't that much)* and from what he subsequently told me, he did try at first. That was until we ran out of food, and he suddenly realised that he didn't have enough to feed himself, let alone a growing child as well. I don't think either that they had viable unemployment benefits at that stage, not at the beginning any way! Also they didn't yet have 'instant', or tinned meals for kiddies, and he hadn't really learned to cook vegetables and things. He ran out of what he could cook, *(baked beans that he could mash up, for one, mashed potatoes for another!)* and didn't really have the where withal to purchase any more! He told me that he said to himself - "Drat - That kid's got to eat. *(charming, wasn't he?!), a*nd I guess that I've got to eat as well. I guess that I'll just have to go on earning some money, to buy the food. I haven't even got enough to have a flutter to try to win some more", he complained to himself. He hadn't really thought of that. - "Oh - Bugger" he said. He watched as a few dejected looking moths, fluttered feebly out of his coat pocket, and he said *(so he told me)*, something like - "I am what a bloke might just call - broke"! *(A pretty habitual state for him, from what I can gather, and I have cleaned up what he is likely to have said!)*

I don't think that he must have given much thought to any of the other problems that there were likely to be either. He possibly had the romantic thought of bringing up his little girl, the way that he wanted, with no interference from anyone. But to make matters worse, there he was, all alone, with only a couple of grumpy old men friends. This of course, was before Peggy arrived on the scene. He knew that he and the men, had had very little training for bringing up a girl child, and suddenly he didn't really feel that he really wanted to learn about it either. He had backed himself into a corner - again! That was a thing that he was evidently very good at, and a thing that I have seen for myself, that he frequently did!

Also remember - they didn't yet have disposable nappies, and his first effort, by himself with a dirty nappy , (or *so again, I was told by him*), was a real Abbot and Costello sketch! He said that I had started to cry, and after having had his nose assailed by a strange unpleasant odour, he finally realised that I might just be in need a nappy change*(clever boy!)*. He said to me, that when he had taken the nappy off my wriggling butt, the resultant excrement was a yellow/ochre colour.

That could, of course have been because we had been eating a lot of baked beans and mashed potato and nothing much else. Do you think?

Just lots of milk in my case! So the 'pongy' excrement ended up all over the improvised change table, and because someone wasn't too good with the washing either *(I think that that may just have been my daddy!)*, the towel that he had placed on a kitchen type table in the corner, went from a 'greyish' colour, *(it had originally been white)* to a lovely, bright mud, yellow. Dung brown? Most classy! Well done daddy! Even with all his concerted efforts at keeping a wriggling child still while he got the nappy to do what it was supposed to do, once he had taken it off of my continually active rear end, the 'poo' had ended up all up the walls, over the floor, and he smelt like a proper "dunny" *(the good old Australian word for toilet)*.

"I know", he said, holding his nose against the aromatic odour, emanating from the nappy! "Maybe I could con one of my mates to help out". But having remembered that they had looked in on him once or twice, joked about the mess and the smell, and scampered off as quickly as they could, without offering any help, he said to himself - "Naah! Maybe that wouldn't be a particularly good idea then"!

He reckoned that that would probably have been stretching the friendships a bit far. After all - his friends would have known almost as little about bringing up babies, as he did! If anyone got wind of the true situation, then neither the authorities, nor mum would have been too impressed! "Watch out in the future little one", dad says that he said to me - "looking after kids is definitely women's work. Why is it that women know better how to cope with smelly infant behinds", he told me he said to himself in his innocence of how the world really works.

"I suppose ideally",he sulkily thought, "that I should try to get a woman to help out, but four days is all I've got to find someone before I have to go back to work. That is if I've still got a job to go back to"!

"Now - let's see - there just has to be someone who would relish playing mother, and who will look after us in the manner in which we would like to become accustomed". He had a very strong opinion of his own self worth.*(Does that sound a bit like me?!)*

Unfortunately for him, there was definitely no way that he could afford to pay anyone. I don't think that he would even have been prepared to forego his 'flutter for riches', but he still needed someone who would keep house for him, his mates and now his little girl. He wasn't feeling too optimistic about his chances though, with so little time available!! Maybe he could leave me with the fella's", he cheekily thought? "I've only got four days too", he says he pondered. "Most things could be organised in four days" he said, but miracles, "I'm not too sure about them! I suppose that they might just take a 'wee' bit longer!"

Then he says that he laughed at his own attempt at humour, remembering the fact that I seemed to be always wetting my pants or my nappy. "Maybe I should try being a comedian, and earn some money that way", he said.

(Just as well you didn't daddy dearest!)

Apart from my real Mum, he hadn't had much luck with the female half of the world so far, and come to think of it, I don't suppose that you could really say that he had had much luck with her either. "Ah, I know - One of my drinking 'buddies'", he thought! "They must know of an undemanding, affection starved woman who loves children. *Yeah!* - that's it! My mates!" He then came to monumental brick wall; he did some serious pondering, and finally decided, *(I'm afraid that I can't know whether it was happily or not) -*

"Bugger - I suppose that I will have to marry the damn woman that I choose though! But then", he thought, "for what is entailed, I don't suppose that's too high a price to pay! Mind you", he says he said to himself, "I'll need someone who won't feel too averse to having two other 'fella's' being around. Nor of our getting married quick smart, if it can be arranged quickly". *("With a bit of luck, if I were to handle it right", he says he thought, "and I appeal to her better senses, I might not even have to marry the woman straight away - if at all!")* Thinking about it now, maybe his luck must've been in, for a change, for he never did marry poor Peg!

He must have figured that there had to be someone out there who was desperate enough to take pity on us all, and help us out. "After all", he thought, "for the right woman, who would really look after us, the real draw card will be Kerrie" *(My mother spells my name Kerrie. I changed to just Kerri for work.)* In his typically masculine thought process of the time, he would have said to the other fellows -

"Women love kids, and I guess that I could probably manage to be loving to someone if they looked after us all! - I am not too good at all that cooking racket anyway, and to tell the truth - I think that I'd hate it!"

Then dad said that one of his mates had said that he maybe knew of just such a someone. Grigor had said to dad, "You know Charlie mate - I think that I know of just the right woman - my little sister! Although for a little sister, she is a bit on the large size, but her size is compensated for by the fact that she comes with a widow's pension. Her deceased husband was a war hero"! Dad must have said to himself - "ah, ah, a widowed lady of means - yes, yes!"

Peggy and Daddy about 1953

He told me though, that when he first saw Peggy he wasn't sure at first whether this was going to be the right option after all. She was *fat*, he told me and he said, that that was just a bit of an understatement. Mind you, at that time she was still only about 15 stone; not a stunner, but not an ugly sight either. It turned out that she was lots of fun when he got to know her, and from what dad and his friends could garner early on, it appeared, mostly up for a good time. *(I have to wonder though, just what exactly they would have called a 'good time'?, 'cause Peggy definitely wouldn't have been 'up for' anything 'different', and morals were pretty stiff in those days, and I guess that she figured that just living with my dad and the others was already risqué enough!!)*

The following are just summations, because I can't really know what was going through his mind, but judging by the conversations that I remember having with my dad, he must have thought -"well, if she is fat, and I guess that I would have to admit that she is, she probably wont be too sexually demanding of me". Some thing that had crossed dad's mind! - "Don't know how I'd cope with too much interest in all that, anyway!", he said. "But I imagine though that I'll have 'to do the job' occasionally ", he must have grumbled, and muttered to himself! Most promising, from his point of view though, had been that earlier comment his 'buddy' had made. It must have intrigued my dad, and it definitely got him very interested. As I wrote - his mate had said - "She comes with a widow's pension". Dad's ears probably pricked up like a fox's, that had heard a noise, or caught a scent! Easy pickings for gambling money? *(I can just see him - twirling his imaginary moustache again, thinking - mm!).* He must have happily thought - "Yes - yes - yes, things are definitely looking up!" *(Little did he know!)* Now I can't really know if Peg genuinely loved my dad at first, and she probably just felt lucky to have found someone to share that part of her life with, but I am pretty sure that she must have done so, or at least felt something near 'love' after spending 25 years with him.

It's funny what kinds of things I do remember though. Sometimes!

Peg and I were having one of our not too frequent mother daughter chats one day, and I was saying that Harry *(I'll tell you about him later too)* and I were talking about having a baby once we were married.

(The thought of her being a doting grand mum, really brightened up her 'not much happening' life, I can tell you. Peg told me sadly, that even though she'd been pregnant three times before her war time husband had been killed, she had miscarried each time at about 4 months. She had unfortunately been told that the likelihood of her being able to carry a baby to full term was pretty small. So she had been thrilled to be introduced to Daddy, and she was positively ecstatic when he introduced her to me.

53

"Just think, instant motherhood", she must have thought.

"I got my baby", she told me grinning from ear to ear, giving me a big bosomy cuddle! *(At 22, you don't really know which way to look amidst a bosomy cuddle, I can tell you!.)* Especially when the bosoms were so *huge*, and hers were *hugely huge!*

Her beloved elder brother, whom she loved and trusted, just happened to occasionally live in the shared accommodation with dad and the others, and he had introduced them, so she must have thought at the time - "He sounds nice enough - been in the army eh? *(that was their first error)*, and what a 'looker' *(second mistake? - although I guess that as I said before, he* was *'goodish' looking when he was younger)!"* Unfortunately he ended up with most of his teeth gone, and those that were left, were brown *(diseased)*, holey, and probably hanging on by the edge of their skin. *(That is of course, if teeth have skin! I don't think that* he himself *was particularly holey, but his teeth definitely were.)* Peg was probably thinking that she had scored, big time! Dad on the other hand must have had 'iffy' confidence in his ability to carry off a relationship with a woman very well, and after my real Mum, if what they have said about him is definitely true, then I'm not at all surprised! "That's ve – r -y interesting about her pension though", he must have thought I'll just need to make sure I don't get lost in her flab," he says he cheekily said to himself. "Damn it, I'm in a bit of a hurry, so I can't let a bit of blubber bother me too much!"

Peg told me that he told her about having to get back to work on the next Monday, and that although he had said that he was a bit disappointed that they wouldn't have more time together, *(a typical sweet talking male?)* both of them had decided that they'd bother about a ceremony and honeymoon later! *(Either he was able to sweet talk her sufficiently well, or she was just feeling desperate!)* Peg would probably have been super eager to get on with her new, exciting future, and she must have decided that the sanctity of marriage would just have to wait for a bit. Knowing how sexual Peggy was as well, even though she was not exactly svelte and 'sexy', I should imagine that dad's 'problem', if he still had one then, was kept under wraps for quite some time!

She probably would have said to herself - "A marriage probably won't be that long a way, not if I have anything to say about it, anyway". It had probably seemed 'so sudden', and 'so unexpected' to Peg already, but I can imagine *(remembering how satisfied she was sometimes, when I was at home, and in between her decidedly cross interludes)* that she probably found it super, and wonderful!!!!! And anyway - dad would have craftily said, "plenty of time", probably not even realising that he *was* being crafty! Peg had suddenly been given her family to look after, and she wanted to get stuck in to playing mother, straight away! But you know, she must have noticed a few little, niggling things about dad, even during those first few days. Things that if she hadn't been so preoccupied with being a 'mother' to me, might just have concerned her a little.*(But I don't suppose that one can tell, after all this time, and it's not really my job to put words in place for them anyway, is it?)* Those rented digs with the other guys sufficed at first, and they moved in together straight away! *(positively unheard of, in those days)*

The other men sharing with dad may have been a bit hesitant about still having the kid about, but they probably also thought to themselves - "Yippee - home cooked meals", so although she didn't pay rent, I bet Peggy well and truly earned her keep! *(Not that way silly)!*

Dad told me that Peggy had made friends with me easily enough, and that he was evidently so thrilled about it, that he had quietly said to himself - "ah - it looks as though I've at least done the right thing this time. Just what we need - someone who'll be happy to look after all of us, and not only that – home cooked meals!" So Dad was happy and probably feeling pretty clever, the boys were happy enough, and Peggy was 'gob smacked.' Peg also told me that she'd optimistically thought - "Well - even if I don't have a child of my own, the prospect of looking after Charlie and this lovely little girl seems to solve a lot of possible problems. I'll have a husband *(kind of)*, and I'll pretend, and lavish Kerrie with love, just as if she were my very own". I guess you could say that, in whatever ways she could afford to, she did kind of spoil me! I did go without a lot of things, but was never short of love and cuddles from her.

"And anyway - you never know Charlie", she probably said snuggling up to him one day, whispering in his ear in a sexy kind of whisper - "maybe we will have one of our own in time"! Dad told me though, that at that comment - he quietly, positively cringed! Peg was the eternal optimist, *(another thing I inherited maybe? - not genetically, but by close proximity)*.

Before dad, she hadn't actually met anyone serious since her husband had been killed, apart from a few 'not right', one night stand, ex soldiers. *(She would have been a bit of a raver – my step mum)* So when her brother introduced her to this good looking, apparently upper class young gentleman, even though she was a bit wary, she was also over the moon. *(Dad was a sort of good actor, who liked to 'play 'toff' whenever he could, and he mustn't have done too bad a job of it, I don't suppose!)* I don't think Grigor could have known anything of dad's sexual preferences before he introduced his sister to him *(he probably would have killed him if he had known)*, 'cause he knew that Peg had wanted a 'family' more than anything. Her own family had seen how desperately disappointed she had been after her own miscarriages, so I doubt that they would have said anything that would distress their precious sister, even if suspicions had come up and bitten them on the big toe. Just as long as Charlie didn't start bashing her! Grigor would have killed him, if he had!

Dad though, had never shown any 'real' signs of being 'different', and had always appeared 'normal' to me, and to the neighbours - again, I think. A bit lovably thick sometimes - but hey! Most dads seem that way to their children, until the child grows up a bit. He did after all, biologically father me , and anyway, Peg had three big burly brothers who were definitely fisty cuff types, so dad would probably have been 'done over' if Peg had ever said anything about not being kept reasonably happy that way.

(But then - maybe she knew them too well to say anything!) I never dared, or even thought to ask, *(didn't do that sort of thing in those days - not any days really!)*, and by the time I moved out at 18 and a bit, it was no longer an issue anyway! Society had moved on, but to be honest, it probably would have created all sorts of trouble if I had known for sure that they weren't married, when I was much younger. I was a typical *(for just about any days,)* young person/ teenager, and it just wasn't done in those days, to have that kind of scandal lurking around in the broom cupboard! Just living together, I mean to say!

Back then though, if they had suddenly gotten married, the talk in the street would have been amazingly derisive, and not liking to be the topic of conversation in the neighbourhood, they had probably decided that it would be easier if they just continued living together. So, for about 25 years, everyone believed that they were married, as they lived together as Mr and Mrs Dyer. *(The relationship lasted longer than most proper marriages do now a days, anyway!)* De-facto partners, long before it became a fashionable thing to be. Now a days, it wouldn't even raise an eyebrow. But can you imagine the trouble it would have caused them in 1953?

In 1978, not too long before my accident, I 'threw' them a 'silver wedding anniversary' party! Most everybody thought of them as a married couple anyway remember, and so a wide variety of friends, 'rellies' and my workmates, were all invited to one of my 'showbiz' jobs *(I'll tell you about that a bit later too),* and we took over part of a working men's, or RSL club for the night. *(Can't remember now, which it was)*

Everybody enjoyed the celebration of their 25 years together. Peg and Charlie had become *so* proud of me!

Their 'little princess' I was! - Not only an entertainer, but one who had worked at the Sydney Opera House, which would have seemed to them, and was, a monumental achievement. What is more - to have *their* daughter on daytime television, performing for Australia, almost every month, even sometimes every week! In their eyes they had done a 'bonza' job. I was making something good of my life. There was no doubt about it, and again not wanting to toot my own trumpet too much, I guess I was a real source of pride for them. Because they had nothing, I guess that the promise of wealth *(through me)* must have lit up their eyes as they watched me perform. Peggy used to grin from ear to ear, with tears trickling from her eyes, while Charlie laughed and cheered with the best of them. At one of my 'shows' one night though, he unfortunately told off a guy in the audience. The guy had become what Dad called, 'a bit too friendly'! *(Towards me sillies, not to my Dad! As I have said, from what I have been told, I'm not too sure if he would have been too cross about the fellow's being too friendly to him!)*

The poor fellow, if he'd been sober, would have been so very ashamed. I was momentarily distraught, at my dad's reaction! But then - you know something? I shouldn't have been. Both dad and the man were actually *so* drunk that they wound up crying on each other's shoulders, about how good the soubrette *(the fellow's word, meaning me)* had been, and what a wonderful and entertaining show she had put on!

Dad was suddenly in his element having already told the guy that I was his daughter! His chest must have really swelled, and he probably felt a bit like a cockerel, standing on a roof top, crowing! The guy had said - "What about her climbing on the tables, and parading right under everyones' noses? Then a big hearty slap on the back followed, along with a raucous laugh! "Wasn't she *great*, and what's more she sings like a nightingale, doesn't she?" The fellow kept heavily patting daddy on the back *(I think that dad may even have ended up with a few very nasty, congratulatory bruises)*. It was almost as if dad had done the show himself! So, Peg and Charlie's '25 year together' celebration ended up a great time, with everyone having a ball. My pocket was a lot lighter, because I had arranged for Peg and Charlie to appear to have a win on the 'pokies' *(poker machines; not all that easily organised; but something that they loved)* and they staggered home drunk via the limo that I had arranged for them. They were both 'well pleased' with their daughter, and with the 'silver *('living together')* wedding anniversary' party that I had organised for them!

Off they had gone, very 'pissed', feeling a bit richer, and having been serenaded by some of Australia's 'star' club performers. What a celebration it was!!! Such a pity I don't have any photos, only those that remain in my brain, which unfortunately are a bit cobwebby!

Peg had chosen that night to tell me again, in an apologetic but totally unnecessarily tearful state, "I - if we had actually been married, as I had originally wanted, I would have lost my widow's pension plus all the associated benefits *(medical etc.)*,and then where would we have been? Your dad is not what I would call a great provider at the best of times, and I am not what you would call an inexpensive mate medically"! I told her that she had been lucky to have received the help she had received, but that when I was rich and famous *(which I of course believed was just around the corner)*, they could relax in the fact that I would make sure she was looked after medically, and that we could even have a 'remarriage' service for them. A kind of 'vow renewal' service! In her final years though, although having grown a little bit more, Peg remained fairly attractive! She was about 20 stone when she died. A state of affairs, I might add, that Peg hated, but obviously not enough. Not meaning to be at all rude, 'cause I could never be rude to Peg, but I would say - and I think Peg would have agreed with me, that 20 stones, and only 5ft 2, is BIG and round! I have been told that it definitely caused the mortuary a few serious problems when she died.

(On her less down days, she used to tell me - "I'm just cuddly, that's all!")

I think that dad just saw it as a positive excuse not to bother with any intimacy, so he wasn't about to complain too much, was he?! Again,I have to say – "I think", because I can't *really* know, can I?

She did have one thing in her favour though *("apart from her pension", Dad would have said)*, and that was that she did always like to be clean and very well dressed at all times. She had always ordered clothes from a catalogue for the more 'generously proportioned' figure. Some of her nightdresses had to be seen to be believed.'Especially on washing day'. Her undies, were also on the 'gargantuan' size, and they used to look a little like sail boat sails, flapping about on the line. *(I guess that was why we never seemed to have a problem with migrant birds visiting our yard.)* Dad did keep budgies and things, but they had grown used to the underwear fluttering in the breeze, so they didn't really bother them,and they paid them no notice! They *(the panties)* were at first, *(while I was too young to really notice, and when Peg was still pulling out all the stops for Charlie)*, large copies of the latest in 'sexy' underclothes. I don't suppose she ever stood much chance of getting thin though - either her mother, or Grandmother was a BIG lady as well! I am not too sure which one was in the photo I saw, never actually meeting either of them. Peg was always there for me though, whenever life got too hard for me to bear, as it often seemed to do for teenagers, especially miscreant ones such as I apparently was!. Whenever I had boy troubles, which seems to have been all too often - guess who was there for me. Not only to remonstrate, but also to try to help me pick up the pieces? My real mum only really found out about some of the escapades, when poor Peg and Charlie suddenly had an 18 year old leave home - to live with a man twice her age! *(yes, that was Ed)* Shock and horror! They were instantly on the phone to her, with their cries of - "Where did we go wrong?"

As I was growing up, I probably caused Peg and Charlie, along with the teachers and people at school,a whole lot of angst, so I shouldn't really be too surprised that Peg and Charlie fought as much as they did! I guess that I was what you might call a 'little devil' *(and that's definitely putting it nicely)*. I did though always feel that Peg and Charlie loved me loads, and that Peg probably never really approved of what eventually became dad's all too frequent outbursts. Charlie used to beat me to within an inch of my life sometimes, and then burst into apoplectic tears of remorse. He would cuddle my bruised, and sore body so closely and cover me with kisses, begging my forgiveness, whilst doing almost as much damage to me, all over again. No wonder I have become such a confused 'biddy'. Peg would try to intervene, sometimes successfully - sometimes not. There were also plenty of good times though, with Peg and Charlie being lots of fun, especially when he wasn't drunk, or when he hadn't lost at the races, and had a win for a change! Peg had tried not to let her weight stop her too often from doing what she wanted to do. We had done a lot of things together as a family, and I have some wonderful photos of us together - somewhere!

But even with Dad's 'oddness' and Peg's size, they probably had some kind of intimacy. After all they battled on together, for more than 25 years, to provide themselves, me and my little foster brother Micky *(I'll tell you more about him a little later too)*, with a relatively happy home. Sometimes I would feel embarrassed, as most kids do of their parents, but I guess that looking back on it now, although it was a good time in my life, and was definitely 'different', I always felt that I had a 'normal mum and dad' situation, with the added bonus of that extra mum! Mustn't forget that extra mum! I figured that I was a lucky kid – two mothers!

I didn't know at that time, that there could be a 'not normal', and I considered that their quarrels about his gambling, although fairly frequent, were normal enough in themselves. In Greenacre in the 50's, mums and dads generally always fought!

Peg and Charlie's 'domestics' though, sometimes had to be seen, or heard, to be believed. Especially if Dad had been drinking. He would not only suddenly get vicious, but as I have already said – he would, after knocking the sense out of Peg, me, or my foster brother Mickey, *(sometimes all three)*, be in tears, begging forgiveness and vowing that he hadn't meant it, and that he would never do it again! *(Oh yeah!)* But to give him his due, he didn't - *(well not until the next time anyway!)*

Such a handsome family!

Now Peggy? Now what to say about that wonderful person?! Peg spoiled me when she could , but she also reprimanded and punished me when I did serious things wrong, and even for just being a bit of a scamp and a scally wag if that scamping, or scally wagging, got out of hand *(as it sometimes did!)*. I hate to admit it, but it was probably a little too often too, judging by things I have been told.

But even though she had enormous hands, as far as this young person was concerned, her punishments were a lot gentler than Dad's. She never really clouted me! *(Well, not too hard anyway)* Her big hands though, did sometimes deliver very controlled, moderated belts about the bum - that would *(lovingly?)* pull you into line quick smart! And although the accident on the 28th July, 1979 *(shoot, I haven't told you about that yet either, have I?)* may have been most unusually, an 'uncontrolled', and 'un - moderated' belt about the head, instead of the bum - it most definitely had the same effect of pulling me into line quick smart!

I was still understandably, a bit cross with the world after that accident *(don't worry - if you continue reading , I'll tell you more about the accident later on as well as some of the other things that, because of my still wobbly memory, I haven't told you yet!)*, but I really do wish that I had been more truly awake when Daddy saw me at the hospital, four and a half months after the accident! He, like everyone else, had thought I was going to die, but I didn't! *(some would probably say – Pity, but we don't care about them, do we?!)* I may as well have done though, for all the good that I was to anyone at first. I also would so like to have been able to reassure Dad of my love at the time. He died himself, the next day after I came too I think it was. Mind you - if his spirit can feel, even all these years later, the love that still emanates towards him from me , then he will know that I still love him loads, and I hope that he would be happy that I have married again. That I am being very well looked after, by the very same man that I ran off to live with at 18. My 'older man', husband. My wonderful Ed!

I must admit though, that that first time of our getting involved, back in 1969, my own Papa had not been too enthused about Ed and I being together. Dad's little girl was only 18 and a bit. He felt that Ed had stolen away his daughter, to live in what my father *(and everyone else I might add)* at the time, called - 'sin'! Dad didn't really like it at all then. *(I think that it was most definitely a case of - 'what was good enough for the male gander, was definitely 'not on' for his darling gosling!)* After all, remember, Ed had been almost twice my age at that stage, which would have been an absolute anathema to Dad and society, at the time! Why I'm not too sure though, when I think about it now.

But – I think that he would be more than happy with the way it has all turned out,and he would be pleasantly impressed with the way Ed looks after his, *(Dad's)* 'little girl', *(not so little any more)* and his 'little girl's' little girl *(also not so little any more!)*.

Ed says now, that although he had initially been caught up in the romance of our 'thing', when I was 18 and a bit, after he had had time to properly evaluate the situation, he had decided that it wasn't fair to tie me down so young, with what he says was an 'old' man. Ed also didn't feel he had any right to hold back such a talented, young thing. At least that's his excuse, *(as if he ever needed one any more)*, and he is sticking to it! He is now my husband, and has been since my daughter was one year old. 20 years, and I know I will probably say it many many times before this book is finished, but that is because I *am* a very, very, very,

very lucky lady, and Charliene has had the best of 'Daddies' for all of her 'rememberable' life. Even if typical of her age, she hasn't yet reached the truly appreciative age!! Almost though! Maybe, in a strange way, it was all meant to be. What they call - Kismet or Karma!

Wherever my daddy went when he died, I and you can rest assured that he's making the best of whatever situation he has found himself in! He should feel happy in the knowledge, *(if only there was some way of letting him know),* that I am finally happy!

By the time they work out how to do that *(have me talk to him I mean),* I'll be dead as well, and then we can have a face to face - or a spectre to spectre reunion! Won't that be nice? That is of course, if we end up in the same place!

I sometimes like to imagine him at the great big, dog or horse racing course in the sky, or maybe down below - the more likely option - *("I didn't say that"!)* with his favourite greyhound winning either the 'Heavenly Angel's Stake' up there, or the 'Devil's Demons Handicap' down below, over and over and over again! He would be eternally, ecstatic, and I guess that he does deserve to be - *(really!)*

There I go again - getting side tracked! I guess that we had best get back to the story - again!

But as I said before though, Peg would often agree that although I had been a naughty girl, and although they sometimes didn't like some of the things I got up to, she and daddy always loved me. "He just has a strange way of showing it", she would say to me!

My own daughter now, is probably tired of hearing similar things from me. She hasn't, though, been spanked since she was about six. Mind you - she doesn't do really bad things, and is no where near as naughty as I was.

She does though evidently, find it a bit embarrassing to have a mother that did some of the things that I have done, even though no one but her and my husband knows of them. *(That is not until I wrote this book)*

But even when she does do something naughty, which luckily is very rarely, I wouldn't dare smack her now. She would probably hit me back!

She is a young woman now!

Charliene has said to me, on a number of occasions, that although Papa can sometimes be a bit strict, and a bit dithery; underneath, she does love him a lot – really. Which is probably just as well, because Ed is a wonderful man that also loves her a lot! Again -really!

I cringe when I hear of men *(or women for that matter)* beating their children. The couple that inflicted 180 broken bones on their little person, and the mother who organised the mass hunt for her supposedly kidnapped child, when all the time she had her locked up in a flat, on starvation rations! Unbelievable! All that was done in the hope of getting a big payout from the media when she miraculously discovered the child.

Luckily my not so little any more girl, never has suffered in that way and hopefully will grow up knowing, that whatever, she is loved more than almost anything else in the world by both me and her step dad. Just as I was, really, by both Peggy and Charlie, and my real mum.

My biological mother told me about 25 years ago that my dad and she had had a 'heart to heart' discussion, the day before he died. They had met up at my bedside in the hospital. He had looked so unwell evidently, that mum, who drives, must have been overtaken by her Christian 'be good to your fellow man' better self, and offered him a lift home. Dad wasn't very well, and was still evidently grieving really badly because of Peggy's death. To make things worse, both Peg and he had been thinking that I was going to die, for ages before this time. Peggy would have been devastated, and now, with Charlie having lost her, he himself must have been absolutely lost. His precious little girl had been in a coma for such a long time. He would have had to handle a funeral for Peg, as well as having to try and get in to see my inert body, all without anyone there to help. Although I think that some of her family, and my mum probably helped out! Not being well himself, dad too had thought that I was going to die; and then when he had seen me the day before he himself died, although joyfully knowing that I had come out of the coma, he must have been devastated again because as I was really only half out of it, and wasn't able to talk properly, I hadn't even recognised him! I didn't really recognize anyone. Can you imagine - to not even recognise your own father! It was bad enough that I didn't recognize my husband, but to not recognize your own dad!! And what is more – he knew that I didn't recognize him! I wasn't exactly what you would call very communicative, either.

In fact I was probably, unknowingly, very 'not nice'!

When I think about it now, there would have been a lot of things that I probably would have discussed with him if I had been able to. I now sit for hours pondering over that whole spectrum of my life. Thinking back on it all, I tell myself that I could do without some parts, and yet am still unable to enjoy again the bits that I desperately wanted to relive! During those first few years in Greenacre with Peggy and Charlie, whenever and if ever I had thought about it,*(I was a little kid after all)* I must have wondered why I didn't have at least a brother or sister at home with us. I had seen how much Peg *(I called her mum, most of the time by then)* loved children, and I used to casually hint, as only 4-5 year old's can hint, that so and so's 'mummy' at the school, had just had a beautiful little boy, or that Jemima had just got a baby sister. Wasn't that nice?

But I didn't dare to ask if I was going to get one, - well you don't at that age, do you? *(Alright - some kids would ask - but I didn't.)* Maybe it was because, I felt that I was already 'special', having TWO mums. No one else that I knew had that, and I sure didn't really want to have to share them with anyone else, now did I? Anyway – much to my chagrin I guess, when dad presented Peg with the opportunity to foster Micky, they both happily grabbed at it with both hands. *(The opportunity, not the little boy. Although I guess from what I have been told, that Dad must have grabbed at him a bit as well)* The coercion to get Peg on side with the fostering hadn't really needed to be all that strong. After all, as I said, at that time she had apparently seen nothing major to make her query his suggestion to foster. Micky was a pretty little boy *(probably not a good omen in the situation),* but he was obviously unhappy at losing his Mum, or as unhappy as a 2 year old can be anyway. He saw his real Dad every four to six weeks. Having had his wife die, I don't think that Micky's father, who had been one of the regular visitors to the flat that dad shared with the other men, had thought that he could look after Mickey well enough by himself. Micky seemed to settle in with us, relatively well at first, and my dad must have been on his best behaviour for a while,a couple of years I would say! Peg wanted to believe that her little family was OK, didn't know that there was any reason for it not to be, and even if the reality of the situation had eventually come up and bitten her, she no doubt would have found some, any excuse or reason to not believe it, and she would probably have chosen just to ignore it.

I wasn't actually living at home whenever whatever happened with Micky, happened - so I am afraid that as I can't really know for sure, I had better not go into it too deeply. I have been told a few things though, and as I haven't spoken to him personally, in over 33 years though, I don't think that I should comment on what I'm not real sure about, do you? But I do know that Dad used to drink, and that when you are a drinker, as he most obviously was when he could afford it - a bit of a serious drinker and gambler, it would have been very difficult for him sometimes, to stay sober and not lose his inhibitions. He could quite easily have become too friendly, *(or rude)* with Micky. And my daddy did a lot of that! *(have his inhibitions disappear that is)*, and without inhibitions, and with his tendency to act before thinking, judging by what I have been told, the things that were supposed to have happened, probably did!

Talk about a strange family to find yourself landed in! Charlie drank and gambled; was reported a bit 'iffy'; and Peggy used to buy things on the 'never never', with payments that she couldn't really afford, spread over 6-12 months or so. Her widows pension paid for a lot of things needed for her, me, Micky and for the house, but she did try never to use it to aid Charlie's gambling habit. Sometimes successfully, sometimes not! She did though, being the lovely person she was, occasionally, sneakily bail him out of trouble! *(Now - either my Dad was very lucky, or Peg was overly besotted!)* If I had spent a moment to think about it at the time, I guess that I already had 'different', and didn't really need to 'wish' for it after all. Did I?

Sometimes good *(bad)* old Charlie would intercept the mail, and forge Peg's signature to get hold of the giro cheques of her pension. *(He learned to be a super good forger in his 'good old, bad old days'! Aw - he was a bad boy!)* Peg, being poor - even saved Food stamps! *(Goodness – I can't be that old–can I?)* Bookmakers didn't then, and still don't, take food stamps!

Go Peggy - wherever your spirit is, know that I still love ya' lots Mum!

Peg had told me that when they had arrived in Greenacre, and had only been there for about a year, she could already sense that Charlie was getting restless again - with 'itchy feet'. Panic set in! *("Ah ah - so I learned my tendency to panic, from Peggy, did I"?)* Because of this, and the fact that she was getting a bit worried that he would have us on the move again, to 'god knows where', she told him - "if you don't get us and the kids settled in the one suburb, with a good school *(which was just up the road by the way)*, then I will have no alternative but to leave", she said. "I just don't fancy traipsing around any more, and it would be just like the Government or Council to accuse us of mistreatment of the children by moving them about so much, and then take Kerrie, and give her back to her biological Mum, and Mickey would go back to his dad"!

She was also a bit worried that they would find out about the fostering, which hadn't exactly been done officially. If that had happened, then Charlie would probably be banned from any further contact with either child. But dad, being a bit like the cowardly lion from the Wizard of Oz at heart, didn't like to rock the boat any more than was absolutely necessary, so he cowed down, and we stayed. We lived in that house until I left at about 18. Micky left just after he turned 16, supposedly under a dark cloud, and Peg and Charlie both died there. Dad had never made a point of bringing his 'boyfriends' home at all, at least not that I ever saw anyway, and he and I obviously never had a chance to sit and discuss it. You never did that sort of thing in those days anyway. Sit and talk, not about anything! And it definitely was 'not on' to ask your daddy if he had Gay tendencies! Being Gay meant something totally different in those days, and dad was dead by the time I might have found out for sure. According to what mum told me about it later on, in the 'heart to heart' discussion that she and dad had in the hospital, when he looked so bad *(though through the years, she probably had acquired first hand information about daddies oddity)*, he had evidently told her that he was, not all that slowly dying of Aids. The reality of that absolutely horribly fatal complaint *(even though it is sort of self inflicted)*, plus the loss of his lifelong partner, Peggy, and the apparent possible loss of his precious little girl, must have made him regret so many things in his life, and it all must have put an absolutely unbearable strain on his already no doubt weakened heart. He had had final closure with my real mum, but then he went and died before he and I had a chance to have that final closure discussion. Now that I think of it properly, I guess that he hadn't really been looking too good that last time I'd seen him and Peg, about a week before the accident. Probably, if I hadn't been so preoccupied with my own life at the time, *(I was evidently totally immersed in the possibility of being EVITA),* I might have taken the time to take a really good look at both of them, and would have tried to ferret out the reason for their apparent unhappiness. Now, come to think of it, when I do look back, neither Peg nor Charlie, had exactly been bouncing for joy last time I had seen them both. But being a typical young person, with my own promising adventure on the near horizon, I was so engrossed in my own world! If he *had* been suffering with Aids all that time, and Peg had been tending him, then she must have been absolutely worn out, as well as heartbroken.

Heartbroken - **1**; at the possible thought of losing him, *(she had loved him to distraction for so many years.)* and **2**; at having to tend to his failing self, without help. Not wanting to burden a daughter with their problems when her own world looked as though it was finally going to be rosy, they mustn't have wanted to worry me with the prospect of an even more money less future for them! Poor people could never really afford to get sick! Because of the situation though, and with dad knowing that I hadn't been driving the car in the accident that had left me unconscious for so long *(Oh god – I haven't told you about that either yet, have I? Don't be like me and panic, I will!),* he had become so extremely full of 'anti my first husband thoughts'. The nurse had come into the intensive care ward totally unaware of any possible adverse reaction from Dad, with the news that Peggy, after having devoted 25 years to bringing me up, was not allowed to come in. As I think I said before - Dad's apoplexy knew no bounds. Something had gone terribly wrong somewhere! "How dare they", he must have thought! *(Although, I can assure you, that his thoughts, and probably his voiced comments, would have been a whole lot stronger than just "how dare they, and nowhere near as polite"!)*

I guess though that I can understand the hospitals position. It had all happened so quickly, and so out of the blue, that they hadn't had time to properly inform the staff about the unusual situation. The hospital rules did, after all, say - blood ties, and relatives by marriage only. Peg had been inadvertently *(not literally)* bashed about the head with the hideous unfairness of not being allowed in to see her precious child. 29 by then I was, and I can just imagine what a devastating effect those words - "You can't go in", would have had on her. To have her little girl *(which I still was, and had always been to her)* in a hospital bed, unconscious, with a dreadful prognosis for her future, or non future, would have absolutely shattered her. The Doctors had said that even if I did come out of the coma that I was in, I was bound to be more than she could have coped with anyway. And then, horror of all horrors, to not even be allowed in! It's no wonder that she died not too long after, and before I had even woken up! If I had known about it, and had had any say at the time, I probably would have risen up, and said in a strident voice, "But she's **my mum**!"

(Now wouldn't that have been a sight to see,eh? A supposedly dying, unable to speak, corpse sitting up in the bed, remonstrating at the unfairness of Peg not being allowed in!)

As I think I have already mentioned, my real mum though, is a really good organiser, and if she wants something, she generally has a knack of moving the world over to make things possible. But then - I don't suppose it would have hurt having once been a nurse herself! I have to admit though,come to think of it, that it was probably the most humane thing for Peg that she did die without seeing me. She would have been devastated by my appearance; she would have coped emotionally with my rehabilitation even worse than I did; and she is now out of her own pain and discomfort, of which she undoubtedly had heaps! It is sad though that she never did get to find out that I had survived, and sad that I never got the final chance to tell her how much I had truly loved her!! She never got to meet her only grandchild either! Oh well! I have to believe that somehow she knows that Charliene exists,and that her second name is hers.

Now dad, although he was around to know that I at least was alive, and that I'd come out of the coma, was because I was still in such a bad way myself, probably still pretty upset by the way that I handled it all. I had as I said treated him in such an objectionable way.*(I mean to say*

- for heavens sake! I was still only semi awake after all, and to be perfectly honest, I guess that I treated everybody abominably!)

I had been however, unable to show him how much I loved him before he died, and I never even got to go to Peg's grave! I didn't have the foggiest idea of how to go about finding out where she was buried! But I think I know now, and I will try to get there, if I can, next time I'm in Australia in 2011. I do though know that their spirits are out there somewhere, cause they are always in my thoughts, still giving me bits of advise, and the wariness that Peggy taught me to have, still raises it's helpful face every now and then. I just hope and pray that they know that I will always love them, and that I thank them both for a wonderful, even if 'different' upbringing!

It was actually almost two years before the reality of dad's death impinged on my poor battered brain, and before I realised properly that somewhere, out there, there was 'my daddy'. He had been cremated while I was in the Hospital. The Crematorium had evidently sent out letters to me at my then address, looking for payment when I was still in the hospital. I, of course, wasn't there, and Andy hadn't thought to bring me up to date. *(Probably didn't want to upset me any more than was necessary. I'll give him the benefit of the doubt anyway, shall I?!)*

The letters that had come to the house, which I have subsequently read, myself, had informed me that dads bill was still to be paid. The last one, had said that if the bill wasn't settled within 3 days, Mr Dyer's ashes would be disposed of. It was dated 10 months previous. The letter also said though that the ashes could be collected once the bill was settled. I was left wondering - "why hadn't the crematorium bill been paid"?

A.L.V.A and THE ASHES!

If Toni, my ALVA mate *(you'll read about her on the next page),* hadn't found the letter when we were clearing out my wardrobe, and made me look at it, and do something about it, then I would never have been able to say goodbye in the way that you'll also read about on the next pages. My first husband had neither mentioned it, nor had he paid the bill, and I had been talking to him, just the day before. Why had he said nothing about it? Hadn't he been home, or collected the mail I thought, and if not – where had he been? Didn't he realise that I'd care? I guess that he probably hadn't had the money, and that he had too many other things on his mind at that time. Me, among other things.

Luckily there was one person who *did* know that I would probably, deep down, care, and that was Toni Stevens as she was working as at the time - now Toni McClean.

**Toni and I probably just out for a friendly dinner,
which we did on more than a few occasions!**

She was the inaugural Queen Bee of ALVA, *(as you already know
- the Australian Ladies Variety Association),* and we had only really, just
been friendly fellow performers before the short time that ALVA had
been formed. For the 5 months since the inauguration, I had though
also worked with her as a founder member of ALVA, so we knew each
other well enough.

I was very lucky to have inadvertently made such a good friend!
ALVA looks after all entertainers, and because they knew that I was
broke after the accident, and laden down with debts for things that
would have been most difficult for me to have done while lying,
unconscious in a hospital bed, they were very concerned. They knew
also that although my mother, and Andy's mother were watching over
me, I wasn't being looked after quite as well as the girls of ALVA would
like, and so they through Toni, and with my permission, had sold some
of my, now unusable things, to help pay off some of those horrendous
bills that I had somehow seemed to acquire. Toni's husband and she ran
a second hand furniture store you see, so they sold some of the things
that I would never be able to use again, so that I could at least have

72

the money from them, to help clear the bills, and thus my name. She helped me sort out all the problems that I had been left with, like unpaid driving fines etc. I mean to say – as I think I said before - I don't think that I could have been speeding, or parking in the wrong place, from a hospital bed - now could I?

Oh, it was definitely my car alright, but there was no way that it had been me behind the wheel! Not unless I had quietly been rising up from the bed, and 'moonlighting' as a racing car driver!

Toni was, and still is, such a good mate!

It was cold in 79/80, and my feet were turning blue because of bad circulation, so she used to massage my feet to get the colour back to normal. She even bought me two wonderfully warm, and very glamorous tracksuits from her own funds! Didn't I feel special? She used some of the money raised from the sale of my things, to sort everything out with the cemetery for me, and after some unwarranted (I suppose) heavy reprimands to the crematorium staff, and after some extensive searching, we were able to collect Dad's ashes just in the nick of time.

After all that time, they were almost on the verge of destroying them! There is no doubt about it though, it must have been meant! Why? - 'cause as Susie (the 2007/8/9 Queen Bee of ALVA) said just recently, - "Charlie was still there!"

I have found out since, that Toni and the girls of ALVA disliked the way in which my first husband had chosen to handle things post accident, and they were a bit concerned for my well being. He had been seen, regularly, with another female entertainer while I was in the hospital, and he had also been seen out socialising when they knew that I was at home alone. They were not at all impressed. No - not at all!

But he would have had his own set of demons to handle at the time, and I can bear him no malice! (No malice at all - not now anyway! Oh, sure – I suppose that I did though, positively hate him for years, but I've decided that to spend even a fragment of a life which, in my case I am very lucky to have, in recrimination against another person, would be a real waste of that life, and a bit of a slap in the face for God! Wouldn't it? Andy probably had as much to deal with emotionally at the time, as I did. In a different way, of course, but I have decided, that it really doesn't bring

73

you any satisfaction whatsoever to berate the other person too much in a situation such as that that we found ourselves in! Especially not when that person had at one time been 'the greatest love of your life'.)

Toni went to my place with a team of girls from ALVA, on a 'let's clean up Kerri's house before she comes out of hospital drive'. Big mistake - for them! They found a truly dirty, smelly, unkempt house. They were so appalled that no housework had apparently been done by anyone all the time I had been in hospital. Just over nine months by that time.

I hadn't been there for the clean up of course, and a lot of this particular information is what I was told. A right mess it was! Rod Little, from 'The Collection', one of ALVA's adopted male members, had just opened his own Carpet cleaning business, and he very kindly cleaned all of the house carpets for me, free of charge. Again - wasn't I a truly spoiled lady?

But, we were talking about Dad's ashes, weren't we? Again, sorry!

Toni phoned the crematorium, and was told - "Oh - hang on", You are in luck! - they *are* still here", but unless someone, anyone, claims them pronto, they *will* be disposed of", *("Oh no" says me, when Toni told me on the phone that afternoon. It was a case of well and truly pa-anic!, all over again!)* Toni rushed to the hospital, got a letter of release from me, and she paid for the ashes with the money from the sale of my things. Then she came back to pick me up, and we took the ashes up to the top of North or South Head, *(I can't really remember which)* in Sydney. You know we probably looked a little 'sus' stood on the hill top, overlooking the water. There was me who was tottering about, not looking too sure footed, and there was Toni giving me orders *(a thing that she would probably have been rather good at doing, but which would also have been very necessary to keep me from falling over the edge of the cliff)*.Ha ha, Can't you just imagine how silly it looked!

I said a few words of thanks to dad for a wonderful upbringing and wished him a 'soppy' goodbye, with a face all crumpled up. *(Remember, I couldn't cry at that stage, and I still can't, so my face must have looked a bit like an air filled, cheek puffed, lips quivering soppy dog!)* Anyone catching sight of us would possibly have thought that I was about to jump, and that Toni, at my insistence, was helping me, or encouraging me, with a mercy suicide! I was, after all, very insecure with my standing and walking, looking most upset with life, and leaning very heavily on Toni's arm as well! It is probably just as well that I then released my grip of her arm a little, moved aside, and took a handful of ashes from the box that I was carefully holding. Like Nefertiti , I majestically threw them out on the wind, over the sea, with all the pomp and ceremony of an ancient Egyptian, river Nile, burial – you know - just like in the movies! Such typical, 'Showbiz drama'! Very regally majestic! - Ha! But my dad being my dad, *(not ever really being into regal)* wasn't about to leave me without his own normal touch of flair. He would have positively loved the drama and spectacle of it all! Maybe I got my love of entertainment 'pizazz' from him, or maybe he caught it from me for a change. I can't really be sure, but when I took that first handful of ashes, and majestically threw them to the wind, the ashes of the 'silly old bugger', flew straight back in our faces. We stood there shocked, and desperately trying to remain suitably pious about what was supposed to be a serious matter. There we were, trying desperately not to laugh at the absolute ludicrousy of the moment!

Now – I figure that he was giving me a final 'kiss and a cuddle', just as he had always done last thing at night, when I was small; he was maybe having a final flirt, with Toni; he had always flirted with the girls at my jobs, *or* he was remonstrating with me for not being there when he needed me. I guess that now, I will never really know?

But I tried a second time *(to throw the ashes I mean)*. I took another pile of ashes from the box and made the full majestic speech and everything all over again. I threw the ashes onto the wind, but once again – he just didn't seem to want to go! The wind blew his ashes back in our faces again. This time though, we were laughing so raucously, and slapping each other so hard on the shoulders,that Toni and I nearly fell over the edge of the cliff, and into the lapping briny! It's a wonder we didn't fall over the edge of the cliff; we were laughing so hard. *(Mind you I have a feeling that I probably hadn't judged the wind direction too well. Don't you?)* Third time does the job, so they say, and I finally managed to set him free to the wind, but with some of him still staying on the Cliff side.

My warped sense of humour can still see him, just as I imagined him that afternoon - dangling on the cliff face edge, and now 30 odd years later – I can actually see him desperately hanging on by his fingertips, over looking the harbour that he loved, but had only been able to actually see a very few times! *(By now though, I reckon that he has probably fallen into it! What do you think?)*

Still - wherever he is now, he must have heard me apologise for my being in my accident. I've told him, a thousand times over the years since, that he should have known I would never willingly have left him or Peg, and that even though sometimes I was a bit of a 'nasty shit I really did love both of them lots and lots, and I would have loved for them to have known their Granddaughter, named after them both – and to know how Charliene Peggy Ann, and Ed have now made my life complete!

MY EARLY DAYS AT GREENACRE

I don't really remember anything much about schooling before arriving in Greenacre. I guess that I must have been involved in all the usual class activities from pre-school up. You know - making lots of silly trivial bits of paraphernalia that seemed fantastic to a little person, and hopefully, equally so to parents. I had three parents to please now, Dad, Peggy, and occasionally my real Mum, and they could, and did all show happiness and pride or displeasure in my efforts, depending on how those efforts effected them. I don't really remember much displeasure though, but there was bound to have been some. I was young and I didn't give it much thought at that time. (*The fact that you were only supposed to have two parents I mean.*)

I just took it for granted that everyone had three parents. I did - and how was I supposed to know that we were 'different' at that time? The kids at school understandably knew Mr & Mrs Dyer as my parents. They also knew that I would go to visit someone else, whom I also called mum, about every six weeks or so, and sometimes at holidays, but I don't think that they paid much attention to that. I don't remember them ever saying anything about it, and anyway, even then, I think that they thought I was a bit mad any way! Things sometimes got a little difficult explaining it and everything, as I grew a bit older, but by then my real Mum, for various legitimate reasons, that generally always meant that it was better for both of us in the long run, said that I shouldn't go to see her or her other family any more. Charlie did his normal 'loud mouth' complain, but I did as I was told, and didn't go to visit her any more.

(*I went back to having a normal 'two parents' family!*)

77

And a little more socially acceptable it was too!

There were often long periods,*(lots of years sometimes)* of time between visits to my Mum's. Charlie used to absolutely love the apparent disownings by Mum. I vaguely remember him telling me that it kind of made him feel a little less inferior!

He really enjoyed being able to say to me - "See - I was always there for you".

(I have always loved him, but there's no doubt about it, he could be such a little boy sometimes!)

Oh damn, - I did it again, didn't I? I do get distracted so easily, don't I? Sorry!

Back to the main story - Having been at Greenacre, in a council home for a few years, Peg started to sense that Dad's mood was getting a bit restless again, and after having always been on the move till then, I hadn't really had the chance to make many friends. When ever I had made friends before, Dad would move us on, and I'd find myself alone again - friendless, which for a very young person is generally a 'not really noticed at the time' situation, but a 'not nice' situation! So as I wasn't very 'up' on the art of making friends, I was surprised and delighted, when a girl *(who was better at it than me)* moved in down the road. She became my first true best friend and soul mate for those early years. That friendship had a real chance to develop too, because we didn't move on again!

Oh joy!

Micky was my foster brother. (*Gee I still haven't really told you about him either, have I? Well - here goes! Not that there's much to tell anyway!*)

Micky was just a charming little boy, with all the 'typical' little boy quirks, except that my Dad, according to some, supposedly took advantage of his youth. But as I can't know for sure - I don't think that I should go there, so I don't suppose that I will be able to tell you much about him after all, except that I do remember him as being great fun to have as a baby brother! As I have said, Micky was a handsome little man, and he and I had always got on great. Together, we had made a point of going to say hello, to the Floyd family who had just moved in down the road. *(Not that we were nosey children or anything!)* We were thrilled to find that they had a son and two daughters. The elder girl had already left school, and was working, while the younger girl Carol, her brother Robert *(a few years older)*, and Micky and I, were all in roughly the same age bracket, give or take a couple of years, and we had a lot in common.

We all liked singing and dancing for one thing, not that Micky could sing much at his tender age. Come to think of it, he couldn't dance very well either. He would just put the odd 'squawk' into a group song, and the odd shuffle, that was supposed to pass for a dance step, with the emphasis, again being on the odd. We did though all like doing good works for Charities, and in those days, good causes didn't make too much of a critical analysis of the people willing to make them money. It was just as well, as we were just four scraggy school kids, but I think that they were just happy to get the money, however little it was, and by whomsoever it was collected. Just as long as it came free of any legal complications, they were apparently happy to accept it! We used to build cardboard box stages on the road outside the houses and we would perform all the latest songs and dance routines from the radio, and the newly arrived on the scene, television! One day, a TV producer who had heard about some crazy kids doing an impromptu street show, *(unheard of in Australia in those days)* just happened to be watching when we were in the middle of one of our street 'box stage' productions. He had stopped on his journey, to watch 'these kids that he had heard about' *(you know what news programms are like when it comes to newsworthy items!)*, and I was asked if I would like to sing on the 'Captain Fortune', TV show. I had thought at first that he wanted the whole small troop - but NO!   Unfortunately, but fortunately for me, he asked if just I would like to sing a song on the show. Talk about feeling embarrassed! We were much better as a group I thought! Television was then a very new medium - a bit scary too, and I was a bit hesitant at first, but the others all said - "Yeah! - go on, go for it"!

So anyway, there I was with my little black doll called Topsy, singing - "Oh my babby, my curly headed babby, we'll sit beneath the stars and sing a song to the moo - oo,oo -oo - oo,oo – oon"! *(Oo - ooh ! How wonderful it felt to be in the limelight, even though I shared it with a scruffy black dolly!)*

I think Peg and Charlie, watched it on a neighbours set! *(They could never have afforded one of those 'new fangled' TV sets at that time!)* They were though just so proud and happy, and my slightly impoverished, black dolly, with hair desperately needing a comb and set hairdo, didn't half mind either! All of 10 years of age I was, and there was me, doing my first local TV show. I got an early taste for hearing that applause, and I must have suddenly, from that moment on and without even realising it, known what it was that I wanted to be!

I was going to sing and I was determined to be a 'star'!

That was it! Kerri Dyer was going to be a singing star! I was also determined to make a lot of money, so that then Peg, Charlie, I and Micky, would be 'rolling in it'.

Oh well!

(The dreams of youth!)

My own little girl was only 40 days old when she was first on telly, with Steve Raymond stopping her crying, by holding her in his outspread arms, and giving her a bit of a bounce. But being on TV at so young an age doesn't seem to have had the same effect on her, as it did on me. If anything it has had the completely opposite effect, more's the pity! - BUT- my wonderful daughter Charliene, is a clever biddy, and far more academically inclined than I ever was *(a bit like her grandad on my mum's side. Must have missed a generation, do you think?)*, and now that she has had her two years out to gain some work experience, and do a teensy bit of travel, she has been accepted to London School of Economics! The business world looks like being her Show business! Depending of course on whether or not the Global credit crunch bashes the world around too much more of course!

But just as I hadn't really decided before the tender age of 10 , what I might like to do in the future, - I, as sure as eggs knew from when I had done my first TV show!

I was definitely going to SING!!!!

By the time I had reached the grand old age of approximately 11, I honoured that decision, as was evidenced by my singing in the opera and the choir at school and also in the Salvation Army songsters. I drove Peg and Charlie mad with my habit of always giving voice to songs of one kind or other, in the most unlikely, and often the most embarrassing places. Whether it was good or bad singing, didn't really seem to bother me too much at the time. In the bath, in the bed, in the yard, and yes, even in our excuse for a garden shed - I used to sing! Dad would come through the back gate, and there to the left of the back yard, he would sometimes hear, what I confess now, probably sounded a more like a cat that had got her tail caught in something than singing. I would though, vocalise away, convinced that come hell or high water, little Kerrie Dyer was going to make something of her life. I was convinced, as only young people can be convinced, that I was definitely going to be a *star!*

I probably had what you might call now, a bit of an ego, *(still got it I suppose!),* but I figure that without even realising it, I just wanted to find the quickest way out of poverty. I didn't feel as though I belonged where I was, and I had always had the belief that someone must have accidentally left me on the wrong doorstep or something when I was a baby. *(Which in some obscure kind of way, I guess that they had!)*

The day came though, when having been settled in Greenacre for a few more years as a family, and not having moved on, it was time for me to go to 'big school'.

(I can't begin to imagine the kids of today calling it anything quite so self demeaning. "What the heck were we before we were 'big' people, going to 'big' school anyway"? 'Little people'? And we weren't even Irish!)

Carol and I had gone through Greenacre Primary school together, and we went happily, but fearfully off together to Wiley Park Girls High. Carol's elder sister was already going to work, and had been paying her Mum and Dad board until she had left about a year before to get married.

Carol's brother, being a 'big boy' *(also one of my earlier conquests),* but not yet of working age, was in High School already, and Micky being still virtually a youngster, was only about 9, and so he was still in primary.

Bestest of friends!

CAROL

Full of excitement, Carol and I were due to set off up the yellow brick road to our own unknown future! A future that really did look as though it was set to produce a truly fantastic 'pot of gold' at the end of the rainbow.

It was a maudlin Monday, after what had been, to kids our age at the time, a fab weekend, but our new *big* School episode was due to start on the Wednesday, so the week ahead at least looked like being fun, and do you know what? Even then – I guess that I had a fancy for fun! Our first problem - if you could call it a problem, was that Carol and I had to find out how to get to Wiley Park High, from Greenacre. Now - for those of you who know anything of the area, you may say derisively, "come on that is not very far", but in those days, and it does seem like an humongously long time ago now, we who had never been very far out of our own street, not alone anyway, found it just a trifle difficult, and 'scare-y' to negotiate! But all the fear aside, it was a major excitement for we 11 year old's.

We suddenly had to get on the right bus, find the right station, the correct train, get aboard it, off at the right stop, and then take a short walk, in the right direction, to and from the station that the train had dropped us off at! *(Tricky stuff for kids!)* Then, when we had managed all that, we could majestically walk down the hill, from the station and into the new school grounds!

Now – I tell you - that that there school was waiting to draw us in, churn us around a bit, and then hopefully spit us out, more clever than we had been when it had sucked us up! But - just to be on the safe side, and to ensure that there were no unexpected snags - full of anticipation, Carol & I had decided, to give it a 'dry run' journey on the Tuesday morning, the day before we were due to start. Well we couldn't afford to get it wrong now could we? I mean - we had always been super careful about such things (*not much else though, I might add!*), and Wednesday was, after all to be our first day at 'big school'! Such excitement! (*We may have been always getting into trouble, but - we liked to at least do it, in a careful, well planned out way!*) After all, - I mean to say - we wanted to know that come Wednesday morning, on our first 'for real' step into the 'not baby' world, the routine that we hoped to plan and map out on the Tuesday trial run, had been safely negotiated at least once. So we, as I said, us being careful, but typically cocky kids, had managed to beg the fares from Carol's parents (*Peg and Charlie wouldn't have stood a chance of being 'hittable' for the fares!*) and we set off, full of schoolgirl enthusiasm, on our first really big, outside adventure together!

We had paper mapped it all out! We knew at what time we would catch the bus around the corner, to the station. Catch the train, and then after about ten minutes train drive from Lakemba station, we would chug into Wiley Park, which was on the rise just above where the '*big*' school sat, gazing out in it's typical, bored looking school yard way! We were then going to leisurely wander down the hill, into the massive school grounds of Wiley Park Girls High School.

The school was open on the Tuesday so that for those bothered(*and I might add that most were expected to be bothered*), an exploratory day could be spent finding out where their class rooms were, and what their timetable was going to be, all in preparation for the next day. All sorted! It must have been an open day, before they actually called them that! As 11 year old's, who in those days were lacking the experience of childhood independence, we had only ever seen schools like the local Primary school, which was walking distance, just up our road, and we hadn't really been this far away from home without our Mums and Dads before. So the new school grounds, with the extensive light brick buildings, seemed gargantuan, and just a 'tad' frightening.

Come the Wednesday morning though - we both felt wonderful! The big day had finally arrived! Both of us had brand new bags, new school uniforms, and shoes, and for the first time for me at least, they weren't even second hand things! (*I have since found out that I had my real Mum to thank for that)* I had been so excited on that thrilling morning, that me being me, had found it impossible to wait for Carol to get to my place. So I rushed out onto the street to briskly walk - no, almost run the 40 yards or so down the road to her place. Carol must have been bitten by the same impatience 'bug', 'cause she was rushing, up the street to our house. We literally bumped into each other midway. We were both just *so* excited! We just about knocked each other over in the middle of the road with all that excitement.

"*Wow*", she sang! - "*you look so fresh and new, and "wo-nder-ful, even.*"

"And you look positively magical"!, sang me.

Then we both sang at the top of our voices, in two totally different melodies,in a truly cacophonous sound -**"Big words in preparation for BIG school"**!

(It was almost completely out of tune, but it was still uncanny how much we thought alike!)

We were commencing a whole new phase of our boringly 'normal' suburban lives. Carol, as my bestest ever friend, knew, of course that I had always loved music and singing, but, both of us had a decided aversion to all the hard work that would obviously be involved in taking on the Music elective course. Carol was to opt for a much less strenuous choice, deciding that for her to just be in the school choir would be sufficient. I though, was already a Salvation Army Songster, and the chance to not only be in the school choir *(which was in itself a fantastic thing)*, but to take advantage of taking part in any shows, *(there were bound to be shows, weren't there?)*, was just too, too exciting, and enticing. It was just too good an opportunity for me to miss, regardless of the possible work involved. I liked to 'ham it up', and although not supremely confident, I guess that I have to admit it - I have always liked to 'show off' a bit. I figured that for me to get a place in any of the school productions etc., I would need to play an active and integral part in the whole of Music elective scene.

A lousy reason for taking the subject I guess - but hey! *(I think that Showbiz must have always been, secretly, in my blood!)*. So cockily and probably a bit unthinkingly I suppose, I said to myself, and the school board - Music Elective here I come!

(The work that would be involved, had been momentarily forgotten, or at least temporarily ignored! Well you don't really look at things in the complete way at that age - do you?) The prospect of having to learn an instrument had just seemed a bit too exciting for words, and I have to shamefully admit, that the work that would be involved really hadn't bothered me too much at the time. It must have just seemed romantic. You know! I'd be able to serenade my Dad when he lost his temper. "Maybe then he won't think about hitting me", I had must have cheerily thought - "I'll just worry about the extra work that will be needed, when and if it comes."

(And boy did it ever come)

So even though I knew that my family didn't have the money to have me privately tutored in an instrument outside of school, and although I knew that instrument 'au fait-ness' would be a pre-requisite for doing the elective course, I was so keen to do music, that I had signed up for it at the end of the previous year without having really had a chance to think it through properly. I guess that I hadn't given any thought to much at all, apart from my desire to do music, and even more importantly - to sing!!

I'd find some kind of way around my being poor! Come to think of it, I don't suppose though that I even realised that I was poor.

I did know though, that a lot of the other girls already had private tuition in things like violin, saxophone and oboe, and I must admit that I had never really given the fact that I didn't, much thought. They of course, selected those instruments to do, but when it came time for little old me, from the less wealthy side of the track to choose an instrument from the by then very much depleted, very limited stock of school instruments, I got left with - wait for it - the *cello*!

Now – I don't really remember my initial reaction *(all those years and an accident ago remember)*, but I probably fought back a tear or two, cause I am pretty sure that the cello would not have been my first choice of instruments I wanted to play.

(In fact – I don't think that I really even wanted to play an instrument of any kind, I just wanted to sing!) I do remember however, having always loved the sound of it, when it was played correctly. But I would have to

say that I don't think that it would ever have been said, that I played it correctly, or at all well! I am pretty sure though that the rousting and humiliating comments that came from the other kid's as I lugged the monster about, were probably more than most kids could have coped with at that tender age. And on trawling through my memories to write this book, it turns out that they *were* a lot more than I could bear! If I was going to have to lug an instrument to and from school, it would have been a lot easier, and so much nicer for me, if it had been a smaller one . But chin up everyone! There was me, struggling on and off the local bus and the train with this 'ruddy great' cello. Even if I *had* been able to lift the cello onto my upturned chin, I probably would have speared myself with the metal spike at the end of it. *(Mind you - the noises that I did manage to get from it, probably sounded as though it had already speared me anyway!)* But - Mr Keen, *(yes, fortunately, but most unexpectedly, my present Mr Keen)* who was the general music teacher at the time, and as such, one of my music teachers, had done an excellent job of 'selling' it's virtues to me. *(The cello's virtues that is!)* It had been his favourite instrument, and he has recently told me that he had always wanted to play the cello at music College, but didn't really get the chance, so I guess that his encouraging me to play was supposed to be the next best thing at the time! I think also though that the fact that there was very little else available, may also have had just a bit to do with my getting it! Don't you?

They were probably down to the dregs of a few percussion instruments. One Cello, a couple of Tuba's and bassoons! *(Come to think of it now though, I wonder if I might not have been better off with one of those?! A Tuba maybe! At least then, I would have got some breathing exercises that would have come in handy with the singing. You can I hope, imagine the fun and games that that there cello brought into my life!)*

My own darling daddy, just about fell about laughing, and that was not necessarily an easy state of affairs to bring about! *(He rarely found anything to laugh about those days. Drunkenness does often impair the ability to see genuinely funny things as funny, doesn't it?)* He definitely found the thought of me playing the cello funny enough though. The kids would take it in turns to try to take kicks at it. I was forever trying to shuffle it out of their range, so I guess that you could say that that way, I inadvertently also got some dancing practice in. *(Pity that it was generally only the 'side step' though.)* One boy even said that if he could get hold of it, he would take it home and chop it up for firewood. I was mortified! I never let it out of my sight after that! But looking back on it now, I hesitate to imagine how anyone's parents would have used the wood if they had known where it had come from. But then - come to think of it - if the parents were anything like the son – well? One never knows, does one?!!!!! I guess though, that when you are poor, as they probably were, living around that area, *(which was among the poorest in the land),*then warm tootsies are of more importance than a good moral sense! Even Australia used to get some cold winters! *(But come to think of it - maybe not quite as cold as England's winters get though!)*

Apart from the more obvious problems concerned with getting a thing of that size, safely on and off the bus and train when you are only a young, almost teenager, I felt that if it could have been arranged, it might have been a 'tad' safer for all concerned if I could have squashed myself inside it. But unfortunately, no go! If I could have though, then no one would have known exactly who was daring to bring a such a monstrous thing onto the bus or train in the first place. Can't you just see it though? Two arms sticking out of the side of it, paying for the tickets, with two big brown eyes peering through the eye holes, *(the already cut sound slits?).* There was no doubt about it though - it was definitely an 'uncool' thing at that time to be seen struggling to school with an instrument of any kind, let alone, it being a 'cello' of all things.

I was even asked once by the bus ticket collector, thinking that he was being clever and friendly, and with a huge smirk on his face as he hung over the door space, glancing back, after winking at the driver -

"And where's the Fiddle's ticket then my pretty one"?

"Fiddle?", says me in a most mock - confused voice. "Oh, you mean my Cello," says me in a pseudo apologetic voice. The conductor smirked, nodding his head.

"Now - let's see shall we!", he says to his driver mate. "It takes up a full space - so it should really be full fare, but as a special deal for a regular; yes - you my pretty - half fair extra I would say!, wouldn't you Tom? Let's say the tuppence a week for you Missy, and a penny a week, for the fiddle"? says Bert -

"No tell you what", takes over Tom the driver - "I reckon that we can do an extra special deal for a well liked regular, like little Missy there".

"OK", says Bert - "What do you say Tom – 'tuppence ha'penny' for the two of them! Can't do much better than that - now can we?"

Tom was just about rolling about behind the steering wheel.

Bert then said - trying not to laugh out loud too loudly- "I know - better still Missy - you can play us a tune as we go along to make up the fiddle's fare!".

My face must have hit the floor, and I, not realising at the time that the guard was having a piece of this gullible school child stood in front of him, and my feeling decidedly unlike playing for the bus lot, said meekly - "Aww - please mister - I'm sorry". "I didn't realise I would need a ticket for it, and I don't think you or the kids on the bus would particularly like an out of tune rendition of 'Frer-re Jacque'". But I did actually open up vocally with - "I didn't actually - bring any extra money, anyway"!

The driver and conductor both looked genuinely surprised at the voice, and then laughed. Bert sent me off with a tap on the 'bum'! *(Funny how I remember someone tapping me on the bum! I can't remember things that matter, and yet I can remember that! But it's a thing he definitely wouldn't be allowed to do these days. He'd run the risk of being had up for child molestation! Just for a slap on the bottom! Sheer madness!)*

At that age though, you just feel so ashamed, and I had probably wished for the thousandth time that the violins, or something smaller than 'this thing,' *(the Cello)* hadn't all gone! Because of my youthful laziness though, and if I am honest, I guess that I was what you might call, a 'bit of a lazy git' when at school, I never really learned to play the Cello very well at all. My husband would probably tell you that right up to today, 2010, I still haven't really grown out of it very well; not liking work too much, and that I can still be a bit of a lazy 'git' occasionally. *(So I guess that maybe the laziness wasn't necessarily just a youthful thing - was it?).* Mind you - I will say this in my defence!

I don't really think that I am what you could honestly call lazy. I just don't like doing, what I don't like doing - or doing something that I can't see being an advantage to me, that's all! I did though absolutely adore and love the mellow, romantic sounds I could *(very very)* occasionally make the instrument produce, and in my own self defence, it *was* very hard to practice.

Dad was definitely not enamoured of hearing me play it either! He said that most of the time, it sounded a bit like a cat with laryngitis being strangled. *(I have always loved 'pussy cats', [I have one now – my daughters'} so I was definitely put out, to think that anyone thought that I was maligning those precious beasts by my playing and my singing!)* At 11 and 12 though, unless you are an aspiring musical genius, from the right kind of background, *(which I definitely wasn't)*, then you don't really have the proper amount of application needed to truly benefit from the work involved in learning such an instrument. I guess also, that I just wasn't focused enough on instrument playing, to take advantage of the fantastic opportunity I had been given.

(Now, in 2009, I definitely wish that I had been though) But back then, it would very occasionally, on the rare occasions that it was being played properly, give off a lovely rich and caressing sound. *(I have to admit it though - that it never seemed to do it all that often. Not for me, anyway!)* But it sure didn't really take too much to make me overly protective of it! If things like cello's had a mind to think with, it also probably would have liked it better if it hadn't been there in the first place. *(But then - I don't suppose that cello's have any thoughts at all, do they? They just stand there, looking majestically beautiful and put up with whatever non-talent decides to make cacophonous noises with them!)*

You know though, all the attempts at humour aside, I really did love the sound of the Cello, but again, maybe I just wasn't disciplined enough to really appreciate it! *(What do you think – eh ?)* Maybe I hadn't had the right stuff to learn to play it well, but I do know, that I definitely didn't have enough of what it took to face down everyone on the bus. So I had very reluctantly, and yet with an almost self conscious sense of relief, given the cello back to the school at the beginning of my second year of High school. Mr Keen was a little miffed that I handed it in, but still - I had persevered with it for a year hadn't I ?*(and even now, at my advanced age, he has to occasionally give me a rouse when I am trying to re learn to sing, and obviously not doing enough practice!!)*

Do you think that maybe - I will never learn!!!

But because I showed a keen *(get it - a 'keen')* interest in the singing, I was allowed to continue in the elective class anyway, even though, at that time Mr Keen himself, hadn't really heard me sing. He didn't get to hear me until the opera, Hansel and Gretel, a few years later! Miss Evans had, and I have to say that it was just as well they let me carry on though!!! Why they did - I can't really remember now, but I must have been *so* glad that they had! When final Exam time came, in year four, years later, I got an A+ in the singing and A' s in the music theory exams, but couldn't really sit the practical instrument examination, and I will however now put it in writing for all to see. The actual musical knowledge I learned while I had the instrument, was to prove more valuable to me than I was ever to realise at the time. It proved to be super useful, both during the earlier years in Australia. 1969 - 1974 when I did my own 'copying' *(writing out of the manuscripts for my 'shows'),* and now, as I re learn to sing – again! The music knowledge needed to copy music sheets, played a big part in my being able to sing and phrase well back then in Australia, and now the little that I can remember *(and unfortunately it is only a 'little'),* also plays a decisive part as I try to relearn to sing properly!

Earlier in 2007, after the first few months of very little response from the vocal chords, and of my being unable to manipulate them so as to make anything like the proper sounds, I can now sing - kinda! A bit like a young child though, *(and I do a mean the simplest versions of three Blind Mice,and twinkle twinkle little star).* But I am a bit like a young child that throws fits of temper while she is singing.

Oh goodness gracious me! Done it again, haven't I?

'You stupid woman', as 'Renee' says on Television!

Let's get back to the story so far, shall we? Now where was I? *(such a long way back)* Carol and I had set off together to catch the local bus to Lakemba Station just as we had planned. We had been confronted with a 'typical', 1950's train station, with it's wooden slat bench seats, two fine pebble dash, concrete platforms with the train lines between them. A ticket and station masters' office, *(remember them?)* proudly occupied the strip down the middle of one of the platforms.

Australia's Canterbury was about the same distance from my home then, as the English one is from my home now – about 30 minutes *(not in rush hour though.)*

There is though, of course, one big difference, in that England 's Canterbury has the magnificent Canterbury Cathedral, doesn't it? How absolutely fabulous it would have been to have had the Cathedral *(with all it's historical significance)* in my own backyard when I was growing up. All I had was the Canterbury race track!

(Almost did it again, didn't I?)

Now where was I? - oh yeah! Carol and I had boarded the Wiley Park train, which was to take us all the way along to the next station. There was an air of expectancy everywhere around! Although the towns and suburbs were all busy quickly growing, back in Australia in those days, abductions or child murders were a decided rarity, if not a non entity, and Lakemba and Wiley Park stations were both, not a lot bigger than large 'country towns' anyway. Almost 'lazy country towns, you might say'! So I would have to say, that things were a lot safer in those good/bad old days.

Now – here in Ashford, where I live by choice, has Canterbury and Maidstone as it's nearest big towns, and they *are* both big towns. They say that Ashford is earmarked to be a really big town soon too, and at the present, in 2009, it looks a bit like one huge construction sight, with cones up everywhere! Mind you – they have been telling us that since 1990 when we got here, so I am not too sure anymore!! But back in those days in Australia though, 1961 - 1965, Lakemba's nearest big towns were Bankstown and, once again, Canterbury. *(Named by homesick Englanders do you think?)* In those days them there towns only catered for about a mere 25-30,000 people each, even though there's a good chance that they would be a lot larger these days. England's Canterbury is already definitely decidedly larger than that! Everything is! Unfortunately, even me sometimes! *(My weight still fluctuates, depending on I don't know what!)* But it's hard to believe that there was a time when kids of about 6+ years of age, could fairly safely wander about by themselves. They were not always allowed to do so, of course, but by the time they got to 11, well there were next to no limits on what they could safely do in those days! -Nowadays the same towns in Oz would probably be enormous, but on whichever side of the world you live, there is, unfortunately a definite air of 'fear for the unaccompanied child's safety'. Parents *(me included)* today, live in an atmosphere of - 'what if'. I still worry about my 21 year old daughter and her friends! Some of those girls are just too good looking for their own good when they are all dolled up!

Emma and Charliene - true friendship!

BIG SCHOOL—WILEY PARK GIRLS HIGH SCHOOL

But I suppose it has always been thus, and even though teenagers today are brought up to realise *(far more than we were)* that there are many dangers 'out there', *(it's on the TV all the time)*, I personally don't think that they really understand just what kind of 'sickos' there really are in this world.

As I said, Carol and I had done the trial run on the Tuesday and on the Wednesday, when the train had pulled into Wiley Park Station we had given a bit of a 'yippee'. We opened the doors, *(no electric doors in those days)* and jumped down on to the platform. You could almost feel the anticipation pulsing in the air! We and, what felt like the air around us, were positively shaking with it! *(does air shake?)* Well *we* were shaking anyway! We showed our tickets to the stationmaster, and grinned from ear to ear, only to be greeted with a curt nod of the head *(well when you think about it, why would he be overly interested in one scrawny, and one slightly obese teenager)*. There we were, studying our reflection in the station mirror, and secretly swelling with pride at what we saw. Off we went in our fresh looking new school uniforms, ready to wander down to the 'new school' grounds that we had 'reckkied' the day before. A new school - new people - new teachers – and new subjects. A new start - but for the same old us! The thought of it all was enough to make one want to give up and go home before even giving it a go. Or was it?

We didn't really think so, 'cause -' *ONWARD TO ADVENTURE'* - had always been our motto, and thus the first few terms at this new school, which were still an adventure to us, were positively fantastic. All the excitement of meeting new people - doing new subjects - it was, *(to steal a phrase that probably hadn't been used at that time,)* - SUPERCALAFRAGILISTICLy great!

Then unfortunately, the 'rot' set in.
And what rot might that be, you may ask!

Well - I had, for some reason, not too clear to me at the time, inevitably, become known as a bit of a rapscallion. I was even called *'the Dyer'* by some of the teachers. *(Can you imagine? I had no idea at the time, just what I might have done wrong at the time, to earn that name?)* After having been on what I considered my bestest behaviour for the first few months, it had become a case of - "now let me see, shall we?" - If there was a rule that could be broken without causing too many problems, then I would look for it, and find the sneakiest, best and safest way of breaking it.*(I didn't want to hurt anyone now did I?- Especially not myself. But I have been told that I was a veritable terror!)* I am exceedingly thankful though, that I never came across a *'me'* at St. Mary's Primary school Ashford, Kent, in 1992-1999.

I taught at St Mary's school 1999 for about 7 years as a fully qualified, voluntary 'Learning Support Assistant'. I absolutely loved it, but now, having been in a teaching position myself, I bow my head in shame when I think of some of the things that I did when I was at school. Mind you, I'm pretty sure that *I* wasn't that much trouble when I was at Primary School. I can't fully remember that far back, so I'll just assume that I wasn't! Safer that way! To me at least! High School though, now, well that was a 'different' matter. I was always in trouble. I never seemed to have done my homework for one thing, and then there were other things! Did I say other things?

Yes - there were definitely other things!!!

For instance, there was one teacher early on, a Miss Brown I think it was, who taught Social Studies and she took it into her head straight away, to thoroughly dislike me. At least that is how it seemed to me at the time! Without so much as a 'how's your father', she had already decided that I was an undesirable! I couldn't understand it myself! (*I was really a very lovable person once they got to know me. Honest! Some of the teachers didn't even give me the benefit of the doubt. Because I wasn't in the tidiest, and cleanest uniform and things, they just branded me as*

96

a troublemaker, and that was that!) *'In their eyes'* - trouble maker was what I was!

In reality, I guess that the state of my uniforms might just have been part of the reason for them coming to that conclusion, of course it might also have been that I *was* a bit of a troublemaker, I guess! Peg had said that the uniforms that my real mum had bought for my first year of high school, had, again, to be kept for best! I of course, didn't really know at that time, that Peggy hadn't bought them, and to this day, it is difficult to know what Peg regarded as best in those days, 'cause even the uniforms my real mum had bought, although they were clean and well made, and *new,* when I got them, were definitely not what I would have called 'best'. *(I mean to say - who would ever consider school uniforms as the best of anything.)* Nerds probably would have, but I'm pretty sure that I didn't! I had failed the 'nerds' entrance exam!

The uniforms I had had before *(those bought by Peg and Charlie anyway!)* were normally second or third hand, and not very well fitting clothes. They were though, like anything else Peg got her hands on, always clean. *(Too clean maybe?)* Peggy saw to that! It turns out that she was a bit of a clean freak of the highest degree! They do say that when you're poor, you are generally clean, to compensate. *(I don't think that you could class me as poor these days, but my husband says to me that it's a pity I hadn't inherited that 'clean' quality from Peggy by proximity).* Back then though, sometimes I'd go to school with my clothes slightly faded, and positively 'reeking' of bleach! *(Most classy, depending of course on just who was doing the classification.)*

With Social Studies though, I just wasn't about to waste my precious time taking notes about, what was after all, to me, a boring subject! I mean to say - what did I need with all that inconsequential knowledge about where the post office or the library was. I mean, after all, I was going to be a star, and live in some exotic, and romantic place, miles away from Greenacre. I was convinced that I was going to get out of those suburbs, asap! *(A bit of a brat - would you say?)*

Even at that young age though, I was determined that I would be able to afford to pay someone else to post my letters, when they needed to be posted! *(Never got there, did I?)* I did though find most of the other classes at school, well, pretty easy - peasy, so I guess that I considered the whole of year 1 as a bit of a 'dos', and consequentially a complete waste of time! But then Year 2 began, and the school decided that they would give us the option of swapping a lesson for, what they called, a 'touch of class'

We could actually learn something that we didn't already know - A taster of French - for a year, instead of Social Studies! Yippee! *(Was I ever a 'happy little bunny' - but I think that now a days, I might call that kind of child a little self opinionated. What do you think? - yeah - we'll politely call her self opinionated, and brat-ish shall we?)* Talking about being self opinionated though!

My dad! - Now - He wasn't self opinionated at all. Oh no! Not my daddy! Smirk, smirk! He was, in reality, what you might call, the most UN self opinionated man that I have ever met - unless of course when he had been drinking! Then – when boosted with alcoholic bravado, he often *(if he didn't get caught)* 'borrowed' the 'two pennies to rub together' needed for his 'exploits', from Peggy's purse! He would wander off to the pub, and get 'blotto'. The whole neighbourhood would hear about it when he came home, if/when she found out about his pilfering ways, which she often did. But then, in the same way that Peg must have absolutely loved my rapscallion dad, even though he was a loveable old rogue, I too had loved him loads, almost as much as I loved them both! There was only one thing that I loved more even than I loved Peg and Charlie though, even at that young age, and my involvement with the Salvation Army meant that I had been able to do it. - and that was - *singing!*

I guess that in a way I was kind of lucky, if you could call it that. Kids in my days hadn't yet become as super fashion conscious as they are these days. Mind you, at any age though, you did become very self conscious over the smallest of things, and although the smell of bleach wasn't exactly a 'smallest' of things, I remember cringing sometimes when I had to go to school smelling like a hospital.

Peg probably put the ones my mother had bought me aside, and out of reach, with what she considered were the best of intentions. There they stayed, kept safely for four long years, with only occasional release for those -'special occasions'! Thus - luckily for them, they had not got too dirty, and therefore they had stayed unwashed *(so unbleached)*, and didn't smell like a surgery whenever what she called special occasions, showed their ugly faces!

Over those four years I had of course, well and truly grown out of them, and they had begun to look decidedly tired by the time I got to the third year. The moths had found them tasty in a few places, and I think that by the time I was in the final year when I still wore them to 'special occasions' and things when I had to, I didn't dare bend over, even a little bit. The hem would have been a mere 'half a turning' wide, with bias binding tacked on the inside, to make up the difference. No longer anything like they had been,and pitted with moth holes, they had at least managed to make it, avoiding the scary bleach pot!

By the time I got to my last year of school, I remember hating her, *(Peggy, that is)* as only 15–16 year old's can hate! The hate of course didn't last very long though. I think they call it growing up! But I did finally talk Peg into splurging on a new, second hand uniform half way through my final year. *(Hey I just thought! Was it second hand? And I wonder if she paid for it, or if Mum did! I guess that will never know now!)*

Carol and I had spent all those years in kindy and primary schools , and then two and a half years years from when we had been just thirteen, in and out of all kinds of typical schoolgirl scrapes, she and I had actually been scheduled to leave school, with little or no expectations. So there we were at the ripe old age of 15 and a bit, at the end of third year of high school, with a lifetime of menial work in a local factory to look forward to. Even with my scatterbrain behaviour, I had somehow, goodness knows how, managed to achieve 'not bad' grades. I think that I probably had talked Carol into staying on at school too. I remember that I could be pretty persuasive if I believed in something strongly enough, and she was also actually a pretty smart cookie. And typical of me though, although she didn't really like school too much either, I selfishly wanted her to stay on with me. Her parents were pretty much for it, they could almost/just afford it, and her staying on as well, meant that at least I was going have a known friend to hang around with. We were halfway through the first month of the fourth year at Wiley Park High School, and most unusually for us, we had made quite a lot of friends throughout the latter months of the previous year. Although quite a lot of the girls had left, a few of them were continuing on too, so we were sort of looking forward to that last year of High School. At least we were still going to have each other to hang about with. The demonic Dyer, and the flighty Floyd. Getting on with the new students who were taking advantage of the excellent teaching facilities there, was a lot easier with no nasty track record to overcome. So we figured that we would be OK. Although, there were of course, some 'non friends' staying on as well! More's the pity!

Even though I had handed the cello back, two years before, as I said, the school had allowed me to continue with music, and I had really enjoyed it. I no longer had to feel guilty about not having done the practice that was needed on the instrument. I took up recorder, and played that instead. It was easy enough to play, didn't take up a seat on the bus, but my playing of it was actually more abysmal even than my cello playing, and as you read – that was awful enough! A more inadequate recorder player you'd have been decidedly hard pressed to find. I got left out of the recorder class performances more often than not! The results of my efforts, even if I do say so myself, were atrocious! The musical notes, *if you could call the resultant squawks musical)* were not exactly what anyone would call very good, and I was always in trouble. *(I wonder if that might have been because I didn't practice enough? Too busy practising singing, wasn't I?)*

But when they told us, that because we were to be in our fourth, and supposedly last year, and that hopefully we would be going on to better things, we were going to be starting a proper full course of French instead of the mini course that we had done a few years before, you could have knocked us over with a feather! Most of us had about as much chance of actually going to France or Paris, and strolling down the Champs aux Lyses, as we had of bumping into the Queen on a Saturday afternoon, in Lakemba! Zilch!

But anyway - 'them that ran the school figured that we should all become bi-lingual, just in case', and it did give me something new to get my teeth stuck into. But I remember thinking at the time.

"Just in case of what"?

"At least though, the new French teacher had a bit of a sense of humour. I even did the homework for her, and I breezed through French. Well I almost always did my homework anyway, and I just about 'swanned' through my classes and exams, and managed to get an Advanced+ pass for French. I even sat and passed the Australian Government's 'Alliance Fráncais' exams, held in the Sydney Town Hall.

Surprise of all surprises - I passed, *and* I won a prize! *(which ,considering that it would have been about 45 years ago, I have lost. Can't even remember what it was. Probably a lovely gaudy certificate, very much admired and cherished by me, and the family at the time!).* I must say though, that it's a pity that I hadn't got stuck into it a little further. *(French that is)* With us now living in England, a more detailed version of French, would be very useful. Very useful indeed! Mind you, I guess that if I were that bothered though, then I would get stuck into learning some more French, now, but I never seem to have the time! *(again - I am just too busy doing things like writing this book, I suppose! And there is just such a learning curve involved with it!)*

Like I said before though - I prefer to do things that interest me. I do however, feel such a fool whenever I go through 'le Grande Manche' *(The Eurostar Tunnel),* and I definitely find it difficult to talk to the people on the train, or restaurant staff on the other side *(France).* English with a French accent, doesn't really cut the mustard - does it? But to tell you the truth - I'm not too sure who would have been the more surprised that I had learnt what I did learn at that time! Me or our French teacher, Miss Bush.

My one real saving grace at school though, was that I *did* sing, *(not, unfortunately in French though!)* and they all eventually thought that I sang OK. I was always singing, and as I have said, I must have driven Peg and Charlie mad at home, and I also drove the teachers at school nuts as well. In fact - my singing, must have been a tad on the disconcerting side for just about everybody. *(except me of course!)*

Students and teachers would be striding down a school corridor between lessons, anxious to get to the next class, when they would suddenly hear a voice echoing through the expected silence, *(everybody having already been told to 'walk quietly and quickly'.Remember?).* Through the corridors though, they would hear a raucous voice, raised in joyous, unfettered song, wafting from the toilets or empty rooms. Although it was most definitely inappropriate at times, the sound that the staff and students did hear, was evidently a 'bit better than alright' for a 15 year old! The general school kid consensus, in amongst the unavoidable teenage jealousy, was that " 'the Dyer' might be a bit of an oddity, but didn't she sing well ?"

The school year had just begun. It was a particularly hot time in Sydney, Australia that year, and the teachers, joyfully thinking that they were imparting welcome news, told us that we would be putting on Humperdinck's opera of Hansel & Gretel at the end of July. *("Aaw" - says us, finding it just too difficult to be as full of interest as the teachers expected us to be - "hopefully it won't be this hot by then", we all complained).* The ensuing talk about the upcoming Opera presentation turned the school into a veritable cacophony of sound. The kids' chatter sounded a bit like a noisy flock of galahs, *(an Australian parrot)* or budgies, chirping away. A great amount of 'trying to be silent and yet not being very successful at it', whispering abounded around the school. For me, who absolutely loved music, the news about the Opera, had been a bit like a birthday present , and I had cockily thought,"it's a birthday present for Australia as well".

You see, my birthday is on Australia Day, and although I never even considered Mr Keen as anything other than my teacher at that time, it is now also our wedding anniversary. The man who taught us all music as school kids, and whom we all thought of as wonderful, is now my husband. Isn't *that* wonderful! *(well I think it is, anyway!)* And what is more, he has been so far for 20 years in January!

What a great day the 26th January has turned out to be for me! I definitely got the best birthday present ever!!!!

But back at the school with the kids - the babble about the school grounds, although very excited, was tinged with a little fearfulness as well. The Opera seemed to us, and others, as if it was a bit of an over ambitious choice for school kids, but Miss Evans *(the music mistress)* and Mr Keen *(now the second in charge),* believed that we could do it! So being the good kids we were?, we squashed our worries in our bags, and figured that as the organisers of it were, after all, the music staff, and they thought that we could do it, then we would just have to accept that we could! They should know, and, of course - as it turned out, they did! *(Know, I mean!)*

"What part are you going to try out for Kerrie?", Carol asked me.

I thought about it for a moment - "would I be good enough for any of the parts? Do I really want one", I asked myself? *(Underneath all my usual bravado, I still wasn't sure that I was good enough)!* Secretly I really wanted to try out for the witch, *(but then I thought that Carol would have realised that, from the practice that I had been doing at her place),* but I wasn't about to actually voice my choice to anyone, not at that time anyway! *(I used to practice all the parts, just to put her off the scent, so I don't suppose that her question should have come as that much of a shock!!)*

Back then though, it just wasn't 'cool' to even intimate that you wanted to play an old 'hag', when you were only 15 and a bit. I don't think that it would be considered cool, even today! But then in a quiet, more like me, embarrassed, head hung low kinda voice, I said - "I don't think mum and dad could afford to get a costume made, or hire one, even if I did get a part. Can't you just imagine the problems that it would cause, Carol"? Peg and Charlie would have been, of course, initially as pleased as punch that I had even been considered for a part. But any pride they might have felt, would fly straight out of the window once I started asking for money to pay for things. I can still hear him - *(dad I mean),* even though he has been dead for many years. - His roll up fag, limply hanging out of the corner of his mouth, and flapping about while it still stuck to his bottom lip where it had left a kind of sore like mark. Spittle would burst forth from his mouth as he yelled as loudly as he was able with the fag still in situ -

"You are joking, of course? Where do you think we are going to get the money for you to waste on your looking good for a school show"? I was desolate! Especially since the witch didn't exactly even have to 'look good'!

For Charlie to have been even a little bit happy about it all, the school would have needed to be putting something on, with a major role that I could do naked. Like 'Lady Godivah' or something!

He probably would have been embarrassed that I was naked, *(at least I hope so)* but at least my nakedness wouldn't have cost him a penny for my costume. Peg, though decided that if I did get a part, she would just have to sob the whole story out over the phone, bury her pride *(again),* and tell my real mum what was needed. Mum would have known that Peg and Charlie wouldn't have had the cash, *(as usual)* and Peg felt that she would just have to do did a bit of 'legitimate, crying poor mouth'

Luckily enough for me, I did get a part, and although both of my mum's were proud of the fact that I had a part in the show, neither Peg nor mum was overly happy about the expected expense, but after it was checked with the school, *(I think my real mum wanted to double check just how genuine this request for money was)* she 'intervened', and actually financed my first true step into showbiz. *(I would say - thank goodness! Not too sure though how my real mum would feel about it now though! She never really liked my interest in showbiz. Didn't think that it was a 'proper' course to follow, did she?But then, I began with an Opera, by Humperdink, didn't I?)* I am pretty sure that her opinion changed towards the end of my singing career though!

(Hope so,anyway!)

Peg though, mentioned to mum at the time of the school opera, that she was a bit scared about bringing the subject up with dad , of where the things actually came from. "It might just rile him up", she said, and they both agreed, and said - "No, we definitely wouldn't want to do that". "We'll just need to make sure that he doesn't know where the money for the costume came from", said Peg, and although my real mum doesn't really approve of subterfuge, she knew from old, that to rile Charlie, would have been like taking a bone from a dog's mouth. Not a very advisable thing to do, at the best of times, unless you had some fingers you didn't need. They both agreed, and so not telling dad that mum had paid for the costume, Peg and mum had come on different nights, and dad just figured that the school must have provided it!

Hansel and Gretel ticket

I said to Carol not long after, - "although he's my dad, and I love him to bits, I have to wonder why he doesn't see"? She quizzically looked at me. "See what", she said? I spun round and petulantly, stomping my foot, I answered Carol, with my eyes spitting daggers,and looking heaven wards to the sky - "Well really! Don't tell me that you can't see either", I said, becoming super cross - "I could become 'famous'", I shouted. "I could make us lots of money, and then I would be able to keep Charlie and Peg in comfort in their old age. You and I could have a right old time too, Carol. Peg would be in her element, with dad able to lord it about among his friends. He'd be able to get some new teeth too", I churlishly said!

"Yeah - he could do with them", Carol thoughtlessly remarked. I flashed her a scathing look, and did a typical kids 'hit out' at her! Those kind of comments were OK from me, but not from anyone else! Then sulkily I added - "I can't see why dad doesn't just invest the little that he wins, when he does win, *(which wasn't all that often anyway!)* in my talents, instead of in that blasted dog that he won a few months ago in place of actual money. At least then he could be assured of getting something back, instead of pouring what little money he does have down the things throat. - *and* - then there's another thing! - That dog should have been called 'almost', and not 'Winner', as it is called, because it only ever 'almost' wins. And do you know what - to make matters even worse" I added nastily - "it generally only ever 'almost' wins the next ruddy race"!

Being typical kids, we both hugged ourselves, in fits of laughter at the vision of this moth eaten dog, stumbling along, a whole half a track length behind the others!

"Giggle, giggle, snicker, snicker", we went. Then said Carol, in between the fits of laughter. "Imagine the drama if the silly excuse for a dog ever actually caught that bunny thing it is supposed to be chasing!" We both laughed in a raucous way, and guffawed a lot more, at the cartoon like vision that flashed, simultaneously through both our minds. We both absolutely fell about! The vision of 'Winner', chasing and then pouncing on the electronic bunny was one thing, funny enough in itself to cause us to hold our crotches to make sure we didn't wet ourselves, but then I stumblingly said through the giggling - "you know - I can just see it -'Winner', all stiff, with his head and his legs wildly shaking, as the electricity transfers from the 'hare' to him". We laughed and guffawed some more!

Carol added, just about falling down at the mental image of it, - "yeah", she said! - "The dog's legs and body suddenly going all stiff, legs sticking out in a petrified 'legs akimbo' state, as the current goes right through him. All the way from his scrawny head, to his elongated, painted by your dad with clear nail polish for strength, toes"!

When she told me her vision, I just about fell about with laughter - "Ouch! that hurts", I said,grabbing my ribs!. We both giggled and fell about, all over again! Eventually we managed to calm down a bit though. Mainly because, as I remember it, although it had got to the end of February, it was still too hot for raucous laughter of any kind, for any reason. So our laughter petered out, and we just stood there fanning ourselves with whatever we could grab to fan with, while the dregs of our laughter rippled through the air! I though, must have been feeling a bit naughty. Very 'anti' everything, and I can imagine that I probably said , repeating myself, because I do remember that the whole thing used to make me so cross, - "It's probably a lot selfish of me, but I could sure use the money that dad wastes on that mongrel 'Winner'. "Why will he not see?" I would have sulkily moaned again!

"That dog is a complete waste of space, and uses up money that dad doesn't really have, but do you think daddy looks at it like that? Not on your Nelly! He treats the dog like it was a baby, and how on earth he expects it to ever win even one race, is beyond me". I guess that I would have let out a big sigh. "He is always feeding it, even though it is supposed to be a thin, hungry enough to win greyhound!

Goodness knows where he gets the money for it's food - probably again, out of Peg's purse", I angrily complained! "Says he feels sorry for it, and that it looks at him with such big, hungry looking eyes"! Even at my young age, I sometimes said to him "aw come on dad, - It is meant to be a racing dog for heavens' sake!" I said to Carol -"dad lives in a dream world! He is always saying that one day he'll hit the jackpot. Can't he see that I could be his 'jackpot'? Out of the blue, in my far off dreamy sing song voice - I added, what had by then become my favourite song - "I'm the greatest star, but no one knows it". Then I would cheekily add - *"YET"!*

Carol raised her eyes, and shrugged as she slumped off! The heat of February had passed a bit, and the school had finally decided that it was definitely putting the Humperdink opera - Handel & Gretel on in the July, so all of the teachers and students in the school were very busy getting everything ready for it. But because it was still a bit on the hot side, no one was putting 100% into the opera at that time. They were still too busy trying to get cool.

Portable fans small enough to carry around with you, hadn't been invented then, so we all just went around, waving bits of paper made into fans, and trying not to sweat too much. Even at 59 (*as I am now)*, I do seem to vaguely remember the 'not so subtle' aroma of nubile, newly menstruating young females, pervading the air!

The rehearsals and preparations for the show that would hopefully prove to all the parents and invited guests just how good we all were, were about to begin. That was of course, if the weather ever managed to cool down enough for everyone to feel like doing any work! The performance would, we hoped, show how hard we had all worked. Also how inspired, and inspiring the teaching staff were. But before the rehearsals for the show, and that hard work could begin, the auditions needed to be had so that the teachers could find, and settle on the cast members who would be doing the rehearsing. So - before we knew it, it was 'audition time'!

GENERAL AUDITION said the notices put up all over the school! So the whole of the fourth year pupils, along with a few upper third year pupils were in a state of anticipation, and questioning. The lower grade kids kept asking me,"Aren't you in the know Kerrie? Who is going to be in the show? You do Music elective, don't you"? Come on - you can tell us". "We won't tell anyone else", they said. "Promise - we promise"!

Questions, questions, questions! Then it really started in earnest - even more questions! Of course, the selection of the major parts was partly done, by the teachers, basically using the class lists and each teacher's own personal knowledge of their own student's abilities. "Come on Kerrie", the kids said - "haven't you heard who is going to be Hansel? And - what about so and so for Gretel"?, they asked. - "What do you think about her? - She's pretty enough" they said, "but do you know if the people in charge might think that she would be right for the part"? That was the general gist of the questioning. "She sings good enough though, don't she? Don't you think so? Who do you think is going to be lucky enough to play the Good Fairy?

I'd like to have a go for that part", said one of the girls. "What do you think my chances would be"?*(I think that we probably all just looked at that particular girl with our mouths open, saying nothing, not wanting to offend!!)* And then finally - "who's going to play the Witch", they would ask? "Who would wanna play a horrible old hag anyhow", said one of the kids in a sarcastic manner? "Ha,ha, ha,ha"! they all laughed.

(I vaguely remember shrinking at the derisive comment, and feeling a bit grateful that I had previously said nothing!) "How the heck would I know!", I would grumpily answer back, each time I was asked, secretly wanting to know myself, because I knew of at least one person who would want to play 'the horrible old hag'! Me! But my repeated assurances that I wouldn't know any more than them, seemed to fall on deaf ears. I did though say, in an attempt to keep them quiet, and not put too many noses out of joint - putting my fingers alongside my nose, and speaking in a quite secretive kind of voice - "I will tell you this much though", and then I would add - "but only if you promise to then give it a rest"!

I have since been told by an other person who was there as well, that I had also said to them in a kind of pronounced stage whisper, *"although it is a very ambitious choice for school kids, the teachers, and head mistress all feel that with a lot of hard work from everybody, the girls of years 4 and a few chorus members from year 3 are 'up to it'".* I too thought that we *were* up to it!

I couldn't really get into any trouble telling them that much could I? After all - I knew about as much as they knew now, and that was still – *absolutely NOTHING!*

(I guess that I just liked to play 'big shot'. A bit like daddy, perhaps! You know - pretend to be someone who is 'in the know', even when I wasn't really! Silly really, when I look back on it now! But I was only a school kid, after all!) But on seeing the disappointment that was still on their faces, and in an attempt to make them feel more involved, *(I unfortunately knew what it felt like to be left out of things)* I think that I had said, full of pupil bolstering confidence - "What do you think, eh? Are they right girls? Are we all up for it, or what? The girls all went '*YEAH*'!, and a very animated, loud vocal discussion ensued, with about half of a very

excited group of almost teenagers, and young people slowly meandering back to class.

Typical of me though, I don't suppose that I had really paid overly much attention to what the kids had been saying at the end of the discussion - I was suddenly lost in a dream about my own desired part in the show. I knew what part I would like to play! I had never seemed to have time for homework and stuff, and yet I had already half learned at least three of the parts. I knew Gretel's part would be demandingly fun, but I said to myself, "I'm not pretty enough to play her".*(There was no doubt about it. I was an ugly kid, with lank, messy hair, and enormously large ears!)* "I have big ears for one", I said out loud, *(which meant that the few kids who were left, just stared at this strange person talking to herself, about something as innocuous as 'big ears,')* and "I know that I do look a bit like an unattractive rabbit", I added, still out loud, vacantly looking around me. I continued on talking to myself , with those who were still there, wondering what on earth I was talking about, or who I was actually talking to, as I added out of the blue - something like, "a little like the ones that 'Winner' chases, and never catches" An unattractive rabbit, without the electric charge, I must have thought. The kids that were left, on hearing me talking to myself again, wondered whether or not I'd gone even nuttier than they already thought I was. Then, out of the blue I quite boldly said out loud, and right to the girls this time - "You know - I wouldn't mind giving them all *(the kids in the audience I meant)* a bit of a shock", and I must have grinned at my own wicked sense of humour! *(I actually smile now when I think of it! The teachers had been right! I definitely was a bit of a rapscallion!!)* Then out of the blue I said boldly to everyone - "I don't think that I would get the part of Hansel, so he would be out. I don't really like playing boys anyway. It only reinforces my feelings of 'lack of beauty, and anyway," turning sharply towards her - I asked "Carol - didn't you say that you would like to try for that part"? A shy, affirmative nod was her reply!

Two days later there was another notice that said 'most of the parts had already been filled. "That was quick", I said to Carol. Picked in two days? That doesn't sound too good!" "Too quick," I thought, again stomping my dainty(?) foot on the ground. "How dare they? I haven't even put my name forward yet". But to tell the truth, I couldn't believe that the teachers would do that though. *(Just take anyone I mean!)* I knew that they were anxious to get it over, but didn't they realise that there was a lot more than just pleasing the parents at stake here. They just couldn't have found everyone so quickly! "They just couldn't have, could they", I worriedly thought. I also sulkily thought again -"Some of us haven't even put our names down yet"! *(Do you think that that comment might just have been indicative of how egotistical I was – even then!)*

Apart from saying that most of the parts had been taken, the bottom of the notice had also *(luckily for me)* said that they were still looking for a witch. *(Phew!)* The successful applicant, it read, would not only need to be innovative *(I didn't even know what that word meant at that time)*, but must have a good vocal range as well. The sign also said that the successful applicant would also need to have a good imagination.

"Now" I thought to myself - "my imagination is always getting me into one scrape or another. "I'm not too sure about it being good though, and I am also not too sure about the innovative bit either. How does one know if one is innovative at our age"?, I asked Carol."I find the word impossible to say, let alone know what that big word means", she answered! And then the notice also said that a wide vocal range with the volume needed to fill the auditorium would also be required. "That is a bit 'iffy' too then", I thought! *(Loud I could do, but did I have the range?)*

But that there morning I had decided, and I then said to Carol, full of youthful confidence "In for a penny, in for a pound"! "I am pretty sure I can do that"! "Well - at least" says me haughtily -"I've actually done all the parts at your home, haven't I? "Nibble, nibble, mousekin. Who's nibbling at my housekin", I sang. "When I sing that at home though, dad is always telling me to shut up",I said. Now - whether that is because it sounds horrible, or because it is too loud and I am interrupting his sleep, I can't really be sure. What do you think, Carol"?

A shrug would have been the reply, I think, *(it normally was)*. I had secretly 'borrowed' a copy of the music and words from the school music room, and I had scrimped, stolen a little bit, *(of money - such a bad girl I was. I guess that I had learned it from dad, and I hoped that Peg would never miss it . She rarely did with dad, after all!)*. But I also quickly saved, and raided the dregs of my own piggy bank to buy a copy of the record of one of the show's performances in a leading Bankstown Theatre, at a local bring and buy sale. It had cost me a whole 1 shilling and 6 pence, which in those days, for a kid of my age, was an enormous amount out of my almost non - existent pocket money. Almost all my savings at the time it was, and boy did I get in trouble when Peggy noticed sixpence missing from her hoard! She reckoned that it could only have been me who had taken it. It just wasn't fair! Dad got away with murder when he 'borrowed' money! But me? No fear!

But - Carol's family had the record player, so I had spent loads of time at her place singing along to it! I had already learned a lot of the opera at Carol's place, again, just in case. *(I seem to have spent most of my life doing things, "Just in case, don't I?")* Still actually do! But I was standing there, looking at the sign, and I read on.

Down at the bottom of the sign - it said in heavy black print -
WE STILL NEED A WITCH!

"O Ooo! Goody", says me to me! There's still a chance then!"

'The Witch will need an auditorium filling sound', had said that latest sign. *(That also in thick black print, and it was underlined for emphasis!)*

"I'm still not really too sure about that bit though", I said to Carol, who replied - "You're joking aren't you"? - She laughingly said, "aren't you always being told that you're a bit of a loud mouth? Now is your chance to put your 'loud-mouthiness' to an 'alright' purpose, and to 'really show 'em', once and for all. After all - you already know half of the show anyway". We smiled a big grin at each other *(she alone knew of how much work I had already put into the show)*, and I was suddenly, from that moment on, totally convinced that she, at least was on my side. There could be no doubt about it. We both thought that I was 'alright', but was I 'alright' enough to do such an important role as the Witch? Carol evidently thought I was - and as she was after all my best friend, who was supposed to be brutally honest *(which unfortunately, she most definitely was, most of the time)*, I had also to believe that I was alright!

We both agreed though, that although I got on reasonably well with most of the other class members nowadays, I was still not the most popular girl in our class. If it came down to a class vote between two or more people for the role - then I would probably lose. But on seeing those signs over the previous couple of days, I had said to Carol - "You know, I think that maybe we have shot ourselves in the foot by not having applied yet". And then it was as if a light bulb had flashed in my head -

"A large part of the practice I have been doing with the record at your place Carol, has been concentrated on the Witch's part, and I think that you of all people probably know just how desperately I have wanted the witch's part all along! That there sign says that the part is still vacant. I might not even get it, but would you mind too much if I did? Apply for it now I mean. As I have said - I can't really see myself as Hansel, nor as Gretel, and I don't think that I'd make a good 'good fairy, now, do you'"? I must have always repeated my thoughts and statements! I posed in a twee way, and we both giggled a bit. I added, "even you would have to agree that I am not pretty enough for a Gretel or a fairy. Also I am definitely not light enough of foot, nor dainty enough! Fairies don't clop about, as if in hob nailed boots, now do they"? We both giggled again! "Fairies are meant to be 'will of the wispy' types", I lisped, flitting around, trying to look as wispy, and light as possible. Undoubtedly it would have been very 'unwispyish' for clod hopper me. "Now - be honest," says me, striking a comic pose - "can you honestly say that you could see me as a fairy"?

Our enmity *(if there had even been any)*, dissolved, and we both did what was becoming all too frequent for us those days, and fell about laughing again. The 'oh so pretty', 'perfect looking, and perfectly singing' Jenny, was bound to, and did, get the part of Gretel. I hadn't really liked Hansel's part, the competition with Carol aside, and it had been out of the question as a part for me to try for anyway! Friendships were paramount at 15-16!

In case she had laughingly said that the witch would be too much a case of type casting, and that it had a much too hard for me to learn vocal part, I had never even intimated that I was contemplating that part before. I had tried all the parts at her place, and I must admit, that I had had a few problems with the witch's part. We had often missed out on something or other before, because neither of us was a quick witted 'doer' at that time! I still am not - really!

Miss Evans, and Mr Keen only had to settle on the gingerbread men, in the chorus, the good fairy, and of course 'the witch'. So a final notice had appeared on the board that very afternoon - 'ANYONE who is interested in playing the witch, the good fairy or a gingerbread man', was to notify Miss Evans or Mr Keen, asap, so that the school could close the auditions, and get on with the rehearsals! Carol and I looked at each other. "According to the sign - we now have no excuse you know", said Carol. "The school is virtually begging us to put our names forward", and then she said - "I could always be a gingerbread man if I get in quick enough. They are not all picked yet"! *(Though I suppose that for me to be politically correct with my writing, I had best write - 'gingerbread person'.)* And she did make an excellent gingerbread person, she did!

TEACHERS' DISCUSSION

So - we had joined hands, and loudly repeated our favourite saying -
'in for a penny, in for a pound'.
(Remember when we had them? "Oooh - I forgot - I've got them again in England! I meant in Australia.")
Carol and I read on. That last new sign on the school wall, advertising the show, and handwritten by one of the art teachers, in thick jet black paint had also said -

"The show will be full of fantasy and imaginative ideas re the presentation, so you may need a head for heights', with our own Mr Keen introducing
some of the international stage effects
direct from
the 'London West End Theatres'".
A show you shouldn't miss! Make sure you're there!
(A bit like - 'be there, or be square?')

"Oooh - maybe he knows a way for the witch to fly a broomstick around the room, and whoever gets the part will not only have to learn how to fly, but will need a good head for heights," said Carol. "How do you feel about flying high Kerrie? Ha ha! "*(And remember, that comment was made in an era, well before Drugs had become a problem at schools, before they were a problem at all, really!)*
Having been a bit preoccupied with my own thoughts, I hadn't really heard the question, and I vacantly said "I'm a bit worried about

the head for heights bit that the notice mentions though". She grinned knowingly to herself. Carol knew that I couldn't even wear short heels without falling over. "I can just see you", she said - "having a fit of giddiness and falling off the broom, right into Mr Keen's lap" she giggled, putting her finger on the side of her nose, and Betty Betty Boop'ing it up again, with big pursed lips - she said - 'Oooo'! Ha Ha Ha Ha, ha ha ha! laughed Carol again, just about rolling around the room.

"No I wont!", I quickly, and angrily retorted, stamping my childish, and disgusted at the very thought, foot on the floor. *(That foot was definitely kept busy in those days, wasn't it?!)* I had never even looked seriously at 'fellows' at that age. But after casually thinking about it, I probably said something like - "Ooh yes please", it was just typical teenage wishful*(?)* thinking, and I think that I said something like - "Mr Keen is a dish! - So clean looking! Can't you just see it!!!!"

Youthful bravado?

"You know something, though? You are probably right Carol", says me cheekily grinning. "I probably would fall off the broomstick but with my luck, I would land most unceremoniously, not on Mr Keen's lap as you said, but on the lap of some poor local dignitary or something!

Then the newspaper headlines would really have a field day, wouldn't they"? I can't remember if the papers would have written about an event such as that at that time, but if it were now, the headlines would no doubt read - ***"Council member cleaned up at Local School! Flying Witch, cleans up the local mess with her broom, during the show."***

Carol and I fell about, all over again.

(Judging by what I have written, and knowing that it is all the truth, Carol and I must have spent most of our high school years either slapping each other on the back, or falling about laughing! How on earth we found any time for lessons, is beyond me! It's also a wonder our bodies aren't covered in permanent bruises!). Come to think of it, maybe they are, I'll just have a look!

(Na - ah - Luckily - not!)

But we had made our decision, and as you should know by now, our favourite saying said – "in for a penny, in for a pound". So as there could be no backing out this time, we rushed off to find Miss Evans or

Mr Keen to tell them that we would like to give it a go, and see what happened! I sang "Nibble, nibble, mousekin" in my best produced, and most lyrical voice, as we laughingly, full of giggles, rushed down the corridor to find someone to officially tell our decision to!

Our adventure had just taken a new, and exciting twist!

THE ADVENTURE HAD BEGUN!

Miss Wylie and the teachers though were in the staff room, still a bit worried. They were all discussing the pluses and minuses of the few candidates that there had been, who might, if they decided that they'd want to do it, be suitable for the main part- the Witch. They still hadn't been able to find a Witch for the show, and the show just wouldn't really be a show without the cackling presence of a convincing witch.

"But which one of the girls available would be able to present a convincing witch", they pondered? The music teachers also had to finalise the picking of the gingerbread fence people, and although the witch obviously hadn't been a popular part with girls, she was absolutely pivotal to the success of the show.

They went through the very short list of available people who they knew 'kind of' met their criteria. Three people I think it was , two of whom had already willingly auditioned, and who, for one reason or another were deemed to be not quite right for the part. Then Miss Evans, the head of the music department, quietly, almost tentatively, said to the other teachers - tentatively, because she guessed that her suggestion would raise a lot if dissent. "That leaves only the one other that I know of"!

She quickly said - "What about Kerrie Dyer, she was on our original short list, wasn't she?"

As she surmised - grumbles and disagreeable sounds of disapproval came from some of the teachers. Miss Evans looked a little worried at the reaction, as she quietly said - "I thought that she was interested, but I don't think that I've seen her name on the student's lists?" "I could have told you that was going to happen! - That's typical, that is", said one! "Doesn't surprise me one bit", said another, "generally is all mouth, and no action". "More trouble than she's worth if you ask me", echoed a few others.

(Goodness, I was popular, wasn't I?)

That was the general reaction from around the table! "Now now teachers, - really!" Miss Wylie the headmistress probably would have said in her autocratic, headmistress way, in answer to some of the more persistent grumblers. Once Miss Wylie had quietened the teachers' moans, Miss Evans added with an understanding tone. "I am fully aware that Kerrie can be a bit of a handful sometimes, but although I have always known that she could sing, I have only just been made fully aware of the other abilities she has."

"You mean she can do something other than just make trouble", butted in one of the teachers?

Miss Evans smiled patiently - "Yes, we have found out that not only does she sing rather well, but I believe that, if given a scripted chance to show off a bit, she might actually just come into her own. The Drama department say that she has shown initial signs of evidently being alright at acting as well. Maybe we could put some of her exuberance to profitable use. How she has managed to 'slip the net' for this long, I am not sure! What do you think Mr Keen?" Mr Keen hadn't had a lot to do with my classes at that time. Not at least, since I had handed in the cello, two years previous! But he had heard a few of the teachers in the staff room, grumbling and complaining about someone called Kerrie Dyer, before today. Because he trusted Miss Evan's assessment more though *(and he also knew where his bread was buttered),* he took what he was being told him in asides by the various teachers with a grain of salt. He quietly nodded agreement with Miss Evans' deduction.

Some of the other teachers however, who had been at the school for a while, and who had actually tried to teach Kerrie Dyer something were showing decided signs of negativity. And how do I know those things. My darling husband, Mr Keen, told me the general gist of the staff room mood, and I, vaguely remembering what the teachers were like, have imagined the rest! I do know personally also though, that I was not a truly popular student. Not with *anyone*. Neither with some of the teachers, nor most of the students! Except for instance, maybe with

Miss Bush, the French mistress who had turned out to be my bestest ever teacher friend in Year 4. But even she evidently used to say - "There must be some way of getting her to do some work. It is such a waste otherwise"!

Unfortunately I have to admit though, that there would probably have been very few others who would have championed my cause. I guess that she must have liked me I think! But then, maybe she recognised a fellow rebel, I don't know! But I like to think, that all things aside, she liked me! I was rather pleased for her that she was due to become deputy head. Even the general student body liked her, and she was affectionately known as "Bushy" by some of them. Having already taken on some of the deputy headmistress's duties, Bushy had been making a point of keeping a close eye on all the students, and every now and then one of them would make a real impression on her. Unfortunately for some of the students *(me in particular)*, it was not always a positive impression, and I don't suppose that I had always made positive impressions on many of the other teachers, either! I was told, again by my husband, that Bushy would take her customary, lo -on -g puff on a cigarette, and through the resulting carcinogenic fog of smoke *(that would definitely not be allowed these days!),* she would say -"Mm - Kerrie Dyer. Now let me see. I am pretty sure Mr Keen , is that girl with the big ears and pig-tails in 4b. She is now in Miss Evan's music elective class, I think. I seem to remember something about a cello too. "Am I right - Mr Keen? - Miss Evans?" Miss Evans smiled an exasperated smile, looked around , and nodded. Bushy continued - "She is one of the pupils who has given us, me especially, a lot of angst. Very bright, but not very well disciplined! Always singing in the toilets! I can't believe you haven't crossed swords with her recently Mr Keen? Meeting up with her again with the opera, should definitely be a pleasure that you really mustn't be deprived of!"

Taking another deep drag on her cigarette, she cheekily grinned, stubbed the cigarette out, and continued speaking, as she peeked out through the enveloping veil of remaining smoke. "There is no doubt about it" she said, "Miss Dyer has the brains needed for the part, but so far she hasn't showed us any sign of using them productively. At least not to me she hasn't!" Glancing at some of the others to see if there was any further reaction she added – Miss Dyer is always in trouble around the school, with problems of one sort or another. Her grades, that she apparently does relatively little or no work for, show us that she is definitely university material, but honestly, I mean to say, the way she cavorts about the school always humming, and singing to herself and continually disrupting class. She is always causing all kinds of problems. If there is ever any trouble of any sort, you can be pretty confident of finding her, apparently innocent, smiling face, smack bang in the middle of it".

She stopped, brushed some fallen ash from her skirt, and then she thought for a minute. "Maybe an opportunity like this might be just what the girl needs though, help straighten her out a bit." she said. "Get her on the right track"!

Miss Wylie interjected, and said - "Yes, come to think of it now that I ponder on it, I think that I've actually heard her myself. Let me think – Yes, I am sure that I had reason to reprimand her for singing in the corridors a few weeks ago, just after we commenced the term, and from memory, she does sing rather nicely. A bit coarsely maybe, but nicely all the same, and with some training from Mr Keen and Miss Evans, she could be just what we are looking for!" The bit coarsely might even be an advantage in this case! She cackles really well too", she added. "I heard her, when she and a few of the students must have been playing about with the some of the songs from the show. And as it happens I have also just recently had cause to speak with her real Mother, but about a totally different matter entirely, and yes - I think that maybe we should find out", she said, as if talking to herself. "Shall we"? Then she added, addressing the staff. "Miss Dyer comes from a 'split' family you know, and there has been a bit of concern about her decided lack of diligence in a few of her other subjects as well. I suspected some sort of problem, read her school reports, and after my recent phone call from, and subsequent talk with, her biological mother, I found out that her parental situation, through no fault of her own, has left a lot to be desired over the years.

Her parents were divorced when she was little, and she lives with her dad and step-mum. It turns out that they don't have much money, and as her father wants her to get out and earn some as soon as possible, there is little, or no academic encouragement from that source." Miss Wylie then said, "Mr Dyer doesn't really have much time for education.

Kerrie's real mother says that he is a very basic worker type. I assume from the conversation that he is the total opposite of Miss Dyer's mother, and that he thinks the whole education thing costs too much money. Money that he doesn't have, to be spent for no real purpose that he can see anyway", he says.

"Oh", she said in answer to a few grumbles – "he realises that the schooling itself is basically free because he is in the lowest of the low income bracket, but for all the extras incurred with any extra curricular pass times, and the uniform and things, he just doesn't want to know. The prime example having been the Cello, and the lessons needed, in year One. Miss Dyer's biological mother, who didn't know about the Cello at the time, tells me that Mr Dyer often says, in a very rude kind of way I might add, that he just can't afford any fol de rol extras. Miss Dyer's mother said that Kerrie wouldn't have received much scholarly encouragement from her dad and step-mum, and that unfortunately she couldn't really help as much as she would like to because she has a young child, and another, from her second marriage, hopefully on the way. She also said that because of her background as a child, Kerrie definitely wouldn't fit in to her current family's lifestyle". Mr Dyer's lifestyle is diametrically opposite to her current situation. Miss Wylie continued, nodding her head in thought all the time she was talking.

"Her mother said that if we thought that there was a good chance that she might achieve it, that she would like Miss Dyer to at least sit her leaving certificate, and would be prepared to help out in small ways when needed, and if and when she could! That is actually why Miss Dyer is still with us for year Four". Her mum is paying for it! She also repeated again that no one would get much positive help from Kerrie's dad on the matter of her staying on.(As much as I have always loved him, daddy wasn't what you might call, too hot on academic qualifications.)

"As I said before", Miss Wylie added "Mr Dyer had said to me, through Kerrie's step mum, that he wanted Kerrie to get out to work a.s.a.p, and bring home some much needed money to help them both out a bit". Miss Wylie paused, thought a bit, brought the conversation back to the Opera, and then continued. "Yes - now let me see. Right, yes!, I am definitely sure that it was her that I heard 'cackling' about something or other when she was joking with one of the other students, the same day that I reprimanded her for singing in the corridor! I hesitate to admit it, but she really does have an almost natural witch's cackle". She added ,"I think she might actually enjoy the challenge of a show like this. Mr Keen will be in charge of some of the stage work, and what he and I have discussed, will definitely pose a challenge for all of the performers", she said silently smirking to herself!

"If Kerri were to get the part, -*(and I have been told that some of the teachers thought, and said – "God forbid"!!),* it will also hopefully give her something to get her teeth into, that will keep her too constructively occupied to waste any more time being a nuisance for this last year of her school life", said Miss Evans.

Quickly turning around, having heard the muttering from some of the other teachers, Miss Wylie said - "Yes, you are probably right Miss Evans". Then suddenly she said, looking at her watch - "Miss Andrews - do you think that you could send a message to Miss Dyer for me please? Ask her to come and see me after school this afternoon please? Mmmh - let me ponder on it a little more! Yes - I think that after all the trouble, we just might have found our witch! Oh - and by the way", she said to the teachers, "I would also appreciate it if you would all be there as well, please".

Moans about the apparently wasteful loss of time that was valuable to them, came from most of them. A lot of the teachers there, were maybe a little hesitant about the head's choice, and some of them were probably more than a bit disgruntled at their late afternoon/early evening being surreptitiously commandeered. But as what the Head teacher says goes, they had probably thought - "Jobs are few and far between", and in those days, *(just as it is now)* you needed to work hard once you actually got such a good one. If you were lucky enough to be a teacher, at a highly thought of school, and in an occupation well loved by those in it, then it was a job that most people would give anything to have! Therefore the message was begrudgingly sent. *(simply a case of - 'She who must be obeyed', do you reckon?)*

Although one of the benefits of doing 'Music Elective' at school was that it's students, if they were talented enough, were usually the ones who performed the roles in any school production, I was still very surprised and naturally excited to actually be given the part later that afternoon. As I have said, I had secretly wanted it all along, but for me to actually be given the part of the Witch, in the way that I did actually get it, was truly thrilling for a school kid, and really *most* unexpected.

Originally, with my not having a clue about what to expect, I was full of fear and trepidation when I was ordered to Miss Wylie's office. I was thinking that I was in trouble for something and trying to remember if I/we had done anything too horrible; anything that would warrant being summoned to the Head teachers office after school!

And it had to have been something pretty nasty, to get Miss Wylie involved in the first place. So totally unsuspecting of what was to come, I slunk in to the office, ready to apologise for whatever I had apparently done wrong! Up till that moment I had often been in trouble, but had never been chosen for anything – not ever!

It seemed as if I had a big sign on me, saying -

DON'T PICK KERRIE!

But this time, Miss Wylie, Miss Evans, Mr Keen, and even though it had been begrudgingly by the other teachers, had actually picked me, and they were soon to find out whether or not they had done the right thing!

All they could do now, was cross their fingers, and hope that the drama department had been correct in it's assessment, and that I could act!

HANSEL & GRETEL

The Opera was the main topic of conversation for days. Whether or not I could act was still a major cause of worry for the teachers!

Miss Evans, was probably the only teacher that had really heard me sing properly, and I still didn't know if she would really have been suitably impressed or not. She had never really said as much to me! The others had just heard me 'mucking around' in the corridors and things, and I hadn't impressed too many of them then, but - no one, not even Miss Evans, knew whether or not I could act? The Drama department seemed to think I could, but to tell the truth, not even I knew if I could, or could not act! "What exactly constituted acting anyway", I would have thought?

Oh sure, I knew that I was always acting the fool, but I wondered if that would come under the same category as proper 'acting'. Typically for me though, although *appearing* very sure of myself, I secretly must have thought that the fact that they wouldn't have needed a lot of work to 'uglify' me up a bit for the part of the witch, probably had had a lot to do with the final decision as well. I guess that I have to admit that I was, what you might have called, as I have no doubt already said a pretty ugly teenager, and I think it would have taken a 'whiz' of a make up artist to make Joan Day or Trisha Lane *(who were both beauties)* look ugly enough! *(They used to make me feel sick with the envy that only a definitely un-pretty, almost teenager can feel!)*

Again Miss Evans asked - "What are your thoughts Mr Keen"? He just nodded agreement again, always liking to be sure of his facts, before he actually spoke *(hasn't changed a lot then!)*. "Yes"! - Miss Wylie stood and thought for a moment. "She might just possess a lot of the requirements needed to play such a difficult, and demanding role. You are right of course Miss Evans. It would, most definitely, prove beneficial for everyone concerned if she wanted to give it a go, and even better if she can actually act.

Then the rather snide Maths teacher, Mrs West interjected! "If this opera is going to be the success that we would all like it to be, it would definitely help if she could". Most of the other teachers shuffled on their chairs, raised their eyes to the ceiling, and muttered indecipherable comments among themselves! But they all seemed to agree that I did at least possess all the qualities of an ideal witch! Especially the angular face! Two enormous *(you'd be able to see them from the back of the room, even without make up)* big, brown eyes that could be made to look positively evil if needed. *(Not too much work needed there then!)*

My classmate, and friend Joan had eventually been given the part of the 'good' fairy, and Trisha was her understudy! So it appeared that my 'suspect' looks had worked in my favour, for a change! Except that, as hard as they searched, they couldn't find me an understudy! Now I wasn't too sure whether it was because they couldn't find anyone else ugly enough, or because no one else could handle the part! And it did turn out to be a very hard part! I wasn't allowed to get sick, and lord help me if I even got the sniffles. The school would be hard pressed to find anyone to fill in for me if I did! They finally decided though, that they just had to have an understudy for me, and as Joan was the only other one who could sort of handle such a difficult part, she finally had to learn two parts - the good fairy and the Witch. *(She was a bright cookie that one!)*

If things did go wrong, and I got sick, she was going to have to do the filling in, and that would have meant some major reshuffling of cast members so that her understudy would get a go! *(So there were probably one or two pupils that hoped I got bubonic plague or something!)* I though, was never the less, under strict instructions to make sure that I stayed out of contagious situations, and people were continually checking that I hadn't caught a cold or anything, and that I was OK. *(I should have been pleased with all the attention, I suppose!)* But I always had to be kept at the correct temperature. They just didn't want the witch catching anything, did they? I knew that witches were meant to have big, wart covered noses, but I didn't at the time think that they really wanted a 'Snozzle Durante' look/sound alike! I felt a bit like one of those 'hothouse' roses, or something! I was under strict instructions not to do so *(catch a cold I mean)*, at least not until the show was finished, anyway! "Then, after the show" - they told me with a smirk, *(horrid people!)* "you can actually go and get the bubonic plague for all we care. You can get as sick as you like"! *(Nice, wasn't it?!)*

The make up for the show was jointly done by someone who wanted to be a make up artist, and a local cosmetics firm with whom she had been given a tentative job offer in the future, dependent on her success or not, with my make up! An early apprenticeship do you think? I was to be her trial case, and it was to be in all the papers. *(Both the make up trial, and the Opera!)* So she went to town!

Imagine, if you can, a wart covered *(lumps of Plasticine)*, false nose. She must have had a truly 'bonza' time, making this nearly 16 year old, *(me)* look like an old crotchety, withered, hag. The 'Hag' part was probably not too hard with my ugly face, but the 'old' just might have presented some major problems! My school girl, long hair had to be dyed green temporarily *(if you could ever dye hair temporarily in those days)*, and green face make up applied all over my angular face. *(I was picking green gunk out of my pores for ages. Out of my ears, my nostrils, every open orifice! Some said, even my 'never really closed' mouth- ha ha!)*

Both the hair and the face were painted, with fluorescent paint, so as to be picked up by the ultra violet lighting. The long black, plastic false nails, that made my fingers look nine, vicious inches long, and apparently looked like they were going to poke and prod at people, as they bent into lethal looking talons *(lethal that is, until I actually poked anything, and then they would fold up, like timid, scared little people, that reacted just like the plastic they really were)*.

My face peered out evilly from under a big black witches hat, and a long twig broom hung by my side. It looked as though I would fly out over the audience at any moment. Truly nasty! - Again, imagine if you can. - There you are, sat in a pulsing with energy, full auditorium. The first act, full of gentleness and introductory type of music, along with the songs, gave the first appearance of wholesome and gentle Hansel and Gretel skipping through the forest. The main plot of the first part of the story is enacted, as they romp into the darkened woods. Then they curl up to go to sleep, and the curtain closes.

Interval followed, where the audience went off to toilets, had cups of tea, munched on potato crisps and snacks, and chatted. A bell announced the resumption of the show, and everyone having so far had an enjoyable, and totally untroubled time, wandered expectantly yet unsuspecting, into what had promised to be a great second half! *(And good, it probably was, but again - it was also 'different')* The music for the second act started. The school orchestra, again excelled itself *(well, as far as school kids can ever excel anyway)*, as the music swept to a great crescendo of exciting, eerie?, crashes and bangs. Cymbal - **CRASH!** Timpani drums - **Boo Boom!** *(a truly overly enthusiastic school orchestra, maybe?)*

The curtains slowly open. -

Then there is an eerie silence heard!? An expectant hush comes over the audience, The lights go down, almost off, and a lone, deliberately quavering voice is heard, coming quietly and hauntingly from backstage somewhere! "Nibble nibble mousekin, who's nibbling at my house kin"? The ultra violet lighting, 'picked' up all of the 'specially painted parts' of the fence and the house, creating an even more eerie spectacle! Absolutely everything was lit up and delineated by UV lighting, and I tell you what - talk about being in my element! It was August 1965, and I was in, what was for a 15 ½ year old - 'Witches heaven'! I guess that I have probably always been a bit of a fool at heart, and even more so once I had realised that I could make people laugh by my acting like a bit of a 'nut'.

Even at that age I liked to make people laugh! People tended to like me more if I made them laugh!

Some of the little ones, had to be taken home very quickly after the show, with wet knickers, and there had been some quick wiping up of the puddles on the floor, as well as some embarrassed looking, surreptitiously trying to cover up the accidents, mums. The students had spent weeks and weeks and weeks of preparation and rehearsal, and after the initial ribbing that I got, from the other pupils, they and the teachers were as thrilled as I was that I had been given the part. The opening night of the show was such a huge success! The mishaps that had occurred during the show though, had to be seen to be believed.

Luckily enough, *(for me at least)* they weren't! *'Seen too much, nor even recognised as faults!*

None of the mishaps had been scripted, and none of them was done on purpose, but those mishaps made for a wonderfully entertaining, and extra humorous school production. The show though, inadvertently turned out to be a series of mishaps! After the opening night, a standing joke arose among the cast members. They would even lay bets as to what particular prop the 'witch' would knock over that night, and sometimes everyone won! Just about everything went flying! If I wasn't broad siding the gingerbread men with my broomstick, then I was bumping in to things with my hands, bottom, or feet. So much of the scenery, and so many of the fence posts ended up flat on the stage, with the gingerbread people *(the kids)*, being inadvertently thrust into the spot lights before they were actually meant to even be there. If there was something that could go wrong, and the witch came within three feet of it, it would either fall over, make an unscripted early stage appearance, or blow up. I earned the reputation of being a 'bit of an elegant bungler'. *(So Humperdink, who wrote the opera, suddenly had a very 'different', definitely not to his 'original idea', 'clumsy' witch.)*

(Was that childhood wish for 'different', being fulfilled, even then?)

"So what", I would no doubt have thought. My witch had made it even more FUN, and far more entertaining! *(At least - that's what I probably said then in my belligerent manner, and it is definitely what I would say now!)* I don't think that the teachers would necessarily have agreed with me at the time though, do you? And I probably wouldn't have really thought so at the time either! I would probably have been mortified! But knowing what is coming in this story, I am forced to realise that, 'chaos reining' must always have been part of my life(job) description! The world around me would seemingly cave in, and there beneath the rubble and destruction would be the same smiling, cheery face - mine! *(The beginning of a party trick, do you reckon? Again, you'll realise why I say that, as you read on).* The children, Hansel and Gretel, did finally get the better of me though. They tricked the witch, *(me)* and she *(I)* ended up in the oven!

('Crispy witchy'?)

Once they had that accomplished, the lights went down to almost nothing, and in the ensuing darkness, the gingerbread people turned back into class mates, who, when the lights went up, all got together, and joined in with the hectic, all singing, all dancing, jubilation at the death of the witch. "Ding Dong - the witch is dead"! *(Do you think that maybe they were pleased I was gone? I do!)*

Using an idea adapted from one Mr Keen had learned while working in one of the big international theatres *(I think it was Paris, France)*,our humble school play had an oven that had been constructed using 8 to 10 pieces of thick, re enforced cardboard, painted with a fluorescent paint. Two or three pieces were attached to clear nylon threads strung from the top curtain gangway. Those pieces could be lifted up, out of view, up and over the gantry's shelving when the oven exploded. Other similarly painted parts, were carried about the stage, by black clad, and thus supposedly invisible stage hands, making it appear that the stove had exploded, and blown into a myriad of pieces. I didn't really have anything to do with the oven blowing up *(except that the witch was supposedly inside it, of course)*, but that tendency of mine to knock and nudge, and cause explosions or chaos, seems to have followed me for most my life.

That is of course except for my present marriage, which has as I said, lasted all of 20 years so far, and fortunately for me, shows definite signs of going on and on, regardless of how much knocking or nudging I still inadvertently do!

But lets get back to the show though – eh!

The witch was traditionally a nasty piece of work, with much waving of arms and casting of spells at the beginning of the 2nd half of the show, in order to turn the children into the gingerbread people that made up the fence of the witch's estate. If ever, and whenever she got hungry or particularly vicious, which she did often I might add, she would quietly cook 'em up, and eat one of them. She was then able to daily, feast on at least one of the 'beautiful, soft, tender' children, *(her description)* and feel totally satisfied! But by cooking the witch - well! Hansel and Gretel had put paid to her vicious intentions, and they had magically freed all the children, resulting in a piece of technical brilliance that was most 'un school play like'.

We, of course, had no knowledge at that time, of what the London Palladium, or the Guildhall School of Music were, but to think that we were going to use 'tricks' that had come from the London Palladium, and Paris! It seemed just too 'fantastic' to the students of our Australian school. But Mr Keen tried, and succeeded as much as was possible, to teach us how to put some of what he had learned there, as well as some of his own innovative ideas into some sort of positive action at our school. *(There is no doubt about it, says me in a totally unbiased manner, he is a very clever, imaginative man!)*

Our humble school performance, was turned into a remarkable tribute to the teacher's patient teaching and to the art of entertainment on the whole! It was wonderful! The kids excelled, and - Hooray - for when the oven 'blew up', *(supposedly with the witch inside)* the oven broke into it's eight or ten pieces, just as it was meant to. So that the bits on fishing line flew into the air, and each of the specially designated class members picked the other pieces up, and wildly ran about with them, as the choir joyously and triumphantly sang a song of elation, and jubilation. A vibrant chorus of singing and dancing took place, with everyone singing - Everyone that is, except the witch, who was supposedly very dead inside the oven!!!

Aww - *No more witch! Y-up, that's what you got - Crispy witchy!!!!*

Such a pity! Or was it?

Joyful havoc had ensued, with the strobe lighting doing it's job magnificently, and 'picking up' the oven pieces that had magically*(?)* exploded into the air. The music had developed into a crescendo of hectic string, vocal and percussion passages, with each of the elective music class instrument players getting the most out of their particular instrument of torture*(?)*, and the singers in the choir, bursting forth with an abundant, mostly tuneful cacophony of sounds, All musical participators were stretched to their extreme limits, and yet, for school kids, they still did an amazingly good job! They played the immensely difficult score with a precision and accuracy, normally attributed to much older, professional musicians, but still with the unavoidably odd discordant, ear jarring sound that reminded the audience that the orchestra were mere children!

There were umpteen days and nights of super intense learning, and sleeplessness, leading up to each performance for those in the orchestra and cast. Most traumatically so for the first night's show, but as a result of all the hard work - three fantastic nights were had by all.

Both the pupils involved, and the audience agreed that,
'The show had been a resounding success'.

That was to be my first taste of almost 'proper'*(?)* theatre, and if it weren't there already, that show really 'set' the 'bug' in my system. My parents were understandably very proud of me, but my daddy did say to me, that even though he thought that the show and I had been great, - sadly and regrettably, because we were of the working class poor - I had to forget all this 'la, di, da' stuff, and get out into the workforce and earn some proper dosh! Then he added rubbing his hands – "And I know that you will be quick smart about it too!" They didn't have enough to finance any venture of mine into an area that as far as he could see - gave no guarantees, and was dependent on fanciful expectations! But - a whole list of exciting possibilities still flashed across my youthful brain. I just loved the thought of showbiz, and of parading my talents in front of millions of people! I was sure, that with not too much hard work, I could be an instant success as an entertainer! "Yeah", I smilingly thought. So forgetting how much hard work it would inevitably mean, and momentarily forgetting about the expense, and how I might finance it, I said in my youthful naivety! –
"Yep ! Showbiz is definitely the future for me"!

But as quickly as that particular light had turned itself on in my head, it went out in my life, at home that night. I had faced the biggest negative force that I was ever to face in my whole life up till that time. Dad truly 'poo pooed' my career intentions and my future ideas! Disappointment absolutely swamped my teenage, super ambitious self! I was still young, and at that time I must have felt that I owed allegiance to my parents and what they wanted for me, so I swallowed my childish pride and headed for the occupation that dad and the school had very kindly made all the introductions for. A job where I would be able to make Peg and Charlie happy, and where I would be able to start earning some money straight away - a thing that would make dad say - "whoopee"!

So - a little reluctantly, yet filled with natural teenage excitement about the fact that 'I'd be working', I uttered boldly, as only young people full of natural childhood to new adult pleasure could -
"Bank, here I come"!!!!

STARTING WORK - AT THE BANK!

The day finally came when all that they had tried to instil in me at school, was to be put to the it's initial test. The Commonwealth Bank at Lakemba had begun enrolling school students who thought that their future might lay in banking, and as was the normal procedure in those days, after discussions with me and my parents, the school had put my name forward with the required references, as suitable for banking staff work.

The Bank checked the applicants' IQ, and School Grades of course, and I was accepted. "Phew!" Peg and Dad were so proud. They already knew my grades were good, *(four A's, and two B's)* but they were ecstatic that someone as prestigious as the bank was willing to give me a job, and as I said before, they were keen to get me out to work a.s.a.p. Dad had even said *(jokingly ?)*, on hearing where I was to have the interview, that if I did get in, to be sure and bring home a few samples! *(I wonder though, how much he would really have been joking?)*

Peg and Charlie had already been thwarted in their desire to get me into the work force once before, when my real mother, thankfully had actually paid whatever costs were involved to keep me at school. So I donned my neat and tidy *(definitely not smelling of bleach this time - I made sure of that!)*, especially bought and kept for work, skirt and blouse, and my white gloves. *(Remember when it was fashionable for young ladies to wear gloves?)*. I very nervously got ready for my first day 'on the *job*'. *(Not that kind of job silly!)* I had the most 'amazing' *(or so they seemed to a 'poor kid')*, first pair of what they used to call court shoes. I put them on, and gleefully, though full of trepidation, set off for work. Timidly and expectantly I turned up at the local branch, ready, so I thought, to take on anything that they might throw at me.

I seem to remember that I spent the first few weeks, sitting timidly alone at lunchtime, in what was elegantly(?) called the dining room. It was a mobile building that was fitted out with a few chairs and a table, and when I think about it now, I probably scared the other staff members off at first, because as was typical of new school leavers, with no real social experience, I guess that I tried too hard. They probably didn't want to run the risk of being stuck with someone that didn't quite fit in, that needed too much looking after, and probably required massive amounts of assistance because of her age. It took a bit of time, but I did make some friends there, even though most of the older workers were what I guess I would have thought of as old fogies in those days. There was only one other person who was close to my age of just having turned 17 that month, and she had already been there a year and a half, and had started straight from lower school, so she was about 18 and a half.

In the space of the next eighteen months however, I went from Lakemba (*a small suburban branch)* to Bankstown *(a middling sized town in those days)*, actually making friends along the way. Not a lot of friends I have to say. Could there have been something 'different', and odd about me, do you reckon ? *(I wonder?)*

And then? And then - I was offered a chance to work at the Phillip Street branch, in Sydney *(a most prestigious, pretty old, yet fairly large city branch – daddy had been so proud!)*. I worked there for about 6 months. Finally, with the bank's insistence, I graced King & George Streets with my presence. It was an even bigger, slightly newer, top notch head office branch in those days. And,and, and, such excitement! It was virtually just up the road from where Mr Keen *(remember him?)* had his teaching studio.

So as 'New Faces', the first of a run of talent quest shows on Australian TV at that time, had just begun, and as I had been cajoled into entering by Carol and a few of my banking friends, *(not that they had had to do a lot of cajoling I might add)*, I figured that if I was going to do that, then I had better go get some vocal betterment training. I mean, I wasn't really even sure if I sang well enough any more. It was one thing to put my talents up on the box stages in our street, the school Opera, and the one TV show that I had done when little, but quite another to even contemplate subjecting them to assessment, and criticism by judges! *(I wasn't sure if they had had me on to sing as an oddity or not, and after all, I was no longer 10.)*

I guess that I had progressed well in the Bank, getting promotions all the way, and it has probably been the only, ever, 'organised' part of my life. I worked for the bank for about a year and a half, and don't suppose that that is too bad really, when you think about it - I at least managed almost two organised, years out of my fifty eight years of chaotic activity!

I had begun my 'bank life' at Lakemba as a 'junior'. A sort of 'dog's body, gopher' who made cups of tea for the bosses, and helped with everything from form sorting, to assistant counter enquiries, and finally a tiny bit of teller work. Those counter enquiriesthat I talked about started with just a few general questions from 'normal' *(?)* customers, and then progressed *(if you could call it that)* to some very disgruntled complaints etc. from those customers who felt particularly 'aggrieved' about something or other. If anyone came in disgruntled and upset about anything, then you could bet your life, that I invariably got landed with the potential troublemakers. A big smile, and a few cheery words *almost always* soothed any rattled nerves and set the punters on the right path. And anyway - what kind of damage would they do to someone who was obviously a 'newbee', anyway?

Then for some reason known only to the bank, I was taken off the counter, and promoted *(again(?)* to 'teller', and accounting machine operator. Either I had upset someone *(wouldn't be too surprised)*, or one of the bosses had thought that my ability with maths was being wasted. Probably though, they had heard me talking to one of the more problematical customers when I, myself, was having a bad day, and had decided that they couldn't really afford to take the chance of it happening even once more!! I could be most disagreeable when having a bad day myself!

They then started me making up the statements for each account and seeing that the customers were notified of any discrepancies. They seemed unavoidably to happen a lot in those days. There always appeared to be loads of them! Remember -

You couldn't even blame the computers then! It was all down to brain power, and early calculators, which weren't always guaranteed to be all that good, or accurate! Especially not the brains!

I don't suppose that I have ever been what you might call a 'normal' bank employee, probably always been a bit 'different', and it must have been very disconcerting for some of the stuffier old managers and staff. They would sometimes be walking along a corridor, past the ladies toilets, when they would hear, just as the teachers and pupils had done at school, either a conversation in boisterous progress, or even worse, hear a voice raised in loud energetic song.

(Well, after all, I mean to say -The bathrooms had tiled walls and a remarkably good reverberation, and as I had considered starting with Mr Keen, I had to practice somewhere - didn't I?)

I think that the bank bosses must have had a 'confab' about the irascible 'toilet singer', and the bathroom noise that had brought me to their attention, again. *(Sound familiar?)* Not too sure why, but for a while, they desperately looked for a job at which I could excel. The next job they gave me was customer contact on the phone. *Aw!* No tiled walls? *(Also - the switchboard was on the upper floor of the other half of the building, and I reckon that they just wanted to get me as far 'out of the way' as possible!)* They must have also figured that as I was a friendly enough soul, who always seemed to be in trouble for talking on the job, that they would give me a legitimate reason for doing so. *(Talking on the job I mean, not for getting into trouble! Did they ever give you legitimate reasons for getting into trouble?)* I was taught how to use a switchboard, which compared to the electronic masterpieces of today was an extremely complicated activity, but I did a 'bonza' job of answering, and dealing with the calls - most of the time! *(Again – sound familiar?)*

Pulling out, and putting back in the various plugs that connected 'different' people shouldn't have been too difficult – should it? I was apparently very good at helping to solve other people's problems. Not too crash hot with my own in those days, and not even these days really, but for some reason, evidently my personality made a 'great' first contact with the bank. I was chirpy, friendly, and obviously eager to please. But again - only *some* of the time! Some days the little red lights on the switchboard would drive me so far up the wall that I would find myself being severely tempted to disconnect some customers. Not all mind you! Just those that were, in my opinion rude or those that I thought had said enough. Most of the time though I didn't. *(Disconnect them, I mean. Almost, but not quite!)* So - combine my temperament with my chatterbox ways, and I suppose that it's not that difficult to see why the Bank and I were not destined to be overly good bedfellows for any largish amount of time!

Couldn't find a proper job for me, could they?

Oh, nearly forgot – speaking of bedfellows - I *did* meet my first very special boy friend who was to be the first of my 'many men' along the way. - Graeme Bouncer, was all of 19 years of age, with me being a grand old age of 17 and a bit.

Out for dinner - young love!

At that age I was still a bit of a 'plain Jane', with my 'pretty suit top that would cover my flat chest up, with collars and decoration, but he was what was considered a reasonably 'good looker' in those days!

Now, in 2009, I don't know? Probably not, but 'hey', he was, when I do think of him now, a truly lovely boy! The Bank had organised, what would be considered 'frightfully old fashioned' now a days, a Banker's Ball, at which I made my 'début'. Remember those! It was very '*in*' in those days, and I think that débuts are trying to stick their nose through the young people's doors these days, but in a 2008, school year 'proms' sort of way! Dressy disco's seemed to be the flavour of the day then! But I must confess, that today even I myself say - Début de -shmoo!

All dressed up and nowhere to go, but the dance floor!

Apart from the fact that it was considered something special; at the time, it was basically just a good, and legitimate excuse to put on a long white dress or a suit, play at being ladies and gentlemen for a night, and get well and truly 'pissed' without *(hopefully)* the old's finding out!!! *(Nothing changed much then, apart from the colour of the dresses!)*

A great night was had by all though, and I even had my first alcoholic drink - a bourbon and coke, I think it was. My first taste of alcoholic inducement at so young an age, meant that I ended up, legs touching the car roof, in the most, unglamorous back seat of a 'specially cleaned up for the probably much anticipated occasion', Vauxhall. *(Do you think that it was a pre planned conclusion to a 'different' night?)*

138

But, weird limb positioning or not, it did turn out to be the most glamorous evening I had thus far spent, and what is more, it too was definitely excitingly 'different'! I had never felt so glamorous and 'special', even though I probably looked a right sight. My legs in the air, and my dress half on/half off my trying not to get cold body! ! I have so much to be grateful to Graeme for though. He actually started me on the long slippery road that led to my present 'different' life! To him the 'ugly duckling' Kerrie was beautiful! Or so he said, anyway! *(But, after the last 30 sometimes hectic years, I have decided that in those kinds of situation, men do tend to say anything to get 'into your knickers', don't they? It is just a pity that we girls often didn't realise until it was too late!)*

As I said, I who had always felt a bit ugly, was made to feel like a swan that night, but young love didn't last too long. Rarely does I suppose! Over our time together though, he had taught me to 'chuck' that ugly duckling feeling away, and I carried the sense of 'swan-ness' that he had brought me, with me from then until my accident. Unfortunately, from then on it was no longer 'swan-ness' that I felt. When/if I could feel anything at all, it had become 'ugly duckling-ness', with a vengeance!

I am only now, after what seems like years of rehab and eventual independent living, starting to at least, 'like' myself again. Not a lot to be sure - but it certainly beats hating oneself. My darling husband does his best to make me feel loved and cherished, and what is more, is does a fantastic job when I am prepared to take advantage of it.

But anyway, while working in the bank, I had also begun going to the 'Become a Star' studio. *(If you have decided to read on, you'll read about that in more detail, later on too)* I had then been going there for about 6 months, but after about a month of hard work at it, *(learning to sing properly I mean)*, I had done New Faces. *(The poor man's equivalent of today's Pop Idol, or X factor.)*

Alright! - I maybe hadn't done brilliantly at the time, but I had done OK! I was a nervous sort of person back then. *(Soon grew out of that though, didn't I?)* I got through to the semi finals I think it was, and I was already starting to question just how much I really wanted to be at the bank anymore? Peggy and Charlie though, still wanted me to be there, *(at the bank that is)* and I hadn't even followed daddy's orders - and taken home any free samples! It seems that the restlessness that I must have inherited from my dad, and that has been with me since the day dot, had raised it's ugly head again! So when I had been at King & George St. branch for a few more months, and just as the relationship with Graeme was swinging along fantastically, I did my soon to prove typical for the time, about face, and asked myself, and Graeme - *"Is this all there is to life"?*

I think that I remember poor, young 'normal' Graeme quizzically wondering what on earth I was talking about, when I asked him that one night! I though, would no doubt have thought - as the new song from the latest popular show at the time had said - *"There's got to be something better than this".* Restlessness was making it's presence felt, in a not uncertain way, and 'talk about my feeling, definitely unsettled'. All that rigmarole that I went through at the bank was not really what I wanted to be doing. I still just really wanted to sing! So I am afraid that Graeme, as adorable as he was, was destined to be 'No1' in what would eventually end up a long, long conga line! *(In 2007 I mildly succeeded with the singing, but in 2010 the desire to sing properly really returned with a vengeance once I got to this stage of writing the book. So my darling hubby has again been looking at the possibility of resuscitating my poor, scared of being hurt again voice. And it is slowly coming back. But it's a bit like a recalcitrant tortoise, munching on green shoots with some of them still belligerently sticking out of it's mouth, unable to be digested properly for some reason! Although the physical pain of trying to make the muscles produce a pleasant sound is sometimes astronomical, my husband assures me that it will be worth all the effort, and I keep on hanging in there! You see, all other things aside, as I can't run, or exercise efficiently, he tells me that the singing exercise will help me regain my once alright figure. And help extend this life that I am not even supposed to have. Isn't that lovely! He must still love me, after 20 years!)*

Mr Keen *(from school)* had actually opened his 'Become a Star School' in Sydney city, when I had only been about 16 and a half and working at the Bankstown branch. When I had first seen it advertised I had thought – Yippee! But for me to attend classes in the city would have meant an early evening train journey of about 45 mins, and a late night trip on train and bus in order to get home. That is of course if the buses were even running at that hour. The trains, although they ran that late at night, probably would have been a bit scary for a single young woman, who wasn't even remotely used to traveling on her own. Peg and Charlie would have definitely knocked that idea on the head anyway. They wouldn't have thought it would be safe. *(And come to think of it now, they were probably right, even though muggings and murders were still a bit of a rarity in those times.)* Also with Peg, being money cagey, as the poor often are, she was also right when she said that the cost of the fares would have taken a big 'chunk' out of my weekly money. And that would never do! It would mean less money for board!

I knew that Peg and Charlie thought that my ambition to be an entertainer was just a pie in the sky idea. I didn't think so though, but still, I had ignored the ad in the paper anyway, saying to myself - 'for the time being'. I was still young, still had Graeme to consider at that time, and I wasn't really prepared to ruffle feathers at home any more than necessary - yet!

Now, as I look back though, it seems as though I was always determined to sing! Still am, I suppose, although I think that this book writing lark is taking some of the time that the the singing should have!

But anyway, 2 years had passed with me working in the bank. I was growing more and more independent of mind, and the last Branch move had taken me to only a short walking distance from Ed's 'Become a Star' studio! No train costs! So I figured - "what can it hurt", and after all, by then I was about 6 months past 18! A big girl, and as I said, I had recently been talked into giving New Faces a go!

The show business gremlin is obviously determined by nature, and as it had tweaked my thought structure when I was doing those box shows in our street, and when I had played the witch at school, it very clearly showed its fangs again!

"Admit it", that gremlin used to say to me, *"you can't fool me-' you want to sing'"*. That there voice was full of tormenting nastiness.

(And you know - it doesn't appear to have changed too much now, either. It's the same today! You would think that we would have become friends by now, but that gremlin is still about, and just as bossy as it ever was! The so and so!)

HELLO

But having finished the day's work one week in July I think it was, as I remember the weather not being real good, I jauntily walked around to the Kent Street address that had been in the add, praying that it wouldn't rain. I wasn't really dressed for wet weather. *(And of course, that was back in the days when I could* jauntily *walk* anywhere – *at all! - 'Aah' - Memories!)*

I went through a ground floor door of the brown brick building, and got into a rickety old lift. Two extremely scary, full of rattling, floors later, I was quite abruptly facing a long dismal corridor. A hobo was staying warm, asleep in the corridor, *(July was notorious for cold days at that time)* and I looked with apprehension at the choice of office doors. I tried to casually, and quietly walk past the hobo, desperately trying to not wake him, on to the room at the end of the corridor. The room had a small hand written sign on the door, saying Eddie Keen's Become a Star studio - Welcome!

It also said - "Just come in". But me still being a 'supposedly well brought up', white gloved *(still had the white gloves on didn't I?)*, hat wearing girl, I thought - "I wonder if he will remember me"?

Straightening my hat, I brushed my clothes down, pulled the fingers of my gloves out straight, and I *(trying to feel confident)*, pushed the buzzer. But just to make sure, I knocked on the door as well! Well it was an old building, and the bell might not have worked, I thought!

Ri - i - ng - knock knock!

After a normal medium length pause, the door opened, and inside stood the man who had tried to teach me music at school. He was looking a little disconcerted.

(Most people didn't normally knock, they did what the sign said, and just went in. He must have been wondering what he would find outside his door! A bill collector maybe?) But back in school, Mr Keen had told me, "if you ever want to be an entertainer when you leave school, just get in touch". So - even though it had taken all this time, I had taken him at his word hadn't I? There I was! I figured that the time was finally just about right for me to take him up on an offer, that I found myself momentarily feeling very nervous about. I suddenly thought, - "I bet he probably glibly handed out the address to any number of the girls in his class". But suddenly, before I had a chance to change my mind and run, there he was - a man who had seemed to a 15 - 16 year old, to be - a doyenne - a God! Now though, to an 18 and a bitter, he just appeared a learned man with an organised bit of fluff around his chin. *(He had definitely **not** had that at school, he had been a clean shaven, 'proper' looking Mr Keen!)* He had been a man who seemed a lot more down to earth. Very 'teacher-ish'. Now, he looked more like a learned elf, than anything else. I guess that you might say that he had become an 'elfish' doyenne!

"Hello" he says, with his eyes looking me up and down with their characteristic blueness, a dazzling twinkle in those eyes, but without even a trace of any recognition whatsoever!

"Can I help you?" Just a blank, but friendly welcoming face. I nervously stood there wondering what on earth I was there for, and what I was supposed to do next.

"Hello Mr Keen", says me quickly. *(Pause!)* "You don't remember me - do you?"

"Sorry - should I?" says he still looking me up and down.

"Nibble nibble mousekin", sings me in the best, un warmed up, witch like voice that I could muster up at 4.00pm in the afternoon, and then suddenly his eyes opened wide. A pleased *(was it pleased?)* smile spread across his face, and he said, "The Witch, Miss D - Dyer isn't it? - Well I never! *(Pause!)* Come to think of it" -*(says he looking at where my ears, which were still humongous, should be, and although well and truly camouflaged by my hair, still unavoidably stuck out a bit)* he said "yes, that's you all right! I would recognise those ears anywhere.

Let me have a good look - turn around for me, will you please!". I did, and then he said - "Well - it's about time isn't it? - took you long enough. But you're here at last - come in properly - come in".

(He has since told me that he lasciviously thought - "Well - what have we here then?") We laughed and reminisced about the hilarity of the school Opera, and all the weird things that took place. We laughed away almost the whole half hour until his next pupil was due, during which time, between the laughs, I had briefly told him that I was working in the Bank not far up the road and round the corner. He asked me if I really liked it, and I said "I didn't really think so, but that it helped pay the bills, helped out at home, and kept my dad off my back". He smiled knowingly at me! *(I guess that he had vague memories of my having to return the cello, and what my old man had been like in my Hansel and Gretel days.)*

He asked me what my ambitions were now that I had so obviously grown up, and I immediately said - "I'd give anything to be able to sing for a living. Do you think I stand any kind of chance", I asked? His next student was actually running late, and so posing a bit, with his finger by is nose, he said to me - "Let's see then shall we". He was smiling as he went to the piano, ready to play a song, and I quickly followed him to the rear of the studio and stood next to the same piano. He got me to sing a few lines of various songs, and having reassured himself that the nucleus of a voice was still there, he asked me how I felt about having lessons with him. I said that I would love to, but it depended how much they cost, and that I probably wouldn't be able to afford them, *(I was rambling, because I thought, "well they were bound to be too expensive for me, weren't they"?).* But on my saying that, he paused a little - thought, and then he said - "oh I think that we can probably work something out"! *("Oh no", I thought suddenly. Surely Mr Keen wasn't going to turn out to be one of them" - I had heard about men who said things like that!)* Realising just how 'sus' that answer must have seemed to such a young girl, he quickly added - "How would you feel about answering my phone, and making appointments for us? "Us", I *(was it jealously)* said?

"Yes, us! Jan, who is not here at the moment, is my presentation/ dancing teacher, and she and I find it a bit difficult to coordinate the teaching with the clerical side of things . Could you work part time for me as a -sort of - receptionist? After you finish at work you can come here and answer our phone etc. to pay for your lessons". And it turned out to be very handy indeed, what with him having his studio only about a 10 minute walk from my day job. I used to go straight down there after work, I would keep my work up to date, and rush out when the knock off bell went at 3 o'clock *(remember those, knock off bells I mean)* and I would get to the studio at about 3.10pm. I still got my bank wage, *and* I was having lessons, virtually for free! *(Sometimes I would even knock off early so that I could get to the Studio ahead of time. I was a bit of a naughty girl, even then.)* It was the best of both worlds you might say! My daddy should have been pleased! *(Please note I said - should!)*

"Hello, The Eddie Keen showbiz school - 'Become a Star' studio. Can I help you"?, I used to cheerily say. If these callers had any problems, they were a lot easier, and more pleasant to deal with than any of those at the bank, and I was having singing lessons, for free, and with my mentor. Actually enjoying learning things, I was. I hadn't really liked school all that much, even though I had done well enough there, I suppose. I had really enjoyed the Operetta that we had done though, and again, as I have said, I was always singing around the house, driving Peg and Charlie mad. Now - my singing lessons with Mr Keen, were a ball! *(A disciplined ball maybe, but a ball nevertheless!)*
(It's just a pity that my then new found love of practising, hasn't stuck with me right through till now though. I could really do with it just now. Life just gets more and more hectic every day, what with having a daughter going to University, writing this book, and trying to fit in singing lessons, there just seems too many things to do, just to get from one day to the next. Planning things for my 60th birthday doesn't exactly make for restful days either! And then on top of all that, this economic downturn that is going on at the moment, has just about everybody worried about where the next penny is coming from! Including us!)
Back then though, there was no book, family, or economic downturn to worry about too much, and the time had definitely come, for me to grab myself by the bootstraps, and actually learn, and do, the correct things to make my 'natural' sound, into a voice that hopefully would actually cause the punters' bottoms to raise from their seats *(as Ed*

had told me I should aim to have happen). Preferably with their hands bursting into rapturous applause!

I definitely wanted their cheers to lift the rafters. I, for my ego's sake, needed to succeed very badly, and I always *(well nearly always)* did what Mr Keen suggested, and because we were spending so much time together, we 'fell in love' with each other. *Aw!!!* Me, as only 18 and a bitters can, and him, with the normal reticence of a grown man, who wasn't really supposed to get physically or emotionally involved with someone so young, nor one of his students! But it was I suppose, unavoidable though, when you think about it. We were, after all, spending so much time together working on my voice, that the other was kind of a natural progression of events, wasn't it?

Talk about funny though, and it did have it's funny moments - but then, come to think of it, I don't think that I should go into those moments here! That's really personal, that is! *(Oh all right - just one of them - a 'kind of' non sexual, romantic one!)*

While I was still working in the bank - during a lunch time one day, Ed had actually come round to the bank branch to see me. I think that it was Valentines day, back when Valentines day was something meaningful to young romantics! Remember, this was before the other girls I worked with had been able to see the definitely 'older man' that I had always been talking about. He came wandering into the branch with a single rose perched nervously in between his index finger and thumb, asking to see a Miss Kerrie Dyer. I am pretty sure that the girls had thought that I had been 'pie in the skying' when I had talked about an older man. Trying to 'big note' myself? Their jaws must have positively dropped to the floor when this quite handsome, definitely 'older than me' man, came wandering into the bank with a lovely red rose in his right hand. And what's more - he was politely asking to see me! 'Little old me', of all people!

Before that monumental event, the girls on the staff had already been having a bit of a typical 'girlie', behind the hands chat about my so called, 'older' boyfriend and as to whether or not he was in fact a reality, or just a figment of my imagination. "There would be no doubt about it," they had said, "if he exists - he would be very 'different' to Graeme", the young man they had seen me with at the Bankers Ball. I had secretly smiled at their comments, and had casually, and mysteriously said, - never thinking that they would - "Oh, you'll probably meet him one day".

I have to be honest though,I was enjoying the bit of the notoriety that came with my going out with someone who was considered *so* mature, and whom no-one had yet met. But they definitely met him that day. There was no longer quite the same sense of mystery from that day on, but it didn't really matter. Red rose bearing visitors were not only a rarity in our bank, but normally non existent, and as such, were bound to create a genuine hubbub of chatter, and a pool of interest.

So anyway, when at lunch time on that Valentines' Day, one of the male office workers came into the staff room to tell me, full of excitement, that there was a gentleman in the main foyer, and he wanted to see a Miss Kerri Dyer please, I was suddenly truly elevated in status in their eyes! The messenger posed in such a twee way, and said in a supposedly posh voice, holding out his poised hand - "And what is more - he is holding a lovely red rose"! "Oooh - La di da", he said as he posed crossing his legs, and sticking his bum out!

Very 'camp'!

Now - someone coming to see me would have been unusual enough, but for a man to be carrying a flower in those macho days! Unheard of it was! And what is more – it was a 'red rose' of all things! All the girls giggled out loud. Some of the older ladies came to the outer door of the staff room, just to have a 'nosy', and to see what all the hilarity, and chatter was about. They had heard the twittering, and had nosily poked their heads round the door, and what was it that they saw?

There at the end of the banking hall, in all his youthful 36 year old, sartorial elegance, and with his curly, tending to be a bit windswept, hair slicked down into a reasonable,shiny shape, stood the then *(and very luckily for me, now after a break, and after all this time)* love of my life. A single stem rose bud wobbled in his shaking hand. Talk about my feeling - 'something special'. I will never forget just how embarrassed, and yet how absolutely thrilled I was. It was the talk of the branch for weeks and weeks. They had raved on about how romantic it all had been, and how they *(the girls)* would definitely have to set about finding themselves an 'older' man, who would lavish them with roses*! (Goodness* *knows what ages their older men would have needed to be though. Some of the ladies were super decrepit as far as I would have been concerned at that time.)* I only just thought though. As much as I hate to admit it, I have become one of those super decrepit's now!

Oh well! I suppose it happens to us all one day!

Ed and I though, had decided about a week before that day, that with all the time spent trying to build my voice and career, it was becoming a little tiresome to for us to be living in two different places, catching trains and buses, and doing midnight drives. So a decision had needed to be made. I had to work up enough courage to tell Peg and Charlie that their 'little' girl *(I would have been, after all nearly 19 soon)* was about to 'fly the coup'. Being a bit of a coward, I think that I actually told them, and moved out, on the same day! *(I guess that you could have said that maybe I was just a 'tad' on the scared side?)* It obviously hurt them, but I must have by then been so full of typical 'normal' teenage angst, that I didn't give it much thought at the time. Now though, looking back, and with a daughter myself, and one who did a similar thing to me at about the same age*(she didn't actually leave, just brought the boyfriend to the house, to share her bed),* I am absolutely horrified that I can have done anything so thoughtless. It would have been a **lot** worse for them in those days too!

I guess though, that what goes around, comes around, and although in my case, my career aims were probably a little high for someone my age, I mustn't have cared about anyone else all that much at the time. I was just following the words of one of my newest learned songs at the time - I did have-"Such a lot of livin' to do, and I figured that I was off to at least give the living a try"!

After all - the future promised to be trés, trés exciting!

So many great opportunities lay ahead, and I was on my way! And after the months of hard work that followed - I finally arrived at the first stop on the way to my 'stardom' destination. - And what is more – I was absolutely loving it!!!

Such excitement – and freedom!!!!! -

OUT THE WINDOW!

So there I was - about to do the first half of my very first paid job ever, and - having only been at the EKO 'Become a Star' studio, about 6 months, I was a veritable bag of nerves. Ed's and my hard work was apparently about to pay off. At least I had thought so, and I went on to that stage full of the teenage exuberance and confidence that inevitably went along with the nervousness of doing your first ever show!

But - after having done that first half of the show, I had decided that maybe I wasn't so sure after all! Not only was I flushed, sweaty with exertion, and looking a bit like I had been pulled through a hedge backwards, but on thinking back on what the previous 20 minutes had entailed, I was also truly embarrassed. I who had had no previous experience to rely on, had walked chirpily onto the stage, to be faced with an audience of middle aged, to older and old men, who were apparently still drowning themselves in their beer glasses from the tribulations of the night before. A few 'clapping seal' like claps were heard ! They seemed as though they were sitting on their hands in between 'hair of the dog' sips from their glasses! Probably still too much in a coma, trying to recover from an inebriated night before. They didn't clap, or when they did (clap that is), I had been given only a cold, to 'moderately' warm response. Almost 'tepid' one could say. I may as well not have even been there, and after slowly slinking off stage to virtual silence, I ran, and found myself standing alone in the comparative safety of my dressing room.

"Alright - they don't want me"..I was ready to burst into tears of despair. "What on earth had made me think that I should ever consider being an entertainer", I thought.

"If I am honest, I am 'no-one special'. - Just a girl from Greenacre! Why had I thought that people's reaction should be any thing special for me?" I felt abysmally small, and now thought to myself, "how useless am I? A scurrilous impostor"! My heart just about broke. The desire and the need to have been a success must have overpowered me again, because I *do* remember that the tears absolutely streamed down my face. My ribs and chest positively racked with upset! I had desperately wanted to break away from Greenacre, and the life of poverty that it offered. I didn't feel that I belonged there. I thought to myself while standing in the empty dressing room, "right Kerri! You just have to accept the truth girl *(as much as I didn't want to)*. Whether you like it or not - you're a failure"! Bristling up, and stiffening my back, and with my apparently habitual arrogance, I thought - "So what"! I spoke to myself - "Come now! - so you're a failure. No tears my girl! Into it – Don't just stand there crying - Remember! Carol's and your motto was always - 'Forward into action!'

I took another big 'sniff', wiped my eyes, looked about the room, and spied a barely opened window. I must have had that 'cartoon light bulb' click on, in my head, as I rushed over to that window, hitching my dress up over my waist, and tucking it in to my pants in preparation for a quick get a way. The dresses, music and shoes for the second 'spot', *(which I had so confidently, and expectantly provided for)* were now looking a bit forlorn, in a pile on the floor. They were inside the room, just within a hands reach of that only window, and there I was, attempting to climb over all the now obviously unneeded performance paraphernalia. I couldn't get 'out the window' till I had managed to climb over the clothes, and then all that I had to do was to prise the window open a bit further than it's present four inches, drag the clothes outside, through the window, and I would be off! Yeah!!! *(Why I wanted to take all the clothes and stuff, I can't imagine! But they* were *my clothes after all, and although I would probably never get to wear them again, it didn't really matter! I guess that I must have inherited my acquisitive nature from my step mum. I wasn't about to give up what was* mine*! I had after all paid my hard grafted wages for them)*

Eds car was parked, very luckily, just up the road, and if luck was even further on my side, I would have been able to get to it before anyone even noticed that I was gone. That audience hadn't really noticed that I had even been there anyway! "They probably won't miss me" I howled, as tears welled up in my eyes, and came streaming down my face, all over again! Just what I would do once I'd gotten to the car I hadn't really considered. "Maybe I can go home - yeah, that's it - I'll go home". But then I suddenly thought - "Oh heck - I can't drive, I'm still on L plates. I'm not even aloud to drive by myself yet"! Yet because I had been in such a hurry to get away, I hadn't thought of just what I was going to do once I did actually 'get away'!! "I know", I said - "I'll run down the road and hail a cab" - and yet almost instantly I said to myself, oh

"Bugger - I don't have any money on me, do I? I came with Ed, didn't I? Who am I trying to kid anyway?" I must have thought, "the best place for me, is back with the bank. At least there I felt 'good for something'. They kept promoting me, didn't they? I mustn't have been too bad, I don't suppose! I wonder if they would take me back?"

I had just managed to open the window a little bit more, and my front leg was half in, half out of the window, with some of the clothes being dragged with me through the now, foot high gap. The bit of the leg that was outside, was waving about, like a dysfunctional antenna, searching for the path. It was being squashed a bit by the window frame with every movement, while my other leg, unfortunately still inside, was tromping around among the rest of the clothes that were still on the floor. Was it trying to give me a firm base? I must have looked a lot like a half landed fish, straddled across the window sill, wriggling, trying to find a secure fin hold, somewhere - anywhere – when -

"And just where do you think you are going young lady?" - says this very angry, disembodied, voice from somewhere behind me.

"Is this the Kerri Dyer, that I thought I knew", the voice yelled, as the body that it issued from, came rushing towards me, kicking the few clothes that were left on the floor, out of the way. He grabbed for my leg just as it was about to disappear out of the window? *Gulp! Sprung, big time!*

He tugged the leg, and with a lot of squealing and squawking, the attached body *(mine)* slowly squashed back inside with it. *("Ow! That hurt" - I squealed!)*

Just about yelling down my throat, he shouted -

"I am thoroughly disgusted with you"! "Where's the gutsy, I'm ready for anything - let me 'at em' - girl that I have been teaching? How dare you run the risk of ruining my reputation with the agent by doing something as stupid as running out"?

Then taking a step back, he added, still crankily but in a slightly calmer voice, "Haven't I been telling you all along, that the first rule of show business is to find out what the audience want, and then, within reason, try to give it to them"?

I was crying, and ranting and raving. *(I guess that I have always been a bit of a drama queen! Still am I suppose!)* "Now calm down a bit", he said. "Come back in here properly and get dressed. Forget about fleeing, and go back out there and give that audience what they want"!

"'Win them over? Win them over?" I bawled. *I'll give them, win them over!!!!*

I have always been a bit 'mouthy', me *(a thing that I'd learnt from Peggy perhaps)*, and I grumpily shouted back at him, in my loudest, and yet obviously most upset voice, *"and just how am I supposed to know what a bunch of crotchety, drunken old men want? Win them over, my foot, I'd like to bash their heads together".*

(And do you know? The strange thing is that I don't seem to have learned a single thing since those days. After spending the last 19 and a half years, quietly acquiescing to everything he advises, partly because I wasn't really well, now that I think that I'm a bit better, I am sometimes ranting and raving again, using my most ungracious voice, and hitting out at the one man who has always only ever tried to make me see the sense of things, Ed. I guess that I will never learn! Just as well he loves me as he does! But I don't suppose that it is really fair to rely on that always being the case - is it?)

But anyway, back at the window - my tears became even stronger! Ed stood there, shaking his head, amazed that someone who was normally full of positive thoughts, seemed to be so 'out of it'. He took a deep breath, put his hands on my shoulders, and then quietly but insistently said - "Come off it! Use your brains! What do you *think* that that audience out there might want?" he asked, glaring at me with a questioning stare.

I shook my head, in a dejected, 'I don't know' kind of way, and then I shouted,

"I am not a stripper!", so if that's what they want - they can jolly well forget it!

He continued, in a little more consoling tone, but more like the teacher that he had actually been, trying to explain 1 + 1 = 2 to a child who should already have known.

"It's a Sunday morning", he said. "Some of those men are hung over from last night, and they may have been listening to their 'little woman' nagging, all week.

Eyes down cast, I nodded, begrudgingly agreeing, whilst trying desperately to hold back the tears that had been running so freely before, and were now, about to well forth again!

"Don't you think that they would like a bit of light hearted fun after a week of work and harassment?" he asked. He shuffled through the now, messy choice of dresses for a second show outfit, that had again been strewn on the floor. He was definitely looking for something! But what? "Here wear this," he said!

"Oh yeah", says me! - "Trust him", I sullenly thought!

He chose the one dress that had the appearance of being an extended 'boob tube', and that made me look like a bit of a 'tart', because it wasn't 'extended' very far. It barely even covered my bum! Throwing the dress at me, he said - *"Now,put this on, and get out there - walk on top of the tables, flash a bit of leg, and wiggle a bit of 'arse'".*

He laughingly demonstrated, prancing across the dressing room floor, merrily mincing, in and out of the chairs and around the strewn clothes, in an attempt to lighten the atmosphere a bit.

Me? - I just begrudgingly giggled! He did look ever so funny though! I was then desperately trying not to laugh, instead of trying not to cry. I struck the pose, and emulated his seductive attempts. "Come on now", he said. - "That's right - that's my little bombshell girl! - *BIG SMILE!* Play at being Marilyn Monroe, better still - you sing so well - imagine you're Judy Garland". *(Now doesn't that show my age? You possibly don't even really know who they were!)* "Judy with 'boobs', bum and 'sex'", he said. "Take them off to see the Wizard and his 'magic' along the yellow brick road if you want, but - **WIN - THEM - OVER!**," he commandingly told me again.

He pushed my cheeks into a big grin on my face, and with me outwardly appearing to acquiesce, I sulkily thought to myself - "What a bossy so and so" - and - "It's all right for him! - He doesn't have to face those unresponsive, beer swilling 'yobbos! "I'm the one who has to do that", I thought. "All he has to do is play the ruddy piano"! *(How ungracious of me!)*

Ed shook his head and as if reading my mind, raised his eyebrows, and then continued on in a more gentle lover like, yet fatherly, conciliatory tone. "Ruffle their hair, sing a few songs that they can join in with, and do a little harmless flirting with the 'silly old buggers', but remember what I have been training you to do, and for goodness sake - *Entertain them!* I took some deep breaths, bravely tried to lift my head up, and berated myself for not being positive enough, while Ed was in the auditorium talking the musicians through my music for the second show.

I quickly went through the planned show in my head, brushing the tears aside, and doing the final touch up of my make up, almost erasing any sign of tears. Then on hearing my 'chaser *(going on stage)* music', I took another deep breath, tried to tug down my *(ever so short)* skirt, and got my head well and truly into 'show' mood. The music had also alerted that same audience of 'dirty old men' to the fact that something was about to happen again. The compère introduced me, and having taken another really big breath to steel my nerves, out I romped onto the stage, in the red glittery mini dress that Ed had chosen. My red glittery high heeled shoes made my legs look ten feet long, and they twinkled invitingly at the audience. *(The shoes I might add - not the legs! Although come to think of it, the legs probably did a bit of twinkling as well!)*

first job mini

SHOWBIZ RACKET!

Those apparently ten foot long legs, in their stockings, probably twinkled a bit too, as I stepped gaily out through the split curtain at the back of the stage. I faced the still 'a bit bleary eyed' crowd of bemused, befuddled gentlemen, and after my initial moment of fear, I looked across at Ed on the piano.

His cheery - 'go get em girl' face helped calm the nerves a bit *(mine mainly!)*, and I opened my second half show with Boom Bang a Bang. Another cheeky and light hearted song followed, and then I slowed it down a little and got a little cheekily mushy, with a gently rollicking ballard, winking at the guys, and flirting outrageously. *(I flirted as only a nearly 19 year old can flirt, anyway.)*

The stage went right up level with the front tables, and for the fourth song, following Ed's suggestion I gracefully pranced straight across from the stage, right onto the first table. Hands quickly moved glasses out of the way of my feet, and some, only some of the guys mind you, were coyly trying to look anywhere but up. Some just ogled as far up as they thought they were allowed to! I was cheekily winking and wickedly grinning at all those 'lovely' drunkards. It was as if I was actually inviting someone, anyone, to complain. *(Nobody did, of course.)* I sang 'Kiss Me Honey Honey Kiss me', and the show suddenly became a lot more friendly, what with me singing a communicative song like that one. *(They positively, lapped it up!)*

There would be sing a long a bit later if they liked my show, but as I was still on the table, and I think the next song was probably Puppet on a string, I got to play 'puppets' on that there table! Lots of 'Betty boop' faces, with the big eyes, and pursed lips!

I seem to remember that I loved being cheeky, and I must have been in my element! I dropped into a curtsy at the end of my song, and, borrowing a helping hand from one of the 'big, macho' men *(and didn't they lap that up?)*, I stepped across the 6 inch gap, back onto the stage. I was able to make a lot of 'business' out of how graciously the gentleman had helped me across that tiny gap, and he was suddenly being really 'ribbed' by his mates! *(well that got about 6 of them on my side, anyway!)* The time had seemed to be almost right for a 'scorcher of a Ballard', but I looked at them and thought -"nah ah - not too serious yet"! I had them on the hook, and had just about landed them in the palm of my hand, so I quietly told the muso's that there would be a change in the programme, and I swapped the songs about!

"Gently does it Kerri! No point in letting them wriggle off the hook before I have a good chance to play with them a little more! The scorcher of a ballad will just have to wait a bit", I thought!

I must confess though, that knowing me as well as I do, and very luckily, remembering what sort of mood the audience would normally have been in by then, I must have really enjoyed holding them ever so gently, just like putty in my hand. I can't remember what ballad I finally sang at that time, I used to sing a wide range of big love songs, but it would have been one that gave the fellows time to think about the show, about life, and love, and for some - even about their wives?! Some of those men were just beginning to smile, a bit like naughty little boys just waking up for the first time, to the fact that they had had a very 'juicy lolly' on their plate. I was in turn smiling, and grinning from ear to ear! The previously 'not too friendly' looking men, who had been either trying to drown their sorrows in, or bathe themselves in, their beer glasses, were now absolutely beaming at me, with smiling faces! You know - to this day, although I find it difficult to remember too much at times, I can still remember those smiling faces! My heart melts at the thought of them! I know that I have said it before, but there are definitely no two ways about it, have been a very, very lucky, unlucky lady!

(Ooh, Sorry - did it again, didn't I? I am such a nut! Let's get back to the story though, before I get well and truly sidetracked again, and get maudlin

eh?! But it really is again, a case of 'Memories, memories'! There are just so many things that I miss, even after all this time. But then, I suppose that I should be grateful for what memories have come back, shouldn't I?)

I had again stepped from the stage, across onto the tables. It was time now, for that sing-a-long with the fella's. Some wanted to sing, some didn't - but eventually I had all 50 of those 'silly old buggers', as Ed had called them, singing along with "My old man said follow the van - and don't dilly dally on the way". I was bouncing along the table top, encouragingly urging them all to sing along again! Stepping back onto the stage though, I continued skipping backwards and forwards, singing all the time, gesticulating and again, encouraging them to sing a long. For the last 30 of the 45 minutes show, and after other similar songs followed, I had those same 'drunken old men', the ones who had sat on their hands after my first spot, now totally involved and rapt, and clapping - shouting and yelling for more. Beer and bits of chips and sandwiches, were spitting forth from their mouths as they clapped, laughed, and yelled!

The applause when the 'chaser', announcing my departure began was ear splitting. *It had been such FUN!*, and I decided then and there - apart from the fact that I definitely liked the FUN of it - that maybe, just maybe - **"this showbiz racket was gunna be my bag after all"!**

There would definitely be no going back to the bank on a permanent basis for me! Come to think of it, not even part time! I was too busy enjoying the cheers and "Whoo-ps", and they were the first of many more to come, and in many parts of the world too! *Ed's* orders had worked! Once I had finally done as I was told - I had - *entertained them!*

Through the following few years, somewhere in the remotest corners of my 'typical enjoying herself mind', I was thinking though that - "One day I'll not only make me happy *(and ecstatically happy I was!)*, but I'll make both Peggy and Charlie very proud of me! And I sincerely hope that I did just that before they died! I only wish that I had been able to give them a whole lot of the things that they went without when bringing me up! They were both dead before I really got into a position where I could share my so called 'good?' fortune with them.

But anyway - there I was, back in 1969/70 , a lass from Greenacre, who was just embarking on what was to be the most exciting merry-go-round ever. Much more exciting than the bank! And when you are only half way between 18 and 19 excitement and FUN were paramount! But as I think that I also said before, I was soon to find out that it also proved to be - *a lot of hard work!*

In the 70's, the 'club circuit' as we entertainers called it was a very lucrative source of regular work and 'shows' etc. Not so these days, so I have been told, and not for some years, although now in 2010, it looks as though it may pick up a bit, so I suppose most things are cyclical though aren't they?

But back when I was working though, there were a lot of venues requiring either a week's worth of shows, like 'the Mandarin Club', and some interstate venues, or the single 'one or two nighters', such as the local RSL Clubs; Bowling Clubs; Worker's Clubs; Soccer Clubs, Golf clubs; and the Leagues Clubs in those days. *(dying days of the 60's and then the 70's)*. Lots of work for those that wanted to actually work!

And I definitely wanted to work!

I began by doing the normal 'club circuit' for the first year and a half, thinking even then that I was looking through a magic mirror when I gradually saw my weekly income go from $40 per show - to $75 - and then to what was in those days, a humongous $85 per show. *(Australian Dollars, in 1969/70 remember!)*

Well anyway, having got that first show out of the way, and having nearly made a veritable fool of myself by running away via the window, I fairly quickly got into the showbiz routine, having definitely decided, as I said, that it was for me after all!

I mean after all, this 'showbiz racket' looked like it was going to make all my dreams come true! But there was still an awful lot that I had to learn, and who better to have teach it to me than Eddie Keen, my ex school teacher, and my then mentor, and lover. He was after all, the man who had gotten me started on this merry go round in the first place. And I loved him, as only teenagers can love someone! Which was more than immensely. I loved him as totally as a young person brought up to believe that love is forever can love!

So I was glad that it had been goodbye Bank, and 'hello' show business. It seemed like I had suddenly become rich! I earned enough to be able to give Peg and Charlie a bit in the way of 'not really living at home board', and still re-invest a little of what I had earned, in me. I might also add, that I was having a much better time earning the money as well. I was enjoying being alive, was with the 'love of my life' *(that will become a familiar statement before this book is finished. Yet again - I can unfortunately guarantee it!)*, and I positively loved to sing!!

I am pretty sure that that must have been the time when my 'speculate to accumulate' period of life began in earnest. When you are only nearly nineteen though, as I was, having a 'good time' is still high on your list of priorities. I was speculating and accumulating, but spending and not investing; Peg and Charlie's precious daughter had, in theirs and their friends eyes though, suddenly become a 'scarlet woman'. I suddenly found myself travelling, and living the life of Riley! 'And what a life it was!'

But even for a 'scarlet woman', some weeks, just doing 'one nighters', I managed to do Friday and Saturday evenings *and*, Sunday mornings, afternoons, and evenings as well. That was 5 performances over just 3 days.

I would find my bank balance bolstered by as much as $425 on a good week. As little as $85 on a bad week, but even so, they were still astronomical wages for a girl my age in 1970, and absolutely fantastic for a girl from the so called, wrong side of the tracks. Even $85 was more than three times what I earned for a weeks work in the bank. Just one of the reasons I preferred to work as a singer you might say! Although Peg and Charlie were upset about my having moved out under the circumstances that I had done so, I think that they were happy enough for me. I was, and would always still be their 'little girl'. Also, on successful weeks like the one I just mentioned, I think that the extra financial help that I gave them, did it's bit towards keeping them onside a bit as well. I often used to give them money to make up for the fact that I wasn't at home, paying board! They were after all, my parents, and they had done their best, but I used to walk around Eds house, when I was there by myself, singing - "I'm in the money", "I'm in the money"!

160

Ed would probably not have agreed, but, just imagine how any young person *would* feel! I had been earning about $26.45 per week in the bank, for 9 – 5, five days a week, and by the time I'd paid the weekly train fare, and allowed for board at home, I didn't have much left at the end of the week. I'd have nothing left to bank - even though I had worked in one. But suddenly I was earning heaps of extra money at this showbiz racket, and I *should* have been able to save loads more than I did! "Why should", do I hear you ask?

Well - I had been working the clubs, and living with Ed for close on about 10 months, and had only managed to save a very little at that time, *(with the emphasis on 'a very', and 'little')*. And then, horror of horrors, Ed suddenly decided, for one reason or another, that because of my age, and the fact that my career looked as though it was 'just about' to 'take off', the age discrepancy between us had the potential of creating some very unpleasant, unneeded, adverse publicity. *(That 'just about' by the way, would unfortunately take about a further 9 years. Could that have been because Ed was no longer with me, do ya reckon?)*

Back at the time in 1969/70, if it had become even small scale media knowledge that we were living together, it would have been the kind of publicity that neither I, nor his only really newly formed training school needed. He said that I would be better off without him, and that I would probably do better, unattached, and on my own! *(Of course his business could definitely do without the adverse publicity that our living together would have brought as well!)* He reckoned that he had taught me what I needed to know to get started, and that all I really needed from then on, was the occasional booster lesson. Talk about a polite rejection!

Even though I was sad, and devastatingly heartbroken *(a state of affairs that I would become all too familiar with over the following years!)*, I accepted the situation *(I guess I was a 'toughie', even then, but then, in reality I didn't really have any choice in the matter, did I?)*. I set about getting on with my life, trying to manage for myself at first.

I would have to admit though, that I didn't always do a 'pucker' job of being an entertainer when I first started, but I did find what appeared to be a reliable agency arrangement to start with, and then a series of 'with it', and clever business managers to follow. But what with their costs, the fact that I hadn't really learned any monetary frugality, even though I had worked in a bank, as well as my having developed a penchant for looking good when I turned up to the clubs, the money that I was earning never seemed to go far enough. *(But then, does money ever really go far enough?)*

Stage clothes seemed to cost a 'bomb' - a lot more than I had remembered. My show music provision costs also increased when Ed and I broke up, as he was no longer scribing the manuscripts for me. Add all that to the normal household expenses, which were no longer shared. It all meant that I never seemed to be able to save very much at the end of the month. The odd bit, here and there maybe, if I was lucky! Without the steadying influence of prudent Mr Keen, my money just seemed to go through my fingers like grains of sand! Still - although as I said, I was devastated over the break up, and that the 'love of my life' had left me, after a few more months, my life was actually going great guns with my shows. They were now proving very popular with the theatrical agents. So I figured that Ed had maybe been right. I was better off alone. They had always told me that I would need to speculate a little in order to accumulate, but Ed hadn't really been into speculating in those days. I was suddenly alone, and I was! *(into speculating that is)* Must have inherited it from daddy!

So it seemed, that although I never appeared to be having much trouble with the actual earning, and speculating bit of the equation *(at the time that I was working, there were always plenty of jobs to be done)* – to tell the truth, it was the accumulating, and saving bit that I was finding difficult to do! Typical of most 19 –20 year old girls though, even one that was earning very well, I was still, always broke! But then, I have to admit that I *was* having a *fun time* even so! For those first few years I don't remember anything outstandingly fantastic happening. I think that I just plodded along. Oh, hang on, I have just remembered! - There was *one* person – but no, I had better not go there, probably a bit dangerous for them if I did! I was also though, invited to do my very first overseas 'gig'. Now that was *definitely,* outstandingly fantastic. The Agent that had been handling my 'book' for the last few months said to me one day - "If you don't already have a passport - you'd better get one, and be quick about it".

"What for", I innocently said.

He actually set the balls in motion for me, and I think he must have fast tracked it or something, because he had no sooner told me that the bookers from Indonesia had already seen my show at the Mandarin Club, and that they wanted me to go to entertain their clients there, than I was on a plane. On my way to Indonesia! "They seem a bit keen", says me! And then I think I thought -

"Oh Oh"! In the same way that I had heard about 'those kinds of men', I had also heard lots of 'sleazy' stories about the kind of 'entertainment' that could be needed in some of those far away countries. I was still only just 20 and a bit, tall and now not at all that bad looking, even if I did say so myself! *(I had been told that I had well and truly left my ugly duckling look behind)*. My boobs had grown, and my shape had filled out! I was still though, very wary at first. But with assurances from both the agents, and others who had already done the booking, I boarded the plane, passport and toothbrush packed, and headed for Djakarta. *(I did of course, take a few more things other than just that with me. - l though think that to perform Cabaret, in the Orient, with just a toothbrush and a passport would possibly have gone down pretty well indeed. Especially in those days, anyway ! But then - come to think of it - maybe a bit too well!)*

My singing, even with my clothes on, seemed to get the crowd on side well enough though, and so the shows all went great!

It all seemed too good to be true. But true it definitely was, and it really did look as if my 'speculating' was starting to pay off. The 'accumulate' couldn't possibly be too long away! Could it?

There was also the fact that 'little 'ol me' got to go on my first aeroplane flight, which was in those days of 1973, an almost unimaginable exploit for a just past teenager from, as I said before, the less 'economically affluent' side of town.

(Now, I can't use the actual paper clipping for this particular job, suffice it enough to say that it would probably disintegrate if I were try to take it out of the album it is in, but I will write a bit of what Mr K. I. Mahmud said in the Indonesian paper when he wrote about my night at the Nirwana Supper Club on Saturday 15th December 1973.

163

"Hearing and especially watching this flaming redhead at the Nirwana Supper Club last evening was a good treatment for the ears and eyes and directly made your mind relaxed after the hard days work. She sang and danced for nearly 2 hours non stop, with only joyful intervals of 'step down, and meet the clients' interludes. The men were more than happy, and their lady folk were made to feel very good and happy that their men folk were attractive to such a good looking girl!"

Only been in the business about 3 and a half years, and already
with my name in lights on the top of the building,
and my picture smiling at me from all over !

I was virtually singing for my supper, and what is more - having a
'fantabulous' supper at that, with all the added benefits thrown in, for

free! Oh sure, even then, some rich families would send their children off on exciting trips abroad, but that little girl from Greenacre, from the lower income family, was in absolute seventh heaven!

Wow! It was a regular free bee! Just imagine my excitement in 1973 when I first arrived at the Hotel Indonesia, in Djakarta to work in the Nirwana supper club, and find my name, written in 50 foot illuminated letters, right across the top of the front of the hotel building.

'KERRI DYER'!

Talk about making you feel 'big time'.

("Only been in the business about 3 and a half years, and already with my name in lights"! Oooh!)

The very sight of that, plus the news paper articles made me feel like all my Christmases had come at once. Especially since - I would actually still be there for Christmas day! *(Unfortunately most of those early photos and newspaper articles disappeared a little later on, during and after the Darwin escapade that you'll read about a little later on.)* But I'll let you see what I DO have.

What a Christmas present that little trip to the Orient turned out to be!!!! I have heaps of memories! Memories that nothing can really take away, even though the accident has had a ruddy good try at it, but memories are persistent little buggers, and every day *(some thirty years later)*, especially as I write this book, another fond memory flashes across my brain space *(even as damaged as it has been)*!

The delightfully caring children out there need to be seen to be believed!

An Asian Father Christmas has to be seen to be believed!

An Australian/English/American/Asian Christmas in Indonesia, just has got to be experienced to be believed!

The other Australian performers that would also have also experienced them will know what I am on about! In the main show /dining room there was a GIANT 80ft tree, and the biggest, lit up **'MERRY CHRISTMAS'** sign I had ever seen. Other signs both in English and various other Hindi and Malay languages, were all about. The signs inside the hotel were 'only'(?) about 10 feet tall but they too were all 'lit up'. The hotel's electricity bill must have been absolutely astronomical, what with the signs on the roof top, and the others lit up all around other areas of the hotel. I don't think that they would be affordable, or even allowed these days, what with power supply prices being so expensive! *(And do you know what? - There would probably be a team of 'green earth warriors', marching up an down, and protesting outside nowadays! Climate change and everything!)*

Their power supplies would probably be strictly metered nowadays anyhow, or they would have investigated, and probably found, a more eco and pocket friendly light source. *(Candle light dinners would probably needs be the vogue these days, if they were still operating, I guess! I would have to say though, candles would definitely be appropriately very romantic, in such a romantic place!!!)*

I may have technically been doing two 30 minute shows a night, seven days a week, which quite often became hour shows, depending on the audience response *(the paper clipping exaggerates about 2 hours non stop.)*, but the thought of getting paid what seemed and what was, at that time, the astoundingly large amount of $375 Australian dollars per month + *airfares*, which were then, and still are astronomical + accommodation, plus free access to the hotel food menu, three times a day, along with free unlimited use of the pool and all facilities. Hot tubs, sauna's, and everything! Everything clubbed together,would have made it equivalent to close to $900 a week. And $900 a week, back in the early 70's was considered astronomical money! Just think! 20 years of age, and earning that amount of money + perks!

Even after my management was paid, I was having a profitable, *fun* time!!!

Let me at 'em! My corner of the Sky!

There were other, garish, non lit up, Oriental signs all about as well, all written in a variety of Indonesian, Chinese , American, and English. The Eastern sign writers absolutely loved, and still do *(from what I have seen on the limited travel that I have been able to do since the accident)*, bright, gaudy colours, and streamers. They were absolutely everywhere. The show room looked very, very Christmasy! *(is that a word? It has a red wiggly line under it, so I guess that it's not, but it does set the mood, doesn't it?)*

"Now where was I"?

Oh yeah! That's right!

I'd do my two shows a night, right there in that room, amidst all the paraphernalia, and each night, under the tree, there would be either a gift *(generally all wrapped up, with ribbons and sparkly paper)*, or there would be a plain white or brown envelope with a garish *'MISSY KERRI'* or *'Miss Kerri Dyer'* elegantly/or not, written on it. After a while, it became almost as though it was my own personal Christmas tree. Absolutely WONDERFUL!!! There were *so* many envelopes under the tree with my name on them, and they would generally contain an Indonesian, or English/American Christmas card. *(All of which have unfortunately been lost over the intervening years, again with the accident, and many moves)*. There was sometimes even some US dollars or maybe some Indonesian money *(which I still have, all this time later!)*. When I had changed the foreign currency, and added it up, I must have received almost two months wages as gifts. Chrissie presents maybe? I would look down at them, smile and say - "They were right! - there was no doubt about it, I thought - this speculate racket, is definitely beginning to accumulate". All I had to do was save it! *(Fat chance I no doubt said!)* When I sat down and counted it all, *(which of course I greedily did straight away)*, and added it to what I had earned, I had never seen so much money. I was sitting on the floor, throwing the money in the air, with the biggest grin you have ever seen spread across my face. I really was 'in the money' as I had once sung, dancing around Eds flat. I finally went home after just one month of pleasurably singing and entertaining, with close on $5000. Nearly 7 months wages, in 1 month of sunning, funning, and enjoying my working. Talk about *FUN!*

(Fancy getting paid to do it, sing I mean, and what is more - to have really enjoyed myself as well!) Wow!!!!

And even though I was maybe a little bit naughty when I was in the East, there was no longer any doubt about it. All my Christmas's had definitely come at once! I hope that 1973 was a fantabulous Christmas for the clientèle at the Hotel Indonesia, because it definitely was for me!

I had never had so much money in my whole life at that time. Not money that wasn't already earmarked for something in particular, any way. Apart from being an excellent showbiz teacher, Ed had also been a very good teacher of the art of saving, and if I had been even half as good as a student of economics, I might have done better from my stint as an entertainer. *(Funny? My lovely daughter is now the economist in the family!)* I think that I must have been one of Ed's better singing students, but I don't think that I would have been one of his better students in the subject of frugality. I never seemed able to properly learn that aspect of life *(I still frustrate him with my inability to save, although even if I say so myself, I seem to be doing a bit better these days!)!* He had been forever rousing me for my slack monetary habits back when I had been living with him, and now that we are married, it's really no different!! My life may be different in that I actually have some money now, but according to my darling husband, I am still as much of a spendthrift as ever!

Once I was living by myself though, there was no one there to stop me, and I tended to live, *(probably learnt from Peg and Charlie)* on the 'never, never', but always with the belief that my singing would one day make me rich!

Because my singing was going great guns, there was always money coming in. It was just that it went out again before it had any chance to build up a 'nest egg' so to speak! I guess that secretly, I was enjoying being single, and a bit of a 'gad about'. In fact I was enjoying it a lot! *(Was that naughty - or what?)*

Peg and Charlie had tried to teach me, along with Ed, that I should to try to stash a bit away for tomorrow', even *(as was the case with Peg and Charlie)* if the 'stash' turned out to be 'not all that much'. But, to be honest, the tomorrow that they had both told me about, had always seemed such a long way off! *(It has very suddenly been here for the last 30 years, and even though I have enough these days to at least survive fairly well thank you, I am having to listen and, what is more – still obey! Drat!")*

When I was working I earned well, but it still wasn't enough to make me rich, and at that time I desperately wanted, as do most kids of that age, to be rich! *(a bit like Robbie Williams - "I'm rich - rich - rich to excess", was what he said! I would positively still love to be **that** rich!).*

I may not have been stinking rich then, but I thought at the time *(maybe a little selfishly)*, that "a girl still has got to look and feel good, eat well, and have a reasonable time while she is becoming rich, doesn't she"? And anyway - I was sure I was going to be famous one day, and then I would be swilling in it – *(money?).*

HARRY

The fact that I was enjoying life to the 'oonth' degree on the path that I had chosen, might just have had something to do with my decision not to go home to Peg and Charlie when Ed and I broke up!

So there I was in about 1973/5, still with visions of the day coming, not too far away, when I would be able to set Peg and Charlie up in a big house, with servants etc. Alright! I was young! It was an exciting world that was just about to open up, with the promise of an almost unimaginable, for me at least, life stretching ahead of me. At the time it didn't seem as though my wealthy days were going to be that far away, and anyway, I figured that Peg and Charlie deserved that 'right haughty tauty place' that I had in mind for them!

I had made a lot of friends over the years between 1969 and 1978, and I had been involved in some excruciatingly interesting, and romantic relationships, *(some of which, don't worry, I will hopefully get around to telling you all about).* Each 'find' though, had turned up in pretty similar kinds of ways, especially with my being in the entertainment game *(and if I am honest, I would have to put my hand up and admit, that there have been quite a few. Although some people might even say, and I would probably agree - that there have probably been even more than quite a few 'finds' in my life!)* I guess though, that without even realising it I grew up in a world of different from birth, and that I must have got used to it without seeing it for what it was.

As I think I have already said, I grew up feeling that I wasn't really meant to be where I was! You know - it was almost as if the stork had inadvertently dropped me down the wrong chimney! But I'd actually had my first taste of different when my parents got divorced *(even though I knew nothing about it at the time)*. My childhood was decidedly 'odd', what with the 'box stages', the school opera, and things. I experience different with my older man - mentor; and then there was Harry - the young 'spunk' who also promised to again be different, but definitely different, in a 'different' kind of way. I don't suppose that I really needed to wish for it, did I? I already had it! And I would have to shamefully admit it – again, in bucket loads full!

Sometimes I used to think that it was a pity that I hadn't stayed around to find out just how 'different' it might have been with Harry! I probably would have been given all that I thought I had wanted, sooner and probably without the dramas that my life has brought me. *(Oh well!)*

As was pretty common with me in those days, I did what had become my usual trick, and ruined what promised to be an absolutely wonderful future. My fervent unknown or unrecognized for what it was desire for that something 'different' had lead me into what was to become for me, the most frightening part of my life.

But - where was I? - oh yeah!

Harry was only about 23. Much more socially acceptable for me age wise than Ed, and he was an accountant by trade. *(Just what I could probably have done with?)* He was also a singer in his spare time, *(we had met at Eds studio)* with a voice that would curl your toes with it's rich husky sound! He was considered a 'spunk' by all the other girls at the studio, and such a good 'catch' if you could 'net, or hook' him.

He was always well dressed, always smelt nice, and looked very fresh, clean, and affluent. Very important factors to a girl of my age at the time. I looked about silently for my lavender scented fishing tackle, and when he asked 'little old me' out for dinner, I was absolutely over the moon. Well, when you think of it, why wouldn't I have said yes? But what about Eddie I hear you ask? Well - a girl can't mope about break ups forever, can she? Especially not at my age. I was single again - and unattached! Yippee! Watch out world! *(Was that destined to be another of my favourite, and most used phrases!?)*

Harry and I went out together *(goodness that sounds quaint doesn't it?)* for about thirteen months, with him sometimes staying over in my flat in Glebe before we got engaged. (*Naughty naughty*)! But we were happy young love personified, and we had both decided that we were meant for each other! There was only one major problem. Technically, when he wasn't at my place, which was only a couple of days a week, he still lived at home with his mum and dad, so we dare not go there except on formal sorts of visits, and after a time, neither of us liked saying good night to each other at all.

I had found myself 'in love' - again! (*difficult to imagine - isn't it?*)

His parents liked me however, and they had decided by that time, what with Harry's age and everything (*his being in his mid twenties*), that he was old enough to do as he wanted, within reason. It was just that our sleeping together in their home, with them only a bed room wall away was not a desirable situation, for either party.

They both thought that I would possibly make a good daughter in law, but they were definitely not in favour of us staying over, together in their home. (*Fuddy Duddies, I remember thinking at the time! They were not though, just of a different generation!*) But then of course, Harry still only had a single bed anyway, and two grown ups in a single bed, gyrating around, had to be seen to be believed, and it also made for a very difficult event to not 'hear'. We had tried the 'old's' double bed when they were away one time, and being typical young people - although we had enjoyed not having to keep the noises down, we had decided that the sooner we got a double bed of our own, the better. So he stayed at my place (*I already had a double bed didn't I?*) more, and more often! And that was another thing they didn't really like, either! Oh well! I guess that you couldn't win with mums and dads in those days! Probably not in any days! Theirs was an understandable reaction to a very 'alien to them' situation

One evening though, when we had gone on a romantic night out, and having 'kind of' discussed it a few weeks earlier (*you know - the "what do you think you might do if"? sort of thing*), he proposed. I coquettishly blushed and accepted, even though I had already decided what my answer would be if/whenever he got around to actually asking me. (*You know girls - you kind of know when these things are about to happen.*) I had sensed the change in the vibes a little while before, and most unlike me, I had bottled my anticipation for days, waiting. Not

173

an easy thing for me to do, and I was positively bursting with joy, and just about bouncing off the chair with suppressed excitement when he finally, actually asked me! My happiness knew no bounds! *("At last", I admit I must have thought - "I am going to be an honest woman"! See – my so called depravity must have worried me a bit more than I thought then!)* I will say now though, thinking back, that the beautiful exclamation mark engagement ring that he popped on my finger - the baguette, oblong diamond with a sapphire dot at the end - should probably have been a question mark, for all the angst that I caused him. Although, maybe he knew something in advance? 'Different' generally does always bring exclamations, doesn't it? And the ring was, after all, an exclamation mark!

There was no doubt about it though. It was the best bit of fishing I'd done up to that date! Unfortunately the sapphire dot on my gorgeous engagement ring, fell off during the first days I was out of the hospital, *(I'll tell you about that later as well)* when I was what you might call 'a bit clumsy' *(a definite understatement)*, but I still have, and wear the diamond baguette solitaire. My present husband, who just happens to have also taught Harry, doesn't mind. At least he has never said anything about it , so I assume that it's alright with him for me to wear it. Ed has actually, bought me some other lovely rings, and I just asked him whether or not he minds my wearing Harry's ring, and he said - "why would I mind? You're married to me, and I say why shouldn't you wear your memories if you can"? *(I am **so** lucky! Ed is truly a wonderful man!)*

I actually have the history of the really serious relationships in my life, all together on the fingers of my right hand. Harry and I had only been engaged for about 5 – 6 months, which meant we had been together for nearly a year, and you know what they say about 1st year jitters. And although I am definitely not proud of how I carried on, Harry didn't deserve any of what transpired within that relationship!

But I really did deserve what I almost got!

NEW HORIZONS?

Why? Well let's see shall we!

I started inexplicably, getting jittery, and there was no doubt about it, I definitely should have known better than to do what I eventually did. That sense of desperation for that something, anything different, must have unfortunately kicked in again!

Life with Harry had been what some might call, gloriously uncomplicated, with lots and lots of fantastic 'that' *(you know what I mean by 'that', don't you girls?)*, but to tell the truth, I must have found life just a tad on the dull side. 'Cause by then, as I said, that stupid, looking for something different Kerri, *(must have been the gremlins)* had made her presence felt, and they *(the gremlins?)* had definitely taken over! *(Yeah – we'll blame the gremlins, will we?)*

It was a bit like my having two me's in my brain.

One 'me' would say in a panicky, kind of 'don't do it' voice *(get married I mean)*, while the sensible voice, which I seldom seemed to hear much of in those days, was saying - "But you're due to marry Harry, the perfect gentleman. Remember! - the man of your dreams"! Please remember Kerri!

The other voice would then chip in again, with it's snide and complaining tone - "Ah yes! That's right! But, if you do marry him, your life will inevitably be, extremely predictable, and very much, 'not different.' - There is a smorgasbord of fellows out there, and anyway – didn't we hear you say that you ask for 'different'?

Then the now turned slightly anxious, good voice, would worriedly interject - "But just think Kerri. Your financial worries will disappear, and with Harry being such a wiz with money, you are almost assured to be rich one day; You'll be able to continue singing, and become famous"!

The practical, and the adventurous sides of my nature were in the middle of an almighty battle! "Oh - help! What do I do"?, says me, to me.

All that I could see in front of me was - a life of Harry getting up - going to work 9 - 5, five days a week. *(He would allot time to pursue his singing of course, wouldn't he?)* I had completely, and momentarily forgotten exactly why I had loved him. He was wonderfully gentle, loved me a lot, and of course, was a great screw, but was that really enough to get married on? I obviously had thought so before those nasty gremlins started in on me.

("What about us", those nasty, looking for excitement gremlins would selfishly ask me? What are we going to do for excitement?)

Because of my all too frequent at that time, unsettled and unsettling moods, the gremlins must have been able to sense that life might just turn interesting for them, 'IF', and as it turned out, the 'IF' was unknowingly sitting in the wings, biding it's time, getting ready to pounce! The first pseudo 'interesting', 'unpredictable' man that I met at that time when my defences were down, was definitely targeted by them, and they aimed their *(my)* man hunting laser beam straight at him! How stupid can you get? Really!

Those gremlins knew me well enough to know that with Harry safely out of the way, there was no one there to hold me back, and that with no one to make me see what a stupid thing I was about to be led to do, I would be 'fair game'. *(I ask you! Can you believe that I could have been such a fool? Fancy convincing myself at the time, that it was not my fault, but the fault of some obscure, imaginary 'someone else'.)*

"But let's just have a look at what I had convinced myself that life probably would have been like if I had stayed with Harry in those early days, shall we!"

I would have been doing my club shows of course, with possibly the odd, exciting overseas show thrown in for good measure. It would also have been a case of us going home at night after my having truly enjoyed my performing; going to bed, possibly having an incredible romp before going to sleep; with that by the way having been absolutely, mesmerisingly fantastic! Very important for someone so young! Then next morning, we would get up, Harry going off to work, leaving me to spend the days at home *(probably doing a dangerous nothing except practising my 'patter' and doing my vocal exercises {which really shouldn't have been a dangerous nothing – should it?}).*

I would have waited like a dutiful wife/girlfriend for Harry to return from his accounting work. The occasional party would be thrown in, if and when Harry had the time. *(I probably would have thought then - Oo, oo, woopy doo! So thrilling! I guess that I had also momentarily forgotten the other good times I had with Harry, and the good times had while I was singing as well. It also appears now, trawling through my memory banks, that I have spent a huge part of my life shamefully asking myself this very same question)!*

"Is this all that there is to be of life?"

Talk about my being a silly girl!!!!

Oh don't get me wrong though! I positively loved my singing work, but at that time of my life,my feelings, well I guess that they - well they would have been very hard for anyone to actually pin down! All I can surmise, is that my satisfaction/dissatisfaction gremlin had kicked in, and that it must have decided things for me, - *(There I went again – always blaming someone else! I seem to have been doing that all my life")!*

"Your life looks like being positively boring at the moment", it would no doubt have said, *(wrong, says me now!)* and that one charming, but persistent little gremlin would also have added, "let's have a bit of fun eh?"

Harry suddenly had to go away for a week, with his accountancy work, *(which to tell the truth, he hadn't had to do too often before, if at all),* and I was all alone. *(Those 'up for anything' (UFA) gremlins must have secretly thought, ah ha! Party time)!*

Not that I am really just blaming the gremlins, - I liked parties, and it was *me* who listened to them, and *me* who took their suggested actions!

But, anyway, Harry was off interstate, and off I went to work in a 'ready to party mood'. That night I was to work at a club where I would never have expected to meet anyone intriguingly interesting. *(I was planning to go partying after work anyway!)* That particular place had always been full of what I considered 'untouchables' at my tender age - you know - 'old fogies'! If it had been one of the other 'young people', late night nightclubs, my warning gremlins *(the* (GGs) *goody goodies!)* might just have stayed on the 'look - out', and they may have saved me from making such a fool of myself. *(That is of course if I had bothered to even listen to their good advice!")* As for the UFA's *(up for any things')* I am sure that, although they knew that that particular venue didn't normally offer them any fun, they might just lurk around for a while – and probably said to themselves, "you just never know, do you?" They no doubt figured that "with 'that fellow' away, *(Harry normally kept an eye on me)*, there was no telling what sort of fun they could have!"

It probably seemed too good a chance for them to miss out on! So there I was, completely unprotected! Those UFA gremlins must have been able to sense that life might just start to get interesting for them, IF, and it appears to me now, that their 'IF' was sitting patiently in the wings - biding it's time, getting ready to pounce! And pounce it most certainly did! There was no one around to stomp on my madness that time! No one to point out to me, the stupidity of the suggestions those gremlins were making to me.

(Mind you they themselves wouldn't have thought that what they were about to convince me to do, was stupid! They probably saw it as that bit of excitement that I had obviously been secretly crying out for, for the last little while! If I am honest about that time of my life - then I was just a fool!) Ooh, and do you know what else?! I should probably never have been allowed out by myself when my 'restless gremlins' were about. If Harry had been there, he would definitely have put the 'kibosh' on them for sure. Come to think of it, I must have been a very 'hard work required' girlfriend, because he had managed to do so, *(stop 'em dead in their tracks, I mean)* a few times before. Harry knew me, and the signs pretty well, but, he unfortunately wasn't about that night, so Kerri Dyer, or 'the Dyer' as I

think I told you I was known as in the business, was about to be let off her leash! Here comes that phrase again! - Watch out world!

Now - Gregory Adams, *(that was the name of the 'different' man at the centre of my next – almost my last, adventure.)*, came up to me at the club bar. I was hot after working *(as was usual)*, and although I was a bit reticent about it at first, he and I had a drink or two together. Although he was technically an oldie, a bit like Ed had been, *(but this time, even a little older. In his mid to late 40's when I was in my twenties)*, he did though seem so nice *(Fatal attraction?)*, and although I initially must have baulked a bit, we chatted, and laughed *(probably a bit too loudly and a bit too loosely)*. Got in I was!

So I got talking with him a bit more! - We had a few more drinks – *(deadly!)*, and then out of the blue he had kissed me. I almost slapped him, but my hand stopped in mid air, *(It must have been like a bit like it is in the movies)* and I just gave him a shocked look, he cupped my chin and drew my face close again, and planted another big kiss on my mouth!. This time I had actually *felt* 'something' when he kissed me.

But I wasn't supposed to feel anything with anyone but Harry!

Yes -'Ve - ry interesting'! Oh dear!

How **very** stupid! Definitely an intriguingly, dumb *'no no'!*

ON THE ROAD TO ——>

When his suggestion of us running away together had fully permeated my *(probably drunken by that time)* thought structure, I figured that, well after all - they do say that "a change is as good as a holiday", and I no doubt thought that I could probably do with a holiday! One of Carol's and my my motto's had always been "On to adventure!", and Gregory's and my chat seemed like it could really lead to a life changing, *fun!* adventure! *(I guess that that will teach me for saying that 'there had to be something, anything better than this'.)* Was I about to find out if there was?

Desperately though, I must have foolishly been thinking again that I wanted that something 'different' *(and boy oh boy, did I ever get it!).* I shamefacedly have to admit , that after quickly finding out first hand, when we ducked home to get my bags, that he promised to be phenomenal in bed when we had a bit more time, I am afraid that I just didn't really see it for what it was. Sheer lust!

I simply threw all cares to the wind. Chucked a selection of my music and clothes into a bag and did it, *(ran away, that is).*

We had already been happily driving along for three days, to a town where lust had, again shamefully, won the day a few times before, singing and chatting *(more me, than him).* We stopped off at Motels along the way, to eat, drink, and do what all young romantic, runaways normally do *(and I still hadn't rung Harry, or anyone else for that matter, to say where I was!).* I ask you, now how bad was that, eh?

Now Gregory may not have been what you might call a 'really good looker', but I am here to tell you, just between you me and the bedpost, that what he lacked in the looks department, he more than made up for when it came to bedroom activities!

(Just as I had surmised during that quick interlude before we had really hit the road, he was, what you might call, very, very good at 'that'. And 'that' after all, was of paramount importance at that impressionable age! More's the shame!)

Gregory was definitely the diametrical opposite of my fiancé in most things. He was not particularly good looking. *(Harry was. Good looking that is! In fact he was stunning!)*, and although Harry had been good at 'that' too, to tell the truth, what with Gregory's 'that' also being SO incredibly good, I didn't spare much time worrying about the chaos that I had probably left at home. *(I think that 'that' must have foolishly been a definite pre-requisite for any of my 'interests' in those days 'cause Gregory's 'that' was not only fantastic, it was also enchantingly 'different'. As you have probably garnered from what you have read so far, apart from my enjoying a good 'that', I also craved 'different'. So with him I had definitely scored! He provided for both of my fantasies from every which way!)*

Greg though, was even worse with money than me, and as it turned out, it wound up the worst possible scenario, *(except for 'that' of course)*. *I* had paid for the petrol, and we had run away in *my* car. But to make things even worse - *he couldn't even sing!*

A definite trio of 'not goods'! Can you believe it? I still can't! Not even all these years later! I have to ask myself, how on earth I can have been so stupid? But, to give him some credit though, he did do most of the driving up to Darwin!

But as I was to find out a bit later, he had a reason, known only to himself at the time, for wanting to pick somewhere as isolated in the scheme of things, as Darwin was. I had inadvertently provided him with a safe, untraceable way of escaping from Sydney. Why? - aw; to my shame, you'll soon find out alright, but not quite in the same way that I did!! I guess that it was a bit like 'toad' of Wind in the Willows fame. "Broom, broom, - hit the open road."

But - there ya' go! Greg and I were on the road to Darwin before precaution, and plain good sense had had time to kick in. Harry and my poor agent must have had a hell of a time. They had no idea where I had gone. I had just disappeared from the face of the earth for all they knew. Left no messages - had I? My agent had had to admit to the irate club managers, for weeks later, that he had no idea where I was. Nor when, or even if, I would be back, so there were some very hurried cancellations, and unexpected bookings in some of the better clubs, for other singers! *(For someone who had supposedly wanted to be a 'star' - running away was definitely NOT the wisest of moves, was it?)*

But at that time, and I don't think that anyone could really argue about it - I just mustn't have been thinking straight! *(crooked maybe, but definitely not straight! - Come to think of it, I seem to remember Gregory having a penis that kinda went 'round corners' too! Bent? Now that was a very different bit of titillation! and could have had a bit to do with what happened. But what was even more important at that time, was that he definitely knew how to use his bent tool to it's best advantage!)* I think that his bedroom antics would probably have been uppermost in my brain at the time! And I'll say again - 'more's the pity'. I have to assume, that I just momentarily mustn't really have cared about anything much else! I was the age I was, early twenties, and sex definitely ruled! Maybe it was my way of committing suicide, but one would have to ask why would I want to do that? *(Commit suicide I mean! Not 'that'? I reckon that by now, and having ploughed through this much of the book, that we would definitely have known why I would have wanted to do 'that', alright).*

We were merrily driving along, and I do vaguely remember saying to Greg, that it should be easy enough for me to get work in Darwin, in one form or other, having just returned from there, and still being armed with my music and clothes. Gregory was sure to be able to find work to do up there too! There was bound to be lots of bar work!

I tell you what though - was that statement ever a *wrong move!* How was I supposed to know that he had *no* intention of either of us working ever again!! The car came to a screeching halt. I sat there, fidgeting in my seat, trying to see what had caused us to stop so suddenly, and with such a shudder. It would have been pre dusk, and I couldn't see any reason for it, but thought that maybe a 'big red - *(Kangaroo)* had bounded onto the road, and had come at us from Greg's side of the car. We were in the Australian desert area after all, so I looked out of the my side window in a further effort to see why we had suddenly stopped. Nothing! I turned in the seat to look across at the driver's side again, and there was Gregory, his head almost under the driving seat, hands fumbling around, mumbling, and grumbling all the time. He suddenly came up, holding what he'd been scrabbling about with under the seat, and I came face to face with a gun barrel, pointed straight between my eyes. My immediate thoughts were - and I beg your forgiveness, - "Oh shit! I'm going to die". *(Again, sorry - but that's what I thought!)*

My world came to the same screeching halt, that the car had come to.

He had turned every shade of blotchy purple, blue, green, yellow and red, with, what I can only assume now, was rage! What had just happened to make him so mad? *(If I hadn't been staring down the barrel of a shotgun, I probably would have, knowing my warped sense of humour, laughed out loud at his hilariously funny look. His face changing every colour of a sunset rainbow, with dribble and drool spurting from the corners of his mouth!)* He looked a bit like an apoplectic toad! *(Not that I've ever actually seen one, of course, but I think that you should know what I mean!)* There he sat, raving on at me, spitting out both spit, and words about my belonging to him now.

He screamed at me - "I don't want you singing in any of those *(to use his words as he pointed at the suitcase in the back)* "slutty outfits".

He yelled that I was to ********** forget about parading myself in front of other men. "You are MINE", he screamed at me at the top of his voice!

The car virtually shook with his rage! *********, I thought! I was totally 'gob smacked'. *(The words were a bit much to type here, my typing fingers blushed enough when I originally wrote them down, before erasing them. So I'll leave it to your imagination will I?)*

My whole short life flashed like a cine film, right in front of my eyes. My heart took a swift flight up into my throat, and I found myself shivering, and quivering with fear, looking this way and that for some possible way of escape! And then, and then, - the click of a trigger resounded in the car, followed almost immediately by the release of a bullet. I must have caught the quickest of glimpses of the movement of his hand just before that click had actually permeated my brain space. *(Luckily, my reactions were a lot faster in those days. I would probably be dead if it happened these days.)*

Instinctively, and just in time so it appears, I dropped my head down to my lap, and between my knees. I was positively terrified, and didn't dare raise my eyes to see what was going on, but I had heard a loud ricocheting noise, and I realised that he had probably, actually taken a pot shot. *(I guess that it really was just as well that my inquisitive nature hadn't taken over, and that I hadn't looked up then - wasn't it?!)*

I was to learn later that that ricocheting noise had been the bullet flying around the metal of the cabin, and that it had finally gone right through a slightly open window, ripping a hole in the glass edge, with it's velocity. My very frightened head had been missed by the merest fraction of a quarter inch. The bullet had *'zooshed'* through that gap in the window, and had lodged in a tree just outside the car. It is probably still there! I wasn't too sure if Gregory had purposely tried to kill me; I mean, no one would have known with us out in the desert, would they? Was it an accident *(some accident!)*; or had it been done merely to frighten me? I just sat there. I was so full of shock, and just too bloody scared, to cry at the time. (*"But I am too young to die"*, *cried out the frantic voice inside of me, that had so cockily been urging me to set off for adventure before!)*

I found out later that he was too good a shot for it to have been anything other than a frantic scare tactic. But how was I suppose to have known that at the time. I hadn't even known that he had a gun! That shot that he had fired, had most definitely succeeded! *(In scaring me I mean!)* I nearly 'pooped' myself! *(Am I allowed to say that? Tough, I've said it!)* I think that I can see the funny side of it now, but I definitely couldn't then!

"There could only have been one explanation for it", I must have thought - "The man I had run away with, may be superlative in bed, but he is definitely a NUTTER!" *(How had I not seen it before?)*

Now I know you will probably say that I was probably only getting what I deserved, but even I must have thought to myself at the time - "do I really deserve this?

I thought to myself - "Maybe I am mad too? Can I have been imagining it? NO! No, no, no. I am definitely not imagining it"! I knew that my imagination was a vivid one, but I would never have thought up what had just happened! Not even in my wildest dreams! Why would

I dream that I was going to be shot? "Why wasn't I safely tucked up at home with my 'used to fulfill all my dreams' Harry?", I thought. "Awww. What had I done?"

But no! I was there, stuck in the middle of the Australian desert, miles from anywhere. No one had the foggiest idea that I was out there, and I had just been target practice for a genuine 'nutter'. F.....h...!!!

GOT YA!

I was positively shaking with fear, unable to speak, and then when I dared to look up - what do you think I saw? You probably won't believe this, but it is as true as the fact that I am writing this book. I saw him - full of remorse, and most disgusting surprise of all surprises, I saw his once blotchy, yellow, red and green, full of rage face, swell up even further, till he looked even more like a toad, and then suddenly erupt into a fountain of uncontrollable tears!

Just like a little kid who had had his prized sweety taken from him, his face was melting, into a trembling mess of crinkled skin, tears, blubber and even more drool!

I felt like being physically ill, right then and there.

Shock and abhorrence flooded through me! He dropped his head down into my lap. There was so much drool, and his tears were swilling all over my legs. He was sobbing his heart out! "Forgive me! Forgive me! I can't begin to think what came over me! Except that I lo-love you," he spat and drooled!

"*What?*", I gasped!

An intense *(immediately suppressed in the name of safety)* feeling of total aversion overtook me, but somehow I could still sense his genuine distress, and a big chunk of my anger towards him momentarily dissipated. *(Note I said – momentarily!)*

Initially I had gone to instinctively pull away, just wanting to get out of the car if I could, but after seeing such a drastic change occur before my very eyes, I was now unsure of quite how to handle the sudden change of situation. My original sense of horror and aversion, had suddenly changed to the most profound compassion when he lifted his face to me again. He appeared to me, to be positively overcome with grief and remorse. I saw the tear stained eyes, the puffy face, and could hear his chest cracking sobs. *(There is no doubt about it - I remember being a bit of a 'sook' when faced with a someone that had suddenly become such a big soggy, lost pug or pussy cat!)*

My feelings though, very quickly changed back to intensive aversion again, when I quickly replayed in my mind, the reality of the dangerous situation I was in. Was I mad?! Why should I have pity for him? After all, "had he, or had he not, just tried to kill me?" Every nerve in my body was twitching, but I made myself as still and as emotionless looking as I could. *(Tough call!)* I had never been up till then, nor have I ever been since, so scared in my whole life! How I gave the erroneous impression of calm, I will never know. Both of us just sat there. I was silently trying not to shake. While him? Him? Tears just continued to stream down his now, suddenly, even uglier looking face! His not really marvellous looks, had suddenly become totally abhorrent to me. "How dare he still be crying", I internally screamed. I was trying desperately to appear normal, and yet trying to console him as well. *(I was however, finding it very difficult to stay calm! For some reason, can't imagine why, I definitely didn't feel very much like being nice to him at all any more! I just wanted him gone from my sight!)*

To him, everything had to appear as normal as was possible! I didn't dare react the wrong way, but I didn't even know what the wrong way was. How was I going to cope with this gross insanity?

Where had this sudden change in his personality come from?

Again, most unlike the normally hyper me, I decided there and then, that I would try to continue calmly. I still don't do calm well at the best of times, and those were definitely *not* the best of times. But things would probably turn worse, I thought, if I didn't continue to act as if I hadn't really even noticed his psychopathic behaviour. Amazingly, so far at least, my acting had apparently worked! Apparently! But for how much longer, I wasn't sure! *(I must have been a better actress than I thought possible - Funny that you can suddenly do a pseudo calm when you are bloody terrified, isn't it?!)*

I, as calmly as was possible in the circumstances, figured however, that if and when we finally made it into Darwin, I would try to secretly *(wishful thinking maybe?)* contact the police station and tell them what had happened. I had to at least find out whether or not he was wanted for anything. To have had a gun so readily attainable *(or at least, stuffed under the seat)*, combined with his eagerness to leave Sydney only signified one thing to me. A criminally dangerous madman, on the run! *(Had I unwittingly become a 'gangster's moll?)* I now just wanted to get away a.s.a.p, but, all the time I was thinking - "take care, Kerri". If he had gotten wind of the fact that I was still scared of him, or of my plans, I might have ended up dead, or even worse for me at the time, bashed about, and scarred! My vanity, which knew no bounds, momentarily took over, and I sulkily thought - "*Any* chance of my continuing my singing career, with a bashed about face would be nigh impossible". And then I thought to myself, "What if he wakes up in the middle of the night, and decides to shoot me anyway" I must have philosophically thought – *(or as philosophically as was possible under the circumstances)* "well I don't suppose that it will matter much what I choose as an opener or closer from now on, will it? If he shoots me, the show would definitely be over - no more Kerri Dyer!" And to tell the truth, I thought to myself, "if he shot me, I'd be dead, wouldn't I? Everyone else would 'hopefully?' be perturbed, *(but knowing how cut throat the business could be, probably not. They just would have thought, after initial sadness, - "Oh goody! More work for us!).* I don't suppose that by that time, I'd have been too perturbed either. I mean after all once I was dead - I would have been dead, wouldn't I? No chance to think about 'nuffin'!

"Probably the better option in this case", I would no doubt have thought!

But - if I were still alive, and bashed about, now that would have been a totally different matter, wouldn't it? I would have to look in the mirror, at a scarred, disfigured face every day! And even now, I'm still too vain to even think about the possible disfigurement that I would have had to face in the mirror every day, let alone endure!! *(Ooh, Now I know that that sounds vain and selfish? But that is what I thought at the time, and now, as long as they don't invent mirrors that can walk behind you, tapping on your shoulder so as to allow you to see your backside from the rear, then I'll remain reasonably happy.)*

I hate the funny walk I have since the accident, and I am still always trying to improve that. I hate my strange voice, but at least it is a 'different' voice that I have. I guess that I should be pleased about that anyway, and I guess that because I don't see my fat 'bum', it doesn't really bother me too much, and so far no one, [except my darling hubby] has dared to even mention it to me!

But, I must have thought to myself back then -"now calm down Kerri, be sensible." I would then have tried reasoning with myself. "No one has ever come back to tell us whether death hurts or not"! *(Although, it must hurt, mustn't it? The actual 'quarking' it bit anyway. Unless you just instantly left this world! Yeah! Some people must be lucky(?) enough to do just that!)*

But there would have been, of course, the even more devastating, hugely embarrassing explanations to be made to people, a thing that I wasn't really looking forward to! I decided though, at that time, that it would probably be far better after all, to admit to my own stupidity, rather than not to have been there to explain anything at all!

But after all the drama had eased off a bit, and as Gregory sat upright behind the wheel again, things thankfully seemed to calm down a bit. We were both just a little bit quiet when we first started out, *(can't imagine why we were quiet though. Can you?!)* But then, in an attempt to lighten the mood, he began joking about a bit. *(I cringed at his efforts at humour though.)* We'd been on the road for about 20 minutes more, and it appeared that he had apparently completely forgotten his criminally erratic mood, *(a sign of mental instability maybe?)*, and by the time we actually made it to Darwin, we were almost what you might call, 'kind of friendly'. I repeat, almost! I don't think that I will ever forget my bestest ever acting job that late afternoon! It would probably have qualified for an Emmy, or an Oscar! I had decided though that I was definitely very much in favour of his driving this last leg! The thought of leaving him unfettered in the car, was more than I could have stood. I wanted his hands where I could see them, and for him to be kept occupied doing something other than working out whether or not, or how he should go about killing me. It had become though, for him, as if the gun incident had never even happened, but I wasn't about to forget his out burst of madness.

When we got to Darwin, he unexpectedly left me alone at the motel for an hour or three, while he went off to do 'whatever'. *(I didn't dare ask what it was that he wanted to do, in case he changed his mind, and shot me there and then, on the spot!).*

Once I had waited long enough to be sure that he was really gone though, I rang the police. They must have wondered what they had on the other end of the phone. The tension release when I got the police on the line, went flooding through my system, and I was burbling and gabbling, and tearfully recounting all that had happened. After a few questions from them, that made sure that *I* wasn't some sort of 'nutter', I was told that although they weren't sure if it was the same guy, there *was* a national arrest warrant out for a *Jeffrey Scott*. I belligerently repeated that the man that I had been with was called Gregory, but the Sergeant having asked me again to carefully describe the guy anyhow, continued, as quietly as he could. He had probably decided that it wouldn't be a good idea to alarm me too much. I may have been an accomplice testing out the lay of the land, or something. They really had no way of knowing, but he said that he thought that the fellow that had been with me in the car, might just be the man they were after? It appeared that he had the same scar! *(I can tell you now, that my stomach almost hit the floor!)* The Police had caught Mr Scott's partner, but they had only found half of the money, and they hadn't found Gregory *(Jeffrey)*.

"I wonder why", I succinctly thought? *("Now let me think. Could it possibly be that he was on his way to Darwin with one super frightened, totally innocent young woman beside him - me"?)* My legs became like wobbly jelly again.

"Ooo, I have just thought", I quiveringly said.

I told the Sergeant that Gregory had stuffed a black bag in one of those mail box things, back at a post office a little way back, in the last town. Greg had said that it was just some personal things, and that he would go back for it later.

"Maybe that is where he is now", I said to the Sergeant?

BACK TO NORMAL?

When a suspiciously silent pause permeated the phone call from his end, I quickly explained that I hadn't thought that romantic runaways should start out by questioning each other too much, especially as the female part of the couple *(me)* was definitely not a 'crook'.

"After all" I said - "With him in the mood that he was obviously in, I didn't want to rile him by my being too inquisitive, now did I"? Then I thought out loud on the phone, "ah ah, if it *was* the money that he had stuffed in the mail box, then it's no wonder that he hadn't been too worried about his finding work, or that he got SO upset about *my* work suggestion"!

"He no doubt thought that you could live somewhere, quietly, and that you both could have lived very comfortably on his share of the hold up money", said the copper.

"I swear, once I knew where the money had come from I would never have done that," I said over the phone, "and of course, at that time, when we had only just 'eloped' so to speak, and he hadn't yet tried to kill me, either, had he", I added!

"Oh, what have I done", I squealed down the receiver?

"Now, now, now. Calm down, you're safe now, the local police Sergeant's voice said, in an effort to settle the mad histrionic woman on the other end of the phone.

I organised for him and some of the constables from the squad to call by, and try to recapture Gregory later on that night when I knew that he was pretty sure to be back.

When I look back on it, it sounds super exciting, doesn't it? *(Pity it didn't feel that way back then)!* From memory though, I was positively petrified! My bowel movements must have been disrupted for weeks after. I can't remember too clearly, about 30 years and an accident later, but I think that it must have been about seven o'clock when he came back. Seven has always been one of my two lucky numbers, and it was definitely lucky for me that night!

The police had been to see me soon after the call, and they had organised for a constable to be outside in his unmarked police car. When he spotted Gregory's return, he was to quietly radio the guys inside the building, to tell them that the everyone should go on full alert. Unsuspecting of anything, he set off along the pavement, whistling to himself, and entered the building!

The Policemen waited for the silent count of 40, and then suddenly the two policemen who had been just inside of one of the two rooms at the top of the stairs, came swiftly out on to the internal landing, guns drawn. They crashed the doors open, and made enough noise to have woken the dead, but Gregory who was by then already half way up the first flight of stairs, hadn't seen them until it was too late. When he did see them, he immediately turned to run, but by that time the constable from the car outside, was coming up the stairs behind him, also with gun in hand. Gregory almost ran headlong in to it as he turned to get away! Suddenly, he was cornered. He took a sideways step attempting a leap to jump off the staircase, but got stuck half way. Three shots rang out, and Greg grabbed his stinging arm. There he was, straddled over the railing of three stairs, his legs all askew, *(just as I had imagined Winner, my dad's greyhound would have looked when it got that electric shock Carol and I had been laughing about!!)*

"***STOP!*** Jeffrey Scott, aka Gregory Adams. You are under arrest. You are not obliged to say anything, but what you do say, will be written down and used in evidence against you in a court of law!" I may not remember the exact wording, but I do remember that the ensuing noise in the apartment block lobby drew a myriad of spectators and inquisitive eyes from the other flats, and that at the sound of a gun going off, all the occupied room doors that had been sneakily opened to investigate, were hurriedly slammed shut again. Faces that had peered out when all the noise had been going on, had stuck their necks back behind the closed doors. Just like scared turtles?!

Thinking that all was clear, I came staggering further out of our room, trembling with fear. On looking around, other room occupants must also have realised that whatever was going on, had finished. They too had all come out, and it seemed as though there were dozens of worried people, looking on in amazement, and in awestruck wonder! They had probably never seen anything quite like it! Come to think of it, I don't think that I had ever seen anything like it either! *(It was enough to make me feel sick! It actually made my tummy turn!)* I don't ever wish to witness anything like it again! I guess that you could say that I was momentarily, instantly, cured of ever again wanting 'different'! I am here to tell you though, that although Greg had missed me with the gun, in the car *(whether intentionally or not, didn't really matter to me at that time)*, if looks could have killed, then I should have been dead on that floor.

Gregory looked up at me as I stood on the top landing, and he stood below, *(handcuffed and at pistol point)*, with the most vicious look of smouldering hatred that I have ever seen on another person's face. I don't think that I will ever forget the venomous flash that came from the man who had once cradled me in his arms, whispering words of love and endearment. To think that I had even found it cute to have been his 'pookie'! My stomach positively squirmed, both at the phrase, and again at my own stupidity. I ask you, "How could I have been so stupid? Yet again"!

The police took him away, and apart from that one more time later, at the police station, when I had to give my written statement, I never saw him again. I think he went to jail. At least I sure hope that he did! And once again, that probably sounds positively vindictive, but it's not really, it's just that, as much as I hate to admit it, prison would have been the safest place for a 'nutter' like him! I also hesitate to say it, but I wanted him as far away from me as possible! "What had I got myself into? What in heavens name had I thought I had been thinking?" If I had been 'thinking' at all!

I blithely, and unknowing of what the future had in store for me, again vowed that I would never actually go looking for anything 'different' again! *(I think that I must have figured that a touch of 'normal' mightn't be too bad after all!)*

Didn't get it though, did I? Why? Maybe you should keep reading and find out!

I had had the perfect future planned out with Harry, and I had well and truly stuffed it up! By now I should have been in the midst of the wedding preparations - ready to be married to a wonderful, definitely non gun toting man. I might even have been able to have the children that I knew Peggy and Charlie wanted so badly to see. I truly must have been really mentally 'out of it'. "And what's more", I sullenly mused, "I probably won't even be able to pursue my path to stardom now".

I would most definitely have thought, "it as sure as eggs doesn't look too likely now! Would I ever be forgiven? Why had I gone doo lally? What a stupid girl I've been"! *(And do you know what? To this very day, all these years, and the ups and downs of life later, I'm still not too sure how I survived! Having been so stupid, I mean!)*

However there were probably some, *(definitely not me though)*, who would say, that it was a bit unfortunate that I did! *(Survive, that is!)*

I finally went back to Sydney by plane, back home to Peg and Charlie with my tail tucked firmly between my legs. It was the first time that I had been back to their home to live since I had announced that I was leaving to live with Ed! *(and I think that I only stayed there for about three weeks.)* I had organised for my little blue Ford Escort car to come back by road train a few days after me. So as soon as it arrived, I was out looking for a flat. Well I didn't really feel like staying with mum and dad, and I couldn't move back with Harry, could I? Peg and Charlie were understandably truly disgusted with me, but refrained from saying too much about it all. They had never said very much about anything I had done since I had been about 18, but being my loving step-mum and dad, they kind of forgave me for being such a prat. As I said, they had called my real mum when I first disappeared, but apart from her helping them to calm down a bit, she had said that there was nothing she could do about it. "Kerrie is, after all too old now for too much parental control", she would have said, something like; "She hasn't, I don't think, broken any laws herself, so you'll just have to hope that she is alright. She is, after all no longer a child", "and you should be used to her doing mad things by now anyway. She has never been known to do things in the 'normal' way! There's not too much we can do about it, but pray that she is OK"!

(And I guess that they were used to my madness by then, I suppose! They had had to put up with a heck of a lot from me over the years!)

When I did get back to them though, their reticent wings provided me with the shelter I needed at that time, and what's more, it was without them asking too many questions either, which was very comforting. I was able to relax, and breath an humongous sigh of relief!

One of my earlier theatrical agents, who had been distraught at my having run off, and who had determinedly and very vocally been heard to say of me to his friends, "she will never work again"; Well he 'kind of' forgave me. I suddenly found myself with 'gigs' in my book again, from both him and other hungry for the commission involved, agents. I think the thought of that commission probably softened their moods a little, and for some obscure reason, it seemed that you made a much more interesting booking proposition when you had a touch of scandal attached to your name. *(Can't understand it myself! But there you go!)*

After about three weeks of my being back, Harry and I had tentatively made contact again. No kisses, hugs, or arms around each other or anything. Just apologetic floods of tears from me, and gentlemanly pseudo forgiveness from him. We both foolishly thought that we might at least try to give it another 'go'. Big mistake!

It was never the same again!

(Maybe the reason I can't cry now, is not just because of the accident, but also partly because I can't really 'deeply' feel things any more. I think that have probably wrapped my heart up in a protective cloak after the Darwin episode, and had cried up all my tears, and blocked out all my feelings then! You never know!)

Understandably enough it was very difficult, if not totally impossible for Harry to 'forgive and forget', and I felt so ashamed that I had done something so horrible. I was definitely not the best of company at all. I just couldn't relax, which made the sex, which had always been fantastic for us before, abysmal.

But then, poor love, neither could he, *(relax I mean)*, which only made the sex, even more, unbearably, super abysmal! *(Well, I mean to say, what else could I have expected?)* With neither of us relaxing, it was bound to be dreadful, wasn't it? He knew that I hadn't been a virgin when we had originally begun our love affair. He had known that I had been living with Ed, but for Harry now, I was definitely, and from his point of view anyway, totally 'unclean'! I can vividly remember almost feeling his body arching up, so as not to actually come in contact with my body. It was positively disastrous. Two people trying to make love without physically touching each other, just has to be seen to be believed! If it hadn't been so sad, it would have been almost laughable! We obviously broke up, and I was alone again! They do say though that he who travels fastest, travels alone, or something like that anyway, so even though I was, so to speak, without a permanent man friend, that didn't necessarily mean that I was alone!

Just as there were plenty of jobs to be done in those days, I unfortunately, or fortunately was never short of male friends to alleviate the so called boredom of being single!

I was also attracting some excellent jobs. I worked with the world famous Marty Feldman in a show called Marty Amok, in which I was able to garner a few tips for the comedy I started doing in my show a little later, and I also performed with, and had a song given to me by the legendary Frankie Laine.

Both of those excellent world wide performers provided me with some fantastic show guidance, and gave me some truly great memories that even the accident couldn't fully erase!

MIRROR TV With MATT WHITE

MARTY, KERRY SIGN UP TO RUN AMOK

1971

Kerry Dyer, a Sydney singer, and Marty Feldman, the English comedian, sign up with Actors' Equity to ensure no union problems with their show, Marty Amok, which opens in Canberra on January 19.

The show, which has a cast of 10 headed by Marty Feldman, will open in Sydney for four days at the Capitol Theatre on February 23.

Kerry was a Salvation Army lass, singing on street corners until she was 18. Later she won a heat in TV's New Faces and became a professional singer.

Marty Amok - Such a funny man – such BIG eyes!

Our Kerri is music to Frankie

Frankie Laine, the evergreen American singer doing the rounds of Sydney's clubs, has at last found the girl to record his favorite song — 15 years after it was written.

By WAYNE GREER

And the "girl with the perfect voice", according to Frankie, is Sydney singer Kerri Dyer.

Laine "discovered" Kerri last week when she was the supporting artist in his show at Ingleburn RSL.

"As soon as I heard her voice I knew she was the girl to sing the song," Laine said today.

"I've travelled the world for 15 years trying to find the right singer, and she's been right here in Sydney."

The song, Pretty Things, was written by the American jazz cel-

list Freddie Katz in 1964.

"It's a song about a country girl who moves to the city but falls into the trap of becom-ing a lady of the night," Laine said.

Laine's problem in finding the right singer was in the tune — a jazz waltz with high and low notes.

Kerrie, thrilled at Laine's gesture, said she had been looking for a song to make her first single.

He'd been looking for 15 years for someone who could sing Pretty things. He reckoned he had found her! I never got the chance to record it though!

I DO!

(well after all this madness - wouldn't you?)

Although my life went on to even greater things, if the situation with Harry hadn't been so sad, it would almost have been almost laughable! Luckily though, for me at least, we have remained friends, although I haven't seen him for about 20 years now. I am though, now excruciatingly happily, *(most of the time)* married to Ed, and living in England, but in the intervening years, Harry married, had kids, and made a lot of money. And again, as I have no doubt said before, maybe I should have stuck around in the first place. But then I was never into anything just for the money! More's the pity!

Unfortunately for him though, his first marriage didn't work out. He got divorced, but found a wonderful partner, and then married again. He and his new wife were both really happy last time I saw them. They were both at my Celebration of life party, and also at my wedding to Ed, in Sydney, Australia, after the accident. They really had a great life to celebrate! *(But more about that party a bit later as well.)*

Going back again though *(I'm sorry, but I did warn you that I write as I think – higgledy piggeldy?!), to* one day after the Darwin escapade, and after a few more years of my youthful 'singleness', getting in and out of all kinds of typical 'Dyer' dramas, I very unintentionally met the man that I was to marry for my first attempt at it. But this time there was definitely one thing for sure. I had seriously learnt my lesson about running away!!

(After all the dramas, I was by then 26 years of age, and I supposed, probably just about ready for marriage! Well, just about! I thought so, anyway!)

You would though think that by then I would have learned a thing or three about life, wouldn't you?! I mean to say, you would think that I would have known that a job was definitely the last place that I should have expected to find a long lasting, prospective husband.

A dalliance maybe, and yes there had still been a few of them, but definitely not the so called finality of a husband! *(And to be perfectly honest, I must confess that after all the dramas in my life thus far, I most definitely didn't think that I would find husband material at any of my jobs, and definitely not that club!! And as it turned out, I guess that maybe I was right!)*

One of my regular bookings, was a club that had remained faithful for a long time after my escapade with Darwin - South Sydney Leagues Club. *(I guess they must have liked my work.)* One particular evening, a couple of years after the Darwin fiasco, the cast and I were doing, what was laughingly called a 'special'. Probably because they were meant to be out of the ordinary, and I guess that in a way, that that particular show definitely was! Unbeknown to me when we began it, that show was to prove to be very out of the ordinary, very special, and very 'different'! For me at least!

We had just finished the first half of a boisterous rock and roll show, and there was me, after that hectic first half, looking very unglamorous, with sweat dripping down my neck and shoulders. All dolled up(?) in a big ruffled, red and white, large polka dot, skirt with dozens and dozens of petticoats. *(Both the polka dots and the skirt were very huge)* Fluffy, curly pigtails stuck out of the side of my sweaty head, and my lips were a shiny, vivid, moist looking red slash across a face that was heavily made up. The perspiration had definitely mucked up, and streaked my make up. So much so, that I must have looked a little like an old bedraggled rag doll. A dolly that had had her face left all lopsided and smeared by the loving owner when they tried *(and failed?)* to glamorize the dolly up a bit!

At interval time, I was very hot and bothered, and in desperate need of a drink, so with a tongue that felt like a piece of furry sandpaper, I was just tramping off to the bar when a relative of the then manager, someone whom I hadn't seen before, sidled up beside me. and calmly, but firmly crept an arm around my waist. I stopped dead in my tracks, and he said to me, hugging me in close, and then whispering in my ear in a 'trying to be sultry, sexy?' kind of voice;

"Hi, my name is Andy, you're Kerri Dyer aren't you? I just caught your first show, fantastic it was too," he said. "A cool girl like you *(grin, grin with lots of clean white, pearly teeth, and a waft of some 'trying to be exotic' after shave)*, could probably do with a 'cool' drink". I cringed at his 'line', and his naff approach, and winced as I wriggled from his grasp. "Not again", I laughingly thought to myself - "wow what an original line. *Not!* " But straight away *(and typical of me)*, I thought!- "what a good looking man".

"Ding, Dong, Ding, Do -oong!!!!!

Those warning bells, that had had no disaster alerts to warn me about for a good while, *(not since the Darwin escapade anyway)*, had been enjoying a restful time, and there had been nothing to be overly worried about for quite a while, because I hadn't *(unusually for me)* been overly interested in giving up my personal space, on even a semi permanent basis for anyone of interest. That is except of course for the occasional night out, with the good feed, and the odd bottle of good wine thrown in.

I think that they called them - 'one night stands'! But it was as if someone had prodded those there bells awake, and they began to chime out, loud and strong in my head!

"I don't believe it", said me to myself. "Where did you come from bells"? Lines like the ones he had just used, had always led to problems for me before, but once again, there was just that odd 'something'; didn't quite know what it was, but I was genuinely entranced. Was it maybe that dreaded 'different' again?

As you probably would have guessed by now, apart from the possibility of an enjoyable 'that', I had always been a bit of a 'sucker' for good looks, and he was just *so* good looking, and me being me, I fell heart first into his unseen trap! Talk about being fished by a 'gossamer' net again! *(and this time it wasn't even me doing the fishing!)*

Even though those protective(?) bells hadn't given up, and were still peeling out something shocking, typical of me at the time I hadn't paid the slightest bit of attention. Normally I would have been up for almost anything on a short time span, and so as far as I was concerned there was no real necessity for the bells. Well after all, why should I pay too much attention? I was young, affluent enough by then, had supposedly learned my lessons, and had spent a couple of years being good after the dramas of Darwin, *(depending of course, by whose assessment of good, and affluent, you were judging!)*. But according to my assessment of matters,I was definitely in a 'good' place. Work was plentiful again, exciting and fun, I had recovered enough from my hurts, and I was by then, ready and up for another round of fun!

the day before the accident!

I also said to myself –

'You can't make an omelet without breaking a few bad eggs!'

Not that that really had anything to do with it, but I said it anyway!

I guess, that I will always be a bit of a nut!

I figured though that I had just about had my share of 'bad', and that this one definitely looked like he would come under the classification of 'good'. So it was a case of 'here we go again'! And then I lovingly thought, "He is just like a red haired 'Adonis', and I have again unfortunately(?) always been a sucker for redheads"! So, as he looked like being of the 'good' category for a change, I shamefully took him! He though, if he were around as I write this, would probably say that *he* took *me!* And if I were honest about it, he was super good at it, and he probably did too!

Now, although there would probably be an abundance of people from the showbiz world of that time, who would have agreed with me that "I had a thing for red headed good looking men", there would also have been others who would have said *(and they would probably have been just as right as well!)*, that I just had a thing for men, period! The almost unbelievable thing was that I who had been in the show business world, doing some really scatty things, for what some people would have said was definitely long enough, should have, again, known better. Having made all the mistakes I had, I should definitely have known better than to 'go there'. But did I? What? know better? No fear! Not me! I went there anyway, didn't I?!

I knew of the problems that could be the result of meetings like this one, and as you have read, I had already suffered quite a few heartaches along the way because of my susceptibility to good looks and that something 'different' about some men. As it turned out, Andy was definitely 'different', lusciously, sexily so, for a while at least! *(Now, that too must be another comment that rings familiar? ['For a while at least'!])*

I not all that reluctantly really, gave in to my 'not better' nature, and allowed him to 'take me out' a few times. After a few more weeks, of being wooed by that full of suavity, and Irish blarney man, he had not only become my new, bestest find to date, *(better even than Gregory)*, but he very quickly became the then 'love of my life'. We moved in together. Again, quick moving you reckon? *(Well - You should know by now, from what you have read, that I had never been one that took their time about anything, especially not when it came to men! I mean to say. If you took your time, then they might get away before you could have any fun with them, mightn't they?!)*

I must confess though that I did think to myself at the time, "Oh heavens, not again. You know Kerri, you must really be a bit of a glutton for punishment!" But as I have said before, in those halcyon days, it had already become quite the 'norm' for people to move in together, and at least this time, it was after all, *my* place that we were moving into, not his, or his parents'! I found out fairly soon after he moved in though that he had recently broken up with the mother of his little girl, and had been living at home ever since, with his very lovely Catholic mother, sister and brother.

(An unmarried, Catholic Dad? I should have heeded the warning!) What was I thinking of? Mind you - *Some* girls never learn do they? And up to that date I guess that you might say that I had unfortunately, been an elite member of the 'some' club. We just 'lived' together *(in my place)* for about a whole year! *(again - naughty, naughty!)* But that love of my life, was not only a 'different' kind of man, but he was also to become my first husband! All legal and everything!

(Unfortunately, there will be only two photos of what was a truly magnificent wedding. My dress and the car! The man is still alive, and it just wouldn't be fair to him, nor his family!!)

I felt just like a fairy princess

But everybody was to be there *(at the wedding)*. Dad, my step-mum, and after not having seen my blood mother for about five years, and after my having cheekily rung to ask if my half sister would be my bridesmaid, along with Angela Ayers *(a fellow entertainer)*, my real mum came as well, as one of the two mothers of the bride! - My two youngest half brothers were ushers at the wedding, and everyone looked fantastic. I had the full works, and the showbiz genes in my body, absolutely reveled in all the 'fol de rol'.

The wedding service itself was beautiful. A typical Catholic wedding service, it was. All religiously correct, with everyone being suitably pious, and yet celebrative. The fact that we had been living together for almost a whole year, was put to one side, and not mentioned on the lead up to, nor on, the day! We weren't too sure how that would actually have gone down with everyone, but because Andy's family were all Catholics, we were signed up for some counseling because I wasn't a catholic, and the priests agreed to marry us in the Church. When I was getting ready to walk down the aisle, my daddy all dressed up in a smart suit and tie, the first new one that he'd had on for about 20 years, smiled a big toothless smile. I momentarily thought, "oh bugger! I still haven't gotten around to having his teeth fixed! Soon though, I promise daddy!" I guess that because I wanted everything to be right, that I was probably being very mean on the day! I wouldn't let him have a 'fag', not even for his nerves, *(I didn't want a half squashed 'roll up' hanging out of his mouth, staining his already stained lips, now did I?)*

they were both SO proud!

He had looked so smashing as he took my arm and then proudly, and majestically walked me down to meet my waiting groom. There stood Andy, at the business end of the aisle, grinning in a 'mock' state of timidity. Peg was on one side of the aisle, all rigged up in her especially bought for the occasion, from a catalog, dress, coat and hat; with my real mum and my favourite uncle on the other side.

My two best mates, from Greenacre, a brother and sister, Robert and Carol - *(You remember - the wooden crate stages in the street, and the charity shows!)* were responsible for the whole catering side of the thing. They had both, a little while before, been married *(obviously not to each other)*, to two other friends of mine. The man Carol had married had been one of my earlier just boyfriends, and the girl that Robert *(who had also been one of my non sexual conquests)* had married was part of our 'box crate' entertainment group! *(A close knit little group, we were!)* The two couples had started up a catering business together, so I, of course, commissioned them to handle the reception for us. Sort of like 'keeping it in the family' you might say!

Three individual hearts overlapping, made the most original, and beautiful wedding cake that I have ever seen, but then I guess that I might have been just a wee bit biased! One heart for Andy, one for me, and one for the families and friends. Beautiful!!! *(the families and friends rightly ate a lot more than the one section of the cake though, I can assure you.)* There were just so many people there. It was a real humdinger of a wedding! Even then I wasn't about to do things small. I wanted 'different' in a big way, and feel a bit ashamed to admit it; but I generally got it!

The car was 'different' too!

The outrageous car decorations!

I think that Robert and Carol had been partly responsible for the outrageous car decoration! It was a typical 70's decoration, with the car completely covered in shaving cream, and with normal wedding messages like 'make love not war' written across the rear window and - 'Just married' sprayed across the boot! Grinning from ear to ear, Peggy and Charlie probably heaved a big sigh of relief when the wedding had actually taken place. Charlie got to have a smoke, at last, and he even raised a celebratory glass. At last he had safely married off his only daughter. He and Peg had disposed of what they possibly considered, damaged goods. They had done their best, but had maybe done too good a job of teaching me to be independent! They had though, very diligently tried to teach me through all my chaotic relationships, that it was important for people to stay together, even if things weren't perfect! They told me, and I guess showed me, that it was paramount to share your life with someone who would stick by you, through thick and thin. They figured that although I'd mucked it up the first time, with Harry, and had scampered off to get hurt in Darwin, they could now relax, and wait for the patter of little grand children feet. They figured that I'd be safe, and that they would find their dreams and aspirations for me fulfilled! They had obviously been a bit worried when I was, what they had called, 'gallivanting about', and after having been a bit suspicious of his motives at first, Peg and Dad had positively grown to love Andy! By their sticking by each other through all kinds of hardship and poverty for nigh on 25 years, they had battled through a lot of miserable times, with only the occasional bouts of good ones. In a truly unconventional way, they had actually, given me a practical example of how it is supposed to be done, even though they themselves hadn't actually been able to be married! I had a chance now to show them that I too had found my mate! *(Little did I know at the time!)*

I had at least though, been able to show them how wonderful I thought they were, before the accident happened. A little while after I got married, I had thrown a 'bonza' celebration party for them at a club, with a whole lot of showbiz people and stars there, along with some of their own friends, *(and didn't they love that! Mum and dad, not necessarily the stars and things though)*! Peg was in her element, in another specially bought for the occasion, tailor made dress! Dad enjoyed playing 'mogul' in his wedding suit. I think that I even bought him a great big, fat cigar for the occasion. *(No fag ends that day!)* How different life could have been for them!

Peg had suffered, and put up with dad's gambling, and his bouts of drinking, but as I said they must have got on, and to have had a little girl to bring up, as well as a little man, was evidently worth any hardships that Peg had encountered. They must have either loved, or happily put up with each other right to the end, because they had stayed together, known as Mr and Mrs, for those 25 years, and that's a long time, in anyone's book! A lot of 'hunky dory' marriages don't last that long, do they?

But married or not, Peg and Charlie's love was definitely till 'death do us part', and a very sad parting it turned out to be for them! Peg had loved Charlie's little girl, me, to bits, and at the time, I was to be the baby she couldn't have herself due to the same medical problem that also caused her excessive obesity. She had opted for a de-facto relationship, a long time before they had even become fashionable.

One of the most miserable things about the way my life turned out, is that Peggy never got to meet her granddaughter. She would have absolutely smothered her with love, and been just *so* happy! But again, looking back, I suppose in one way that it's lucky that Peg and Charlie weren't around for too much of the 'hospital trauma', for the 'getting better' dramas, or for when Andy and I finally got divorced. I think though that they would be stoked now though to know that my first 'older man', teenage love, is the man I am more than happily married to today, and that he took on a newly unmarried, wounded soldier, who had become a disabled mother with child. He has looked after both of us super well, and again I reckon that it's a case of 'what goes around, comes around'? I must have done something good sometime in the past, and there was possibly some small part of good, done in amongst all my gallivanting. I really don't know, but I am just so glad these days!

But, as I said before, *(goodness, as I said; I am scatty!)* back to the story -

Andy and I had only been actually married, wait for it, just over 6 months, when the accident that changed my life, happened. Well, alright - 8 months, but what's 2 months between friends. It was close enough to that dreaded 6 month time scale that seems to have haunted my life, from the year dot! The 6 month thing, seems to have followed me around a lot over the years. A bit eerie, isn't it?

Peggy and Charlie brought me up to try to understand both sides of a situation where I could. At the time, just after I had come out of the four and a half month coma that I had been in, I was still 'out of it a bit'. Actually, probably a bit more than a bit. I guess you could say that the subtleties of the situation Andy found himself in, hadn't really impinged on my sensibilities. It took long enough for me to recognize him as my husband even. So the problems that he had incurred, hadn't really made sense to me until much later, when it was too late for me to have done anything about them anyway! *(I couldn't, unfortunately, undo the accident, nor the way in which I reacted to things!)*

I was just *so* preoccupied with my own problems of survival and readjustment, and what is more, I have to admit, that I was sometimes truly objectionable due to the effects of the brain stem damage sustained in the accident. I have subsequently read that it is a fairly normal reaction in a marriage where the husband has to watch the lady that he married, change right before his very eyes, and yet find himself unable to do anything about that change. I think that the fact that he had been driving the car at the time of the accident, might also have played a huge part in what was to happen next! There was probably a degree of a sense of guilt. I don't really know, but there shouldn't be any more! Everything happens for a reason! What that reason might be, often remains a mystery. It had been though, as if during the time that I had been unconscious, a whole hoard of those same '*devilish* gremlins' that had been corrupting my life before, had suddenly, for some obscure reason, decided that they had best become surreptitiously, 'caringly protective'.

It seems to me as though they had rushed about like the mad things that they were, putting a stack of plugs anywhere they would go. Anything, to keep the girl alive. It appears to me now, that I must have had 'gremlins for almost everything'! *(And as it turns out, thank goodness for it!)* Once I had come round, and their original goal of keeping me alive had been achieved, I sometimes found myself reacting disproportionately to something that I wasn't meant to react to at all. And then sometimes when I *was* supposed to react, I couldn't. *(Or wouldn't! More often than not, the second one!)* Mind you, there would most definitely have been some people who would have said to Andy, about me; "Well you shouldn't really expect Kerri to always do as you ask you know Andy. You yourself say that she was always a bit of a 'stubborn bugger', doing what she, alone figured was right for her". Others said, "Oh, you mean Kerri Dyer. She was always searching for love and attention".

(Oh, so that's why I had the accident is it?! Attention? I don't think so; do you?)

Oh jot! I do get side tracked, don't I? Again – I am so, so sorry!

Let's get back to the story though, shall we! Now where was I?

Can't really remember, and it would take me ever so long to track back through my writing, so we'll just go back to my showbiz diary eh? Yeah – that's what we'll do!

My showbiz career had been 'managed' by a wide gambit of theatrical agents over the 9 and a bit years that I had been working. I had thankfully performed in just about every kind of venue. Some bad, and some exceptionally good, but most were either sort of OK, or abysmally horrible.

My last agent, well and truly after my escapades to Darwin, had brought me to the notice of those people who could really do something positive to further a person's career. I think that they figured that it might just be a trifle late for a 27 year old, and I think that I had only been with them in a personal management way, for about 6 months *(there's that magic time period again)*. For the 6 months before that, I had been with them just as one of my booking agents. I had managed myself at that time! But they had been doing a wonderful job of getting my talents noticed by the 'right' people during the time just prior to the accident. Older talents weren't necessarily the flavor of the day back in 1979, but Warren Smith and Associates had made a very positive move towards getting me and my talents, under the noses of anyone *(generally already stars themselves)* that could help further my career. Because I had been popular with audiences and managements around Sydney and interstate for such a long time, Warren had to acknowledge my ability, but he did say however that I was just a 'tad' whale like. *A tad whale like!*

'Really', what girl in her right mind wants to be told that? I mean to say!

'A tad whale like'? Now I ask you! Did I smell fishy? Did I have a blow hole?

The best classical diva's were generally always on the large size, but as Warren very succinctly told me *(and I guess that I had to agree)*, I was definitely not singing classically, and I would not have been classed as a diva at that stage! He and his partner Carol had also told me that for my own ambitions to be reached, I would need to go on a diet! Full of self protective ego, and much to my shame, I screamed at them - "But I am

213

not fat". *(Self denial?)* But I guess that I was! And it wasn't the first time that I had had to really face the realities of what was needed to succeed in the way in which I wanted to succeed. I had to assure myself, and Warren and his partner that I was prepared to do almost anything to achieve stardom! It would require a lot of their time and effort, and they didn't want to be wasting time with someone who wasn't truly serious about achieving those goals.

But I didn't really understand any more, what I had to do! I had actually already tried to lose weight once or twice before, but had failed. This time however, I was super determined that things were going to be a bit 'different'! After all I didn't want to just get on any more - I wanted to be a star! I seemed though, to hear those damning words at semi regular intervals

So there was me, running around the large Maroubra blocks at 6a.m. in the morning, in a tiny pair of shorts, with my almost obese thighs squeazingly peeking out of them. "Do I hear you ask why so early in the morning"?

Well, I didn't want anyone to see me heaving and sweating as I bumbled and stumbled around the blocks, did I? I mean to say, a girl has to have *some* pride, doesn't she, even if she is told she is fat? I was trying hard, and after all the hard work, and the running around the blocks, my obese thighs were getting more sexy looking, at least I thought so! By that time I was also going to a gym four days a week, having the dance classes and also doing elocution lessons to lessen the ever so slight Aussie tinge of an accent that I had. Warren had told me that although I had a basic raw talent, it was just that! *RAW!* "There is still plenty of work to do for you to organise your talent, and reach your desired goal". I will never forget those words, but somehow I had a feeling that I had heard them before. And do you know? I had!

Ed had told me the same thing about working on the raw talent, years before at the Become a Star Studio, but then I had been a svelte, definitely not 'whale like', teenager. Ed had also told me all that stuff about ticking the right boxes too, when I had been going to his Studio. It seemed to me though, as if that had been a million years before. I had taken it in sufficiently enough then to enable me to actually get started on the circuit, but then, you know, once the enjoyment of the showbiz whirl took over, I must have put all that knowledge in the 'I'll get around to it sometime soon drawer' or something. (*as you do!)* It seemed then though, that that 'sometime soon' had suddenly arrived. Probably a bit later than it should have, but it appeared that it was time to maybe find that drawer, and set about ticking the right boxes on a more regular, decisive and organised basis! That I was working a lot, and that the audience reactions were great, didn't necessarily mean that I *was* always ticking all the right boxes, and Warren had told me as well, that I now had to learn how to be a bit more of a 'lady' on stage. ???? "No more 'smokos'" *(all men Sunday morning shows),* he said. "A bit more careful selection of the proffered jobs, and of your stage clothes, is what is needed my girl"!! Yippee said me about the smokos *(can't say that I particularly liked doing them any way),* but it would necessarily mean a slight reduction in weekly income at first. I was told though, that it would pay off handsomely in the long run. *(Or so I was assured, and I guess that in some obscure kind of way, I suppose that it eventually has!)*

With the abundance of work I was still allowed to do, and with the necessary expenditure on extra vocal practice, my voice had improved, even beyond my, and Eds expectations. My wages had also suddenly been decidedly advanced again. My fee had risen to *(again remember, this was still only 1978)* $190 / $225 per show, and according to my book, some jobs were even in at $885 for a three day stint of individual shows. Astronomical figures for a girl such as I! Some of the leading artists were, of course earning much more, but I was out there doing the same venues, and I was chasing them fee wise, and often, even doing better on the same jobs than some! Towards the end, even on some Sundays, I would earn $600, in that one day. I was earning considerably more than a lot of the other 'non name' club talent in Sydney in those days. I was no longer doing Sunday morning smokos, but sometimes I was doing a 2.15pm Sunday show, and even an 8 o'clock night show.

I couldn't believe it! *(I have been told that unfortunately it's not like that these days though!)* Again though, my bank balance, had the effect of convincing me! Warren's comments had shamed me into action, and I seemed now to be forever in rehearsals etc. for shows in large venues like South Sydney Juniors, Revesby Workers Club, and a multitude of prominent interstate venues.

I was also being nominated for the prestigious MO awards. Twice! When it had been the Variety Awards but even more importantly when it became the MO's.

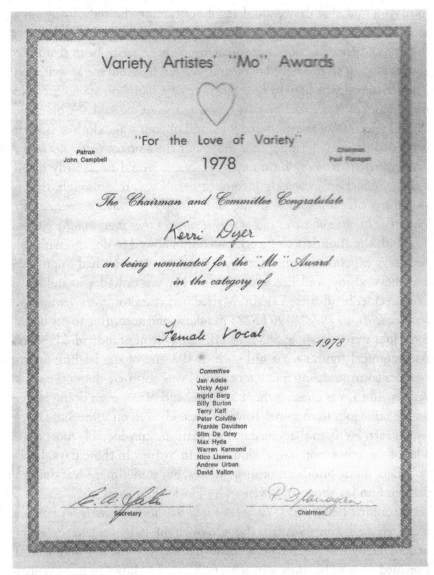

Variety Artistes' "Mo" Awards

"For the Love of Variety"

Patron
John Campbell

Chairman
Paul Flanagan

1978

The Chairman and Committee Congratulate

Kerri Dyer

on being nominated for the "Mo" Award in the category of

Female Vocal *1978*

Committee
Jan Adele
Vicky Agar
Ingrid Berg
Billy Burton
Terry Kaff
Peter Colville
Frankie Davidson
Slim De Grey
Max Hyde
Warren Kermond
Nico Lisena
Andrew Urban
David Vallon

Secretary

Chairman

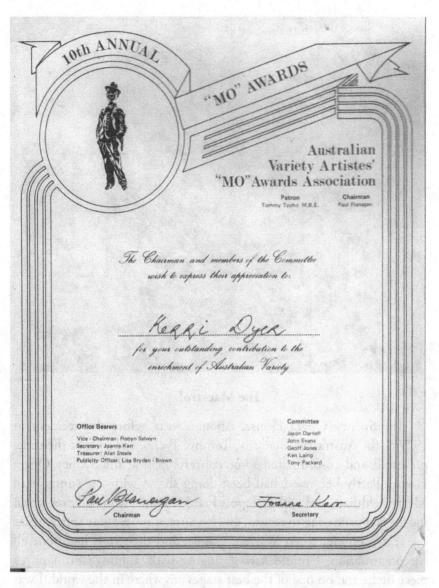

10th ANNUAL
"MO" AWARDS

Australian
Variety Artistes'
"MO" Awards Association

Patron   Chairman
Tommy Tycho M.B.E.   Paul Flanagan

*The Chairman and members of the Committee
wish to express their appreciation to:*

Kerri Dyer

*for your outstanding contribution to the
enrichment of Australian Variety*

Office Bearers

Vice - Chairman: Robyn Selwyn
Secretary: Joanne Kerr
Treasurer: Alan Steele
Publicity Officer: Lisa Bryden - Brown

Committee

Jason Darnell
John Evans
Geoff Jones
Ken Laing
Tony Packard

Paul Flanagan
Chairman

Joanne Kerr
Secretary

(So I guess that the shame that I had been submitted to, had paid off!) But then came the most prestigious gig of all time, on home turf, and it made me positively ecstatic.

The Maestro!

The Sydney Opera House. About a year before the accident in 1977/8, the Australian 'maestro', Tommy Tycho, not a Sir at the time, produced and co-ordinated some concerts held at the Sydney Opera House. Partly because I had been doing shows with the funny man Marty Feldman, and with the great Frankie Laine, who had even given me his favourite song to record, and because of my regular appearances on Television etc, when Warren, Carole, and their staff had done all the organisation, I found myself singing with Tommy's brilliant 44 piece orchestra, on one of the best stages anywhere in the world. I was working with some of the crème de la crème of Australian Talent, and what is more, I was more than 'holding my own'. I couldn't believe it, and Peg and Charlie, who were chauffeured in to see the shows, were ecstatic!

To be chauffeured in, in an enormous limo, especially to see their little girl perform at the Sydney Opera House, was more than Peg and Charlie could ever have imagined for me, or them. Dad had, of course, made a substantial amount of noise, letting the neighbours know of the arrival of the 20 foot limo. Not that you could have missed it anyway! It was a most unusual sight in our Greenacre street, and a magnificent achievement on my part that had made them super proud!

It was much more than I could ever have dreamed of achieving at that time.

I may have thought all my Christmases had come at once, and that I had finally made it when I had seen my name in 50ft lights across the Indonesian hotel, but now, Warren and his staff were most decidedly looking after my 'book' really well indeed. I felt that 'stardom' was just around the corner! I suddenly felt again that all my Christmases, but this time with all the Easters, and Birthdays as well, had landed on my lap!

soaking up the atmosphere of the room.

BIG BREAK

Having managed to lose the weight and thus supposedly looking 'good', I found myself doing quite a range of good television shows. Not that there were very many bad television shows at that time anyway, and because Variety programs were the flavour of the day *(just as they were in Britain, in 2006-8 – and are again in 2009/10)* everyone and anyone watched them. Most fortunately for me, my talents were placed before the producers of some of the biggest concerts both in Sydney and nationally. I was even getting to the stage of sometimes commanding $1000.00 - $1800.00 per week. But the most exciting, and thrillingly unbelievable thing was still to come. My stint at the Opera House, and the high television exposure had also bought me to the attention of the producers of the soon to begin Australian production of Evita.

Due to her own hectic entertainment schedule, Elaine Paige couldn't do the Sydney season of the hit musical, so they needed an Australian replacement.

"Yippee", says me. "I can do that", I self assuredly must have said to myself.

I had done my school girl trick of actually already having started learning, and practicing songs from the show. I had been thinking about doing an 'Evita' medley in my club show anyway! The news of their possibly looking for an Australian Evita hadn't even been made public before then, but always having to be on the improve with my own club show, and needing to stay one step ahead so to speak, as I said

I had been thinking of incorporating a medley of the songs from the then very popular, overseas show in my repertoire anyhow. The Movie of 'EVITA' was yet to come, about three or four years later I think, but the London stage show was the talk of Sydney entertainment circles at that time, and underground news of possible auditions for the Sydney production had reached all the possibly interested people.

So Warren had again done all the following up, *(I mean that is what he was paid that extra percentage for, wasn't it!)* and I evidently went off to the auditions. I don't really recall how I got to them, where they were or very much about them *(my TV shows, and word of mouth would probably had played a big part in the auditions)*, but knowing me, I must have been super confident of getting the part. I'd learned by that time that you ended up with nothing, if you didn't go in sure of getting something and anyway, in those days, but come to think of it, in just about any days, I thought like the words of the song said - "I'm the Greatest Star, I am by far, but no one knows it"! Then as I am sure I told you before, I used to cheekily add, yet! *(I would deal with rejection if and when it came, IF it did! And do you know what? After all this time, because I haven't wanted to admit the loss of my voice, even to me, it was really only in 2007 that I was starting to sing again. It required a lot of work, and now in 2010, I sing primarily for my own satisfaction these days, but I still think that 'I'm the greatest star' sometimes!)* Sick eh?

Odd bits of auditions where I would sing with other girls vying for the part, will occasionally flash through my mind, and it must have seemed that at last, judging by what I have been told of the events, that the speculation and investment I had made in myself, looked as if it was really about to pay off, *big time!* It appeared that all the hard work done by everyone was getting ready to bear fruit! There must have been such an air of excitement among the contenders!

(I really do wish that I could remember it better! But hey - at least I have 'been there, done that'!)

And anyway, knowing me I was probably in a bit of a mental quandary. Never really having been, deep down, overly confident of my own abilities, desperation would definitely have set in as with the other shows and things I had done over the years. I had always thought that I was/might just be good enough, but would they think so? Although my TV performances would probably have been enough to get me through the first stages of the auditions, it was probably a little like the Pop Idol, or X Factor auditions, or the Sound of Music, and Britain's got Talent auditions that were held in England not long ago, positively nail bitingly exciting!

(But for all the excitement, I never even got to go to the show to watch the girl who eventually took the part. I was still too unwell when the run started, and the show had unfortunately ended by the time I was well enough to stagger out to the theatre.)

But they do tell me that she 'done good', even though the show apparently didn't last all that long. I did though see the Movie of Evita, having taken years to steel up the courage to watch even that. Having seen it, I decided *(and some might say that this comment is my protection mechanism kicking in)*, that I would possibly have been a bit too tall for the part anyway. I don't think that they would have wanted a 5 foot 7 inch, red haired Eva Péron, do you? The red hair I already had, but they would probably have needed to cut a rut in the stage, so that I could work down it, or else have had a super tall Juan Péron, and from memory, he was not a tall man in real life. I must have thought at the time though, again as the words of another song say - *'it could have been me'!* Oh well!

But back in 1979, while they were still deciding who would take the lead in the proposed show, one day in mid to late July, I had evidently excitedly run into Eds studio, and I was just about yelling with the excitement of it all - "I think I've done it! I think I got the part"!

Luckily for all concerned, it was in between his teaching sessions, and there was no one else there. He grabbed me by the shoulders in an attempt to get me to stop bouncing about, and slow me down a bit so that he could make out what I was trying to gush out. Ed tells me now, that back then, I was evidently almost screaming with the excitement of it all. "I think I got it! "But it's a secret for a while, so please don't tell anyone", I had said excitedly.

"Tell anyone what? How can I tell anyone what I don't know yet! Got what"? he retorted, bemusedly. He obviously didn't have the foggiest idea of what I was yelling about, and so I evidently told him through a mouthful of excited gurgle. "I think you already know that I am in the final five contenders for the part of Evita in the stage musical", says me positively wriggling with excited tension. He nodded bemused agreement. "My international career is assured" I had said, jumping up and down again.

Poor Ed still wouldn't have known what I was on about, but evidently, he politely watched me carrying on, unable to keep myself still. "I think I got it, I think I got the part", I kept saying! I must have been so excited!

The selectors for the part of Evita had whittled it down from the available contenders to a hundred or so - then fifty. It got to twenty - and then with the help of video clips, it got down to the final five girls, suitable. All five of us would have been super excited about the prospect of actually getting the part. The prospect of my being a star, even though I had always craved it like 'billy oh', was quickly becoming a frightening, almost reality. Having always been a bit of a gossip monger, especially when the rumours had anything to do with me, I was absolutely bursting with the gossip I had heard, and as was pretty typical for me at the time, *(and to be perfectly honest - I guess at 'any time'),* I inevitably took it as 'unofficial' news. *(Well wouldn't you?)*

Now, I knew that Ed disapproved of gossip, and that he was bound to pooh, pooh the information, but I just had to tell someone, or I would positively burst! I had of course already told Andy, but with his being a typical, non-musical husband, even though he would probably have been excited in his own way, his reaction wouldn't have been quite the same as that of my mentor, Mr Keen. And by that time, we were definitely not involved in any way, other than instructor, pupil! I can't be sure of the exact words, but the following is written just as erratically as I must have recounted it to Ed at the time.

"Just listen to this" I would have said. "You know that I have made a lot of friends in this business"

"Yes", said Ed, frowning. *(He has never been in the business of acquiring 'friends'. Too much like hard work, he reckons!).* I prattled on.

"Well one of my 'sort of' friends, is also a 'sort of' friend to my best friend."

"Got it", he said - "Yeah - I ----- think"!

Good", says me, butting in quickly. "But there's more"!

"And what's that", he asked, frowning, probably thinking - "I wish she would hurry up, my students are late but will probably arrive any minute!"

I continued on. "Well this person who is a 'sort of' friend to me, and also the 'sort of' friend of my best friend as well, is also the 'lover' of one of the final assessment panel members for Evita. My best friend's 'sort of' friend, who, by the way, knows nothing of her friend's friendship with me, told my best friend in confidence *(snigger, snigger)*, that the panel of assessors for the show *(Evita)* had just about made their decision".

A pregnant pause ensued! I wasn't sure quite how Ed was taking this phenomenal news, especially as there were a lot of 'sort of''s, and 'best friends', and he generally frowned on any information garnered in this way. I was though, just so excited by it all, that I went on anyway!

"Well - my best friends' other 'sort of' friend, had evidently been told in the middle of some 'pillow talk' with her lover, you know, the one who is on the assessment panel, and then again in general conversation, that it looked like the panel had decided, and that after a lot of 'umming and aarring' were thinking seriously about calling back, and after checking it out a bit more, offering the part to a singer called 'Kerri Dyer'".

My best friends 'sort of' friend wouldn't have had even the slightest of inklings that when she passed on the news to her 'sort of friend, that that 'sort of friend's' 'best friend', *('me')* would also learn before the news was even supposed to go out there. I guess that you could have said that that 'sort of' friend was inadvertently about to let the possible winner of the part know before it was even to be announced publicly.

But – I'll tell you what! Talk about my being 'gob smacked'!

My chin must have very nearly hit the floor.

(I might add that that piece of nonsensical sentence formation is just typical of the excitement that I was feeling at the time!)

"Ooh! - Can you believe it", I excitedly said to Ed, jumping about like a mad thing as he just unbelievingly stood and gaped at me. But you must promise to tell no one"! "The restrictions she made me promise to, in her exact words I might add, were 'you must tell no one'. Now, I know you're not 'no one', but I figured that I could safely tell *you*. You though must give me your promise, as I did to her, that you'll keep it a secret, and that you also will 'tell no one'!

I know that you are better at keeping secrets than I am. Too many 'nice' people will get into humongous big trouble, if you are not". Just don't run into anyone called 'no one', 'cause then you'll have to tell them! Then suddenly I was rolling about at the humour of my own joke, just as I had done with Carol, at school. *(Stupid things amuse stupid minds I guess!* "Tell no one!" Then I think I said - "Get it! - *NO ONE!* - Got it? Good! Ha Ha ha"!

You know, I can just see myself, carrying on a right treat! *(Such was the idiot that I was, but I was just so excited!)* I guess that my friend, who also had been told, with strict instructions, to tell no one, would have known how drastically my acrylic nail extensions would have suffered while I had anxiously awaited the news. *(Chewed and mangled fingernails are definitely not a good look!)* Good, or bad news, it didn't *really* matter, *(much)*, but she knew that I would have preferred good news. Even if it was a 'no go', and I had missed out. I would just have had to wipe my tears, and try again with another show. As far as I was concerned, I was going to be a 'Star', and that was all there was to it! *(Even if it was a bit late in my life!!)* I had though, been given the bestest of news, and it was made even more special for me, because it had come from my bestest of showbiz friends. It definitely, after all those years of hard work, looked as if all my speculation was really about to provide the most unimaginable accumulation that I had been hoping for, and as I mentioned before, I had actually already started learning and practising songs from the show anyway. Now it looked as if I might be playing the role for real! "I am going to be playing Evita", I yelled from the end of the room!

Ooo! Such excitement!

Unfortunately, as I said I don't remember much about them, if anything at all *(the auditions I mean)*, but knowing me though, also as I have no doubt said, I must have been super confident of getting the part. I generally was super confident! They, and Carol and I did say - 'nothing ventured - nothing gained'.

I though was about to venture into the 'big time.

I wondered if the same rules applied there!

29th July, 1979

A friend of both Eds and mine, John T. had arrived at the Studio for his lesson, and he and Ed found themselves having a very strange, and mixed up conversation. John was also a student of Eds, and a lover of mine once from a time before he got married. It's fairly understandable, from what you have read, when I say that he was also a fellow Entertainer. Most of the men in my life were!

John had asked if Ed had heard about Kerri, giving no indication at all of what Ed was or was not supposed to have heard!

Ed said no! *(keeping his promise to me?)* They almost came to blows because of their wibbly, wobbly conversation, where neither of them knew what the other was really talking about. Eds last words had evidently been "they were not supposed to announce it until next week". "Announce it? Announce it? Announce what"?, said John, "what are you talking about Ed"?

"'*It*', whatever '*it*' is, doesn't need to be announced" said John crossly, *"it's all over the front page of the paper!"*.

Then with some disgust, he threw Ed the national paper he had been reading. And sure enough, - there it was - in bold, front page type -

EVITA HOPE UNCONSCIOUS AFTER CAR ACCIDENT.

Ed's jaw just about dropped to the floor, and in a studio that was normally ringing with singing, piano, and happy jovial chatter, you could have cut the silence with a knife!

227

Suddenly John sorrowfully realised what had been going on. Ed hadn't known after all! He mustn't have seen a paper, nor heard the radio and Television announcements. That explained it then. John apologised if it had come as a bit of a shock, and started talking to Ed about his and his ladies' own plans to maybe go visit me at the hospital. "If we are allowed in, do you want to come with us to see her at the hospital?" he said.

There would undoubtedly have been silence from Ed! Why? - Well there is no doubt about it, that question would have instantly put Ed on the spot a bit. Ed, poor love, has never particularly liked hospitals. He still doesn't. Previously unhappy contacts with hospitals, that I don't think that I'll go into at the moment, involving his family and things, had reinforced his aversion to the places. So he wasn't too happy about the prospect of going to see someone he cared so much about, and respected as a really good friend, and ex lover, lying in the bed, unable to do anything at all! He suddenly got a bit fidgety, and looked worried. And Ed said - "It says here in the paper that she's in a vegetative state. Is that so John"? John sadly nodded.

Then Ed, trying to ascertain the true situation properly, but all the while trying to lighten the depressive mood that had settled on them both, began acting the clown *(a thing that he is still good at, at 76)*, and said in a singsong voice - "so, doodly dumdee dee - she wouldn't even know it was me, would she"?

(Ed has always been a bit like a little boy, and whenever he gets worried, or feels awkward, he still, instantly becomes his alter ego - Peeko, and comically sings and dances his way out of his worries!) John, not fully realising Eds self defence mechanism at that time *(I don't think that Ed does, even now)*, must have looked almost astounded at Eds answer, and would have just shaken his head in utter disappointment. All the time Ed was busy trying to avoid Johns decidedly unpleasant looks. "And anyway", Ed said, "she will need me later on".

He tells me now that he is not sure what made him say that, he just somehow knew that I would! That conversation had taken place between the two of them on the 29th July 1979.

On the previous night of the 28th July, 1979, I had been due to start work at the Mandarin Club, where a weeks work had lain before me. A week when I would have been able to break in my new show, and knowing what a week of hard work lay ahead of me, I had been really looking forward to enjoying a family barbecue lunch on that Sunday afternoon at Andy's and my favourite Uncle and Auntie's place before going to work at the Mandarin Club. I think that the Mando's must already have liked my old act, because according to my work diary, I seem to have been there on a regular basis, and I must have hoped that they would also enjoy the new show that I was about to launch on them. Even though the club may have been one of the lesser paid jobs in the city, the ambiance of the room, along with the mixture of excellent, music reading, and yet great 'lugging' resident musicians, more than made for a most enjoyable gig. It had an excellent four piece band, and singers and muso's often dropped in for a 'jam', as well as for a drink or two – or three – and sometimes even five! Ha ha. It was not unknown for we entertainers *(and others)*to go in there for a great sing or play, and then come out of the Mando's, in the early morning - paralytically boozed!

That was part of the reason it *was* such an enjoyable gig, but it was also an 'in' place to work. If any agents who either had never, or not for a long time anyway, booked you and wanted to assess your work, then they could very easily do so there. Occasionally though, you would be working away, and you'd notice a very well dressed, cigar smoking, *(so therefore, very smelly)* stereo type of one of those big wig theatrical agents, and you'd say to yourself - I "wonder"!

229

great gig – what 'gas' musicians!

It could of course, just have been a 'crook', having a night in!

(But then how was I to really know? Some, not me, would say that there was relatively very little difference between the two anyway, but that if anyone could tell the difference, then that 'anyone' should most definitely have been me! Some people figured that I hung out with 'bad people'! Could never understand it myself!)

Most times though, you wouldn't even have known whether there had been an agent there, or not. Not unless they had liked your show. You would only find out when a booking came in for a venue that a 'new'*(?)* agent handled. Very occasionally, an agent who hadn't actually seen you work before, would cancel a booking that he'd already put in your book. On his actually seeing your show, he had maybe realised that you weren't going to be quite the 'right kind of show' for his/her/their venue. But that only happened to me twice, and twice in nearly 10 years, isn't too bad I don't suppose! The particular venues involved in those incidents, really wanted a semi - stripper, and after seeing my show, the agent concerned realised that that definitely wasn't me!

(So I wasn't going to feel too bad about that then, was I?)

The venues I did work could have been just about anywhere in Australia, or overseas, and I have to admit it, it was a 'different', and very exciting life. *(My childhood wish having been granted again maybe?)* But just why was the Mando's a good job to '*work in*' new material and routines?

Well, when you worked two shows of the same performance each night for a whole week, as you did there *(allowing for the odd alteration to suit the particular crowd and time of night)*, the regularity of it all, turned out to be an essential ingredient for 'breaking in' a new routine. Having the audience seated around you, each at individual tables and bar cubicles, with the fantastic band being off to the rear side, was very mood setting, and could be very personal and sultry! Sort of like those old fashion 'speak easies' I guess!

I am not too sure if it were still operating whether the place would have been all that good for your health though! I doubt that it would get through Health and Safety checks these days! The room was underground, with poor ventilation. That meant that the place was continually filled with smoke, very noisy, and a hang out for all kinds of weird and wonderful people. Predominantly a Chinese club *(not that Chinese people are weird they're not, they are generally the 'wonderful' part of the equation).*

It was very well run, by mostly friendly staff who looked after you super well, most of the time! It did though, always seem to have an excessive amount of what looked to me, as though they were Triad members about. *(Mind you, looking back on it now, that impression may have been just a tad prejudiced, but that is how some of the 'business' thought about it at the time. Did I know what Triad members were supposed to look like? I didn't then, and still don't have the foggiest idea about it.)* It was though, a standing joke between the showbiz artists at the time, that if they said they were working the 'Chinese Mafia' club next week, then just about everybody in 'the business' knew that they really meant the Mandarin Club. It was what you might have called, an '*in*' joke. But come to think of it, unless you were an entertainer at the time, I don't suppose it was all that funny really. You had to be there to see the humour of it, I guess!

Anyway – let's back to the barbecue, eh!

Andy, his Uncle Pete with *his* wife Joan, Andy's brother Sam, and I, were all in the back garden, setting up the requisites. Joan and I were the only feminine touches in a male orientated get together that day, and as was typical of Australian men in those days, the women did all the preparation, and the men all the cooking. Generally only for barbecues though. *(For some reason it didn't seem to apply to 'normal' meals.)* In those days, probably like today, you couldn't get a man to even look sideways at a saucepan or fry pan under normal circumstances! But, this was a 'barbecue', so come lunchtime, steaks, and king prawns the size of Barramundi, *(the staple Aussie celebratory food at the time, and probably now, except for the price!)* were sizzling on the barbecue grill, tantalizing us all with the aroma of 'just about ready'-ness. Joan and I went inside to set about serving the salad that we had, between us, already made that morning. Because we hadn't had a chance to get together since Andy's and my wedding, there had been much jovial talk about it. Everyone threw in their own odd humorous quip, and for some reason we all had lots of them!

Not least of all, Andy and I!

Everybody was relaxed and having a good time. There didn't appear to be a lot of booze around, just the norm, *(just a few tinnies, as they say in Australia.)*, and as far as I knew Andy hadn't drunk too much. He definitely didn't appear to have done so to me, so I have to assume that he hadn't. I mean, I had seen him legless a few times. Before. I had even been legless with him myself, *(but never before a show though).* Sometimes after a show, but if that was so, then it would become taxi time. I definitely wouldn't have got into the car with him driving if there had been even the slightest sign of his having drunk too much. Andy was normally a great driver. I had a show to do, for heavens sake, and anyway, I knew I was sober, and if it had come to that, I would have driven myself. At that time, I was a fully qualified and accomplished driver of a Mazda RX5, and I had only had one wine and lots of coke, because I knew I had to go to work! Andy had been safely driving me about for just over a year, and especially so since we had been married, so I didn't really give it much of a thought! Everything seemed pretty 'normal', except that both of us were complaining that we had had to leave the 'do' so early to get me to my job. Also I was probably getting my normally edgy self, and also a bit worried about the lateness, and the closeness of the show time.

It was fairly likely too that I would have been becoming a bit 'tetchy' you might say!!! I was notorious for my quick temper in those days, *(any days really!)* and was possibly 'throwing a strop' *(probably was!)* about the fact that it was very important for me to be on time, or even early for this particular job, and that because I was doing a whole lot of new songs, I would need the extra time gained by arriving early, to 'talk through' routines and songs and things with the musicians. *(I wasn't even too sure about some of them myself, for heavens sake!)*

Andy would probably also have put his two cent's worth in about some of my song choices for the new show. But what I wanted to do, was really up to me. There was only ever 'one man' whose advice I would have taken seriously concerning material, and he hadn't been a round to consult, so I was probably doubly nervous! I seem to recall that there was no doubt about it, I could be a tad 'impossible' at times, especially where my work was concerned. *(As you have read, I guess that I have always been a bit of a 'hard work' person, evidently right from day one!)*

My present husband *(who just happens to have been the 'one man' I just mentioned)* would probably say that I still can be. *(A hard work person, I mean, and do you know something? Even though I am no longer working, I guess that I have to say, that I would probably have to agree with him!)*

I think that Andy and I must have been driving for about 5 minutes when an intersection that we had traversed a thousand times before, came up. I am not really sure what happened next. I don't remember seeing anything out of the ordinary, but from what I have since been told about the circumstances, it must have been one hell of an accident. I guess it was a case of a momentary lapse of concentration on his part. I don't even remember the screech of brakes, or breaking glass. There must have been some of course, but to this day, almost 30 years later - I really don't know! Not that it really makes any difference now any way, but evidently a car whacked into my side of our car, and sent us flying sideways, about 50 yards up the road, where we hit another car. Whether that other car was moving or not, I can't be sure, but Andy wasn't physically hurt himself, and visibly, although I was unconscious,

I initially just had a small bruise or two. I think that he was probably justifiably amazed to find that I was as damaged as I turned out to be. But I stayed unconscious and unable to breath for myself for three months, with a further 6 weeks of breathing, unaided, but nothing else. *(6 weeks this time, as opposed to 6 months)*

But do you know something? Knowing me as well as they all did back at the time of the accident, the families on both sides, probably would have thought - "Aww - she'll be OK. God will look after her. Just give her a bit of time, and she'll be back with us, enjoying another 'barby', with a truly exciting story to tell! *(They all knew that I enjoyed parties, and being centre stage. They knew too that I also enjoyed hearing, as well as telling a good story, and to tell the truth - I still do!)* Also knowing Andy's family, although they each, personally would have been very concerned, they probably would just have said, purely in order to ease Andy's panic, and because of their strong Catholic faith of course. "Don't worry too much Andy, she's a 'toughie' is your wife! God will look after her"!

And, in a way, I suppose that God did. Of course if it wasn't God, then someone must have, 'cause - look - I am here, 30 years later, to write this book aren't I?

Oh, please don't take any offense at my apparent lightheartedness. But I feel that if I can't laugh at some of the things that happened, then who can?

Although the accident was not a nice thing to have happen, and I have lost some things very dear to me, my voice being the main thing, I am still very, very grateful to be here, and be able to tell you about it with such an air of – 'oh well, it could have been worse'! *(I could not be here to tell you about it at all, couldn't I?)*

And do you wanna know something else? What with *my* mum, Andy's mum, as well as others praying, then heaven must have been bombarded with a lot of 'Lord, help Kerri please calls'! If God himself hadn't had the required amount of time to stay on the job after the initial life saving actions, then the message must have been well and truly put out there among God's 'minions', and luckily someone of influence had received it. He/she/it has maintained their 'working on the problems highlighted by the prayers' for all this time, right up to the present day in 2010. They are probably still at it while I finally write this book. But I have to wonder why God would spend all that time looking after all that goes on in the world, with the world not really showing a lot of gratitude. He must still be prepared to devote his time, 24/7 for months, sometimes years on end. The reason behind the devotion of his precious time to just one person is hard to fathom? And I might add, to have devoted that precious time to a person who wasn't even a fully paid up member of his elite club, as I have said seems to me to have been incredible! Take it from me though, I am definitely not complaining!

I know what possibly happened; Gods' job list had probably become oversubscribed with all the problems that needed to be sorted out, and once the initial urgency of *my* case had passed, one of the lesser but never the less, still holy angels would probably have been delegated the job of trying to make some sense of my problems. That Angel would though of course have been overseen by Him whenever He had a spare moment.

They must have a very well organised and effective system going on up there, and after all this time I would have to say, that I for one, am glad that they appear to still be winning. Partly because of their intervention, and my and their hard work, some would say *(and I would have to agree!)* that I have made astounding progress.

Andy had known that I had so much to look forward to, and that all our dreams looked about ready to come true, so I am pretty sure that he would never have dreamed of what was about to unfold! And to tell the truth, I don't think anyone would ever have believed that I would spend the next 5 years from July 1979, desperately relearning how to talk, walk properly, and just learning to cope in a very different way. And then to spend the next however many years to 2010 adjusting to the varying stages of a disabled life,would surely have been something that no one expected! Least of all me!

It all seems too unbelievable to be true, but to tell the truth, again as I was told I must, it's almost as if I have lived two lives so far, and I like to think that as 2009 draws to an end, it not only marks ALVA's 30 years, but I am also into my third life! So again, as I once said on the Ray Martin Show - "watch out world"! - So far so good! Who knows? It might just be as they sometimes say - 'Third time lucky!'. Let's hope so!

But let's do what has become my normal trick, and go back - to the hospital, when I first woke up. As I wrote, I must have wondered where on earth I was, and what is more, what on earth I was doing there. The last thing that I even vaguely remembered was that barbecue!!

When I had actually come too, the Hospital staff, very firmly, and very decidedly 'plunked' me on a treadmill. A completely alien to me, treadmill that even though it would eventually lead to a totally new, and sometimes frightening, but delightful existence, was still a formidable piece of equipment! That treadmill would safely guide me even more interestingly towards the further granting of that childhood wish of mine, for 'different'. Not really understanding why I needed to do so *(get on the treadmill I mean)*, I sometimes unwillingly, set about rescuing what I could from my old life! That 'split' second that had been required for a light to change, had turned my whole world upside down and inside out.

Andy and I no longer had any need to agree or disagree about the choice of songs for my audiences any more. The only audience I was to have from then on, and for quite a while at that, were other individuals trying to make some sort of sense out of the lives they had been left with! I had no idea that the next 30 years to this very date would be spent in varying stages of success, defeat, and self improvement. But we are almost as far as we can realistically wish to get, and where I 'am' at the moment is not really too bad a place! But me being me - I want more, and will get there!

This time it is not 'I think'. This time, it is *I know!*

LIFE 2

I sincerely hope that there hasn't been too intolerable an amount of too-ing, and fro-ing for those of you who have no personal interest, or for those of you who have just risked possible boredom and persevered this far! All of these next chapters, are about the post accident time, and you will probably notice a bit of a difference in the writing. I was as bitter as hell to begin with, but then I looked at it realistically - I was at least alive! There have though been moments when I sincerely wished that I hadn't been.

But now - again not wishing to temp fate – I doubt that there would be anybody more glad that I have survived than me. I have tried to encapsulate the devastating change that occurred in my personality with the accident, and all the trauma's immediately post accident. I guess that you will just have to judge for yourselves as to whether or not I have succeeded, but from having been a self confident entertainer, one who could just about beat the world at it's own game, I had become a continually apologising, disabled person. I did a lot of 'why me-ing' *(must have caught that, from dad)*, and to tell the truth, there was a long period of time when I just didn't understand, *(and I'm not real sure that I do yet)*, why this particular event 'had to happen to me, at all'!

But, tell you what! I have learned this much!

Even if it doesn't appear so at first, I have found that you really should take the life that you have, run with it *(talking figuratively of course, because there are those of you, as well as me, who still can't run!)*

237

and do your very best at making your life beneficial to others as well as to yourself.

For me, fun now would now daftly be being able to cry with tears of joy, at what my life has become so far, nearly thirty plus years later and what it could become in the future! I am ready now, to grab life by the neck, and shake it *(just as I shook that monkey that you'll read about a bit later!)*, until it spits out some of the good things that it has to offer. And it does still have a lot to offer for those who care to work for it. But I have also learned that you really do need to pour a lot back into the pot before you can hope to scoop even the smallest anything out! I guess that I would have to say again, with all the 'nasties' aside, and not wishing to incur anyone's anger for repeating myself, that I *really* have been a very lucky, unlucky lady.

Firstly monetarily because of the so called profit earned at the end of of all the years of hardship *(definitely a 'different' and 'not a nice' way to earn a million dollars)*, and secondly, and probably even more importantly though, lucky most of all because of the daughter, parents, friends and relationships that I have been blessed with.

(Yes, and even the not so nice ones!)

Charlie, my daddy, who although he had his own demons to battle with, has implanted in me, the strength to cope with most things.

Peggy, my stepmother, has taught me *(by example)* that you just have to stick at life and make the most out of what it dishes up for you and - My birth mother, who has surrounded me *(maybe belatedly because of my own stupidity)* with the strength and conviction of her own faith in God.

Just as I feel that I have had three lives, I have had three towers of strength to lean on through the years!

LIFT– PUT DOWN - LIFT - THEN ALL FALL DOWN

I know that this story is a little like a trip through a maze, and I do apologise,but as I am sure I have said before, never having previously written a book, I am learning on the job so to speak! I find the whole exercise very exhilarating. I also appreciate that you, the reader are probably used to the normal format for a book. But as I said before - books should entertain, as well as be a good read! If you can combine both of those aspects, you have it made. Now I am not saying that I have succeeded in doing so, but please know that even though my life has been nothing special compared to some, it has I think had it's moments, and if nothing else it makes for a reasonable read when you are un 'occupied' and desperate for something to keep you entertained!

I guess that I would have to pull myself up short, put my hands in the air, and admit that both I and my life have indeed been different! Sometimes unexpectedly so! But I ask you now to take my hand and come skip with me *(washing our hands first of all though)* through even more parts of the maze of my life.

But while you are getting ready to take on more, please try and remember right back to the first chapters, when I told you about my coming to, and the new challenges that that miraculous event brought with it!

Well, there I was, having survived it all, and then, none too gently I must say, and in a sense of despair on the part of the nurses and doctors, I had been plonked in a wheelchair by the bed. Remember?

That there chair, which I understandably, not too affectionately called 'enemy', was among the many things that I positively hated at that time! But I was lucky *(if you could call it that)*. Having been unconscious for so long, I hadn't moved, so the doctors hadn't seemed to think that there was any need for straps to keep me in the bed. They must have though, weighed up the pros and cons once I had progressed to the wheelchair. But because they knew, and could see that I still had very limited use of, and lack of strength in my arms, and that I couldn't have propelled the beast anywhere out of their sight anyway, they decided that it wasn't really necessary to strap me into the chair. Clever thinking if you ask me!

But I did though tend to slip sideways a lot, and my left arm still felt numb, and tingly all the time; *(and it still does!)* My right arm was continually hurting at the elbow *(still unfortunately does!)*, and the fingers were forever shaking, *(hooray! - fixed now!!!!)*.

I also had an arm with virtually no strength in it, *(wonderful! Time and determination have fixed a lot of things, but I still have that weakness, and the associated arthritic pain, like you wouldn't believe!!)*.

Oh don't get me wrong! I am not complaining too much, but I suddenly knew for sure that I'd been in an accident alright! The doctors had of course, most efficiently explained that piece of information to me. But I still didn't have the foggiest idea why things should have been as they were for me. Not me! Not the great Kerri Dyer!

But they definitely were!

The hospital always brought me up to date with my progress, but I just wasn't prepared to admit to any kind of defeat. Never have been! Never will be, either!

I guess though, that I must have very stupidly been trying, but failing at first to convince myself that I hadn't even had an accident. For some reason it didn't work though! Couldn't possibly! Not as long as every time I opened my mouth to try and sing, nothing happened. And I don't mean that it was just a croaky sound at first that I could have worked on to make less croaky. Absolutely *nothing* moved into place internally so as to produce any kind of singing sound at all for about 5 years. Singing had been my life since I jumped on the box stages in our road, and now for those first 5 years, I asked my self time and time again, "since I had never asked for the accident to happen in the first place, why do I have to put up with any of the 'crap' I find myself having to endure. What in the 'frig' had happened to my lovely voice"?

(I must say though, that luckily {again?}, after years of patient self rehabilitation; intensive singing work provided by my darling husband when ever I was ready to do it; and after periods of 'sit down, and just let the world 'go to hell' playing a prominent role, the tingles in my left hand side aren't so bad now. They are though still there, and my voice is showing delicate growth buds. I no longer have time for, nor the patience with, my right hand and arm, and I like to avoid the tremor that is still in evidence there, so I have had to teach myself to use the computer mouse in my left hand. And luckily again, the tremor is no where near as frequent, nor as violent as it was. It's still there, but it's almost just bearable!)

But you know, even though the hospital may not have actually strapped me into the chair, they did most considerately allot me a 'keeper' to push the chair. I felt a bit like a 28 year old baby in a pushchair. All I needed was a 'dummy' to suck on!

Goo, Goo! Gah Gah -

Humiliating but probably necessary I suppose!

Bundling in behind the chair, my allotted pusher of the 'person in the chair' began to manoeuvre me along the bustling, disinfectant smelling corridors, towards the 're learn to walk' bars.

Only three weeks had passed since my re-entrance' into the world, and I was still very groggy, but I think that they wanted to get me on the road to recovery a.s.a.p., and as was my want, I was also still making my presence well and truly felt. *(who - me? Never!)*

But anyway there I was being jauntily pushed down the ward corridor, to the rehab unit to see what/if anything positive could be done about my physical state. As the nurses gaily pushed me along the ward, there was me blithely saying 'hello' to the other patients, full of bonvivante!

Well, I didn't see any reason not to be friendly, did I?

The medical staff were sure that something could be done but as I was told time and time again, the efficacy and amount of that 'something', lay completely in my own hands! *(Oh yeah! A very nice thing to tell someone who could be as lazy as I could sometimes be, wasn't it?)* At the other end of the ward were the people who weren't quite ready for those bars yet. Among others, they were the amputees getting used to using their prosthetic legs or arms. There were also paraplegics who suffered with mental problems as well as their very obvious physical ones, and then there were those who had already progressed far enough to be able to ride one of the stationary bicycles set up at the end of the ward. The Rehab ward was a veritable ant's nest of activity. It was a world that I had never seen before, except when I had done shows in the hospital wards, *(I even remember thinking at those times, 'there but for the grace of God go I'!)*

I now had to wonder why God had changed his mind, I suppose?

Had I maybe done something he didn't like? I wouldn't be at all surprised!

I guess that I must have decided there and then though, that I didn't wish to actually be this much a part of it for any longer than I could help. I wanted out, as soon as possible! The nurse took me to the walking bars, and once she had carefully lined me up with the end of them she gave me 'that look', *(you know, the nurse says - "you'd better do as you are told" kind of look)*, and instructed me to lock the brakes of the chair. I innocently asked by making unknowing, and imploring faces, "Where are the brakes, and what are they for"? *(well I couldn't really talk much at that time, could I?)* The 'look' that she had flashed my way, was tinged with understanding, but it was also a kind of 'disobey at your own peril' look that led my eyes to the things down at my side. She was though very definite about what I was supposed to do. But do you know? I couldn't do it. I just didn't know what, exactly, she meant. *(Had I suddenly gone stupid or something?)* Brakes? What the heck did they need brakes for? Was the chair going to go on a two mile dash down the ward or something? It was almost as if I had somehow been carelessly stuffed into some stranger's body, and had been plunked into the middle of a scene in the movies or something! Most disconcerting, and I am here to tell you right here and now, that although I had been into acting*(up?)*, for some reason I wasn't in the mood for the apparent

242

scene in the movies that I was now unexpectedly playing! I just didn't comprehend what had gone wrong!

But finally, taking all that they had told me into account, I just had to surmise that the doctors didn't want the chair to take off backwards *(probably with me still in it, and wouldn't that have been an interesting turn of events to see. Even fun maybe?!)* Once I had done as the nurse was instructing me to do though, and had braked the chair, I grabbed hold of the walking bars that she was gesticulating to in front of me. I was soon to find out what it was that they wanted me to do!

"Grab the bars! Just put your hands in place, one hand on each bar," says the Nurse to me. *("Oh, so that's all is it", thinks me? Can you believe it?)*

I suppose that it does sound easy enough, doesn't it! But how was I supposed to know that it really was, as I sat in that wheelchair, full of frustration!

"Come on Kerri", the nurse implored, "be a good girl, and take orders". "Lift those levers down there at your sides", she said, as kindly as she could this time, while still insisting, and pointing to them, "and then we can really get stuck into fixing the problem"!

"Problem", squeals me to me. "So they *do* look on me as a problem then, do they?" How was someone who couldn't even talk properly going to explain again to the staff, that I just couldn't, not wouldn't, do as they were asking.

Repeating the instruction, she said, "Just pull the handles up towards you.

I have to give her a bit of credit though. I am sure that if I were faced with someone who had become as irascible as I had, then I would have found it difficult to remain calm as well. But then in a decidedly louder, almost *(ut not quite)* exasperated shout - she barked - **"LOCk the brakes - please!** *(Again – please note that she did say please! Nurses don't normally shout, but they do have a most decisive tone of voice – don't they? From what I remember, it sure sounded like a shout to me!)*

Cringing at the severity of the instruction, I must have grumpily looked down and noticed the brakes that she had been pointing at. I said in the most agreeable manner that I could manage at the time, trying to soothe the situation a bit - "oh them?"

I suddenly realised that there were two short handles, one on either side of the chair, next to my thighs. Hadn't noticed them before - had I? "Derr"

"Yes - them" she frustratingly barked at me again.

Reigning in her annoyance, she said in a much quieter, but still insistent voice - "Once you lock the brakes, you then pull the foot plates up and away, leaving a gap and space for your feet on the floor! Then – having done that, you first just put one hand on each of the bars in front of you, and grab hold. Then you just need to lift your bottom up, making sure that you keep your feet flat on the floor."

She pointed, adding - "right there where the foot plates were before you lifted them up". She paused to give me time to take in the instructions, and then said - "Now – you must just get your balance when you stand, being sure that you keep a firm grip on the bars. Then you just swing one foot alongside the other foot to start a step".

"Oh yeah" thought me. - "Just! Just! Just! Everything is *just!*

That's *just* all there is to it, is it"? It was easy enough for her to say!

Even sounds easy enough to do, doesn't it? We do it every day, don't we?

"Well why couldn't I bleeding - well do it", I cryingly asked myself? I was suddenly so fed up, and once again feeling immensely miserable. I couldn't understand it! "Why me", I cried again?

(I knew that I was starting to sound like my dad, but I was beside myself with angst!)

The Nurse though, ignoring my plaintive grizzle, as truly good nurses generally did, made sure, again that the chair was lined up properly just inside the bars.

She had said that I needed to gently lift myself up, but how on earth was I ever meant to lift my big fat bum off the seat? It felt as though it somehow had a lead weight tied to it!

UP AND – RUNNING?

She had also wanted me to swing a foot that felt as though it wasn't even there, and then put it down into some kind of walking position. I silently wailed to myself, "Who were they trying to kid"? Again, I just sat there, looking even more than usual, like a bit of a petulant kid. *(And I am here to ashamedly tell you, that being a petulant kid was something that I was getting pretty good at, by that time !)*

The Nurse sighed a big exasperated, but yet encouraging sigh. I felt as though my whole left hand side, my face, my feet, and my little fingers didn't exist. "Oh bugger! Why don't they understand" I wailed to myself! *"I just can't do it"!*

But I guess that the nurse must have understood, in her own way of course. Even though her way was a bit indecipherable to the likes of me, and she was probably getting justifiably impatient with my non compliance, she did though have enough nurses understanding of the situation, to actually stand behind the chair. Just in case? *"But just in case of what'*, I thought. - *"Isn't life ever going to become sane again"*, I wailed?

Well, I guess that I was about to find out that it wasn't going to be wasn't I!

After her at least warning me this time that she was going to lift me, she kept on muttering instructions to me that I didn't really understand! Instructions on how to safely continue the forward movement once she had placed her strong arms around my waist, and had lifted my body

245

up. They were muttered in words that meant very little to someone who hadn't expected to ever be in the position where she would hear them, and I found them almost incomprehensible! On seeing that I had evidently forgotten about shifting the foot plates, she kindly, but impatiently, lifted them out of the way for me, making sure though, in no uncertain terms, that I realised that I had forgotten them. *(Talk about her being bossy!)* With two well trained arms going under where my arms met my shoulders, she ever so gently set me up on my feet in front of the chair. Her big strong nurses arms were still safely holding me up.

"What do they think I am, surely I hadn't needed all this, even when I was a baby", I thought? *(This thought was well and truly before I had had my own little girl remember!)* I teetered back and forth a bit, almost falling back in to the chair, while she was left struggling, only able to use one of her arms to hold me upright. Her other arm was being kept busy coping with my wobbly body chucking one of it's all too frequent at the time, erratic spasms! The nurse waited until the tremor that had chosen that particular moment to attack my right side and arm, had done it's thing. My right hand, the one with the relative amount of strength in it, *(even though it too chucked tremors every now and then)*, was then carefully placed on the top of the bar. She made sure that my wrist was locked into position.

Nature is sometimes super unfair. It gives you a relatively strong right arm, and then decides to chuck a 'tremor' in with it, just for good measure of course! *(Can anyone tell me why?! Devious pleasure maybe?).*

Then the nurse did the same with my left arm.

(no tremor in that one, but no real strength either. And as I have previously said, why does nature do that?)

I am sorry to repeat myself about it, but it is one of the things that I still don't fully understand!

The nurse was watching very closely that I wasn't about to slide sideways or fall backwards again. Once I was actually up though, she took a deep, relieved breath, and heaved a 'ginormous' sigh of relief! In fact, both of us did, and we both even managed a weak smile, and a bit of a laugh. We may have been laughing but at what?! After nearly falling once though, and looking decidedly shaky a few other times, I was apparently up! "Next step - a step", she said to me!

"Oh yeah"? - says me sarcastically to her?

That first day at the walking bars was a real hoot. - Lots of fun was had by all -

"I think"? *(again, depending of course on what you would call fun!).* I seriously felt as though the whole ward was monitoring my progress, partly because of my extrovert displays of pleasure whenever I did do something right. - *(My 'show offness' was really in it's element you might say!)* Suddenly a voice would abound in the ward with phrases like, "look at me, I am standing", even when I wasn't really *(not without the bars anyway!)* I just couldn't get my 'ruddy', fat and swollen legs to do anything much at all. It looked to me at first, as though it was going to take what seemed like an eternity to get even my first step accomplished. The medical team knew that technically there was not really any reason why I shouldn't be able to do it.

All *I* had to do, was actually *DO IT!*

Again, nothing much - really! *(Really??!!!)*

I just couldn't understand it myself! My legs had always done what they were supposed to do before. I must have thought to myself, "oh for heaven's sake, hadn't I been learning a complicated dance routine not all that long ago". All I was trying to do in this situation, after all, was walk! Just take one step after another! There were no two ways about it though. I may have wishfully asked for different, but there were no two ways about it! I sure got 'different' in bucket loads! Now though I guess you could say that I was really paying for ever having asked for it in the first place!

When I began walking at the bars though, they *(the bars)* were doing most of the supporting, but the nurses all told me that I would eventually have to loosen the hand hold a little, and put the strain on my legs, if I could. *(If I could ? They had to be joking didn't they?)* But the staff apparently seemed to have far more confidence in me than I had in myself, and it was just as well someone did, because at that time I had none! Zilch! Nothing seemed to want to work. At least not in a way that I would have called 'normal' anyway! After a while though, as I have probably said before, I guess that the same determination that I had rustled up to become a singer in the first place, was again being called upon. But this time though, it was for a far more crucial purpose! I didn't need to learn songs or even how to sing any more, I just needed to firstly re learn how to walk, and exist in this strange new world!

That's all, and as I have also no doubt said before - "not much then"!!!!

But then I thought, "even plain old walking, would be wonderful! Never mind the complicated dance routines that I had just been learning a few months ago".

As it turned out though, just being able to walk at all was something that was going to be super difficult, and as complicated as those there dance routines were!! That which had always come pretty naturally to me ever since I had had the normal 'all fall downs' of being a toddler, was now proving to be an almost unattainable talent! There I was, being faced with those same 'all fall downs' again. But no longer a pliable toddler, to whom falling down was just a natural part of the job description. I was a 28 year old adult that ran the risk of breaking something each time If fell over!!

About 6 – 9 months later I started walking independently. That is of course if you could even have called it walking independently. I still had to use a walking frame for a further 6 months *(about 15 months in all)*, but I was at least able to look at life from a completely different angle. I could face life head to head – eye to eye!

But my life had been thrown totally askew! I looked a lot like a little person that had suddenly acquired height, but nothing else. I was no longer 10 months old, so why then did I look like a baby meandering about with a great big smelly deposit in her nappy! *(You know - the way toddlers walk?, when they have just 'relieved' themselves. All embarrassed, and not wanting to spread the deposit too much, they stumble along with their feet miles apart, and the cheeks of their bum desperately trying not to make contact!)* I must have thought - "I know the proper way to walk, *and* I know the correct place to go to the toilet", but do you think that I could get my feet or my body to do as they were told? *(I have never been as embarrassed as I was at 28/29! I even actually pooed my pants one day! And wasn't that embarrassing! Oh the shame of it all!)*

248

But regardless of how much effort I put into it at first, I still seemed to be going almost nowhere. I was unable to get my wretched feet to comply with the orders I had given them. The nurse persevered with me though, but whenever I did manage a few feet or so, I would come to a sudden stop, swoon a little again, with the blood rushing all the way up to my head; stars would float before my eyes, making me feel dizzy, and as if I was going to fall over again! I felt so stupid! There were of course, times when I did.

(Go to fall over that is, and talk about my feeling stupid!!!)

If it hadn't been for the bars, and the wheelchair that the nurse had very efficiently, and cunningly kept directly behind my wobbly self for the first few weeks, I would have wound up plastered. Unfortunately not drunk *(which might just have been super nice for a change!)*, but necessarily plastered from head to foot, to help set the broken bones that I would have inevitably received. But that nurse had though needed to be super watchful as well as quick. One time, she must have been distracted momentarily, and I completely missed the chair!

Wound up on the floor didn't I! "Ouch, that hurt"!

(And that I might add, is the polite version of what I would no doubt have said.)

The world did an about face spin, Galaxies and stars burst across my area of vision whilst the nurse, firstly having made sure that I was alright, just stood back, folding her arms, and almost, but not quite, tapping her foot! Oh, they were clever alright, those there nurses!

"Let's just see what she does", she must have said to herself, all the time watching me with her eagle eyes?!

I didn't actually break anything! Neither in the accident, nor in the hospital efforts to get me right, but I did though have a thing called 'foot drop', which had to be put in plaster for six weeks. Not from that episode, I think it was maybe from having just lain there, unmoving for 4 and a half months when unconscious!

But anyway there I was, sat on the floor, and thinking about bawling.

Couldn't though, could I?

249

I was though, politely *(I bet it was impolitely)* wondering why I couldn't even enjoy the release of tears. I decided again, there and then, that the sooner I got the whole sorry thing over and done with, then the sooner I could leave.

But "leave to what", I thought? I still wasn't too sure!

I like the nurse, had heard some startlingly disturbing rumours about what had been going on outside the hospital. But as I was only recently married, I either wasn't really listening, or I was blindly thinking - "Not my Andy"! *(Fatal delusion or what?!)*

But anyway, back at the walking bars, where I'd fallen, I crawled up off of the floor using the braked chair to lift myself up. But because I was having difficulties actually lifting my frame off the floor and into the chair, the nurse took over, and I was most ungraciously plunked back into the chair by the nurse. My legs and arms, looked a lot like one of those Hindu figurines, and on looking back on it, it does seem a rather harsh way to have treated me at the time. They had though learned, through many years and many patients, that it was generally the best and only way to teach a patient to cope with whatever else life was going to throw at them! *(To leave them to it until it was vitally necessary to intervene.)* Among my hospital 'team' though there came the day when there was total elation for this 'suddenly become a bit of a celebrity' patient. Firstly, when I finally managed to traverse the complete length of the walking bars six months later, no longer needing 'ENEMY' behind me.

(Was it another good 6 month period for a change?)

I 'whooped', and 'whee'd' all about the ward. Or as much as was possible at the time. I was just SO excited. I guess that I have always been a bit of an exhibitionist!!!

One of the most inspiring things that I was to learn from the whole episode though came from seeing how differently each person coped with their own disability. Even though it may not have seemed so to others, just the fact that the damaged people were alive at all meant that each one had an obligation to themselves, and to their medical team.

They needed to grab at life with open arms and find some positive way to enjoy it. Even if they couldn't actually make the arms embrace anything, there had to be a reason somewhere for enjoying just being alive! Didn't there?

The ability to find some way to enjoy each achievement, no matter how small it may have seemed, was something that was very highly encouraged by the staff, and there was always some kind of small celebration going on in that ward! Oh sure they understood that a little self pity was OK, if not necessary at first, but once each patient had finished their wallowing in self pity, then the staff made it quite clear that it was up to each of them, individually, and no one else, to make the most out of the life that they had been left with. They would help as much as they could, but basically as long as there were no medical reasons for something not working, it was our baby!

Thanks to the encouraging, consistent support from my medical teams in the five years previous in particular, the staff in the first hospitals, as well as the Queen Elizabeth 2, Rehab Center in Sydney, I was actually, finally ready to be discharged, and it was an elated case of - *"Home here I come"!*

HOME HERE I COME!

Everybody had done a wondrous amount of helpful things for me, both while I had been in hospital, and in preparation for my going home. My family had been wonderful. I had, of course, lost Peg and Charlie by then, so technically, having worked hard to get to this point, it was now up to me, Andy and his family, my Mum and the kids, and ALVA to help get me back into a 'normal' kind of existence.

(Goodness, on reading these ramblings back, I actually had more people to help out than most, didn't I?)

When the hospital said that I could go home, it had become a case of 'all hands on deck', so to speak! *(And am I ever grateful that all the hands wanted to be on my particular deck!)* It had actually been 'all hands on deck' once before. About 18 months after the accident, in 1980 to be exact, but in a slightly 'different' way. It was a long time before I was ready to actually go home from hospital.

ALVA was having an annual Ball, and although I was still technically 'in the hospital' and barely doing what kinda' passed for walking, let alone dancing, Toni Stevens and I *(probably against all orders I might add!)* organised for me to 'go to the ball'. I was just *so* excited!

I was what you might call, just a little out of shape, both bodily and facially, and believe it or not, I had gotten 'fat' again. *(All that laying around, stuffing my face with 'yummy'? hospital food I 'spect. What do ya reckon, eh? Yeah that's what it must have been!)* One would have thought though, that with all the hard work I had been doing, that I would have managed to lose some weight. I just couldn't understand it myself!

(I guess though that I am what they call a 'fatty', but then as I said before, "I am not really fat! I must just be BIG BONED"! Yeah - that's what I am! It sounds better, doesn't it?)

It was actually not long after the ashes business with Toni, and although she wasn't too sure if it would be advisable for me to think about dancing when I wasn't even walking too well, and I had come so close to falling off the cliff when 'tossing' daddies ashes out to sea, Toni knew that I had always reveled in being the centre of attention. She also knew that with me being a true 'showy' at heart, even the mention of the ball would make me definitely want to go! I knew how important it was to my beloved ALVA. It was the main money making event of the year! She tried very hard at first not to mention it in my presence! But it was the talk of the ALVA meetings that she was giving me the minutes of, and talk of it was in all the ALVA newsletters that I was getting brought to my bedside by friends. I found out that it was due soon, and after a bit of heavy selling from me of the idea of how good my going to the ball would be be for ALVA, what with my situation still being a newsworthy item, Toni finally decided that maybe, just maybe they could make it the right time. I think that it had probably been in the back of hers and the ALVA committee's mind the whole time though!

She thought that my going would be well and truly worth any possible risk. Especially when I didn't really see it as being any kind of risk at all!

And, of course, it wasn't! She was after all the inaugural Queen Bee of ALVA and as it turned out, - what great publicity it was!

("The almost dead – dance!")

My eldest younger brother *(I have more than one you see!)* even escorted me to the 'showbiz' function, and I think that as he was only about 19 at the time, *(If that!)* and with the Showbiz world being a completely alien environment for him, I think that he definitely found it all a bit OTT. But he was there for me then, just as he is there for me today, even though it is from the other side of the world!

Toni knew that apart from Andrew escorting me to the ball, I would also need the arm of a strong adult male, used to dancing in the 'old fashioned way!

Preferably a show business great.

Barry Crocker - Grande Entrance to the ALVA Ball

Toni had thought that it would probably have been a little more than Andrew, being of such a tender age would want, or be able to handle. Anyway, being the Grande Dame of showbiz 'terrah' that she was, Toni and the ALVA girls had organised for me to make a 'Grande Entrance' into the actual ballroom, on the arm of the very well known, Australian entertainer, Barry Crocker. *(Now he definitely knew how to make an entrance!)*

I am pretty sure though, that Barry, who is 'quite famous', *(understatement?)* definitely wouldn't have been used to being the 'support act' that he was about to become! He was a 'star' act, and I am sure that he hadn't quite realised just what he was letting himself for, when he agreed to escort me into the ball room! I am also sure that he had never envisioned himself as a *support* act, to a singer who could no longer sing! But I can die happy now - and Australian entertainers from that time will appreciate my excitement most when I say - "Barry Crocker was *my* support act"!

(I wish!)

Still - being the true 'pro' that he is, he put on his biggest show business smile, took my arm, and supported my wobbling, done up to the nines body, through the main door and in to the ball, where, on entering we were given a standing ovation that lasted for a full 3 minutes! Unheard of, in most circumstances, unless you were famous, or on a stage performing! Barry himself, would have been used to that kind of thing when doing his show of course, but it was a long time since I had experienced a buzz even similar to that, and I was totally elated. It had been so long since I had actually performed, had forgotten just how wonderful such a thing could be, and to tell the truth.

'Me found it 'mazing'!!

We were greeted by the most soul stirring applause and cheers, and I was just *so* flabbergasted. Suddenly though, Barry found himself really and truly, having to support me - I got my quarter inch heel caught in my dress, *(at least that's my excuse and I think that I'll stick to it!)* and he had to put his luscious, strong and beefy arms around my waist, to stop me falling over. It was positively marvellous! Made the embarrassment of the tripping, well and truly worth every blush, didn't it? Well worth the trip! *(ha ha!)* We then danced the first dance, *(which was a giggle in itself - he tried to dance, keeping a firm hand on my waist - I barely shuffled. It had to be the wobbliest waltz imaginable, and what with the in co-ordination that I had been left with, and that had not improved at all at that stage, it would have been a right giggle!).* It was just as well that he was there though. I am pretty sure, that even with all my physical problems aside, the fact that I got a bit 'overcome' by it all didn't really help either! It was astounding for me to again begin to realise that there was so much respect and love in the room, and that a lot of it was for 'little old me'! I could be a bit egocentric at times back then, but I honestly had to wonder what on earth I had done to engender so much affection!

That Ball has given me memories that I wouldn't be without for quids, and I guess that I am very lucky that I can remember it at all! *(It is probably just as well that I couldn't cry at that stage. I would have truly looked truly stunning - I don't think!! My misaligned face, with the left side a full quarter inch lower than the right, would have looked even more abysmal if I had had tears streaming down it as well. As it was, I looked like a tearful, yet happy, facially lopsided hunchback of Notre dam, dressed in blue, pleated chiffon, but it is a wonder what you can do with makeup!)* But the grin I had from ear to ear, would no doubt have been lopsided, and probably looked as though it had been chalked on with an indelible crayon!

Even though I now know that Show business people are sometimes renowned for being be a bit on the selfish and egotistical side, some of it's members can also be astoundingly big hearted and caring , both of it's own, and of other people. I guess that the establishment of ALVA, and what they do for members of the business, is among the biggest indications of that. *(Some of we entertainers/ex-entertainers aren't bad old sticks really!)*

But as is my normal trick - back in the hospital though, back before I had even learned to walk independently, the naturally 'eager to have you improve' nursing staff, must have been spurred on to even greater efforts when someone told them that I lived above a shop, with stairs. But then, I suppose that having had to put up with me for as long had, they probably just wanted to get rid of me asap!

And - get rid of me, 'they certainly did Ollie'!

The stairs at my abode, were not just any old stairs mind you. They were stairs that went up in two flights of about 12 stairs each, with a 90 degree turn onto the 2nd flight. It definitely wasn't wheelchair accessible, neither indoors, nor out, and it had been disastrous on the few occasions that I had already been home. Poor Andy had had to just about carry me up the stairs wheelchair and all whenever I went home.

I didn't dare think about going outside, or even down to the shop underneath us for a loaf and to say hello. A lot of responsibility for a young man of 29. No wonder the time came when he had had just about enough!

Andy had made a valiant enough effort at trying to look after me at first, but as you will read a little later, I had made a massive personality change. I was taking a lot of what I heard as fact and to heart, even if it were the truth or not! His being a fit young man, I think that he found looking after such an obviously damaged, disabled wife, just a bit more than he could, or even wanted to cope with! To have your wife, who had once been an energetic, sexual, good looking(?), into everything, singer entertainer, turn into the shell that I had become. It must have been a hell of a trauma for him! Thus, our marriage was destined to be a truly a major casualty of the accident.

The obvious place for a girl to turn in such a case, was to her mother! But as I mentioned, in my case my particular Mum hadn't really had much to do with me over the years. She had not long before lost her own beloved husband, and she and the kids lived in a house that although definitely big enough, and at least all on one level, was no more wheelchair accessible than my place had been.

I still, even at that time, would have needed a lot of supervision, and help and as she had rightly surmised, *('cause I was not the most amenable person just after the accident!)* it was best for me to try to live as independently as I could. Also my lifestyle had been so very 'different' to hers and her other children's. I wouldn't have fitted in at her place at all at that time. I of course had not really known anything about that assessment of the situation until much later.

(I would have to agree though, that I probably would have been a bit of a handful at the time!) Also, except for the wedding, as I wrote, she had had very little to do with me since I had been about 17, about 11 years. So it wasn't really a normal kind of mother daughter relationship! Again - a bit 'different' you might say! So in reality, having me about with her family would not only have been impossible for her and the kids, it would probably have been most 'un-nice' for me. Not that I had become a truly unsociable leper or anything *(nearly, but not quite)*, but the way I had developed directly prior to, and after the accident, was with a most severe personality change! I had probably always been a 'tad' difficult just before because I was always chasing stardom pretty seriously, but after the accident, I had become super stroppy in the extreme! In fact - as much as I hate to admit it, but I have to, - "I guess that I had become rather a bit of an obnoxious git!

Definitely not an ideal guest, family or not!

I had also been brought up in a totally different environment to my half brothers and sister, and Mum was justifiably concerned that no one would benefit by my trying to fit in at that time, nor by my possibly *(most definitely)* introducing a completely alien *(to them)* moral code. The kids were still at that impressionable age *(you know – late teens and things!)*, and it was really a bit late, and inappropriate, for me to be a 'big sis' to them by then!

The hospital staff, and Mum and I had decided that Andy's and my flat was also not the right place for me, *(mainly because everyone knew that there was a pretty good chance that Andy wouldn't be able to cope with me in the future, and that I ran the risk of being left alone too often, as had already been evidenced on more than a few occasions!)* I still needed somewhere to go though! *(Couldn't just camp in the hospital grounds - now could I? Although that might have proved a bit of a giggle, now wouldn't it have?! That would probably have provided me, and everyone else, with some more of what I was fast becoming enamoured -* 'fun'*!)*

Through the hospital though, I became involved with a lady who was the then secretary for an association called the Total Living Foundation. One of the T L F's aims, was to create a secure sense of independence for disabled individuals, but with the regular attendance of people who could help out when/if needed. Living in one of their houses also taught the residents to share with others, *(something I definitely needed to re-learn)*, as well as the art of independent living within the society, which was learned whenever we went out to get our provisions and things. Each of us was supposed to attempt to come to grips with our own disability, and learn how others cope with theirs. At least that was the general idea! Sometimes it worked - sometimes it didn't, but in a household of four adult, disabled people, there were often things that one could do, and that someone else maybe couldn't.

TLF, the Total Living Foundation, provided a few different homes, at very affordable *(for us on invalidity pensions)* rents, with each house adapted for at least two wheelchairs. There were enough rooms for four disabled people at a time, each person with various degrees of disability. It was supposed to, and did I guess, even though we each lived in our own 'different' world, give us all some preparation for the big 'horrible', 'normal' world outside. Whether or not the others wanted to help you with a thing, was always a moot point, but if someone couldn't do something for themselves, then Russ, *(another of the house members, a wheelchair paraplegic, with whom I was destined to have another of my flitting affairs)*, or I would have a go at it for them. *(You'll get to read a bit more about Russ a little later on, too.)* What with Russ being in a wheelchair, me being 'not too sure on my feet', and with my diminished strength in my limbs, there was no doubt about it - sometimes living in those houses, truly was a 'total living' experience! *(Russ and I were a bit like a disabled Laurel & Hardy, and we were always getting in each other's way.)* One thing is for sure though - In a 'different' kind of way *(did I get my wish again?)*, I suppose that it could almost have been classed as *fun!* Although even though I may think that now, to again be perfectly honest, I definitely didn't think so at the time, and because I still couldn't actually cry, my knuckles and wrists were often battered and bruised from my tantrums. But there we all were, sharing the normal day to day household worries, and discovering new, and 'different' ways of doing things.

The accident had been in July 1979, and for the following 6 long years, although I had been granted my wish, and I suffered a very 'abnormal', and **definitely** 'different' existence, I hadn't really envisaged different in quite the ways that I had been asked to cope with it! So many years had been spent in and out of hospital, with the last year and a bit having been spent in that 'halfway house', with four to six other disabled people, that I was finding it difficult to remember what life had been like before!

Now that I was definitely out of the actual hospital, and having to pay for normal everyday things like food, soap, and cups of tea for instance, I was 'broke again! Stony cold' broke! It did though seem like a bit of a 'normal' state of affairs for me. I seemed to always have been poor, even when I had been earning well. As I said, I hadn't been able to save anything during my singing years, and I definitely hadn't been able to save when I was living off the state. I was now on the invalidity pension that the Government gave out. The Australian disability allowance system, even though it all had to be repaid from the final award money, had been very helpful during the pre-settlement days, keeping me alive, *(just)* and, to be fair, I suppose that it did momentarily teach me the money keeping/management skills that I had been lacking. *(again - I think!)*

'Good on ya Aussie Government'!

Even when I had been earning well at my singing, I had been, as I have no doubt already told you, supposedly 'speculating to accumulate'.

Underneath it all though, when I had been an entertainer, I was just enjoying life while I could with no real thought for tomorrow. But suddenly tomorrow had come, and because Andy had understandably found it just too hard to cope with the dramatic change that had occurred both in my physical being, and in my personality, I found myself alone, *(kind of - can you imagine me ever being totally alone!)*, and my disability definitely had had a lot to answer for! To be a bit fair to him *(Andy)* though, and I suppose that I should be, because he *(whom I had loved more than life itself at the start)*, had after all originally married a soon to be a 'star', fit and active young woman. He was a young virile man. He hadn't married a bed wetting invalid, with all kinds of weird problems. *(Still, I also don't suppose that very many people ever really think about the "in sickness and in health" vow that they make when marrying, nor of the fact that it might just, all too quickly bounce back, and smack them right in the face! Peggy and Charlie had had their problems with it, and now Andy and I were having our own problems!)*

I must confess though, that I sometimes wonder if I would have reacted too differently if the tables had been reversed. If I had been driving the car, and it was him with brain damage. I wonder? But I do think that you would have to say that the pressure encountered at the time of the accident, most definitely bounced back and slapped both Andy and me in the face!

As I said previously, *(sorry to repeat myself so often)* we brain damaged people, *(or at least* this *brain damaged person)* sometimes reacted towards things in weird and wonderful(?) ways. I definitely did, and while I was still what might have been called a bit 'sick', and unable to logically work things out properly, I filed for divorce when told of a few things that had supposedly been going on. I was just so gutted. How could he? We were only newly married after all! Oh sure, we had lived together for a whole twelve months before that, and we were supposed to know and love everything about each other. We had vowed to take each other in 'sickness and in health'!

To make matters even worse for me at the time, most of my friends who were in the business, and half of the nursing staff knew of Andy's peccadillo before I had even found out about it. It had been an entertainer who wasn't even a friend of mine, who had taken great pleasure in *(unknowingly?)* imparting the news to me, that my husband had been seen out and about with another singer. *(Maybe she hadn't even known that Andy was my husband? [We can of course dream, can't we])* But then again, I actually know that he had also evidently consoled himself with one of the nurses. That little lapse didn't have as severe an affect on me though. I guess that my pride was inevitably, doubly hurt with the show business fling though!

"How dare he", I thought, and how dare she! *(oh not the girl who told me- although she was a bit of a turd for doing so, but Andy's singer mistress!)*

The whole business was truly assured of finding out about it. It hadn't been him that had had to put up with all the strange undesirable side effects; the inability to walk; the strange voice; and the loss of my *much loved* career and voice. A voice that brought me, and others such joy. Although I suppose, come to think of it, I think that he did lose his job. *(Poor boy!)* The car we were driving at the time of the accident was his company car, and their insurance had had to fork out for the compensation, so the company must have decided that he was just too much of a liability. I don't suppose that they were very pleased so it does seem pretty likely, doesn't it?

I was told though, *(vicious showbiz grapevine?!)* that he had said to this other singer, *(the one that he was openly having an affair with, while I was in the hospital)* that he couldn't divorce me until after the court case was finished anyway, because he didn't want to risk losing out on his share of the compensation money. *(None of us would have known, firstly if I was going to live or not; whether or not I would even get anything in the way of compensation; nor how much would be involved!)*.

As I got much better, I knew not whether that was in fact the truth of the matter. But having seen how the whole thing apparently affected Andy, and knowing how his life since the accident has panned out, I prefer to think 'not' these days. It was more likely, come to think of it, her way of justifying it to herself?

But at the time because I myself was still 'not well', I must have petulantly thought - "his share"?!!

"His share"??

I was so understandably, terribly hurt, firstly by the fact that he had turned to someone else so early in the marriage, after what would have been the first real test of our marriage, and secondly that he had had the hide to choose another singer. And I mean to say! Not wishing to appear nasty at all, but if he was going to be so mean, and have so public an affair with another singer, then why couldn't he have at least chosen someone who was a really good singer? *(I didn't think that she was all that hot at the time, but then I suppose, who was I to really judge?)*

I had probably done enough of marriage invading in my own days, but I will say this though. None of the 'men' in my life ever had their home lives threatened by my presence. Most of the wives don't know to this day, and I didn't really like the tables being turned, and me being the one to whom all the rigmarole was being done. I guess that I hadn't really given the matter much thought at the time of my gallivanting about. I must have selfishly thought, amidst all the fun that I was having - "I'm alright Jack!" I still feel ashamed. But I would have to admit though, that there would have been some very hurt women, if they had known!

But on a completely different subject, I can hereby assure you, that I won't be at all disappointed if I never see the inside of a hospital ward again.

It seems such a long time ago now, and I guess that in reality, it is really, but it's still as if it happened to someone else *(and I sometimes wish it had!)*. I go to do something that now, even these many years later, I find I still can't do, and the frustration I feel is just unbelievable! It may not even be anything difficult, either! Just simple things like putting stockings or socks on!

Shoot! – I've done it again, haven't I? Sort of started something, and then took off in a completely different direction. Such a klutz!! Sorry, but I did warn you! - I guess that my inability to put things in a 'sane' structure must have been with me since the day 'jot', and that the accident can't really be blamed for everything, can it?

It has probably just reinforced it!

I had spent months with my lawyers and solicitors, and with friends helping me out occasionally by assisting me to compile a solid evidence base. I dragged out 'stuff' from what memory I did have at the time that could be used in a case that was, according to all reports, the biggest court case of it's kind, at the time!

My QC had stated at the beginning of the court case, and it was agreed to that 'liability was not an issue, and that the matter was to proceed purely as an assessment of damages only'. "Phew"! We hadn't known that, even earlier that first court case morning, but the assessment of those damages was to prove very difficult for the legal teams to assess.

I knew what the nearly ten years of pain and 'wobbliness', the loss of my voice and career, and the constrained future was kind of worth to me, but it had to be proved, which was bound to be - 'not easy'.

I had my own valuation of course, already worked out in my mind. It was possibly, and understandably a trifle over inflated, but then, I didn't really think so, so I stuck to it with the determination of a bulldog that has his snarling teeth around a juicy bone that someone is trying to take from him!!!

(Singing had been my entire life, and even if I did still have a kind of future in front of me, which was according to the doctors an 'iffy' enough issue in itself, it would be very bleak indeed without my ability to sing!)

ALL RISE PLEASE!

For the months before, and for the 'in court' day I never faltered in my belief of what I thought the loss of my beautiful voice was worth, and what is more, why I thought that I should get it. I would have to admit though, that there were some who must have been getting very annoyed with me towards the end of the 'in court' days. Those on the opposition team, as well as some on my own team!

The lawyers for the other side, who were out to pay as little as possible, kept coming back with 'settle out of court' amounts after they made their first, what I considered derisory offer *(I think the first offer was a measly $250,000. No court costs or anything!)* I of course rejected it, as well as rejecting the next few further offers. I think it was four or five times all together, and each time I sent them back, saying no, and cheekily telling them, as I had from the beginning, the sum that I thought was fair. I would have to admit that there were some in the court that were getting a little uncomfortable when I had rejected the $750,000-00 + costs offer. *(Hooray – they had finally agreed to the costs being on top of whatever amount they offered!)*

But as much as I wanted the whole thing over with, I was still upset enough about the loss of my career and my voice and all the nasty side effects that I had had to put up with, to hang out for my original personal assessment amount. I mean to say - The money had to last me the rest of my life, didn't it? Now, alright they said that I wouldn't live that long, but I wasn't falling for that. Although predictions of a foreshortened life abounded *(to which I have now, obviously paid no attention whatsoever)*, I had repeatedly told everyone at the time, my legal team as well, what I figured that it should be worth. I personally intended to be around for a long time *(and very fortunately I have been)*, but if I got proof that I wasn't going to be, then I wanted to have enough to all the things that I had been unable to previously due to lack of money! I figured that $1,000,000-00 plus all court and ancillary costs should just about do it!

Well, I didn't want to have to pay the costs from what ever amount I finally ended up with, did I? $1,000,000 clear was what I thought of as the minimum that I would be evenly reasonably content to accept for the loss of my voice and career. I had to live for however many years I was going to be allowed to live, and the necessary adaptations to a house *(which as it turns out, were never really needed)*, cost money. There was also 'pain and suffering' that had to be taken into consideration, and although I didn't wish to sound stroppy, *(even though I probably was being very much so)*, I had had more than enough, and more than my fair share of that so far. If I didn't live a long time on this earth, I wanted what ever time I did have, spent doing whatever I was able to do without any money problems. And doing things, whatever they are, costs! I knew that some travel groups took disabled people to all kinds of fantastic places, but it was not done cheaply. Totally unexpected, and un-asked for pain and suffering, was what I had endured at the time, and was, and am still enduring. And as I had told them each time how much I wanted, and what I figured I deserved, I couldn't really understand why men that were supposed to be as clever as they were meant to be, couldn't understand what this battle scarred little girl wanted! A million dollars clear! *(A little bit cheeky, eh?)*

Now though, this many years after the event, I am glad that I stood out for what I finally got. The money, shrank a lot because I went a bit mad! It stagnated for a while, and then because of some clever management by my husband, has risen a bit again. So I am not as rich as I could maybe have been, but I have sure as hell had a great life!

I just wish that I could properly remember some parts of it!

I can't really be sure after all this time, again not really knowing how those things work, but I like to think that they finally must have just thrown their arms in the air, *(if legal profession members ever do that sort of thing)*, and said, "Aw go on - we may as well give it to her. She is obviously not going to change her mind as to what she thinks it is worth to her, and there really is just too much good evidence *(which you'll read a little later)* in her favour - I don't think that we stand a chance of altering her determination to get what she thinks is a fair amount"! *(Now, I know that that couldn't really have been the case, but it does make for a good surmise, and for a little more interesting read. It does though make you wonder just what went on, doesn't it? Well alright! It does me, anyway!)*

I guess that after all these years I will never know for sure, and I am not too sure that I really want to know, not now! But whatever happened out there among the legal eagles, was for me and for those that had given such good testimony on my behalf, a truly 'bonza' result after all the time invested. I guess that the 'wobbly' had suddenly become an Australian dollar Millionaire. I had achieved what I had held out for.

Mine was one of those cases where the outcome was to prove reliant, not only on other knowledgeable people's opinions, but also on verifiable fact, and with the Video's of my working etc., luckily I was able to come up with both!

Some people said after the court case that I had just kept rejecting the offers, because I wanted to listen to what other nice things the witnesses would say about me, and that I still had my showbiz ego, in bucket loads. I thought for a while that maybe they were right, I do still have my showbiz ego, but having re read the court docs, I don't think that that was actually the case. There was some fantastic evidence given, for sure, and I have to admit that it was great for me to hear it, but at the time I must have been feeling so very angry at some of the very necessary, *(but un nice)* opposition, cross examination. It took a heck of a lot of restraint by my lawyers and things to stop me from calling out in the middle of the court case at certain spots! I was positively seething at some of the comments from the opposition, but even though I know that a court case isn't normally thought of as great, I suppose that that one was!

For me at least. Eventually!

For someone with such a bleak life prospect, I have actually far exceeded my predicted life span, but as I think I have already said, he pleasure of the money diminishes when those small 'niggly' things make their presence felt! There are no two ways about it, I think that I would have to agree with those people who say that "you can't buy health"!

I can 'kinda' sing now, and although I can no longer do shows, what with all the wonderful witnesses that came forward at the court case, I guess that the court case was a bit like a show of it's own, with me taking center stage. And I didn't even need to sing a song!

A kind of non musical 'Grande Curtain call, or finale! Although I suppose that there are those videos of me working when I could sing!!!

On re reading the draft of the court case however, I have decided that most of it is what my daughter would call "too much information Mum", so I will try to break down bits of the whole court case for you. And why bother you might ask! Well as I have no doubt already said, it really was like a bit of a show in itself, and I would like to thank those that are still alive to be thanked, *(even this belatedly)*, for helping me to bring about such a successful outcome!!!!

The show consisted of the Australian showbiz greats of the time *(the 80's)*, with some excellent support acts. But again --"let's do as that songs says again, and start at the very beginning, a very good place to start.

Let's just have a little think about it, shall we? There was me. Recovered -*(Kind of)*. I took a cab that first day, to the Supreme court of New South Wales. *(Well I couldn't afford to be late - now could I, and the driver knew where the courts were - I didn't!)*

I'd been advised to go alone that first day, but I intended to bring the others for moral support once I'd got day one out of the way! I needed to 'sus' out whether or not I could handle the stress of it by myself!

Staggering up the steps with one of my legal team supporting my arm, I was to discover that what went on inside that courtroom was destined to shape the rest of my life forever

THE FIRST DAY OF THE
REST OF MY LIFE

<u>Tuesday 8th October - 1985</u> - **The First day of 'the rest of my life!**

<u>pre show 'intro' -</u>

We got to the courts, I did a quick dash to the toilet and then I sat and listened while eight doctors gave evidence about my injuries. There were some excellent and detailed reports from the three hospitals that I had been in, as well as from the wonderful Queen Elizabeth 2 Rehab. Unit in Sydney. *(In those days, every 20 - 30 minutes or so, I had to keep asking the judge for a wee break, or run the risk of wetting my pants. I knew that I had to be in court while the evidence was being heard, and I must confess that after that first day, I even considered wearing nappies so as to cut down on my need to go to the toilet so often. [Tena pants, about which I knew nothing then, if they had even been invented, would have been VERY useful!} I thought though that I would try and brave it out. But my frequent trips to the 'little girls room' thus far, must have driven them almost as batty as it still drives me.)* But at least it is not every 20-30 minutes anymore. An hour to an hour and a half these days! Yippee!

QE2 *(the rehab unit, not the boat),* had been absolutely fantastic! They gave a detailed account of my damages, and the normal expectations of people who suffered with them. Pretty 'normal', humdrum stuff, if you are a doctor, but not, I suppose, if you are a 'plebe', like me! And now - **Strike up the band! Get ready with an humongous fanfare! - it was - SHOWTIME! Tarr-ah!!!!!!!!**

Not having performed for such a long time, I was nervous at the thought of facing so many interested faces, especially with a face that was still a trifle lopsided! *(was that vain, or what?)* I very tentatively, and in a self-effacing manner, steeled myself to be the opening act! I was still mentally in a pretty 'knocked about by the accident' state, but looking *(at least I thought so, anyway)* fairly 'normal' and nicely attired. *(I had had VERY LOPSIDED FACE but it had 'kind of' straightened out a bit by the court case).*

I was grilled pretty harshly, but considerately the whole time by my own legal team, as they set out the basics of my case, from our side. We had been in court for about four hours *(excepting, of course, for those frequent toilet breaks when I had put my hand up, and run(?) off to the loo, and run(?) back again).*

That's a laugh, that is! I don't think that I'll ever run again. *(Walking moderately quickly I can just manage! I felt a bit like a toddler at school.)* We had had lunch and then done another four hours, *(again including wee breaks),* and then *(without the opposition even questioning me yet)* they finally called - Session closed for the day.

(So much time had been spent just settling everybody in, and getting the whole thing under way, so that even though they hadn't been able to really get down to the nitty gritty of the case, they had 'run out of time' for that day. We all went home. The legal team all went to their respective homes, and I went back to the halfway house, supposedly to help myself and my friends get ready for a good night's sleep, in preparation for the next day.)

It wasn't really possible of course, but we tried anyway. A good nights sleep had really been very much needed, because the whole group were all coming in with me that next day! Purely for moral support of course!

Wednesday 9th October - 1985

It was truly a 'real sight and a half' to see!

269

Russ in his wheelchair, and the two stroke victims that I shared the house with, arrived with me in a special wheelchair taxi. A wheelchair user, and three very 'different' looking ambulatory people, made for a 'very' interesting quartet! It was just as well there was a ramp at the court building. They had just recently made it law to accommodate disabilities. Previously it would have been even more hilarious than it actually was. If someone had had to lift Russ and his chair up the steps part, then he/she would have to have been very strong! Russ was a big boy, even without the added weight of his chair! There he was, puffing as he wheeled his chair up the ramp, *(his enjoyed too well, boozing, had diminished his body strength, as well as his stamina),* and there the two stroke victims and I were, attempting to climb the stairs without making too much of a display of ourselves. Trying to look 'normal'. Ha ha!

(We were all as bad as each other in that we were too proud to use the hand rails for support, so we were supporting each other, up the stairs, looking decidedly like a trio of drunks after a good night out. It would really have been a case of 'pride go'eth before a fall' if we had fallen up the stairs. None of us had what you might have called - 'a good sense of balance' at that time, so we just about tumbled backwards on each step.) For me – the balance is a bit better these days, but still not really marvellous! Don't know about the other two though! I haven't seen them! I'll have to try and look them up when I go back to Australia for a visit, and to celebrate my 60th birthday, in 2011. But Anyway, the initial excitement of the first day of the court case had well and truly dissipated, and although I was still very nervous, Russ and the other two house members, kept smiling across the room at me, in an attempt to help me keep settled a little.

I was re sworn, and cross examined by the opposition lawyer - who no doubt did his job very well indeed, but I though, personally found it very upsetting! Talk about trying to make you feel like a criminal who was trying to get something for nothing! It was of course his job though, and he did do it very well!

'But something for nothing'? I ask you! I think that I would quite happily have changed places with him at the time, even though he was an 'oldie'!

(I think that, against all predictions, you would have to say that I have actually become an 'oldie' myself now! Life is just too wonderful for words,

isn't it? Who would ever have thought that I would be glad to be able to be called an oldie! Unbelievable eh?)

After what was a long, and slightly harrowing session with him, I was re examined by my own QC in a much less aggressive way, and then retired.

(Now I just had to wait - for what exactly, I wasn't really sure, but I am here to tell you, that the final out come was really well and truly worth the wait!)

The opposition lawyer, wouldn't really have been doing his job properly, if he hadn't tried to really get to the truth, and hopefully break my determination to get what I considered a fair judgement. After all, as I think I said before - his team *(I guess understandably)* wanted to pay out as little as possible!

But "'I told the truth, the whole truth, and nothing but the truth"!

My darling, now husband, was the first individual apart from myself and the legal eagles, to actually undergo cross examination on my behalf, and although we had once been lovers, and had been friends for years, we had no idea at the time that we would end up married years later, nor for such a long time either! At the actual time of the accident however, he had been living with someone who was, along with him, really good to me just after the accident. I had known her fairly well, because she was a fellow entertainer, and I had even helped her out when she was first getting started.

They went through all the normal establishing who Eddie Keen was routine, his qualifications etc.,and then they asked him questions going right back to his having taught me at school. Edson *(as he chooses to be called now)* and I had, as I said, merely been teacher and pupil at first. We became lovers a few years after I had actually left school, with him being the mentor and me being the mentored. *(He has always been an excellent teacher, in all aspects of life!)* We had broken up emotionally, but had remained friends for years, with me occasionally seeking his advice for in the entertainment world. He told the court that he had first come into serious contact with me when they were trying to find a student to play the part of the Witch, in Humperdinck's 'Hansel and

Gretel' opera, at my school. He then said in the court- *(taken directly from the court notes)*

"One of the reasons I remember her IQ so well, having had hundreds of pupils passing through over the intervening years, is because the operetta that the school was planning to put on was a very difficult one for school children to perform, and required some very careful casting. The chosen pupils had to, not only perform well, but they also needed an ability to memorise and learn a wide variety of things. The selection pot had been reduced rather drastically by a number of things, and Kerrie was one of the very few remaining. At that stage one looks at the IQ to see if she should be able to carry the kind of load that a part like that created. Kerrie obtained one of the prime parts, if not *the* prime part in the operetta, and completely sold the show".

(At that time, in the court room, I have to admit that I didn't remember much about the actual getting ready for, or the performances of the show themselves, but from what I do remember now, as more and more of my memory returns, it must have been a truly great time, back then!)

At the time of the court case, Ed believed it would be impossible for me to sing again. Not just because of the possible damage done to the vocal chords, caused maybe by the tracheotomy operation, but also the actual brain stem damage, and the lack of muscle sustenance and co-ordination. He wasn't sure that I would be able to have the patience and concentration that would be needed.

He was questioned about his qualifications, and after telling them that he had studied the teaching of Music at the Guildhall School of Music, and had graduated GGSM - AGSM - LGSM, he went on to discussing his work with aspiring entertainers

When asked about singers, he said - *(again from the court room notes)* "Muscles are very important for singing, and not just those of the diaphragm. Vibrant, easy and correct use of that particular muscle is of course essential, but facial muscles must also be quickly made flexible, so as to form the correct sounds". *(We have been again working very hard on those muscles, for the last few years [2006 - 2007 – 2008 – 2009, and now 2010], we are now in 2010 trying to get my blasted tongue to 'bounce' correctly, and Ed was correct - it is also hard work, which I have, unfortunately, kind of grown out of the habit of!)*

When Ed had been talking to me after the court case, he did say to me back then - "You won't be able to sing - but you should maybe keep your creative nature focused and active. You should learn to write". *(I don't think that he ever thought that I would though.)*

But, I did do a writing course not long after *(funny how I had always done what he suggested, isn't it?)* I didn't though, do wondrously well at it then. I think that it might have been because my powers of concentration were hopeless at the time, and I guess that I wasn't really in a proper 'work effort' mode at that time. I couldn't use a manual typewriter at all, and I definitely couldn't have written it by hand. My handwriting at that time, still looked as I have probably already said, as if a bird had jumped feet first into an ink well, and then danced an erratic samba or Mexican dance across the page.

(And it looked like a pretty drunken samba, at that! - Now it only sometimes looks as though the dancer is a little bit on the 'tipsy' side! It can though, look quite good if I take my time with it, and I mean really take my time, but it is still a little difficult for others to read it when I don't, and I would never have finished the book if I had been writing it by hand!!) My interest in writing was rekindled once computers became so popular, and thus less expensive. I have been using my trusty computer for all kinds of things, at different levels of competence for the last 20 years. I have certificates of achievement on my office wall, of which I am very proud! I made myself learn to use the mouse, and the electric keyboard. And - Oh oh – almost did it again didn't I - got side tracked again? Very sorry! You would think that I would keep track of myself, wouldn't you?! Again - sorry!

Back in the courtroom, Ed gave some fantastic evidence, and was excused and retired, and I asked the Judge for one of my, even by then, famous after only a day, - wee breaks! *(Phew! Just made it!)*

Next up was my lovely friend - **Barrie Stuart** the then proprietor of the Texas Tavern, in Sydney Australia. Barrie didn't actually meet me until well after the accident, in November 1983 at a party. He knew nothing of me at that time, and when he arrived I had already been there for a while. I was sitting down having a chat with another of the guests that I already knew, and that knew me, and of my circumstances. I got up from the 'lounger' that I had been securely sat on, and because the lawn was uneven, and the lounger was just a teensy bit on the low side, I fell back, quite sharply into the chair. My companion must have given a worried gasp, but once she realised that I was OK, we both had a bit of a giggle about it, and knowing her, and remembering her wicked sense of humour, *(a bit like mine)* she probably even jokingly said to me - "I don't know – will you never learn - 'pissed' again"!

Barry had arrived at that precise moment, and on hearing that comment, or something like It, had said to Warren, that he would like three of whatever 'that girl' *(pointing at me)* had been drinking. But Warren quickly, and brusquely explained that I had been drinking soda water, and the reasons for my doing so. He also said that he *(Barry)* would probably enjoy meeting me, so Warren brought him over to me. At that stage though, Barry would have been understandably pretty sure that I had been really drunk. *(After his initial blush at misinterpreting the situation, it didn't take too long for him to realise, that contrary to appearances, I hadn't been at all drunk, and a great friendship began!)* He learned all there was to know about how I had become as I was, later saw a few of the videos of my work, and from then on, Barry always went out of his way to make sure that I was able to socialise and enjoy myself within the business.

(I hate to admit it, because I don't like anyone doing so, but I think that, at first, he probably felt a bit sorry for me, after having seen those videos!) I did my best to eradicate that feeling, quick smart! *(His feeling sorry for me, I mean).*

He knew that Jerry Queen and I had been old, long time mates, and yes, even at one time, a long time before, lovers. Because Jerry was 'piano bar - ring' at his restaurant – the Texas Tavern, he asked if I would like to go and see him at the club.

I said - "ooh -yes please"! I loved his voice, and his singing!

Barry would usually go out to my home at - I think that I was still at the Maroubra flat at first, and then later at the halfway house. He would either pick me up himself, or arrange for a chauffeured car to pick me up so that I could go into the tavern on a week night. *(didn't that cause a stir at the halfway house? To have a chauffeured limo turn up at the 'normal' looking Petersham house! Very twee!)* But then it was generally

Barry himself, or one of his staff who met me at the top of the stairs of the TT, and take my arm to support me in. I couldn't really manage the 25 outside steps down without assistance at that time see. Nor the ten inside! *(I don't think that I could now, if it were still operating. Not without a handrail at least, and do you know, not only had I once been 'a hard work girlfriend' to Harry, I had suddenly become a 'hard work friend' as well to Barry. But this time it was 'hard work' for a very different reason!).*

I would sit there with my orange juice, and listen to Jerry play piano and sing. Barry and I were, unusually for me in those days, never an item! It's just as well that Barry hadn't found me a too much of a hard work friend though! I really loved going in to the Texas Tavern! But you know, I must admit, even though what I am about to say doesn't really paint me in a good light, that it must have seemed a funny thing. If one was honest about it all, then I guess that you would have to say that I would probably have been one of the very few people among the crowd of many that frequented the place, who would arrive looking as though they had been there all night. At that time I couldn't really drink you see. *(The provision of my quota of orange juice, soda, and the very occasional glass of wine, must have raised a few eyebrows among those who didn't know the real situation.)* But when it came time for them to 'chuck' me out - which they generally had to do because I was having such *fun!*, my departure must have made a very interesting sight. Even sober as I normally was, I was still wobbling all over the place, looking as though I had had a boozingly good night. Maybe in some obscure way, I was good for business. Who knows - maybe it was advantageous in some weird and wonderful way, to have a client coming out, looking as though she'd had a really good night, and yet not ya hooing, or raising the roof!

Jerry, whom I had actually gone to see, sang and 'played super good' and he also usually sang all my favourite songs! Along with his normal repertoire, of course! He was a super great singer, and entertainer!

(You know - I seem to have made a bit of a habit of 'collecting' good singer musicians as lovers and friends, don't I?) Some times, if Barry was busy, or out of town, I would even use my half fare cab facility that the Australian government had kindly given me as a disabled person. Very useful for my getting about it was too.

A big thank you must go to the Australian Government for their great attitude towards encouraging the needs of disabled people! *(I sincerely hope in 2010 that it is still actively supportive of any form of disability!)*

Barry too was always encouraging me to 'have a go at life', disability or not, after the accident. He even escorted me to another ALVA Ball, *(I guess that I had run out of brothers to do it!)* By the time Barry accompanied me, it was about three years after the accident. *(oh his poor toes!)* They both *(Barry and ALVA)* always went out of their way to make sure that I was able to socialise and enjoy myself within the business. Barry had said though that he was never really worried about being seen with me, nor about my wobbliness *(and I have to admit that I was still pretty wobbly at that time)*. I appreciated his saying that, more than I can say.

(Back in the courtroom though it was toilet break time! What – again? Yes again!)

Next up in the show of my lifetime, was the business and personal partner of the man who was my agent and personal manager at the time - **Miss Carole Wright.**

Carole, young and vital, made an excellent partner for Warren, and although they both had high expectations of any artiste that they actually managed, she had been particularly good to me when I had been just working through their agency. She also, *(along with Warren)* gave some very beneficial and informative evidence at my court case. *(Toilet break - not so soon!- yes, when you've got to go -you have got to go*

Then came **Dr. Burniston**. What a lovely man!

He was in the dock for the rest of the day. He was a legally qualified medical practitioner, who worked at QE2, and who carried on a practice as a consultant physician in rehabilitation medicine. He was *(and I guess if he is still alive in 2010, still is)* also a really nice man! He could be a bit of a pain in the bum though sometimes, whenever he used one of his mental tricks on me, to get me to try harder, but he did get some good results.

I guess that I actually have him, and some of those tricks, used by both him and the QE2 staff, to thank for my being able to walk, talk, or exist at all! ***Dr B! I sure owe you a lot!***

But to tell the truth, I hadn't really realised that I was as ill as I was, till I recently re read some of the court drafts! Oh I knew I had been sick alright, but I didn't realise that I'd been quite *that* sick - I knew that I had been unconscious for four and a half months, but when I woke up, I evidently had to be on soft, almost liquid, food for a while, because I couldn't swallow properly. I'd completely forgotten! But - *"Couldn't swallow properly"?*

I was horrified when I first read that. But then I realised that I must still, unfortunately suffer the same, or similar, lack of co ordination, and reflux problems when it comes to eating, these days. *(Very luckily no where near as badly as then, but bad, often enough to occasionally frighten people.)* I still in 2010, get food caught in my throat, and I worry everybody sick by coughing like a lunatic when I do. Especially my husband and daughter. Oops! There I go – nearly side tracked again! Back to the courtroom yet again, eh?!

Once again, the day had just seemed to fly out of the window, and we were again sent home, *(again - just in time for me, ended up with damp pants I did! So, so embarrassing!)* to reappear the next morning at 10o'clock.

Thursday 11th October - 1985

First up - **Mr Warren Thomas Smith** - My Show business Manager at the time of the accident - now deceased. An ex musician himself, who had worked with a myriad of big names, and was associated with the great **Johnny O'Keefe,** *(JOK - also deceased)* and with the birth of the Australian recording industry.

Warren had been musical coordinator for a great many things, including the Army shows, in Vietnam, Darwin and Hilton telethons in Australia, and he was entertainment consultant for *Ernie Sigley*, and *Chris Kirby*. He was also Australian Agent for the American, *Don Lane (evidently also deceased a few days ago in October 2009)*, whenever he was in Oz. Warren gave details of his involvement with Julie Anthony, Marcia Hines, Lyn Rogers, all big names in the female artists section of Australian entertainment in the 70's.

Warren and Carole had spent the last 6 months *(my bad luck amount of time?)* of their twelve month association with me, *(just prior to the accident)* especially grooming me, and preparing me for the kind of stardom that I had told them I wanted. They figured that with hard work from me, the maintenance of the required weight loss *(which fortunately I had thankfully achieved again at that time)*, and with the requisite amount of luck, there was a good chance that with the business as it was then, I might just achieve my goals!

Warren listed his qualifications, and gave a good insight into my prospective earning capabilities prior to the accident. He was dismissed, I rushed off to the toilet - again! - and then we all had lunch! *(no – not in the toilet, but I must say that listening to people saying nice things about you doesn't only make your bladder active, it also makes you very hungry!)* The show continued after lunch, and now they introduced - **AUDREY YATES! Managing director of the Ted James Theatrical Agency.**

Audrey was asked a whole lot of questions relating to the earnings of some of the girls that she and Ted had been managing in the early 80's. She was able to indicate the kinds of fees that I might have been able to command, if I had still been working. *(and do you know something - from what they said – if I had still been working, then I would have been rolling in it!)* She also told of how she was on the MO awards committee *(named after Roy (MO) Reen)*, and that she had had my name come up before her, a number of times, relating to the actual MO award presentation show. But that at that time *(1978)* she hadn't actually seen me work. She said that even though she hadn't, she remembered that Kerri Dyer, had been nominated – specifically in the '75 MO's, and 1978 for the '79 MO's. "Kerri was also very much in demand, was working well and frequently, and because of persistent selling of the idea by Warren Smith, she was of course, on the minds of everyone when it came to selecting a female for a solo spot at the 1979 MO Awards presentations", *(direct quote from the court docs)*.

She said that "many entertainers can go on at the same level all their lives and make a very reasonable income out of it. There are those that have that additional drive and force which is really needed to succeed. Very few actually do. *(have it.)* But Kerri had all the ingredients - no doubt about it! Kerri could have been a world performer, because she had that ability". *(again a direct quote)*

(A short toilet break was again required and taken), and after that - Audrey was then cross - examined by the opposition barrister. *(and a trifle perturbing it was too.)*

Apart from establishing the fact that I was not as attractive as some, and that Kerri Dyer hadn't had the acting and dancing skills of others, as hard as he tried, he just didn't really seem able to discredit my abilities. But, to justify his wages, and as was his job, he had at least tried! Witness was then retired.

Lynne Rogers , for whom I have always had a great admiration as an entertainer, took centre stage next. A place where she well and truly belongs - *(centre stage that is!)*

She told of how she had worked in places like the Pigalle Club in London, and Chequers nightclub in Sydney. She had worked in Europe, Spain, Portugal, and up to Germany, and then back to London.

We hadn't actually had cause to work together at that stage, *(In fact I don't know if we ever did)*, but from having seen a few of the videos of my TV shows, Lyn said that the aforementioned venues were all places that I would have been likely to do if it hadn't been for the accident. She recounted how the earning potential in those places was very good, and how she believed that I would have had no trouble commanding high salaries. Videos of my television appearances were shown to the court. Lyn said after viewing them that there was little doubt that I would have been signed up as a regular for conventions, in Sydney and Melbourne. Then she said something that I found very flattering indeed because as I have said, I had always had the greatest of respect for Lyn's work!! Evidently I reminded her a little of herself when she was just starting off, with the same enthusiasm and energetic, accurate voice control. I evidently had an ability to do technical things with my voice that no average singer could do, and that I "beamed right in on the audience". *(Is that what I was doing, was it? Beaming!)*

Off to the toilet again for me *(my feet knew the route so very well by the end of the in court time, that I even began having races with myself, to see how quickly I could navigate it)*, and then, we all went home again.

I have just realised that all this court stuff, even though I have tried to trim it down a little, probably does still seem a bit like "too much information". Sorry!

My daughter was probably right. If this does seem like too much, boring, information and if you wish to skip ahead, feel free! But I crave your understanding and perseverance. There were *so* many people, who gave *so* much good evidence, it just wouldn't have been right to have left anyone out. So if you have decided to read on, please bear with me, and help me thank all those wonderful people for putting themselves out on my behalf, even though a lot of them are no longer with us. You will hopefully though, find that some of the court case stuff still to come, is full of some gems of humour anyway, and I would hate for you to miss out! But don't worry if you find that you would rather not hack it! I will understand! *(I think!)*

We all trundled back to the court room the next day, after spending a night back at the halfway house. Now that was fun - that was! But diplomatically, I don't think that I had better go there!

<u>Friday 11th October 1985</u>

This time I thought that I would be try to be sensible, and go to the toilet just prior to going in. *(Not that it did all that much good. I still found myself with my hand up at the most inappropriate moments!)*

But anyway, first up was - **James Glennon Brookes** (Jimmy Brookes)

He was the Managing Director of James Brookes and Associates, Theatrical Agent, and manager of some very highly thought of 'name' acts at that time. He drew some favourable comparisons of my work with that of some of theirs, *(acts in their 'stable').* I had done jobs for Jimmy at various venues over the years, and he had a very high opinion of my talent and abilities. I had always done super well at his venues. For some reason though, known only to the legal eagles, he was not permitted to pass a comment on what I might actually have earned if the accident had not happened. *(Maybe they thought that he would be too full of praise).* He was dismissed, and then they called - **MIKE ANTHONY WILLIAMS -**

Now - my darling Mike. *(definitely not one of my previous conquests – unfortunately!)*. He was the talent coordinator for what was the leading TV variety/interview show at the time. The **MIKE WALSH** show had been running in in Sydney Australia for a number of years before I actually had the accident. I had worked with both Michaels many times whenever I did the show, which was fast becoming about once a month. Mike Williams, who kept an eye on the local talent, so as to 'sus' out any suitable acts and things for the show, and also helped out with any overseas acts that the show used while the acts were in Australia. The fact that he took the time out to give evidence for me, was truly fantastic.

Oh yes, I know! - I am fully aware that most of those people were probably subpoenaed, but they were under no obligation to give such good evidence, and Mike gave some that was *excellent*. (*For me that is!*). (witness retired.)

Now I feel that there should really have been a fanfare for the next witness.

BARRY HUGH CROCKER - *(what an incredibly talented man he is!)*

(Barry Crocker) had been a top name all through my late teenage years when I had been getting ready to 'tread the boards', so to speak. We were fellow entertainers, but he was one whom I considered so far above me, that it wasn't funny. I actually saw some of his great shows, from when I had been just starting at 18 years old, so to me he too was a 'doyenne'. I had watched him on Telly, and Carol's Mum *(remember the girl down the road with the TV and record player)* - had a few of his records. Sometimes I would borrow the whole thing *(record player and all)*, or Peg and I would meet up in town, leaving Charlie at home, and go to see Barry in the films at the local cinema! Big time stuff! Peg used to enjoy our 'mother daughter' escapades together, and in those days it only cost 6 pence a ticket *(at the back of the cinema of course, miles away from the screen)!*

To have someone like him give positive and very complimentary evidence in the court case, and on TV, was for me, not only positively invaluable, but it was flabbergastingly wonderful. He had been trained vocally at the Australian Conservatory, with a guy called Stewart Harvey, and he *(Barry)* had his singing exercises on tapes, so that he too could practice whenever he felt like it. I had trained with Eddie Keen, and I also took exercise tapes with me to keep 'in voice', so both of us had been in very good hands! At the time of the court case, Barry was the then winner of Two MO Awards, for best male singer. He had been nominated three times before he won the first one. *("People rarely win it on their first nomination", he said in the court room.)* He also said that the first time that he had actually seen me perform, had been at the MO Award presentation held at Revesby Workers Club, in February 1979, a mere , nearly 6 months before the accident. He said that I had been *(quotes from the court case notes)* "someone who was like a raw ball of talent that last time he had seen me, but someone who was showing signs of becoming quite refined. For any artist to have received a 3 minute standing ovation at the end of their spot, with an audience made up of 'showies', is a rarity that can't be ignored" he added! *(quote!)* "Kerri achieved just that", he said! witness again retired.

(I was able to duck out to the toilet, during the 'dismissal' break, so I missed nothing that I should have been there for. Wasn't that wonderful?)

Back I came with a very relieved look on my face. Then the next fantastic person called, was - **Geoffrey John Harvey** *(another positively masterful, and talented piano playing musician - Geoff Harvey!)*

He was the musical director for the Channel 9 network, in Sydney, as well as all over Australia at that time. He said that unreliable performers didn't last very long in the business. When asked if Kerri Dyer was a reliable performer he said *(quote from the court scripts)* that "she was a definite 'family' member, and could always be relied upon to present the right kind of material, the correct sort of way"!

They liked the way in which I was happy to 'fit in' wherever and whenever I was needed. "If we wanted a bright, happy kind of song - she would do that", he said. "If on the other hand we needed a ballad, be it a big torch like ballad, or a light lyrical song - she had music for that too, and the bosses were assured that she knew how to perform those kinds of songs, and to sing them well", he said. *(again, direct quotes)*

"The Bandstand families (about 10 –12 people), and Mike Walsh families (4 or 5 maybe) are a chosen group from the thousands of singers available. Those who make a 'family', as Kerri did, generally get on very well in the business!

Kerri was considered part of the Mike Walsh 'family', and from working with her at the TV studio, and after seeing her at the MO Award presentation, there is no way that Kerri couldn't have gone on to be a star", he said. (witness retired)

Then came my great friend - <u>Christine McLaine - aka TONI STEVENS</u>

Toni, whom I had met on 'the circuit', and had worked with through ALVA, smilingly told the court room, *(giving me a reassuring grin,)* that she had worked all the major venues in UK, France, Germany, Italy, North Africa. She had been a support act for international names such as Dusty Springfield, Tom Jones, Morecombe and Wise, Bill Haley and the Comets, and Billie Eckstein.

Now - Toni had mainly worked the club scene when I had been working, but had become very involved in theatre restaurants by the time of the court case, and at the time of my accident, she owned and was hosting her own theatre restaurant. She was a great Comedienne/ singer! I actually envied her, her ability to make people laugh! *(I had always wanted to be able to do that, and I had been able to achieve it a little towards the end, but not necessarily with stand up comedy. More through the routines I did, and the various costumes)* We first met in 1976 when she founded ALVA. *(The Australian Ladies Variety Association)*, and I had been a founder member.

Q. How did you rate Kerri's performances?

A. "I saw her perform at the MO Awards Ceremony for 1978, held at Revesby Workers Club, in February 1979, and I would say that it would be the most outstanding performance I had ever seen her do. It was just incredible - it really was. Very few people that I know of have ever received a standing ovation at the MO Awards but Kerri did that night. It was incredible! Kerri was leaning towards the Carol Burnett kind of comedy, and she would have succeeded with it very well". *(direct quotes)*

Fees involved with musical theatre were debated, and they agreed that anyone working in them, on even a semi regular basis, regardless of the fact that there had been a bit of a slow down at that time, could look forward to earning anything between $500pw, and $1500pw.

Toni also told them how after the accident, soon after I came out of the coma, she had visited me at Prince Henry Hospital. She told of how I had been sitting up in bed, supported by pillows, so as to keep me upright, with a black patch over my right eye. "There Kerri was", she said, "diligently trying to *(apparently)* murder a pork chop with a knife and fork". *(direct quote) - (Not only did I have ataxia, but I also suffered with double vision, and was very glassy eyed. Please remember - I was in a terrible state I was, looking very unaware of anything much at all.)* Toni had bustled into the hospital room, she said, and when she had evidently asked me if I remembered who she was - I had said sorry -"no" - so she told me. At that time, because I couldn't use a knife and fork properly, Toni also cut my food up for me. I couldn't use my right hand very much at all anyway, and I hadn't been doing what could be called, a very good job of preparing my food for it's final journey - into my mouth! She said that a lot of my food used to end up on the 'bib' that I wore from necessity. *(If there had ever been such a thing, I really needed a second 'radar directed' fork to actually guarantee getting the chopped up meals into my mouth. It is hard to appreciate now, that I was actually no better at 28, than my lovely little daughter had been at 6 months.)*

Toni had been to visit me at my Maroubra flat not long after after I was released from Hospital, having been hospitalised on and off for nearly 5 years. After finding the flat in an abysmal state, she straight away, organised a 'working bee', where the girls of ALVA all got together, and cleaned up my flat for me. I hated being so dependent on other people's help, but in a way I am fortunate, in that I don't really have very clear memories of that time. I must have still been 'out of it' pretty badly! *(Can't imagine where Andy was. We weren't divorced at that time!)* He was probably about somewhere, but about 12 girls went in and they cleaned up"! And when I say they cleaned up - they evidently spent the whole day cleaning. Even Carter Edwards, the Taubman's man, in Australia in those years, came in with his ELNA ironing press, *(he had been made a temporary, honorary ALVA member)* and he did the ironing for me. *(Now if only I could actually remember it clearly, that must really have been a sight and a half! Carter Edwards was as I said, The Taubman's man, and as such, was a husky, muscle man, and definitely not a 'doing the ironing with an Elna Press' type of man)*

My ironing had built up, because it was easiest for me to just wash things in the automatic machine, dry them in the dryer, and put them straight back on, or neatly put them in the 'to be ironed' *(which I was unable to do)* basket. Most of the time though, I just put them straight back into the dryer to stay warm, and thus be ironed by the warm air.

It was truly in-cre-di-ble! - not just the clothes being ironed by the dryer, but the love that was shown by all. I could never forget that! Nor this! Carter Edwards *(remember - the Taubman's man)* also bought me a microwave oven, *(definitely a new fangled thing in those days)*, so Toni used to save and freeze some of her Sunday roast, or weekly meals for me. - I could then just heat them up in the microwave. She knew that I was not too hot on the cooking thing at that time. Couldn't co- ordinate the food things to make up a meal, could I?

I took advantage of those made up meals, and I also used to use the microwave to make myself cups of tea and coffee etc. I didn't have enough memory or co -ordination to use a stove or a kettle. I had done a good job of burning my hands on one or two occasions, and ran a good chance of blowing up the house, because I would forget that the kettle was on the stove, and that the stove was ON!

It was a gas stove as well! *(Ooo, I was a well looked after biddy, wasn't I?)*

Q. Did you actually help her by doing things like massaging her legs?
A. "She was virtually immobile, just watching Television, so her legs used to turn blue with cold. I stood her up, and walked her about, supporting her arm all the time, and with her permission *(I was after all an adult - a 'crook' one maybe, but an adult nevertheless,* my husband and I used some of the money from the sale of a few of her things, and bought a track suit for her. She had put on a bit of weight, and was told by her husband, when she did see him, that she was fat and had to lose some weight". *(Again? I must have been fat - thin - fat, for most of my*

life, mustn't I? and I guess that I was, and probably still am.) She hadn't been able to buy anything new for ages, so I organised with the girls for some spare clothes, and also took her shopping for a few new things as she slowly got better.

"Toni also told the court that she had organised for me to spend Christmas with them for a few years, and that she often took me out to shows and things.

(Most of my most memorable evenings, those fabulous nights out, shows etc, all came with her excellent guiding hand A better, unrewarded friend, a person would be hard pressed to find!) She was also asked in the court -

Q I think at the ball at the Wentworth, of which you spoke before, she was in fact, accompanied by Barry Crocker into the Ballroom?
A "Yes"

Q. Was she well received?

A "Exceptionally well! I had told everybody that our guests for the night included Michael Parkinson, as the guest of honour, but just after I told them that, I said - "Here is a lady who you have been waiting to see for two and a half years", and Barry brought her in on his arm and five hundred and sixty people stood up and gave her a standing ovation. They were so glad to see her."

(Now, I haven't included this particular piece of the transcript for any other reason than to try and show you just why I loved, and still do love, the 'showbiz' industry, [even though I have had almost nothing much to do with it for years.] The majority of it's members are made up of 'great stuff', and I have always been absolutely staggered by the warmth and affection that I have always received from the girls of ALVA, and the business in general!, even before that horrible accident.) The opposition cross examined Toni and actually, inadvertently, *(I am pretty sure he hadn't meant to do it)* benefited my case by asking questions that, although they were meant to show deficiencies in 'the business', and the lack of prospects for the future, actually showed things that would have definitely been to my monetary advantage, if I hadn't been in the accident. We were all then 'retired'.

(Even though very few of us were actually of retirement age at that stage.) It was all to start again on the following Monday 14th October 1985 at 10 o'clock.

I rushed off to the toilet again – *(again I just made it. - Do you think maybe that I had what was called 'a weak bladder'? Didn't realise that one could be so weak, and yet be so active.)* Anyway we all had a jolly weekend at home? I wonder!

Monday the 14th October, 1985 was to prove, for me at least , the most monumental day of the court case so far! My second favourite musician was next - *(with ED obviously being my favourite, but for a very different reason)* **THE MAESTRO, *TOMMY TYCHO*,** was sworn in, and examined next.

(Maybe those sceptics earlier on had been correct. Maybe I <u>had</u> *kept rejecting the figures for out of court settlements, because I wanted to hear what was said by those who testified. Mind you - I didn't know who was actually giving evidence for me, until either the day before or the actual day, so if I had accepted earlier sums, not only would I have been untrue to my own beliefs, but then I would never have found out that I had been so highly thought of! A fact that I will cherish till the day I actually do die! The memories of what people said will keep me going when life gets almost too hard to bare. I will be eternally grateful to them all for aiding and abetting the final, astronomically wonderful results. Their time most definitely hadn't been wasted. For so much good to come out of something so bad, it's just phenomenal. At least I think so!)*

Tommy Tycho *(Australia's equivalent to, or maybe even better [at least I think so, anyway] than England's Jules Holland)* gave a short resume of where he had worked, and of his fantabulous credentials. He obtained a diploma of Music in both conducting and composing from the Franz Lizt Academy of Music in Budapest, in 1947, and he had been deeply involved with both skills in the intervening years.

(I have also just found out from the court docs, that it appears that he actually came to Australia in the same year that I was born, 1951. Oooh! Is that spooky or what?)

287

He told the court also of how he had been on a number of adjudication panels for many singing competitions etc. and of how those kind of programmes have benefited from his very capable presence, all over Australia. *(Justifiable self praise, I think!)*

He told also of how he had been the compère for a show called "You're a Star" for Australian TV. *(now well and truly no longer on air! It must have been like a very early version of X Factor, that is now world wide, and offers artists an incredible start, but without the monumental monetary gains!)* I guess that I was very lucky!

Warren Smith had put my name forward to let Tommy know that I was interested in doing one of his shows, and Tommy who had seen some of my TV shows, *(so I guess that they acted as auditions - what do you reckon?)* asked me if I would perform in his "Golden Era of the Big Bands" show, in March 1978. It was scheduled in for the Sydney Opera House, The Dallas Brookes Hall in Melbourne, and the Festival Hall in Adelaide. I do remember being 'over the moon' at the time, but Tommy had implied in the court room, that if she *(me)* hadn't 'cut the mustard' *(my phrase by the way)*, then "she would have been very politely dropped from the show, and – before it began touring too", he said. I don't suppose that he could have afforded to have a flop associated with his well established name. Six weeks were spent before each new concert, what with the rehearsals with the musicians, and the on stage rehearsals for the lighting etc.

The most exciting thing for me though, were the rehearsals with Tommy at his home, on his own grand piano. I was learning the songs that he had selected for me to sing. For me it was like working with royalty. *(Thankfully, I had 'cut the mustard', and hadn't been 'cut' from the show! Tommy has, of course, since been made a 'Sir', and an extremely well deserved honour it is, too. He evidently has not been very well for a few years now).* He was full of praise for my ability to sustain the vitality of a song, to sing it well, in tune, and to 'sell' it to every member of the audience, even in a big room.

(I probably blushed when he said that.)

I will directly quote from the court case notes for a bit again, if for no other reason than to make me feel a little better than I sometimes still do, about it all. And right now is one of those times when I could do with a bit of cheering up! So here goes!)

Q.....is there some quality of voice which goes beyond the concept of technical competence?

A "Yes, there is. It is that indefinable sound that I described a little while before, which makes for an instant recognition by the people when they hear it, as to who is doing the singing. It is hard to describe! It is just one of those elusive things that only happen a very few times - seldom seen in the world market of professional singing - that separates one particular person, from all the rest of them. It is this indefinable, elusive thing, that when people hear the voice, they say - Ah! - that person is such and such. Barbara Streisand - Judy Garland - Julie Anthony - Kerri Biddell, to name just a few.

Kerri Dyer was that good. She had great voice production - that struck me from the first time I heard her sing - "there is a talent there that does not need a great deal of improvement to be able to become National, and eventually, an International Star! With her seldom found talent to be able to communicate with an audience via the intensely intrusive camera screen, as well as readily across the footlights, she could very reasonably have gone onto world wide stardom! There is no doubt"!

(I had been nominated in the best new act category of the MO awards in 1975/6. Then I was nominated in the best female artist category in 1977/78. It had taken me those two years to no longer be a 'new act', and to have improved my performance ability. I was nominated again for the 1978/9 awards, having already performed with the dancers six months before, but by then the accident had happened, and I stupidly, sullenly and petulantly said to my ex husband that I didn't want anyone voting for me out of sympathy. A comment I now regret with bells on! How could I have been so dumb as to believe that my entertainer mates would vote just out of sympathy!?

My then husband, thinking that he was doing it for me [I think], withdrew my name, and I could kill us both!) - (It was just as well that we stopped for lunch after Tommy's evidence, 'cause it was time for a 'Miss Dyer wee break' anyhow!)

Then next came - **Robert Limb - (Bobby Limb)** band leader, involved in music, radio, radio recordings, live theatre, television, film and rock and roll events, was next. He studied under a scholarship to the Adelaide College of Music, where he studied saxophone for six years. Subsequently he played in big bands, and in his own band in other major capital cities. He was awarded an OBE for his services to the industry. Enough said about Bobby.

He was fantastic, as was Tommy Tycho. *(He was not quite in the same league as Tommy though, but then I am of course ,a bit biased. Because of Tommy, I got to perform in the Sydney Opera House, which for me was wonderful!!!.)*

Dr. Kerrie Powell was next. She was a clinical psychologist, and a Bachelor and Master of Arts at Sydney University.

(She helped me incredibly with my original coming to terms with what had happened to me, and also my being able to cope in the world outside. So I couldn't leave her out. I will always be eternally grateful to her for her help at putting me back together to form a solid, proper, starting point for my self improvement).

But then there should have been - another 'big fanfare' > - **"B-Dum – tadah!"**

"Richard Foster. From Dick Foster Productions."

(I had no idea at all that my team had asked him to give evidence, but to tell the truth, I was ecstatic that they had, and what is more, just a bit gob smacked! He was Julie Anthony's international manager, and he had been handling her work in America, and I think in Britain too.)

He explained who he was, where he lived in America, and what his credentials were. He had been a singer dancer to start, and he had worked on the show 'Leave it to Beaver', and with Andy Williams, Roger Williams, Judy Garland, Dean Martin Specials, as well as the Donna Reed Show (America and International).

He had also performed on stage with productions like Gypsy, West side story, The King and I, Point of view, Damn Yankees and a Tree Rose in Brooklyn. All the major Casinos and nightclubs on 'The Strip', in America had benefited from his performances before he became involved actively in the creating and directing of stage and television performances. He had, at that time, been in the creation and packaging of shows and talent for about 20 years.

Originally brought to Australia in 1977 to advise in creating and also making programs suitable for o'seas audiences, he saw Julie Anthony perform at the MO's *(the year before I performed there - drat! How truly 'different' my 'different' life could have been then!)* and he took her under his wing. He organised her first US television special, and it won a Sammy Award. *(Lucky girl! I would have given my left leg for an opportunity like that. But - hey, come to think of it though, it probably wouldn't have done me much good without a left leg would it? But I think you know what I mean anyhow!* A recess was called *(Can you guess why?).*

Mr Foster viewed the video of my working while I was in the loo!

Well I didn't need to see it again, did I?

I did though come back in half way through it, and when asked by the opposition lawyers, a little later, for an opinion of it - Mr Forster said - **"Well - mostly I do normally, form my opinion of an overall performance, on seeing a video tape, and I did feel that she was an excellent singer."**

He continued on - "I thought beyond that though, as I had done with Julie Anthony. What I saw with Miss Dyer was that she had the potential of being a well rounded performer. Her voice was very secure, her movement was very secure, and actually when compared to Julie Anthony, the movement was much better. Her looks, her composure, the lack of fear of looking into the lens; all those factors combined, spelt to me a very, very good performer. She had the ability of handling extremely well, the various degrees of types of songs. In addition, I felt her emotion, particularly in portraying the lyric of a song, which is very important, was that she tells a story as well as singing, and that she told the story very well in the material I viewed". *(again directly quoted from the court notes).*

Mr Foster then faced the opposition lawyer, who had said this to him a little later - **Q With respect, Mr Foster, that last answer you gave is very vague.** *(The answer to the previous question had been - 'There are certain singers who can handle the lyrics better than others'.)*

A -**Mr Foster answered:** There are few artists who come to audition for my shows who can sing that song as well as Kerri Dyer did! *(I think it was a medley of Feelings and The Way We Were that he was talking about!*

Not too sure which one he meant though.) He had been in the creation and packaging of shows and talent for many years. *(On reading all this fol de rol back in 2009, it does sound a little big headed of me, doesn't it? Sorry! It was essential information at the time, and it is in the court records - as is.)* He was retired after the barrister had continued doing his job of trying to discredit my witness's testimony for a bit. Thankfully, for me though, the opposition lawyer wasn't all that successful. Then after another wee break - *(again, there was me with my hand in the air, and my knees crossed.)* I came back, and they then went through a whole lot of stuff to try and assess what I might have been earning if the accident had never happened. Mr Foster was dismissed, and then came - **David Samuel Bell - medical practitioner.**

He gave lots of evidence concerning brain damage, and what I would or would not be able to do. *(It was very interesting to read the drafts from the court case, and to realise that some of what he said would be permanent, I have already managed to overcome, but I am continually working on all aspects of my disability, even nearly thirty years later, and I have only just, in 2009, got my voice kind of singing properly! It may be quiet at the moment, but it is almost starting to sound little as it used to! It will never be the same again. Hopefully though, by the time I turn 60 in 2011, I will have it back well enough to actually sing a little something at the party I hope to throw to celebrate my birthday,and possibly have the Australian launch of this book! Always been a lover of celebrating – me! Especially that birthday! I will be 4 years past my 'use by date'! Ha ha!)* But - I guess though that I would have to admit, and agree with Dr Bell, that even the omnipotent me, can't correct some things! I am still a wobbly. Not as much of one to be sure, but still one, never the less. And I still have a 'different', distinctive speaking voice! *(It's a voice that could only belong to one person – Kerri Dyer-Keen. It may not be internationally known, as I dreamed of, but at least I got my immediately recognisable voice - didn't I?)*

But anyway - after a bit more kafuffle, we packed up our things, and all went home again, to return on - <u>Tuesday 15th October 1985</u>

The sixth and final day.

(Do-n't panic! As Jonesy says on Dad's Army. I promise that it's almost over!)

Noel Ferrier - Entertainer and producer of entertainment shows in Sydney and in Australia generally. A most unexpected *(for me)* witness. Although he was not a singer himself, in his job as a production manager, he was always on the lookout for artists to perform in any of his shows. There was no doubt about it he said - he would have been looking for someone just like me, who according to his evaluation, had a good, strong, lyrical voice, as well as being someone who knew how to move well, and to sell a song.

He had also been very impressed with the videos of me singing. Then came **JULIE ANTHONY - female entertainer extraordinare**

Now you don't normally get a beneficial - to you - kind of testimony given by a fellow female vocalist. Most of us *(singers that is)* are always a bit full of ourselves, and full of self confidence in our own abilities, and are not normally keen to praise anybody else. Not so Julie though, and a few others that I know about. Now - Julie justifiably had cause to be proud of her own abilities, so I was doubly pleased that she gave such excellent testimony in my court case.

Julie gave a general outline of all the things she had been doing in the business - where and when she began, and her present management status. She gave details of her London England work, in Irene, *(in which she had the Star role)* and as the Mother superior, in the Sound of Music. She told us of the convention work she did, and the Television commercials, and of being the voice most associated with the leading Building society in Australia at the time - The St George Building Society. Julie shared top billing at that time with the St George dragon!

(And they say you should never work with kids or animals! I think that she proved them wrong that time - don't you? She must have made a small fortune out of that one commercial alone!)

She told the court that she had first seen me in 1975, and that my confidence, struck her, along with *(her words from the court evidence)* her "extraordinary vocal quality". She also said that for one who was just beginning in the industry - "Kerri's confidence and presentation was also outstanding". And then she commented - "Combine that confidence with her theatricality in presenting a song for television - it was as if she was singing right to the individual watching". *(I guess that my writing is similar. I try to tell the story as if I were telling the reader personally.)*

But she added - "It is very difficult to sing that way to a piece of machinery".

(I think that she meant the camera, and she gave some other fabulous {for me} evidence. As with all of the others, I will be eternally grateful!)

Julie and Tommy both said that I had a voice that would have been immediately recognisable as belonging to me, because I used inflection and tone, in a way that would make the voice immediately recognisable as that, belonging to - only one - Kerri Dyer.

"Not only was Kerri nominated,in '75/6, she was also asked to perform for the '77/8 in '79 presentation evening. That is a highly prestigious thing in the business", she said!

"Kerri had been nominated once before, with me, but very few people win on their first nomination. The artist concerned won't come to the particular notice of the voters that first year. It is generally the latter years where the impact is made".

Next up was - **Anthony John Brady**

Principal of ATA - all star artists PL, was also an entertainer, as well as an Agent. He provided information as to the payment for certain performances.

Q - "Have you seen Miss Dyer work before her accident"?, asked my QC.

A - "Oh yes, our agency - well Kerri was one of our regular, what I call performers. She was one of the artists we regularly selected for our venues. Sir, I would most definitely say, that had the trend continued, and been allowed to continue, Kerri Dyer would have been commanding very high fees indeed.

She would have achieved 'name status' (as we call it) and she would have been commanding very high fees indeed. Kerri was a unique performer, but Kerri was, certainly prior to the accident, rated with Julie Anthony, and with one or two other top female performers".

Then there was James Howard Bryant-_Professional Building Appraisals. Basic information given about building requirements for a house for me. Ramps and things - *(but luckily they weren't needed!)*

THE MATTER WAS VERY SUCCESSFULLY SETTLED.

Six 'in court' days!

*(I finally got what I had held out for all along - AUS. $1000000-00 +
costs (APPROXIMATELY about $380000-00 all told, so they told me.)*
*I guess that I can be a very belligerent person, when I think/know that
I am right!)*

Evidently it was the largest court case of it's kind at that time. At
that time! *(it's probably chicken feed compared to many more recent cases
though)*

But a major thank you must go to everyone who played, even the
smallest part in it!

I WILL BE FOREVER IN YOUR DEBT!

THE END OF LIFE 2, START OF LIFE 3!

So here we go again, *(but I won't say sorry this time, you should know by now that I truly am!)* - with me doing my navigational trick and sticking with the courtroom stuff!

There I was having sat through all of the 'let's evaluate her true worth' stuff with my knowing what I thought my talent had been worth, but still trying to be a bit 'kind of' realistic as to how much I could reasonably expect the final assessment to be. I must say though that it was fun! I'd never had to evaluate my talent before. I had never really had to think about it much. I had just turned up, done the shows, and dreamed of one day making it big! *(So I guess that secretly, I must have always believed in my ability – really! Mustn't I?)* It had been though, still a bit of a chore to assess just exactly what kind of monetary value should be put on 'little ol' me. I think sometimes *(especially when I am feeling down)* that it would almost have been worth having the accident all over again, just to be able hear how highly regarded I had been - but then, come to think of it , maybe not! *(I think that I would have preferred finding out in a far less dramatic sort of way, and anyway, I might not be so lucky(?) next time! I might end up properly dead!)*

But anyway - after having gone a bit 'wild' with the money back in the late 80's, by having had a 'bonza' time *(tell you more about that later too)*. I knuckled down when I got to England, and after some clever money management supervised by my lovely husband of nearly 20 years, I have done well enough thank you.

I am now asset rich, income poor maybe, but still living very happily in England with my wonderful husband, and my delightfully attractive, intelligent daughter who is off to the London School of Economics (LSE) next week. I have had a great time, and at least now my daughter will be well trained enough to know how to make the best of whatever amount she inherits when the day comes! But just between you, me, and the gatepost – regardless of what they say about how long I have got, I feel that I am destined to be here for long enough to see her well and truly established, married (maybe) living a wonderful life. Since her getting straight A's and A+'s in her A level exams at school, my daughter has worked for two years, stored up some life skills, and is finally off next week! Off to LSE and the fantastic future that lies ahead of her.

I will miss her dreadfully, but the future is looking very rosy, and exciting for her. For both of us really, as thanks to a wonderful start to 2010, it also promises to be an interesting 2010 - 2011 for me!

So I guess that in 'different' kind of way, I am doubly rich! - Financially because of the settlement, and also because of my fabulously clever family. Who would ever have thought it eh? Me? - A Millionaire! (*Australian, was at least!)* but that still sounds good though, doesn't it"?! Even though it probably doesn't mean quite as much in 2010, as it did in 1979.

But do you know something else? I am not only doubly rich, after all the bad times, I would say that now, that I am in my third life, I am suddenly triply rich!

And how's that?

Well -**1.** I am alive and about 3 - 4 years past the 'use by date' given me after the court case;

2. I finally have someone whom I have genuinely loved more than life itself for nearly 20 years of the 54 year friendship. Someone that I can not only love, but someone with whom I can share the money, when he lets me; *and, and, and* as well as all that -

3.I have a clever, not so little any more, girl.

Life has never looked rosier!

It is now hard to imagine that it could have turned out SO differently.

If not for the encouragement I have received from my lovely husband, and his original 'go get em Kes' training in Australia, that he has surreptitiously continued right through our marriage, I could quite easily have buried myself in a life of torment, and spend thrift ways!

If I am honest though, before I got married to Ed, found this happiness, and got a bit tamed by my man, the truth of the matter is that my selfish streak must have come through in heaps. After all the lead up to the case, I felt that I was owed a bit of a splurge straight after. *(Just to help me get over all that I had been through during the previous 9 years of course. - You understand - don't you? Please say that you do, because I have to admit that sometimes even I don't fully understand some of the things I have done!! It was though, everything 'not nice' put aside, **fun,** and as I have continually said - I DO LIKE FUN!!)*

But anyway, I finally got the chance to do some of the travelling that I had always dreamed of doing but hadn't been able to afford to do. And, typical of me - I figured that if I was going to do it, then I would do it in style! So, I thought at the time that now that I could afford it, it was to be 'first class' all the way!

At first it didn't seem quite right though, *(without Andy by my side I mean)*, but I soon got over that! *(That may sound horrible - but at the time, I hadn't come through it all to let someone 'do me down', now had I?!)*

After all this time though, I am kind of appreciative of just how hard it would have been for him to watch the woman that he had loved, and I can say now from afar that he did love me, turn into the shell of what she had once been. As happy as I am at the moment, and as much as I love the man I have been married to for 20 years, I guess though that I would have to say that my marriage to Ed, is a kind of mixed blessing.

As he correctly says to me now - "if you wish to keep hold of money these days, you can't spend it. *(So somehow I don't think that I'll really be tripping the light fantastic, any time soon! Maybe I'll manage to sneak in some small little nibbles though? Especially around my 60th birthday!)*

When he says that to me, one half of me says - yes my love - you are, of course right my darling, but the other half says - Such a shame. My day will come - maybe!!!

I did *(still do, maybe?)* like spending money, and before I got married to 'Mr Parsimonious, *(as I cheekily, but lovingly call him)*, in the gazebo in my back yard in Australia, and before he was continually around to make me see the so called error of my ways, I saw glaciers, and seals, enjoyed the sunshine, and thoroughly enjoyed cruising part of the world, on the Sea Princess. It was a fantabulous ship, and what is more, I did it with a great escort, a Mr Paul Waite. *(That was after my tempestuous fling with Russ, and before I got married again, of course!)*

Unfortunately, and most unusually for me at the time, the cruising with Paul, was done just as friends, and he is still one of my better friends. He is also my daughter's Godfather though, and he always still 'drops in' when he is in England on Business! *(Which I have to admit, is not all that often these days, but then with the global credit crunch, it is not all that surprising. That is one expensive trip, from Australia. Especially with the collapse of the world markets!)*

I had remembered from previous general discussions with various people, from my own visual experience *(limited though it might have been)*, and from what Ed had reminded me of just after the court case - that "one of the best investments that a newly moneyed person could make, was in real estate. Bricks and mortar, and I guess it still is, as long as you own those bricks and mortar, outright!" But -

Because I wanted to have some fun once the court case was finished, I must confess that I kind of put that information in my *(still had it)* 'get around to it later' basket, and until I got the chance to take Eds good advice, and because I was a suddenly wealthy woman alone, I had to be very careful with the money. There were of course people who had some of the most sensible sounding, ridiculous ideas.

"Only thing is" they would say, "the idea *(whatever it was)* just needs that extra $20,000 - $50,000 for it to be truly, outstandingly, successful"!

"*Oh Yeah?*", says me in my most understanding, yet 'no way' voice. *(I definitely upset a few people very badly by not investing in what they had guaranteed (?) were sure things! Whether or not they turned out to be, I am not sure, but I doubt that they would have made me any richer. Richer in angst maybe!)* There were also the stocks and shares, which I had never really liked, but that my solicitors had organised for me. Somewhere in the back of my brain I told myself that when I got back to Sydney, I would cash in some of the shares, and was definitely going to build a house to live in! That was real estate, wasn't it? That's what Ed had told me to do, wasn't it?! First though, I was going to have some fun!!!! So Russ and I went off to Hamilton Island!

Now - the sun and sand of Hamilton Island had been wonderful, and Russ and I both went back to Sydney, the most adorable shade of 'summer gold' that you can imagine. Lying about on sun drenched beaches, catching a few rays, definitely proved to be more like fun, than pushing a wheelchair in the snow would have been! *(Our other option at the time.)* - "Yeah! - at that time - 'Fun was definitely the name of the game'!

off we go!

Now, I cannot put my hand on my heart and say that Russ and I were 'in love', because neither of us was really capable of loving anyone but ourselves at that time. We had met at the half way house I told you about, and so what began as a friendship between two disabled people, slowly turned into a so called 'love' interest. Having spent so many years actively craving 'that', *(you remember what 'that' is, don't you?)*, I figured during my time with Russ, that it was about time to investigate what other alternatives there were in life, and we *did* find some very imaginative ways of enjoying ourselves sexually. Apart from the travelling that I organised, I also got persuaded, *(not too difficult a thing to do in this case)* to invest in a night club!

There was my name on the publicity blurb as one of the owners, *(Ego tripping maybe?)*,oh yeah, and that's right, I also had a horse race at an ALVA race day named after my darling Daddy - The Charlie Dyer Handicap! That little bit of indulgence only cost me - $1000-00.
Only a thousand dollars?

I think that I must have been truly, off my trolley! I didn't think that I had ever inherited my father's love of horse/dog racing, but I figured that if he could see from his cloud ,or oven, then he would have been so thrilled! Also my little excursion into the nightclub owning world must also have managed to lose me some more thousands of dollars. I can't really remember, but with the depleted amount that I was able to bring over here to England, and the loss on the exchange rate must have gone a long way towards my no longer being a millionaire, mustn't it? Oh well! I think that I must have had a good time! Unfortunately - I can't really remember much of it too well from back then, can I?!

Friends later consoled me by telling me that at least the $1000 I had spent, had gone to a good cause. And of course they were right!

ALVA always helps selected entertainers who find themselves in need of assistance, and they had definitely been there for me when I needed them! I have given them donations since, in appreciation of their help when I needed it, generally when I flew back to Australia on fleeting visits. Charlie, my Dad,who as I think I mentioned was eternally poor, would probably have blanched at my spending a lump sum of $1000 on anything, but I don't think that he would have considered money spent on *The Charlie Dyer Handicap* as an exorbitant amount, or waste of money. Not to have had a race named after him, anyway. He must have had a real giggle from his 'cloud' above, or from his 'oven down below'. And as I had said - it *was* only $1000. But really, a $1000,was a lot of money at the time, and it still is now - I suppose. It's strange what suddenly coming into money can do to your sensibilities! *(I guess that there must have been more of my Daddy in me, than I had thought!)*

The holiday that Russ and I took though - the thought and preparation needed for Russ and I to go to Hamilton Island for a week had been astronomical. But I would have to say that at least the weather had been lovely, and the added help given by the tour organisers was fantastic. Trying to get a wheelchair and me in my extremely disabled state, on and off planes and boats, was a true giggle, for us! Not necessarily so though for the Travel agents, and we must have made very interesting yet super worrying holiday makers for them! But what a sight it must have been!

A wobbly and a wheelie!

Russ and I sure found some wild ways to enjoy the money, and have a 'ripper' of a time while we were at it! Whoa – yeah! I think that I bought him a car! I think too that I probably bought car for Charliene's father as well. Can't really remember!

But I do know that I had a good time and lots of fun, which at that time was all that counted when I was with Russ!

(I had definitely also become very self centered by then.)

But once we had come home, a decision had to be made as to where we should live! We couldn't really go back to the halfway house. Well we couldn't, now could we? Mind you - it probably would have been the best financed halfway house in the land, if we had! But I sort of convinced Russ, no - I guess that I told him that we were going to move. *(Horrible person that I had become, and I assume that the thought of all the money, and the occasional present, helped sway him a little, anyway!).*

I began trawling the 'homes for sale' part of the paper, and in the auction brochures. Being keen to live not too far from a beach, and on seeing an old house come up for auction at Monterey, ten minutes *(even for me)*, from the beach I figured that I had maybe found the site for my dream home. So - I went to see it, eventually bid for it, and managed to buy it!. Neither Russ nor I really liked the 'normal looking' weatherboard house, that wasn't even as good(?) as Peg and Charlie's rented, fibro house that I had been brought up in BUT! -

The site itself was absolutely to die for, *(nothing like Greenacre)*, and already my fertile mind had started imagining and planning. Russ just let me dream on. He possibly found the whole thing just a trifle obscene! He was a pretty basic sort of man, from a pretty basic background. I can't really remember the price of that weatherboard home that I had knocked down *(maybe the fact that Russ knew that I was going to have it demolished, was why he had found it all a trifle obscene.)*, but foolishly, I mustn't have thought that I had to pay too much attention to 'how much a thing cost' at that time. After all, I had the money, and If I wanted it, I bought it! That amount of money from the court case, would last forever, wouldn't it? Silly - wasn't I?

The original weatherboard house, that I was going to have knocked down, had been at the side of a reserve, with the parkland built right up to the side of the house, and a small rivulet thing meandering along, among reeds and things about 20 feet below. The house was horrible, but the setting? Oo yes, the setting! It was beautiful, and I immediately fell in love with the site! Slavishly so! The house virtually had miles of lovely grassy land at the side of it, which was all graciously mown for us by the Council. Just right for we two, who would never have been able to use a mower.

But you know? Come to think of it, that would definitely have been a sight to behold, wouldn't it? Either of the two of us mowing all that lawn

(Although one of those sit on tractor/mowers might have been fun! What d' ya reckon? I can just see Russ and I, ensconced on our ride on mower, doing wheelies outside the house, all in the truthful pretense of - 'mowing the lawn'.) Mind you - we probably would have been fighting over who's turn it was to drive, and would have been falling about laughing! They do say though, that small things amuse small minds!

Not too sure what the council's reaction to that would have been either!

But then – I guess they would have been happy enough as long as the grass was mowed!!!! The house was at the end of a cul - de - sac, lovely and quiet, and it was the open land of the 'reserve' that had entranced me from the first viewing. I mean to say, after all, I definitely didn't want normal, did I? Even then, even after all that time, and after the accident, I still wanted *'different'*, and that house was definitely that!

(Do you reckon that some people never learn?!)

My architects, who I think were 'friends' of a friend of mine, *(which could have been disastrous, but which turned out really good!)*, must have secretly thought that I was nuts. "A loony lady, with money", and that "here is an easy buck or three". And I think that the thought of the 'gold' to be winkled out of the mad woman, must have meant that they weren't too worried about anything much at all! So any suggestions from me for improvements etc., were greeted with hearty approval, because it generally meant more money for them!!

They happily helped me tear down the original weatherboard house, after the not really too unpleasant, but a little tired looking, old house had been very inexpensively 'titified' up for the first party that I threw. A whole lot of food was also brought in by Mr Caterer, especially to provide for what I called a pre 'demolition' party.

AN INVITATION

very 'goth'

Brown, almost black invitations with bright yellow writing, were sent out, *(very 'Goth', before it ever became a fashion statement)* - Ms Kerri Dyer, requests the pleasure of.............. at her pre - demolition Party. Dress smart casual. So all these glamorous, entertainer type people turned up for what was in reality just a lavish excuse for a 'touch of madness, and an excuse to party, and get drunk!' Unlike the 'titifying' up of the house, the catering was unfortunately, *not* inexpensively provided, but at the time, I thought - "What the heck", and in actuality,

I felt that it was well and truly worth the cost. After all – I was the one paying the bill.

Mr Caterer and my builder's young vivacious partner, did an astoundingly good job! They even provided a big mallet, which sat in the corner, with a 'ginormous' pink ribbon tied in a bow around it. *(lost the photo of it somewhere I did!)* It sat there, waiting, while everyone feasted and got hyper, and drunk enough to take big whacks at the house! Which we all did with gusto!

My 'celebration of life party' later on, as well as my wedding tea, when I married Ed, were also catered for by Mr Caterer, that's how good I thought they were!

The builder's girlfriend though, had that touch of glamour that, at the time, I was a sucker for, and so at the party we all sat around drinking *(yes, even me);* I even did a bit of dancing; *(Again, if you could call what I did at that time, dancing! - Actually I don't think that you could ever realistically call what I did, and still do, dancing!);* We all talked a lot - occasionally about the waste of what had once been someone's home; and then all of us, the builders included, took turns at swinging the mallet at the house, until we had partly demolished it. *(The house that is - not the mallet! I don't suppose though that I was ever one for doing anything by halves! Especially not then anyway!)*

Some people probably thought that I was mad. And they were probably right!

A bit bonkers you might say!

1. We all had a really jolly time, bashing that poor, not really all that bad, old house to 'smithereens'! We let out any aggressions that we might have had!

I know that I still had a lot, but evidently – so did everyone else have plenty!

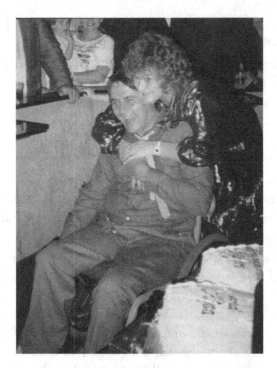

**double celebration - together a whole year
and house demolition**

On the following Monday, the builders came in and finished the job that my 'pre - demolition' party had begun, and about a week after that, during which time I went there every day to watch and look over the final plans being realised, they had finished laying the foundations of my individually designed dream home. Well, after all, I had nothing else to do anyway - right? Such excitement! I even left a hand print in it. "Personalised it, you might say"! *(The concrete base that is! The new owners of the house will never know, not of course, unless they read this book, or the house is blown over by one of the new gigantic wind storms that appear to be happening around the world!)*

Where the original front door of the old house had been, they had built in the automated garage door of my new home. It would now be possible to drive straight into the house directly from the cul-de-sac.

OK - OK, OK, pretty normal nowadays, but very la de da for an ex Greenacre girl, back then! We are talking about 1988 here! Over 22 years ago.

Half of the bricks arrived one afternoon during the first week, and Russ and I spent the last part of that afternoon fooling around, getting in everyone's way by building large 'Lego' houses out of a pile of bricks. There was Russ who's legs looked like a rag doll's, having slid out of his wheelchair onto the ground. His two useless looking legs, splayed out before him, and then there was me, finding it just a tad difficult to sit cross legged on the ground, so my legs were also askew at the weirdest of angles. But weird positions or not,we were there just like two little kids in a sand tray, with bricks and sand all around us. Talk about us never having grown up, and do you know something else? I am not too sure whether or not I have to this day!! *(Not that I would sit in sand playing with Lego bricks any more! I don't think! Ha ha)* We were building all kinds of oblong shapes, padding them up with sand, and laughing, probably a little too raucously as the first lot crumbled under the weight of the next ones. Getting sand all over us, and also, unfortunately, getting in everyone's way as they tried to lay the foundations.

We understandably got roused on something shocking and so, both of us were sent back to the halfway house so that the men could get on with it! And I am here to tell you now, that most dejected we felt about it all too. We weren't really doing anybody any harm - now were we? Bit by bit though, the house began to take shape.

I must have driven the builders mad, and was always underfoot, complaining about it taking so long, *(which of course, it wasn't)*, and asking for last minute alterations, *(which they incorporated if they could)*, but which now that they had actually begun were generally ignored. I was there so often it's a wonder they didn't just tie me up and throw me in the river that flowed past the house. But once they finally gave me the keys to my new home, under a huge amount of pressure from me to do so I might add, I felt such elation! Now I felt that I could really get on with my life! And get on with it - I did!

I very quickly set about finishing the purchase of all the furniture and carpets and fittings. Well Russ *(yes he was still with me at that time!)* and I, who had definitely become a bit of an item by that time, couldn't exactly camp on the concrete floor, among the dust and the emptiness now could we, and I was super eager to move in now that it was done, wasn't I? Patience has never been one of my better virtues, and not even one of my worst, I suppose, but maybe I was a little too eager. There was still a lot of finishing off to be done, and I don't really think that owners are supposed to have taken up residence quite so soon. But they had given me the keys after all, *(no doubt sick of my pestering!)* and had done so only probably so as to shut me up for a bit. They just silently grimaced, and continued working around us for the last little bit!!

I had already bought, and had installed from midway of the build, a huge spa bath that matched the one in the end of the outside pool, except that the bathroom one was a lovely shade of bathroom green. It was actually about five times the size of the pool one, and you could just about have done the Australian crawl in it, *(the bath silly! I'm pretty sure that you definitely could in the pool itself.).* Come to think of it, that bath just about was my en suite! *(A restriction on the amount of water you could use had just come into force those days, but I justified that bit of expensive luxury, by saying that it was a necessary medical aid for administering to my already evident arthritis, and our joint body pains. So it was a tax– deductible commodity!)* OO – I was naughty!

If Russ and I had been able bodied, and able to move about , and climb in and out easily, we probably would have been able to have camped out in that there bath for a while, but both Russ and I would have found it a little too hard to get in and out of every night and morning. More's the pity! No where for us to sleep yet!

The water bed hadn't yet been installed. So unfortunately, it was back to the halfway house each night for us! Once I had moved in to the house properly though, and after I had evicted Russ, *(read about that a bit later)*, I used to sit in that bath, with soap suds bubbling all around me, a plastic glass of champagne in my hand, *(plastic for safety sake)*, thinking how I would have loved Peg and Charlie to have still been alive. I toasted them, and spoke to them, as if they were right there in the bathroom with me, *(all of us in our swimsuits of course - otherwise the mind positively boggles!).* I said how much I missed them, and how they should be there with me, enjoying the benefits of the house and the money.

WHY A BAD MOVE?

They had done so much for me when I was growing up and now, it just didn't seem fair! But come to think of it – There was still nothing that seemed very fair at that time!

To them I had been their little singing princess! But now, even though the purchase of the house should have made me feel a little like a princess, and I suppose that in an obscure kind of way, it did, I was technically, a Princess without a Prince, and what's more - a Princess that could no longer sing! Oh sure - I guess that there was Russ, the wonderful man with whom I had been sharing my house, and with whom I had had a tremendous holiday, but as I was to find out, he had posed two teensy weensy problems for me. Not only did I miss 'that', *(I think. We couldn't do 'that' in the normal way)*, but he drank.

Now - when I say drank, I don't mean, just the odd 'over drink' session. But he used to get paralytically drunk – *all the time! (There were bottles all over the house. Behind every cupboard door, you would find a bottle of something or other. Either empty, or full! Generally 'empty')* Drinking too much was what actually led to his becoming a paraplegic in the first place! *(If you remember - He was drunk after a party, and was playing his favourite game - 'chicken' with a car. The car won, and that first time he hadn't been able to run fast enough to get out of the way. Unfortunately he ended up as a para, and with his own special set of wheels!)* Never having fully accepted that it had been partly his own fault that his state was as it was, he insisted that it would be rude of me

309

to make him drink alone, and that I had to join him! So he insisted that I do, and me being the weak person I was at that time, and still suffering quite considerably from having my own brain rattled, used to drink with him. *(Just to keep him company of course. You understand how it is'!)* I don't really drink now! I have ½ of a French beer with my dinner, that's all, except for the odd glass of wine, occasionally. But at that time I obviously needed to feel needed, even if it was just as a drinking mate! We had had our holiday to Hamilton Island, and there was another cruise planned and paid for. Paid for by me, of course! Do you think that I was just a tad OTT! Trying to buy love? *(I think that I might just have been. Silly, wasn't it!)* But anyway, we partied, and then we partied some more, and we were both supposed to be feeling rich, and content. But then for no apparent reason, his drinking 'really' got out of hand. *(I guess that mine was getting pretty close to doing so, as well, but for some reason, I held my booze a bit better, and I didn't get aggressive either - did I?)* When he wasn't drunk, he was a lovely man, who drove, a specially adapted, hand controlled car very well. Because of his problems *(paraplegia being just one of them)*, if ever we had been drinking away from the house I would never allow him to drive us home. *(I thought to myself- "I've been here before, haven't I"?)* I figured though that if something as horrible as the accident that had left me in the state I was in , could happen with a driver whom I thought to be sober, then there was no way that I was going to get in a car with a driver that I knew was drunk! I would call for a special half fare wheelchair taxi, and we'd get a cab. I would go back for the car the next day! I guess that I was fortunate in that even if I myself had had a bit more than enough to drink, there was enough of my sensibilities left to be just a little aware. I would never drive if I had been drinking even one glass. His car was an automatic, and after much consideration about my ever driving again, I decided that I would, if I could, and had sat for and received a license to drive. But again, like Russ, only automatic cars! Therefore his car was easy enough for me to drive, but if I had allowed him to drive in his state at the time, I could have ended up dead - again! I just didn't feel like taking the risk of it probably being for real next time! I also knew that that particular driver would never have admitted that he was even a tiddly bit over the limit, and would probably have started a row with any policeman that apprehended him! But cars involved or not - You would have thought that by then that I would have learnt just how monumentally unlucky a period of six months could be for me, for about six months after we had moved into the house together, we were spending a rare night in, and drinking alone at home.

(To tell the truth, I wasn't actually aware of the 6 month thing until I started the preparation for this book.)

Staying home should have been be safe enough, shouldn't it? No cars or 'muggers' to contend with! - You reckon? Take it from me, it was a bad, bad move!

And why exactly was that so, I hear you ask?

Well - there was no one there, except for him and me, was there?

No - one else for Russ to take his aggro, *(which could be monumental at times),* out on. And once he had had a few drinks, he *did unfortunately* become extremely aggressive.

RUSS, STAN - TRAVEL
WITH PAUL – STAN!!

Russ had actually taken a swing at me during one of our previous drinking bouts, and I had screamed at him then *(I was pretty good at screaming – I definitely couldn't sing, but I sure could scream!)*, that if he ever tried to hit me again, he would be out of the house, so quickly that he wouldn't know what had hit him.

Me? Well I of course, probably wouldn't have dared hit him. He would definitely have smashed me back, and if he was still drunk, which, chances are, he would have been, he probably would have run me over with his wheelchair! I don't think though, that he had really heard or even believed me! He was drunk enough this last time to have forgotten the warning, and drunk enough to have forgotten how vulnerable my head was. He took an almighty swing at it, and that is not a really a good thing to do to someone who suffered from any kind of brain injury. Luckily he only caught it a glancing blow, but it was hard enough to make me reel! With me not being too sure footed at the best of times, I flew about three feet through the air, and fell, face first, flat onto the luscious looking cream coloured, kitchen floor. Unfortunately for me, and for Russ at the time, the kitchen area was all paved with cream, marble tiles, and although absolutely stunning to look at, it was definitely not too good a place to fall on – especially not when you are in a drunken stupor as I was! A one inch gash opened up across the top of my left eyebrow, and blood went absolutely everywhere. And when I say everywhere, I mean everywhere! The white/cream marble tiles had suddenly turned a bright shade of patchy red! I still have the scar, above my left eyebrow, to always remind me. *(that is of course, as if I would ever want to be reminded!)*.

In my half delirious, blood soaked state, I staggered to the new fancy touch phone, pressed the wheelchair cab number button *(it was one of the earliest phones where you only needed to press one key to dial a pre-entered number)*, and ordered the cab. *(Well I didn't really want the police there, not with my being so inebriated as well)*, and I quickly stuffed a few of his things into a bag.

"Beep-beep", went the cab! I called Russ from the other room, caught his scathing look as he belligerently rolled into the room, sticking his front fingers up at me.

I got behind the chair and pushed him out of the already opened roller garage door. I stomped out as best I could, and politely told the cab driver where to go *(giving him directions to the halfway house I mean)*. I warned him that Russ might be a bit of an unruly passenger, and he would have been able to see my 'bloody' face, that there had probably been a doozy of row. I gave him $20 *(I think it was)*, which would more than cover the fare back to Petersham, thus packing Russ off.

Josephine, who lived next door, had heard all the noise, and she had rushed in, saw me, and she immediately called a medic, who sent me off to the hospital to get the gash stitched up. Josephine was later to be kept busy, running me back and forward to a very different hospital, and for a completely different reason. But you will read about that a little later.

A few months later, miles away from the house, evidently Russ had again been drunkenly playing his favourite? game, that of 'chicken' with a car. But this time, he and his wheelchair really lost! The result wasn't more paraplegia that time, he just lost.

(Be at peace Russy boy)!

When I heard about Russ, I had felt a tad of remorse at having evicted him so unceremoniously, but I thought - "well - he shouldn't have hit me"!

(Again the unfeeling reaction of someone who had spent so much time wondering what had happened to their own life!) I was very disappointed

in him for doing something as stupid as playing chicken with a car again.

(Winning at 'chicken', which was a pretty forsaken objective, was far outweighed by the chances of ending up as 'chicken chow mien' yourself!)

But with the effects of his disability having played such a big part in our conversations, I think that I at least, understand where he thought he was coming from. He was so cross with the world, and he refused to accept that maybe his drinking was to blame! I have to assume though that he just didn't care one way or the other. "What's the bl....dy the point - Who would want to be in this state?", he would moan at me, bashing his useless legs! *(Now I guess that one could say that he is in 'no state' at all.) (Sorry!)*

But after coping with his disability for so long *(about the same 9 years as as I had had to cope with my life altering adaptations),* he had probably just got 'jack' of all the associated problems. *(He had far more severe physical and mental problems than I was left with, that's for sure, and not just his inability to walk!)*

Also - I wasn't really what you might call, a good shoulder to put a complaining head on - not at that early stage of my own injury anyway, and I feel that I might just have been a teensy bit harsh on him! I still haven't been able to work out quite why some people, after an understandable self pitying amount of time, seem to be able to get on with life, and others can't! I unfortunately think that my super caring and compassionate gene must have been squashed in the accident too. I still *(in 2010)* don't make a very good shoulder to cry on! But anyway, moving on -

I'm not too sure how Stan Forth, came to be living in my house, but he was definitely there. Oh yes, he was definitely there! He had arrived during one of my 'not really with it' times I think, his having moved in while Russ was still there *(Russ was, unfortunately, always bringing strangers home!)* So maybe Russ had met him in a Pub or something, and with best of intentions must have brought him home. Stan was probably out on the night of our drunken, 'scar creating' revel - I think! Yeah - he must have been. I seem to remember that he was very caring of me for the next little while though. Probably a little too caring!

314

I can't really remember now, but I think that Stan must have had a normal teenage disagreement with his father at the time, had been thrown out of home, had come home from the local with Russ and somehow he had found himself living upstairs in the attic of my house. We had vaguely been discussing the need to acquire an 'ablebod' to live in the attic , which was set up as a self contained flat. So maybe Russ thought that he was doing something good! Boy oh boy, did it ever turn out to be a 'good' thing that he did! For me, at least! On finding out about his being evicted from his home by his dad, his mum, in looking for him, had got to know me pretty well, and we got on great.

Being a typical mum, she wanted to know that her son had landed on his feet after being thrown out by her husband. His parents separated, and divorced not long after, I think it was! I haven't spoken to them for years! Stan had his own bed/lounge/bathroom up in the roof of the house, and paid a peppercorn rent, along with a share of the food bills, and he ate and cooked downstairs. He told me later, that while he was immensely grateful for the place to stay, and the opportunity to get away from home, he did though, think that both of us *(Russ and I)* were a little - what you might call – strange!

Russ, through their drunken state, had probably thought upon hearing Stan's tale of woe, that as Stan was young and muscularly endowed, and an able bodied person who would be able to move quickly and protect us, that I too would think it a great idea if he were to move in! Russ, knowing that Stan was in need of somewhere to lay his weary head, and that we were in need of someone to protect us if there were to be a break in, obviously figured that he would be perfect for the job. I don't recall ever actually offering the position, but I later thought that that should satisfy Dr Burniston, *(from QE2)* as well, and that maybe he might even have been very proud of me, at how I had solved the problem of added security! Even though it was actually Russ who had drunkenly organised it! But, because of Ross's pub activities, I had both the independence that Dr B. had advocated for me by living in the house, and at the same time I still had the extra secure protection of an able bodied man.

The Monterey house, although stunning, was a lone house, with very few other houses around, and although I absolutely loved it, it was if I was being 100% honest, just a bit secluded. A big posh expensive looking house, apparently set in the open, with two easily overcome people in charge. Mmm!! When I think about it, it did make an easy target for someone with malicious intent! The house was well and truly alarmed, but alarms didn't always guarantee your safety, did they? Maybe Russ thought that he was doing a good thing! *(I'll give him the benefit of the doubt, shall I?)*.

Stan even looked after the house for me, when I finally got to go on my Arctic Cruise. Oh damn! I've done it again haven't I? Left a big bit out, didn't I? I'll tell you about it now, shall I.

As you will have read, I had talked about doing a half world cruise with Russ before the hitting fracas occurred, and I was now faced with a major problem! I had actually done something that I maybe shouldn't have done! *(And as I have said before, what's new, some would say?)* I had, actually already paid for what I looked upon, as the cruise of a lifetime. I could still go, but who was I going to get to use the other, already paid for ticket? I may like spending money, but I definitely didn't and still don't like *wasting it!* But I figured that Stan was too young for me to be gallivanting around with, and what is more, I don't think that at that stage he would have come.

People seemed to like to talk too much about what I did at that time, and that would really have set the tongues wagging. After all, Stan was only 19 when I was 37, and I wasn't into 'toy boys', so I didn't even consider it as an option at that time. Mind you, it was fast becoming a fairly common state of affairs at that time, so it probably would just have been the case of an older lady with her young Gigolo. But as there was nothing like that between us at that time, and I figured that we would both have been horrified. His mother would have been mortified, but I wasn't in the mood to take just anyone though! *(Now was I? Well was I?)*

But - I couldn't really go by myself - *or could I?* No, probably not! Too easy to 'mug' a 'wobbly' on board a ship that wobbled as well. And then there was the fact that the cruise went to all sorts of 'sus for the unwary', places.

Quandary extremus!

So I approached ALVA, but sadly none of the girls had a spare month to go on a cruise. They were all busy doing shows and things. *(Lucky things!)* But *(and this time I was the lucky one!),* it just happened that one of our associate members, a Mr Paul Waite, who was financially well enough off, would juggle things about a bit, and fit the cruise in. He very kindly agreed to come as my escort instead of Russ. He paid the added supplement involved because we didn't share the same cabin *(we did go just as friends remember),* and it turned out that he was the travel companion to die for!

Because he had been a ship steward, he knew his way around a ship alright!

He managed to get a wonderful cruise for himself, for the cost of a cabin only, and I got an incredible escort. An escort who was determined to 'look after' me.

(But unfortunately not in that way, sillies!)

what a great travel mate!

We were sitting at the bar, when a waiter asked Paul what we would like to drink. Paul told the waiter what he would like, and then said in his most polite, wanting to appear caring voice - "And miss Dyer would like an orange juice please"!

"Oh, would she", thinks me, being bitten by the 'naughty bug'. On hearing that, I smiled, and said with the cheekiest, widest lopsided grin that I could manage, and in the most commanding voice that I could muster,

"PUT SOME VODKA IN IT WILL YOU PLEASE DEARY"!

Paul cast me a strange, disapproving, 'you really shouldn't you know' look.

I thought, and said to him, in my typically Aussie way, giving him my defiant *'DYER'* look, - "Now really Paul m' old mate; There is looking after, and there is looking after"!

But apart from our seeing the icebergs I mentioned, we also saw Asian marvels; each of us rode on an Asian camel. We went canoeing, and I had been able to do it all without my needing to have an 'ENEMY' with me. No wheelchair! I was walking about, and in low heels too! True it may not have been walking all that well, but, *I was walking!* And believe it or not - *I was even (kind of) dancing!!!!*

sailing down the river

Poor Paul though! He got dragged around to some most unlikely places for him. Fashion shops, and boutiques! *(Every man's nightmare?)*

We went out on a walk about, you know, to see the 'natives' so to speak, and as we were walking about we came across a man doing wonderful ticks with this monkey.

A real, 'fair dinkum', and as I was to find out - very well trained, thieving monkey!

I had bought some jewellery while on my trip, and me who had not really ever owned any good quality gems before, *(I had had a lot of costume jewellery when I had been working, but I had never had much of the 'Good stuff!),* took great pleasure in actually wearing some stunning pieces of jewellery around as we walked.

(Well I didn't want to leave it all in the ship's safe, did I? What's the joy in that?)

well trained thief!

That charming, flea ridden monkey, whom I had thought was *so* funny, *so* entertaining, and trés chic, was as it turned out, also very well trained, and an excellent thief. Or should I say, *almost* very well trained,

319

and an *almost* excellent thief. It just hadn't come across a brain damaged 'Kerri Dyer' with her first lot of 'goodstuff' jewellery during it's training, had it? It did some tricks first to get everyone watching him.

Which they did! Everyone, including me, was completely distracted by his antics. He'd been jumping on and off shoulders for the previous ten minutes or so, we were all laughing at this cute little thing, when suddenly I felt him jump onto my shoulder. Amazed at my luck, I was initially surprised and delighted, but because I was still very conscious of my new found wealth, hanging out of my ear lobes, I just happened to feel him take my hoop earring from my ear. Now, my reflexes were not real good at that time, but I was just in time to see him put it in his mouth. Well, I ask you? I was flabbergasted! Goodness knows how many others he had collected from unwary, unsuspecting victims! But because I had only just bought my earrings and was still very conscious of their presence, I had actually felt his caressingly thieving fingers take it from my earlobe. Also, I had never owned anything as beautiful, and as they were my brand new, sapphire and diamond earrings, I wasn't about to let him get away with that.

Well I wasn't – was I? So I grabbed him by the foot, just as he was going to jump off, grabbed his neck, and with him turned upside down, I screamed like a banshee myself - "Spit it out you mongrel! Spit it out"! *(It's strange what possessiveness, and a desire to protect what is yours can do for your reflexes, even severely disabled ones!)*

Paul was suddenly aghast! - I know that I shouldn't laugh, and I am here to tell you that I didn't at the time, but it really must have been super funny, looking back on it now. The Monkey's owner was also bouncing around, arms flailing left and right, as Asian 'monkey men' do as I held it *(the monkey)* upside down, hanging on to his feet.

I had one hand around the monkey's throat , while the fingers of my other hand, tried to prise the earring from its mouth. "My, my", I must have thought - "they *are* athletic little buggers, aren't they"! *(and that also is definitely cleaned up a lot!)*

In order to get free when I just had him by the legs, the monkey kept doing mid air sit ups in an attempt to bite my fingers, to make me let go. But – he had my lovely earring still lying in his drool filled mouth. I shook him, and shook him, screaming at him at the top of my then still very strange voice. "Give it back! Give me back my earring you flea ridden mongrel of a thing! "Spit it out"!, I screamed at it - *(shake shake)* "Spit - it - out"!! *(I might add again, that you will need to forgive me. The language was not quite so polite at the time!)* Paul just stood there trying to look as if he didn't know this mad woman shaking the gibbon. He was watching, but unsure of what to do; he stood there laughing at the ludicrousy of the situation that was unfolding before his eyes, all the time thinking - "I am definitely glad that I am not that monkey"! *(as he told me back at the hotel, when we were reminiscing about our trip)* The monkey finally spat the earring out, and scampered back to it's owner, desperately, or so it appeared, begging for forgiveness for not doing the job correctly!!!!

Episode over, jewellery restored, along with two other earrings that he had also managed to steal from others, we boarded the ship again, laughing ourselves silly. Ships were a really good mode of travel for me. I didn't get sea sick *(well not very, anyhow)*. The normal 'riding the waves' movement of the ship probably went a long way to diminishing my wobble, whist on board, but not even the 'wobble' mattered to me at the time. For the first time in a very long time, I felt beautiful. I had bought some stunning clothes on shore, and I found myself sat at the Captain's table with Paul. *(His having been a steward definitely had it's advantages, didn't it?)* Although it was probably naughty of me to do some of the things I did on that cruise, I don't regret one single minute of it! Won't risk boring,or titillating you with the details, but suffice it to say that I didn't hurt anyone, a marvellous time was had by all, and I didn't catch anything, even though for a little while later, I had thought that I had!!

Finally though, the Cruise was over. Paul and I had come back to Australia, both having had a wonderful time. I was though, still determined to fit in as much life as was possible, and as quickly as I could! ALVA provided me with many opportunities to live life to the full, and one particular function that I went to with ALVA was to play the most crucial part in the next, and probably the best segment of that part of my life, so far.

I was without my garage remote control because I hadn't driven myself to this particular do. So on arriving home, we pulled up giggling, having had a tremendous time, and I said goodbye to the girls. I tottered semi drunkenly around to the reserve *(park)* side of the house, arriving at the front door at about the same time as Stan. *(And just who is Stan, again? Surely you remember him. He was the one who had had a row with his Dad, and who baby sat the house for me while I travelled!)* He had also just returned from wherever he had been, and he too, was what you might call, a little the worse for wear. We both went "boo", at each other, and then we drunkenly reeled about giggling. I almost wasn't quite quick enough with the alarm code. You only get ten seconds, and when you are drunk, ten seconds seems to flash past very, very quickly.

But once one of us had actually remembered it *(the code that is)*, the door of the house had opened without the alarm going off. It would have woken the neighbourhood, but even worse, it would have summoned the police! "Phew"! I must have thought - "we really could do without their presence, especially in our present state"! After having another slightly drunken giggle, we thought that we might just as well have a quick 'nighty nite' drink together, and one thing led to another. 'As they sometimes do!'

My poor water bed didn't know what had hit it! *(Talk about 'la cookaracha!)*

Now, I definitely hadn't disliked *that* wobble! He was a young man, and although I was old enough to have known better, and to have almost been his mother, I figured, as I had as a youngster at Greenacre - "well in for a penny, in for a pound"! And because it had turned out to be so enjoyable, we mutually agreed to continue it whenever an opportune moment presented itself, and most enjoyable it was too.

(I don't suppose that I should admit that though, should I!)

But after all the problems that I'd had since the accident, it was absolutely wonderful to be able to truly enjoy 'that' aspect of life properly again, and with someone so young and athletic! It was wonderful! *(unfortunately, no photos of that either! Ha ha!)*

But - I should have known that fate wasn't about to let me get away with it.

(Being happy and untroubled I mean!) 'Cause why?

Well - I have to confess that I was probably only mildly concerned when I missed my first period, and began having 'women's problems'. Although technically I wasn't quite old enough to have hit the change of life at that time, they had told me that because of the accident, it might start about my age. So when my periods didn't arrive that first time, I just put it down to that, or to the effects of the travelling. Everything had been a bit strange since the accident anyway, and then there was the oriental food from the trip. I have to admit though, that I began to feel very strange, and when I missed a second period I decided that I'd better go to the doctors. I had been told that I couldn't fall pregnant, or at least, that the chances were 1 in a 1000, so I never even thought about that as being a problem. My super pleasant cook -ara -char-ing hadn't even really crossed my mind. But there was a lot of talk at the time about sexually transmitted diseases. I knew that Stan was too clean, and innocent to have given me anything, but I was though, a teensy bit worried about whether or not I had caught some incurable disease like AIDS or anything aboard the ship during my few indiscretions at sea. AIDS had really only just come into the news headlines at the time, and to tell the truth - I was petrified of catching it. I had shown no previous signs of any STD's since the cruise, but poor Stan, what if I did have AIDS? He was only a relative baby, with his whole life ahead of him! Was I going to be responsible for his never being able to live life normally again? I worried that if I had caught something in the East, then I would need to know, straight away! And not only for the obvious reasons - but -

1- If I *had* caught something that was going to shorten what I had already been told was a shortened life anyway, I would want to know straight away, so that I could do all the things I had ever wanted to do, and spend the money, and -

2 - even more importantly, and for a far more altruistic reason, if I had caught something, then poor Stan had to be told asap, so that he could get some medicine, and hopefully reduce the germs aggressive nature.

He would need to know!!

How absolutely catastrophic if I had given him something". If what was meant just to be fun, would make his life unbearably horrible! How awful! I had lived my life *(or at least a big part of it)*, and had

had a relatively good one at that. I had travelled, lived life to the full, really enjoyed my youth and had sung at the Opera House. My life had looked positively rosy, that is, at least to me! Then, I had had to bear the consequences of the accident. But he had his whole, un-lived yet, life ahead of him! He definitely didn't need to have caught anything strange from his older 'bit of fancy'! It would have been a huge price to pay for a bit of what, was as I said, supposed to have been, just a bit of uncomplicated fun!

So off I went to the Doctors, and had a vaginal check. I really needed to know that I hadn't caught anything! But, after five days, of not having heard from the doctor, panic again set in, and my over active brain kept coming up with weird scenarios. Maybe they hadn't rung yet because no one really knew how to break the bad news to me. Or maybe it was, oh I didn't know what it could be, so I thought that I had better ring him myself and get the news. Good or bad! At least then I would know where to go from there! So, a bit hesitantly I did, and I tentatively asked for the Doctor, and then when I got him on the phone, for the results of my tests.

When I finally spoke to the Doctor that morning, there was a bit of a silence. He was a friend of a male friend of mine, and he soulfully said to me - "I'm not too sure quite how you are going to take this news". *("Oh O", thought me!)*

"I was actually thinking of dropping around this afternoon to tell you", continued the doctor. "It's not good news I am afraid! But I suppose that now that you have rung, then you had best come in to see me, as soon as you can - today if possible"!

So there I was, a half hour later, in his sterile clinic.

"Right" says me, steeling myself for horrific news. "How long have I got, and can I have given it to Stan?" After a bit of a pause, he stared at me, and then he barked at me - "What do you mean how long have you got? And can you have given what to Stan? And not wishing to sound like your father or anything - who, by the way, is Stan"?

I smiled at this sudden parental kind of questioning, and quickly filled him in.

The age difference and everything!

"Oh, that's why then", laughed the doctor!

Through the laughs he said - "No my dear, I don't think that you can have given it to Stan", he said. "But I have a decided feeling that Stan should break out the cigars, and that he probably gave it to you"

I sat there looking totally bemused! "Stan couldn't have had anything - could he", I said to myself, and why would he want to break out the cigars? He didn't even smoke!

"Against all assumed odds", said the doctor, "because technically you shouldn't be able to be", he told me in his hushed voice, suddenly sounding very concerned, "You are pregnant my dear"!

Well, I am here to tell you here and now, that you could have picked me up off of the floor! Andy and I had tried a few times after the accident. Or should I say that I had tried, *(with Andy, of course)*. Through necessity the hospital had taken my coil out while I was unconscious after the accident, but obviously there hadn't been the will between us to try hard enough after the accident. I guess that neither of us had been all that interested in sex at all. Most unusual for me, some might say! Mind you the fact that it hurt me, and that he knew that it did, would have been enough to put any man or woman into a 'no thank you' kind of mood. Wouldn't it? And it didn't really matter that I tried to hide it - he knew!! I think all the unusual, 'different' moans and groans just may have given it away - Don't you? Now wouldn't it?

But I had not exactly been living like a nun for the years since the separation and divorce, and I hadn't been even remotely careful. Nothing had happened, so I had assumed that the medics and people who are supposed to know, had been right.

They had said that it was highly improbable, if not impossible, for me to have a child in my disabled state.

"Lets get this right, shall we", the doctor said. "You are"- he looked again at his notes - "Thir-t-y seven years old. Almost biologically past it wouldn't you say; Well wouldn't you"?

I glared at him, and on realising that he had offended me, he tried to make things a little better. But with every effort at it, he just put his foot a bit further down his own throat! I sat there and just shook my head back and forth at the hide of the man!

(If it hadn't been so serious, knowing how weird was my sense of humour, I might even have found it hilariously funny, sitting there watching him dig an even bigger hole for himself every time he opened his mouth.) But then, as far as I was concerned, he made things totally abhorrent - by suggesting that I think very seriously, about having an abortion!

"But if, as I can see by all the head shaking that you are doing, you are determined not to do so", he said "well I should, if I were you, at least consider having an amniocentesis. Just to make sure the embryo isn't damaged in any way. From reading the hospital notes, and of seeing how you have coped with your own disability problems, I don't believe that you would want to be responsible for actually bringing a disabled child into this world! Now would you"? I sat there with my eyes downcast, shaking my head!

So I had the test done, ran the risk of miscarrying because of it, and found out that I was only about 6 weeks pregnant.*(Ripper, it definitely couldn't have been from the ship then. I'd been back for much longer than that. Wonderful! - A good 6 for a change.).*

"Ripper", I said again, holding my not yet swollen tummy, and hugging myself to myself! But then I stopped and thought! That meant that the father could only be one person! O-oh, how oh how on earth was I ever going to tell Stan?

The Gynaecologist, 'ammnio' doctor had told me that I was going to have a little girl, and that she was going to be AOK. Wow! A baby, all of my own. To love and to cherish, till death us do part. *(Now that was definitely a long term commitment, but a very different one to the one I'd run away from before!)*

"I am up for that", I thought with a self satisfied grin on my face! I had always wanted children. I had almost gotten used to the fact that I couldn't - *(have any I mean!)*, and had even considered eventually adopting, or fostering, just as Peggy had done. But now - *I was pregnant with Charliene.*

(I'd already, decided that even though the baby was a girl, that she would still be named after my darling Daddy!) Charli, Charliene, sorted!

Being a bit cheeky though, I will say that I had thought, but didn't think that I should voice it, that "maybe, just maybe, the pregnancy might have been the result of, young, virile spunk,"! *("Well, you never know, do you"? Well, you don't do you?!)* The doctor must have considered it too when he had said to me, thinking out loud to himself - "That's why then", but you know, I don't think that he had considered it quite in the same way as I did.

My mind did a very nice little wander! It seemed that my thoughts weren't damaged at all by the accident. Even then I had a very creative imagination! I could just envisage the sperm being shot into the viaduct *(a pleasant enough image in itself, remembering the sensation!),* and it swimming along, scooting around any barnacled, old looking obstacles that may have been there. Then it must have spotted an appealing, 'up for it' looking egg, and with a twiddle of it's long moustachioed tail, and a grinning, determined 'well well', it would have gone whammo!! Result - Charliene - *(O the joys of creation!)*

Sitting in the office, and drifting further off, into a world of my own, I thought -"O Goody! I will paint the room next to mine, oyster pink, a delightfully cream shade of pink, and decorate it with 'girlie' types of adornments". Mentally singing to myself all the time - "I've got a daughter! - I've got a daughter"!

Then I came to a crashing halt! How on earth was I going to tell Stan?

To say that he would understandably, be mortified, would definitely have been the understatement of the year!

I told Stan, and after his initial "'I am stunned" comment' *(which I expected and won't repeat!),* he said "but you said you couldn't fall pregnant.

RAT!

I said - "I'm sorry Stan. It came as a bit of a shock to me too. They told me that it was not at all likely, and that the chances were 1 in a 1000".

I knew that I enjoyed 'that, but as I had never envisaged myself having a thousand nookies in the shortened life span that they allotted me, and as I hadn't taken any precautions for ages and ages with nothing having happened before, I had naturally enough, assumed that I was safe!

But after another week or two, which would have made me about 6 weeks pregnant by that stage, I was actually starting to feel very pregnant. Very luckily for me though, it must have helped correct some of my wobbliness. I was also lucky in that I had the pool in my back yard, and that I could do all the exercises that I needed to do, in the comfort of my own pool and spa. It meant that there was no one to see this fat, whale like person stumbling into the pool. *(Except of course, Josephine when she came in to do the cooking and housework, and she didn't mind!)*

At least at that time I had a legitimate reason for being fat, and whale like. Fat again, but for a totally different reason. The exercises were done regularly, and I even started to take the pregnancy very seriously. I began being a good girl, and started drinking lots of soy milk, and eating lots of fruit. And no 'that', the doctor had said, although he hadn't called it 'that', he just said NO SEX! But all things aside, there was no one about any more to have 'that' with any way, so it really didn't matter, did it?!

About 6 months before, I had taken a course of Chinese herbs. Things like cockroaches, worms, butterfly wings, gnats, bits of special herbs and spices, and spiders legs. Josephine had also been making me lots of Chinese food, and rice dishes. I had been taking the herbs in an attempt to try and remedy aspects of my disability, and then just recently I had become a really well fed and well looked after, disabled, pregnant lady. The only trouble with all that was that I actually started to put on a little too much weight, again! *(Hard to imagine, isn't it?)*

The Doctor did keep warning me, but whether I, or he liked it or not, I was going to be a chubby mummy! I had apparently hit one of my 'fat' stages again! But I felt that at least this time, I had a legitimate reason for it, and this time it wasn't all that bad, being a bit overweight! Was it? After all - *I am having a baby"*, I squealed to the house!

During that first few months of my pregnancy, I became friends with a lady who, with her husband, had formed a security company. They were in need of accommodation, and where better to move into, than Stan's upstairs apartment since he had vacated it. Stan had decided that he was too young to take on the responsibility of a new, very unexpected child that was the result as I have already said, of what was just supposed to be bit of good fun. So we both decided that it would be best if he were to leave! But I would still need someone living in the house with me, especially with me being so far into my pregnancy.

So they moved in, and I had them as well as Josephine to look after me!

(But you know, security people or not, I did take some risks, didn't I? I didn't really know them all that well. They were friends of friends, and as I said before, that can sometimes be disastrous. I really only had their words at first, for the fact that they were indeed security guards. Even my friend didn't know for sure what they did!)

The pregnancy itself went fairly smoothly enough, until about 6 weeks before the babe was due. *(6 days, 6 weeks, 6 months, it seemed at the time that 6 is either my unluckiest number, or one that I should bet on. Now it is one of my luckiest numbers. My precious daughter was prematurely born on the 6th January, 1989.)*

But there I was, at about 10.30pm one night, just getting ready to go to bed, when suddenly, and most unexpectedly, I found myself doubled up with pain.

Panic stations, Big time! And I think that I must have startled Dianne out of her sleep when I called her on the intercom. As I said, she and her husband worked, separately sometimes *(he was at work)*, and they did truly weird hours with their security business. She had had to make herself wake up, because she had worked a late shift the day before, and so she had been trying to catch up on her z's. Josephine didn't finish work at the restaurant where she worked at night, until later that evening, so she wasn't at the end of her phone line at that time either, and I didn't think that her husband or children would have been of much help under the circumstances! They probably would have run around like headless chickens, in opposite directions to this wobbly, doubled up with pain, pregnant duck! Dianne put her slippers on the wrong feet, and staggered down the short flight of stairs. I called out to her, and she answered, "where the b***heck are you?"

"In the bathroom"*(which was tucked away, right at the back of the downstairs part of the house)*, I yelled back, and when she took one bleary, still half asleep look at me, my ashen face, and the big puddle of blood, sick, and sticky water that was on the bathroom floor, she turned grey, and panicked!

And when I say panicked, I don't mean just a little flap about, getting things for the trip to hospital - I mean panicked 'big time'!

You would have thought that she was the one having the baby, instead of supposedly being the stabilising force for the 'wobbly' first time Mum.

She rushed about looking for towels and things to use to wipe up the mess on the floor *(I hadn't realised she was such a 'clean freak')*, and also some to help stem the suddenly voluminous flow of sticky, blood tinged fluid, that was absolutely bursting through the 'poppers' of my pregnancy suit and gushing down my legs.

Dianne was running around like a chook with it's head cut off, while I stood rooted to the spot, looking positively terrified! I am afraid that I just stood there, looking like death, very badly warmed up. I had lost any semblance of my normal Australian 'she'll be right mate' attitude, and I was looking like a frightened, helpless bird, who was trying desperately not to 'puke' all over her, and everything else!

She was also panicking because a decision had been made to get me to hospital 'quick smart'. Her car was an open topped jeep type car, which was fine for her running about, and would have been OK if the pregnancy had gone to plan, but it was definitely not 'OK' for taking a very pregnant, possibly about to miscarry, older, disabled, first time mum to the hospital.

To make things worse, because it had just become January, which is almost always super hot in Sydney, and although we had at first thought about throwing me into the pool to cool down, we then thought that the pool cleaner wouldn't have been too impressed with the mechanism being clogged up with spew and pieces of expelled, blood soaked vagina. So we sat me down somewhere cool, which was of course, on the bathroom tiled *(therefore cool)* floor. Well away from the blood and gloop, of course!

I had also raised my legs on to the side of the bath, in order to ease the pain. So there was me, dressed in my red and white striped, knee length, pregnancy jumpsuit *(hadn't had time yet to get changed even had I?)*, lying on my back, with my pregnant belly poking up to the roof. I was - on the tiled floor, looking a lot like a beached red and white striped whale, with it's' *fins flapping around on the side of the three and a half foot tall, green, spa bath.* A truly classy position it was too, and what was more - I had my feet up on that bath, with my body just to the side of that great big pool of sinewy, red coloured 'gloop'. *Positively stunning!*

Typical of most pregnant mums though, I wasn't able to stay still very long, and I kept on trying to stand up. I would take a few steps, only to end up doubled up with pain again, and back on the floor with my legs up on the bath. Up and down like a yo yo! It truly must have been a sight and a half to behold! I almost wish I could have sat detached, and looked on! *(I probably could have done with a good belly laugh by then!)*

I would struggle up - stride out and wobble about. Then it would be - scream, grab my stomach and double up with pain again, spewing the vomit, just about all over Dianne - again. She yelled at me - oh - *"FOR GOD'S SAKE - BLOODY WELL SIT down WILL YOU, AND FOR HIS SON'S SAKE - PLEASE FACE THE OTHER WAY!"!*

Never having heard her swear before, and being initially amazed that she did, even though I have been known myself to let rip occasionally, it was still a matter of - "easier said than done". I would no doubt have screamed back to her, while I kept getting stabbing pains, that felt like a mass migration of 'jumbucks' *(Australian kangaroos)* was going on in my abdomen. That there baby was having a field day, changing position and turning. In a hurry to get out, maybe! It felt as though the babe was doing a gymnastics course, preparing itself for it's own excercise class or something? Never having had a baby before, I didn't really know! I just knew that it *'DESPERATELY, FRIGGIN-WELL HURT'!*

No sooner would I sit down, as Dianne had told told me to do, than my stomach would heave up into my throat, and I'd want to be sick all over her and the floor again

She and I had, of course, rung Josephine at her work to let her know what was happening, along with Dr. Grey, and he had said to me - "That there baby obviously wants to get out, so we had better make it a quick exit for her. Sorry Miss Dyer, no natural birth this time"! *("This time" says me? "He must be frigging joking", I thought. "This time? he couldn't possibly think that I would ever contemplate a next time".)* Then, full of helpful medical remedies, he said? "Just keep walking till the ambulance gets there!" I wanted to scream down the phone - "that is easier said than done!"

(But at least he didn't want me to stay still, or sit down!)

Oh yeah! I followed orders, and walked around alright! I had 'wobbled' about until I had another 'jumbuck stampede' in my tummy. Then I doubled over in pain, and I remember screaming very loudly, very very loudly, "where is that bloody ambulance?"

Diane reminded me that Dr Grey had said that he'd have a caesarean care team waiting for me when I got there, so not to panic. *("Not to panic", thought me. Don't Panic?)* She also said to me in a 'trying to be calming' voice, that Dr Grey had also said to me on the phone, that he'd call the ambulance, and that he would meet me at Paddington Hospital - the Neo Natal ward!

"Chin up", he had said, "Chin up - see ya there"! "Chin up? Chin up? What does he think I am", I said to Dianne? Mind you I thought, "maybe he meant it as some sort of medical remedy for the 'up chucking'!

It is very difficult to be sick, with your chin up in the air!

But I yelled to Diane -*"Where the heck is that ambulance"*?

In what seemed like an eternity, but in actual fact, was probably only a minute or so later, the ambulance arrived at the house. "honk honk", it went.

"Thank bloody goodness", says me!

I don't personally remember a lot of the getting to the hospital bit, but I have been told that Josephine, who came rushing in just as we were about to leave, and Dianne, handled it all wonderfully. After I got over the original sense of panic when my waters had broken, I think that although I would most definitely have been terrified, I must have been secretly enjoying the drama. Some of my friends/enemies would tell you that I can be definitely a bit of a drama queen at the best of times, and I suppose that that was destined to be one of my better best times. As I was only ever likely to have one baby at my age, and my not really wanting to go through all that palaver again, I guess that I had enjoyed the event being as dramatic as it was. I also guess that they had been right – I probably was a bit of a 'showy' right down to my bootstraps!

Now though, when I sometimes see a natural birth on a television show, with all the screaming, perspiring and pushing that those Mum's go through, I have to say - that even though Dr Grey had decided it for me, a caesarean section really was the only way to go! I would definitely have to agree that "Caesarean has got to be the bestest way to have a baby, ever"! It truly is the only way to go. For all cowards at least!! And after that episode, I would definitely have to be classed as a coward! I remember, that after their putting me in the birthing ward, they gave me a local anaesthetic, and sat me on a table thing. I think that I must have been out of it a 'lot'. They put a pile of cushiony bits and bobs behind me, got me to spread my legs in a most unglamorous way, and then placed a purpose made, metal (?) kind of barrier across, and over my lower abdomen.

Very clinical, but pretty effective - I couldn't see a ruddy thing!

Dr Grey checked that the 'local' had taken effect, and then sliced across my numb, desensitised womb area. There was evidently only a little bit of blood, lots of rushing about by the doctors, and then the next thing I remember clearly is hearing this bawl, and Dr Grey holding up this blood soaked, howling, long armed and long legged, big brown eyed blob. A few bright red tufts, that passed for hair, stuck out of the blob's ginormous head, and it is probably just as well that newborn babies can't actually hear or understand some mother's first comments. My first words on seeing her were - "God - she looks like a little 'rat'"! But in what must have only been a second later - I said through a numbed 'stab' of pain in my abdomen - "can you give me *my* little rat please?" My heart melted as I looked into her enormous, unusual for a newborn, big brown eyes. Bright ginger stubble, poked up between the few bright red tufts, and the 'rat' had a very swollen tummy. Two big brown eyes peered out at me. Peered out in awe and wonderment at the new and wondrous world that she had suddenly been lifted into! Gone was the previously, extra tumultuous, water world that she had lived in for the past seven and a half months. Five faces looked her over, from all angles! They cut the umbilical cord, and put her on my tummy. A strong surge of emotion, that I had never really felt before, overtook me. I fondled this funny looking, blood covered being, that was my new daughter, while the birthing team got on with the cleaning up of the area.

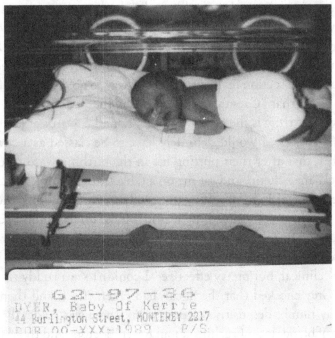

Baby Dyer – 6-1-89

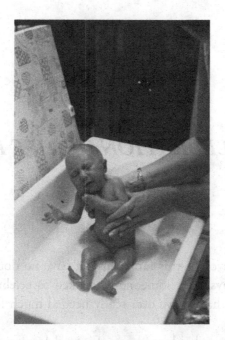

where do I start?

Because she was 6 weeks premature, *(there's that blasted 6 again)* they had to take her away, to an incubator, but once I had moved into the ward proper, they eventually gave her back to me. I had had to express some milk for her first feed, but all the others were done at my breast.

The feeling that overtakes you when that little mouth suckles for the first time, is just indescribable. To have this helpless little face, with two enormously big brown eyes, greedily taking hold of my milk filled breast was just incredible. Little stretching fingers on helpless little hands, grabbed at my swollen, milk filled boobs, while her mouth nuzzled about, searching around for the nipple so as to enable the first breast feed of many more to come for the next year. And having that little mouth, find, and latch on to my boob, was a truly, indescribably wondrous feeling. My own little 'rat', had suddenly become the most precious thing in the world to me. I was relatively newly disabled, but there I was holding, a bit shakily to be sure, a precious little person.

Against all odds - *'I WAS A MOTHER'!*

THE CELEBRATION OF LIFE PARTIES

Now , if you have got this far, then you have no doubt already read that I have always been someone who liked to celebrate things, and I don't suppose that I have ever really needed much for me to have a celebration!

Now though - what better cause for a celebration did I need, than the birth of my own little girl? The one that I wasn't supposed to have been able to have!

so precious!

And celebrate it I eventually did! I also figured again that I would set out to enjoy this extension of life that I'd been given, as well as the new 'little life' that I'd been entrusted with! I had tried not to listen too hard to all the 'behind the hand' whisperers, as well as some of the 'well, and correctly informed Doctors', as they talked about previous indications showing that I was not going to be able to expect to live long enough to see her grow. Ha Ha - *fooled ya!*

I have been here, making my presence felt ever more as each year goes past, and what is more, I did something else that they said was highly improbable when I had her! So although I had previously decided, rightly or wrongly, that I was going to have a 'bonza' last hoorah, I now *had* to stay around. I had a daughter, and what better excuse did I need for another party. *I HAD A BABY DAUGHTER, AND, WHAT WAS MORE - I was still alive!*

Just before the christening

(Somehow I had defied all medical predictions at the time, 'twice')

I had survived the accident, and then some. And I had given birth to a whole new life!

What was more- I was still there. The time had come - ***"TO WELL AND TRULY CELEBRATE "***

Back at the time of Charliene's birth, I had breathed in the newness of her, and spent a few very pleasurable minutes contemplating how she had been created. *(And weren't they lovely images too? Probably shouldn't admit that - but Hey!)* Me being me though - *(a bit of a party girl forever!)*, once everything had calmed down a bit, I organised a Christening party, and it was fantastic! -The invitations went out to all kinds of guests, both Showbiz, and what I used to call 'normal' people, but who were in fact basically just 'non showbiz nutters'. The Salvation Army had agreed to christen Charliene, so the Sally Captain welcomed my little girl, into the Christian world, and some of my favourite Salvation Army friends from when I was young, were there to help me celebrate as well! What a great time lay in store for us, and what a 'bonza' time was had by all! Once the Christening party was done and dusted - a little while later, me again being me, had what I liked to call my - *"Celebration of life party"*.

Some of the same non crazy people came, but with a slight learning towards the showbizzy, and more OTT group of my friends. Out came the 'embossed, silver engraved' invitations. *Again! (New ones of course)*

Goodness, there is no doubt about it! I must have been a true showy!

But then I guess though, that as Mae West used to say and I am loathe to admit, but in this particular case, the saying applies to me as well - "Goodness really had nothing to do with it!"

But - having survived the accident, and having sat through that monumental court case, listening to how highly thought of in the business I had been, and then to have truly beaten the odds, by having my beautiful daughter - I wanted, again to show the world just how thankful and grateful I was to everyone involved. Many of the same big names of Australian showbiz were there, *again* - a lot of the ALVA girls were there, all decked out in their best formal gear!

By order of the invitation, everybody was looking SO glam! Mr Caterer got the job, *(Again? Of course! Anyone would think that he was really good, which of course (he/she/it/they were!).* They had done such a great job with both the demolition party, and Charliene's christening party, so who else would I call on, for what was going to be, for me at least, the party to end all parties! *(except that, as it turned out - there was to be yet another, very unexpected at the time, but absolutely wonderful party to come.)* The christening party had been held in the house, but the

Celebration of life, and the later to be held 'special' party *(tell you about that later too),* were held over the 'floor covered' pool. The *Celebration of Life party* was, once again *fantasmagorical!*

party on pool outside house

Firstly they had created the solid wooden floor that covered the pool, and then they erected a white silk tent over and around it. Coloured lights were strung all around, and the house and pool area must have looked like they were decked out with Christmas tree decorations. The place was full of entertainers, but there were also a lot of non show business people there as well.

My paediatrician, my accountant, as well as a lot of strangers, that now, all this time later, when I look at the photos, I can't remember the identity of. But I reassuringly tell myself that they must have all been fantastic people too! That was a fantastic part of my life, so all my friends were immediately elevated to fantastic as well! As far as I was concerned at the time, the house was positively full of really nice people, who agreed with me, that being alive sure beat being dead! And anyway, they couldn't have been 'un nice'! Not if they agreed with me about that, anyway. - now could they?!

A few of my musician friends formed a band for us, and some of the show business people that were there, got up and did a spot or two. Everybody took it in turns to hold 'Pickle' *(my daughter's nick name, which now at nearly 21, she feels is just a bit gross when I use it!)*, especially the girls, and Charliene was as happy as any three month old, surrounded by a whole lot of 'done up to the nines' yahoos could be!

A wonderful time was had by all, and I was feeling fantastic. I had a fantabulous house, a wonderful daughter, and a lot of good friends. Alright! Some of whom I could probably have done without, but I won't bore you with that! We all enjoyed a true –
CELEBRATION OF LIFE!

Charliene at Celebration of life!

Did I do that?

But prior to the court case finally coming about *(I do apologise, and I know that I told you I was scatty, and that this book was a bit like a maze because my memory is so disjointed, but I sincerely hope that none of you are getting queasy because of all the about faces, and forward marches. Please forgive me, and try to enjoy the book anyway!! Maybe you could treat this book like a conversation you were having with me They too can be a bit 'queaze promoting'! Ha ha),* apart from all the girls of ALVA, and a few other people that stuck with me, there was also Ed, who had been living in Australia at the time of the accident, but who had come over from England to help out with my court case. But right from the very beginning of my being 'let out' of hospital, he and the girl he had been living with for a while, who later became his second wife, used to come and pick me up, and take me food shopping. He has always been a true friend! *(I am his third wife, and it looks as though what they say about third time lucky, is being well and truly proved!!!)*

But anyway, originally it had just been me that I had to feed, but later I would collect the 'food kitty' from the other 'halfway house' members, and head off to the shops to get in supplies for the week. *(Oh for the days when you could feed four people for about $26 -a week. $6-50* *each.)* Russ *(remember him?)* had been one of the tenants in the half way house, so he had been driving me about when Ed wasn't around. Soon though, because Ed got married, and moved to Wales, it would become almost all of the time. I hadn't seen or heard from Ed and his wife for a couple of years, when I think my legal team must have written to him and asked him if he would come, at our expense and give evidence at my court case. Ed and and his wife altered their already planned trip a little to incorporate the court dates, and all I can say, is thank heavens they did! As you read, Eds evidence, along with all the other notable people's, was instrumental in the court case having been so successful. I would have to say though, that Eds testimony made for a very convincing and secure start for my side! Although they had to be on the move soon after giving evidence, it was wonderful that he had been able to come all that way across from England at all.

The legal team, having organised the trial so well, and achieving the result they did, were definitely not going to let me get my maulers on the bulk of the money at that time, and it was probably a good job too, at first. I would have been no good at managing all those bits of paper, as was evidenced by Ed, a little later at my Monterey house, when they had come over from England on a visit.

Eventually though legal eagles begrudgingly said that I could, *(have a more 'hands on' I mean)* but that they were definitely going to keep a bit of an eye on me. And I guess that they as sure as hell did.

They were probably worried all the time, yet unable to do much about it really!

They watched me as I took the money out to build my house, and do those two fantastic trips, and were probably cringing a bit the whole time!

They should have trusted me a little more?

AN OLD? OLD FRIEND *(I don't think so!)*

Ed and his lady had flown back to England a few days after the monumental court case, and it must have been about 20 months later that I heard from him again. I had made sure that he had already been told of the courtroom shenanigans after they left, and of the outcome! He said that he and his wife were coming back to Australia again, to see her family and to catch up with other friends. I invited them to come and stay in my house, which had been 'kinda' finished not long before his letter, so Ed and his wife were the first guests at my lovely new home at Monterey.

It was going to be Ed, his wife, me and Russ. For me it was so exciting! He had, after all, told me to get into real estate, and that was what I had done. Hadn't I? Alright! I had probably gone a bit overboard, tearing down the original old house, and having my dream home built, but it was still in property wasn't it?

Unfortunately, I think that the situation must have upset his wife a little when Ed started paying as much attention to my apparent mismanagement of the money as he did. *(Couldn't understand it myself! If he had been showing **me** attention, then I could have understood. But he was more concerned about, how in his estimation, I had been doing a rotten job of handling the money, with little or no supervision).*

She, quite justifiably, got a bit miffed when he couldn't go with her to do 'whatever', because he was too busy trying to sort out what he considered 'the so called mess', that he reckoned I had made. He was full of disgust with the legal team for having let me have as much control over the money as I had had. *(He assumed that the legal team would still be running things.)* They probably would have been, except for my domineering nature. *(ooh, I was a bad girl, wasn't I?!)*

Ed reckoned that I would lose the lot! That I'd be like the English lady, whose motto had become "Spend, spend, spend". Spend, spend, spend, is what she did until she went broke, and ended up back in a council house! *(And what's wrong with a council house, anyway, I say, - As long as she had some fun while she was here?)* Mind you, Although I personally have never lived in a council house, if they were anything like the house in which I grew up in *(which was an Australian equivalent to a council house I think)*, I must confess that wouldn't like to end up back there!

OK, I will put my hands up. I probably *had* done a few things that he didn't like, and that were probably a little on the 'sus' side, but I didn't think that I had done all that badly. I had inadvertently followed his instructions after all, and I had invested in real estate. I'd just gone about it in a typical Kerri Dyer manner!

Overboard, and with a touch of Dyer flair?

I owned another flat as well as the house that I had built, so the flat had provided a bit of income, apart from the few shares that I hadn't turned in. I had a lovely, purpose built home that was also a great capital asset, and I still had a bit of money in the bank.

But right from the beginning after the court case, I still had my image to keep up!

(Well - didn't I?)- So there maybe wasn't as much in the bank as there should have been, was there?! But I had figured at that time, that you only live once, don't you? I also still had, baby or no baby, and according to the experts, who had very consolingly re-informed me, a pretty for shortened future ahead of me. Charliene would of course inherit the houses when I died, and would receive what was left of my jewellery and things. Unfortunately, they said, I might not be around to see her grow up, and if that was going to be the case, and if, as was the general medical consensus, I would die early, then I was determined to enjoy life where, and while I could. Someone would have looked after Charliene, *(with all that money, I was sure that someone would!)*.

But, not wishing to tempt fate, I am still here! My daughter is now 21, and I am not exactly feeling as though I will quark it any moment!

Again, not wanting to tempt fate - "so much for their for shortened life span - eh"!

Ed and his wife stayed around for a little bit longer, but then I think that the tensions of the situation got a bit terse. The implied accusation of his paying just a bit too much more attention to the problems he could see around me, rather than to her, made their visit uncomfortable for both parties. But I swear on a stack of bibles, that most uncharacteristically for me, there was absolutely nothing going on between Ed and I at that time, and I must confess that I was more than a little bemused by it all. I was kind of enjoying a relationship with Russ, this was well before his eviction from the house, and anyway - Ed was definitely 'out of bounds!'. He was married for heavens sake. Oh I realise that I had never let worry me to much before, had I? I must have grown up a bit by that time though!

So I said farewell to my first visitors, and once they had left, Russ and I were left alone at the house. Not too long after that, the drunken, eyebrow cracking episode I told you about before happened, and after that, I was all alone, except for my uninvited, but welcome tenant, Stan.

For a little while everything went along smoothly enough, but then Stan became a bit more than 'just a tenant', also as I wrote. Dianne and her husband had come and gone, and I was again alone. That is except for my precious little girl! and Josephine living next door, of course. *(Mustn't forget about Josephine!)*

I'm not too sure what I would have done without her. That long suffering lady was the only constant thing, in my then, ultra turbulent life!

I hadn't written to Ed for quite a while. I was pretty slack in those days. *(Come to think of it, I'm not that much better now!)* The last time had been about two months previous when I told him that I had a daughter, and that I had named her Charliene Peggy Ann, after my parents!

One bright and sunny day, my daughter, who although having just 'pooed her nappy, an occurrence that invariably tended to leave her upset, woke in a good, happy enough mood for a change, and I was looking forward to Josephine coming in to have coffee, and do the house work.

On that pleasant summer's day, I heard the postman's whistle, *(Remember when they used to whistle to let you know they had delivered the mail? Come to think of it, shouldn't admit to remembering that! Surely we are not that old, are we girls?).* It must have been about 10.00 o'clock in the morning, when on hearing that whistle, I casually waddled, *(which I still did a lot of in those days),* out to the mail box, and among some of the still all too frequent, statements from the solicitors, and the banks, and bills, *(mustn't forget the bills)* there was an airmail letter from Wales. My first thought had been - "Now - who do I know in Wales"? *(But I figured that the only way to find out who, was to open, and read the letter!)* Derrh!

Then I thought - "Hey hang on, wasn't that where Ed had written the last letter from"? I paused, and no longer rushed to read the letter - 'cause to tell the truth, it had been just a 'tad' unpleasant at the end of their last visit, and I wasn't really expecting to hear from him again. I immediately panicked! - "Don't tell me they are coming back again", and I thought? "I don't think that I could handle that at the moment"!

"Na –ah, that couldn't be, it's not that long since he left, and it is an expensive trip", I said to Charliene, who just watched my lips moving as she tried to poke me with her fingers. It was also definitely not like the Ed I knew, to be spending freely on plane trips like that. Maybe there was another reason for his writing. I picked Charliene up, and looked into her ginormous big brown eyes, and said. "Maybe it is just a polite answer to my letter telling them about you, Pickle". *(Goo, goo. Gah gah, she went, as she sat astride my hip, with my arm holding her none too securely. Two enormous brown eyes looked up at me trustingly, wondering what on earth I was saying?)*

I figured that the only way to find out why he had written, was to open the letter, and read it! Again -"Derrh"! Even allowing for the fact that I did at that time forget a lot of things, I don't think that I will ever forget the words that he had written. Maybe not the exact words, but definitely the intentions behind them.

(Unfortunately a copy of that letter got lost in amongst all the loose paper around the house. I was what could quite rightly be called, 'slack', not only about writing, but in keeping things, for a long time after the accident.) The letter said though - *(and as I said, maybe not in these exact words),* that he was surprised to hear about the baby, but that he knew that I had always wanted a child.

He wrote also that as he had said before, he had been very sad and cross about my accident and was sad for me too, about Russ and I breaking up, and of what had happened to Russ. He said that even though he hadn't thought that it would have worked for long with Russ, he was nevertheless still sad for me. He was though happy, that my own inclination to drink had passed; also thrilled for me, about the baby, and that it looked as though my world was finally coming together after the accident. He was though, a touch unhappy to hear that I was by myself, and that I was going to try to bring the child up alone. He said though, that if anyone could do it - he was pretty sure that I could. He also wrote, that unfortunately he and his missus had been divorced, almost as soon as they arrived back in England.

My chin just about hit the floor!

So he said - that as he didn't really like being alone, if I felt in need of someone who had always loved me and my courageous attitude - that if I would allow him to love me, and help with the bringing up of the child, then he was offering me his help, and his hand in marriage. *(When I think of it now, I say to myself - "oh yeah - what a sus reason for getting married? Doesn't like being alone - eh"? Just as well that wasn't the only reason then, wasn't it?)* But back then though, I couldn't believe it - I had always loved Ed!

(After nearly 20 years of marriage, I definitely DO believe it, and I am ecstatically happy that he chose me to keep him company!)

I pondered on the rightness of the prospective outcome, and then in the afternoon, completely forgetting about the eight hour time difference, I rang him, full of positive feelings about the whole thing! All he would have heard when he picked up the receiver, was a voice yelling Yes ! Yes ! Yes! - No "Hello - this is Kerri", or anything! *(I guess that I have always been a bit of a nutter!)*

Poor Ed! *(It's just as well it wasn't a wrong number. Can't you just imagine if it had been! [a wrong number that is]. The call answerer would*

347

have been even more confused than Ed was, and he was confused enough to last a lifetime!)

It took a few more seconds of pregnant pauses, before Ed must have eventually caught on as to who it was on the phone, and then he said - "Oh - hi there - *(pause)* Look, it's about 3am in the morning here. I can't talk at the moment, I'm still half asleep, and at this hour of the morning I think that I would like to stay that way. That's good by the way! - I'll call you back when I wake up!"

"OK", a dejected me said, "Sleep tight - talk to you later". I paced about all day, as nervous as heck. Was it still on? Was he still going to ring me - Did he really still want to marry me? Had he changed his mind?

Come on Kerri, why would he have in such a short time", I said to myself?

("Oh, why hadn't I checked the time there before I rang", I wailed to myself? "When was he going to ring? He will hate me now, for waking him up. Did he have my number"? And then I thought - "Of course he did, he'd taken it before he left last time!" Were my pushed aside dreams of long ago really about to come true?

I picked up the baby, and nuzzling her neck, I told her about this wonderful man, who was going to be her Daddy! She goo goo'ed', and gaa gaah'ed accordingly, and then I joyfully rang and told Josephine next door, worrying all the time that Ed might call, while I was on the phone. Josephine came in, and after her voicing her momentary concerns, she must have realised that as I was so thrilled about it, she, by rights, should also be over the moon for me. Or at least as over the moon as any practical Chinese lady can be! The phone rang later that afternoon, and it was him.

Even though he hadn't said more than hello, and definitely was nowhere to be seen, every bit of my blood rushed up to my face, and I blushed the most 'humongous' blush that you have ever seen. He, of course, couldn't see what kind of effect just the mere sound of his voice was having on me. *(Just as well! Well a girl shouldn't appear too anxious - now should she?)* He didn't need to know that I had had doubts during the day, and that I was frankly terrified all over again at the thought of commitment.

Was I ready for marriage again?

That inner voice from when I had been re - learning to walk, suddenly came back again -"Of course you are - you silly thing", it told me, in a most disgusted voice, "I really don't believe you", the voice said!

I inevitably wondered though, whether he had thought, *(something that I knew that my family and friends would warn me about)*, that "there is this lady who had been given all this money, who suddenly has a baby, and will need extra help. People said that he probably thought that I would provide a nice little nest egg". I laugh about that now. - I don't think that I have ever met a fairer, protect both me and the money kind of man, than my Ed. *(It is largely because of him, that my money has grown at all! Knowing me, I probably would have spent it all by now. Well alright, I possibly would have done at that time, but I think that he has taught me enough for me to be very careful with it from here on!)*

I guess that I worried about it for a while that afternoon, but then I wound up thinking, "well how stupid are you then"? "Isn't that exactly what Ed had been warning me about back at the court room? Why would he warn me, if he now intended to be one himself?

"He is suddenly alone, I am alone, and I am going to need a little more help than Josephine can give, to bring this baby up correctly", I said to myself!

Then my 'little girl excitement' took over. "Oooh! I can't believe it! I hope he wants to come over soon"! I couldn't wait! But I had too *(wait that was)*.

Again, I can't really remember how long after the call he arrived, but I don't think that it would have been much longer than a month, if it was that. All I do know is that my phone bill was astronomically high while we were apart. *(I was just soooo excited! He doesn't particularly like phones and things, and he wouldn't have spent the money from his end"!)*

Life went on though, while I waited. The baby goo gooed, and gaga'd some more, poohed her nappies after eating her 'luscious looking'(?) baby meals, that she had interspersed with her breast feeds. Typically for a small baby, she was more often wet than dry, with smelly nappies throughout the intervening time, but the day eventually came when after changing her, so that she was all sweet smelling again, she and I excitedly drove to the airport to meet Ed. *(at least I did the driving, she chirruped happily enough though in the back, in her special back to front, rear seat car seat, and anyway, I knew that I was excited!)* It had taken me till about four years after the accident, to gain enough courage to sit for, and pass first time, my driving test, so I had only been actually driving for about a year. But Charliene and I headed off to Kingsford Smith Airport, to meet the man who was to become the omnipotent, one and last 'love of my life'

So - *(where are we now?)* - Ed had flown over from England to Sydney; we had survived the excitement of that first meeting after such a long time apart; and that meeting was, by the way, indescribably, romantically wonderful. I recognised him straight away,and we stared into each other's eyes, with the electricity that flashed between us almost knocking me off my feet. After his meeting his white bonneted new stepdaughter, we all left the airport, and headed to my house in Monterey. Ed was a bit relieved that I had apparently sorted out the accounting problems that he had seen when he'd been there with his ex - wife, things like unattended bills etc., but there were still a few things that made him a little uneasy! *(As much as I love him to bits, I have to admit that I have found out, after nearly 20 years of marriage, that Ed doesn't appear to be really content, unless he has something to worry about! Sometimes I think that he actually looks for problems. But we soldier on, together!)*

Anyway - Ed had been with us for about a fortnight when he made it official, got down on one knee he did *(so regal, and formal!)*, and proposed to me in person, instead of by letter. I actually had the honour of selecting my own engagement ring, which is a little like a bunch of diamond grapes, and then Ed decided on the two bands that surround it.

we are going to make such a great family!

One band is my wedding ring, and the other was a bit like an early eternity ring. He also bought me another eternity ring, for our 15th wedding anniversary. It is two hands cradling a gold heart, with a silver crown sitting on the top of it. Beautiful! - so romantic. *(Am I a spoiled lady, or what?)*

Spring arrived along with my man, and we were to be married on my birth date – the 26th January. As I have already told you, my birthday is also Australia Day, so this little Australian found that that day in 1990 was truly a 'bonza' day.

So, against Eds normal disinclinations to party, the invitations went out again, but this time to an even wider mix of people. A lot of the entertainers were away working at that particular time of the year, it being around Australia Day. It was also smack bam in the midst of a busy time for shows, but there were more than enough showy's at the wedding, along with other friends from all the different arenas of our lives.

Family and friends! A great time was had by all! *(about 40 people, I think)* We actually got married in the house gazebo, beside the pool in the back yard, and Mr Caterer had once again built a wooden floor across the pool top. And, as with the Celebration of Life Party,

351

luckily no one fell through the floor. Even when people got a bit drunk, *again!*, as was only to be expected, and started to go to town with their dancing! It was a fantastic wedding, and with the photos that I have, I will never forget that monumental Australia Day, which wouldn't mean quite as much to me now that I am living in Britain, except that it is also my birthday, and more importantly, our anniversary. 20 years this January 2010. It definitely turned out to be a truly monumental occasion, especially since it preceded the most monumental decision *(and as it turns out, the most profitable one)* I had ever made!

signing my life away?

happy happy day!

my whole best childhood friend's family were there!

dancing by the door!

Ed, Di, me, mum, Garry Who, Roland Hastings!

Me Charli & Mum three generations.

Lyn, Sandy, Carol and Tutti Venuti!

Sharyn and Lynne

MONUMENTAL DECISION

Soon after we were married, I sat down with Ed, and much to his surprise, *(I think that he thought that he was doomed to stay in the house, [which I have since found out, he secretly thought of as an expensive, danger zone for both me and the baby], forever more,)* I said that I thought that we should maybe put the house up for sale, and head for England. He was 'gob smacked'! Where had that come from? Ed says that he definitely hadn't expected that! *"WHAT"*, says he to me? "I have just left there."!

"A new start is needed", I said, full of a young person's *(which, of course I wasn't)* enthusiasm! I explained where I was coming from, and how that although I now had a great husband, and a beautiful daughter, I felt that I could no longer really be a proper part of the showbiz world. And that although I still had a lot of showbiz friends, I felt that because I could no longer sing, and walked a bit like a waddling duck, I could no longer play a worthwhile part in show business. Oh sure, I could probably make some very useful donations, but I thought that I could do with a complete change. Show business friends told me that I probably could help in some way or other, but - in reality, could I? And what was more to the point - did they really mean it? *(As much as I hate to admit it, show business people were renowned for telling you what they thought you wanted to hear! I was even guilty of that myself in my show days!)*, and so I didn't really think so!

I couldn't sing - I couldn't even walk, or talk properly at the time - and it would have been very risky being on stage even if I could sing or speak! I didn't exactly look my normal, *(and this comment is probably going to make you smile)* 'good looking' self. I also felt that the then situation of loads of showbiz friends, would possibly be the wrong atmosphere in which to bring up my little girl. So we decided *(or, again, I did really!)* that it would be best to emigrate to England. Ed probably would have preferred France, but I was a chicken. I didn't want to have to re-learn that wonderful language.

I was having enough trouble making my English understandable in those days. Charliene probably would have learned it really quickly though - children always do learn new things fast, but I wanted her to first learn a language that I could help her with. Was that selfish? As it turns out now - it is just as well I maybe was! Those first few years in England were full of baby crèches, and getting myself re established in a completely alien town, and, what is more, where I was like no one else. Just imagine what it would have been like in a society where I couldn't have understood them, and they couldn't have understood me.

Then Charliene got to Primary school age. Lots of kid's parties ensued, where Ed was able to resurrect his creation from his entertainment days in Australia - 'Peeko', from "Peeko and Poppy". He was in his element, clowning about to amuse the kids.

We had apparently lucked into an alright situation!

Life is just too much LIKE FUN!

He soon became the towns' main singing and piano teacher. Charliene could be proud of her Dad, and his abilities, but I wanted to create a world in which Charliene could be proud of me as well, and not hear kind friends, saying things like "poor Kerri can't do this – or poor Kerri can't do that", as was said in Australia. I didn't want to be poor Kerri, especially since, technically I wasn't! My self worth had been crushed by the fact that I felt that I could no longer contribute to what had been my world before, and I needed to learn, firstly to like myself, and then to do something constructive with what I considered as, the 'half life' that I had been left with after the accident.

Back in Australia, England had handed me a life line, as the obvious place to go, *(Ed being English and all, and my being entitled to British citizenship because of my own dad)* and it was suppose to provide a springboard to just about anywhere in Europe. And do you know, it probably would have - except that - me being me and having developed, unusually for me, a profoundly non adventurous nature, we have stayed in Ashford Kent ever since getting here in 1990!

Ed didn't really fancy developing a 'map of the toilets' across Europe either, so I haven't exactly been full of anticipation to go anywhere. *(Although the toilet map book would probably have made a small fortune!)* So far we have been in two different houses, and now in 2009 are in our third, but it is still in Ashford. We actually bought it 20 years ago, have had it rented out while we lived in our other house, but have now gutted and redecorated it, and are very happily living in it ourselves, with the other house rented! So having arrived and been settled in Ashford, we then spent the next few years not doing very much, just getting used to the place. But then one day while dropping Charliene off at school, I was once again, bitten by the 'showbiz / gotta do something productive 'bug. Edmund had been Peeko at all of Charliene's parties, and I thought - "There just has to be some way for me to get on side with the children. "I mean to say", I cheekily said, reversing the old saying, "what is good for the gander, also has to be the right thing for the goose", doesn't it?

My showbiz determination was back temporarily, with a vengeance!

Charliene's school was crying out for volunteer Mums, to help with the kid's reading skills. "I can do that", says me, full of showbiz arrogance, completely forgetting about my 'different' husky voice! I had also forgotten all about my having an odd kind of waddle, and that I was technically very 'different' from the other 'normal' Mums! But did I care! Not on your Nelly! - "In for a penny, in for a pound"I say, again! *(Well at least, I can thank my Daddy for that saying, and I seem to have been using it since the day dot!)* I figured that having got my youthful wish for 'different' *(and might I risk saying again, "in bucket loads"),* I had to work out what exactly I was going to do with the 'different' life that I now had!

I knew that I had a strange voice, but I confidently said to Ed - "how about I practise at home over the next few weeks"? I can do a great *FE FI FO FUM*", I told him, laughing! So I used the Hall that had come with our second house, and that had a stage, and I did *(practice that is).* At the start of the new term at the school, I was in there reading to this little group of 1PS moppets, both in class and during their lunch breaks, portraying the fearsome, child munching ogre, and feeling as though I had, at last, found a way that I could maybe be useful again.

Charliene used to grin, because at that 'not self conscious age', her 'mummy' was not the embarrassment that I was to inadvertently become a few years later. Her mum was telling great stories to all her friends at school! And they were loving them!

(I felt alive again!)

What began as a group of children to whom I used to read in class, became at first, two or three of the same children coming in during their lunch time break with their sandwiches and things. Then it grew to five or six, and then just before the time I no longer did the 'readings' to the classes, and was doing other things in the school, there were about ten to twelve, from various classes, coming in especially for the lunchtime reading breaks. My showbiz determination was back, just in time, because the school wanted me to begin helping the children with their adding and subtraction!

So my long suffering husband and I, *(he quite willingly put his own important work to one side to help me - I think maybe that he loves me, don't you?!)* decided that as all children liked 'farm animals, *(at least we assumed so)* we devised a basic *(up to five)* counting board game.

Why only up to five times? Well there was me, with my shaking hands, working out ways of doing the illustrating. It just wasn't practical to think about paying to employ someone to draw for a game that basically was meant to give me something to get my teeth into, now was it? I would just have to learn how to draw them, or go without illustrations. I though, couldn't fit more than five of my drawn animals into the squares. They were just too big they were, weren't they?*(the animals not the squares, silly!)* The individual player's boards would have wound up far too large with any more of my drawn animals on them, and those there boards would have wound up bigger than the children themselves! Also, back when I first started, everything was still in twelve's and £'s shillings and pence, as the world hadn't yet become decimalised, so we would have needed a minimum 12 of my animals, which would truly have been a sight to be seen!

FARMYARD'©, *(the game Ed and I invented together)* was a complete success with the kids, and the second year Primary kids were bounding ahead with their counting and times tables, even if it was only up to five! Ed went back to his neglected work with even more than his usual amount of vigour, and I set about inventing a series of slightly more grown up games for the upper second, and third class children. I became Granny Kiddles *(one of my husband's book characters)* in reality, and over the following 3 or 4 years, she became very well established at the school, and with the kids. Now whether it was because of the colourful, 'different' outfit that Granny Kiddles wore, the especially invented maths games themselves, or the sense of fun, I didn't really care.

I used to set of down the street like this!

The kids were happily learning what could have been a real chore. I set about devising other games to help even further with their learning, so 'Hot Potato'© , and 'It's The Same As' (ITSA)© were born, and surprise, surprise, they were both really successful with the children as well. They were also, of course, a bit easier for me, because hey only needed one or two animals, or a witch's hat, or just one enormous 'Hot Potato' on each card. The aim of all the games, in order to win, was to be the player with as many cards as possible in your own collected pile of correct answers, and because the world had gone 'decimal' by the end of my time at the school, the children's job *(as well as mine as illustrator)* was made a little bit easier, in that they now only needed to have learnt all their tables, *both ways* to 10, instead of 12. 20 tables in all. *(Some of the more able students though, even learnt their 11x and 12x tables as well.)* That may of course, have been because they had an 'old fashioned' teacher? - Do you think?

362

They won prizes, of specially made *(by me, on my trusty computer)* certificates, and book marks.

What a success! I even had local newspaper coverage.

KENTISH EXPRESS

MIKE BENNETT'S NOTEBOOK

Thursday July 28, 2005. (K)

with Mike Bennett

WINNING FORMULA : Competition makes lessons fun for youngsters

Innovative board game is perfect learning tool

INNOVATION is essential in schools if they are to comply with Government policy on numeracy, but few can match the methods bringing success to St Mary's Primary in Barrow Hill, Ashford.

Mental arithmetic is now part of the fun for pupils in the inter-class championships for a board game invented by volunteer learning support assistant Kerri Keen.

Her Granny Kiddles Farmyard maths game, launched five years ago, is now so popular that youngsters are regularly swotting up their times tables in the playground in an effort to win matches.

Backed by head Sue Parkin, competition has been fierce since back in April to decide the heat winners who have been earning bookmark prizes for learning tables correctly.

Last week they held the final with Mathias Trilbach beating Richard Aryee in a good-natured contest.

Mrs Keen said: "All the teachers and pupils involved must be thanked. My fun game is based on the farmyard and encourages youngsters to learn their basic tables in the old fashioned way which they enjoy reciting.

Australian-born Mrs Keen from Hardinge Road,

Ashford, a former singer who has been disabled since a horrific car crash, concentrates on inventing learning aids for children.

■ Granny Kiddles (Kerri Keen) shows her new game to St Mary's School Year 3 pupils
Picture Dave Downey
pd852548

Ooh, I used to love seeing them learn!

MUM TAXI - (BUT NOT AFTER DARK!)

Life got rather hectic for a while from when Charliene had passed her 11plus, and when she progressed to Highworth Grammar School, suddenly needing to be taken here and there more often. *(Boyfriends, and sleepovers with girlfriends and all that.)*

Unfortunately she had to go places with her friend's mothers and fathers doing some of the driving, because it involved driving at night, and as much as it galls me, even now, I am still unable to drive in unfamiliar areas once it becomes dark. Papa doesn't feel confident enough at night either. Both of us are getting on you know, he more than me, and I didn't want to be responsible for multiple deaths! Too horrible, and then - what is more – even in 2009, I still have a habit of getting lost!

(I got lost today, going to my best friend, Alison's place. I had been there a hundred times from our Hardinge Road house, but do you think that I could find the way from the new Queen Street address? The houses are only 10–12 minutes apart, but I was on the road for 40 minutes before, shelving my pride - I called Ali on my mobile telephone, to rescue me, and maybe give me directions from where I was! Completely lost, wasn't I?)

Back in 2007 though, I didn't really matter quite so much, 'cause Charliene had reached the real boyfriend stage, and he drove her about. *(After all - did you want your Mum about when you were 18 and a bit, and 20? Now of course, she's at UNI, so I don't have to take her anywhere. She has become independent, and I struggle sometimes to be allowed to pay for her train fares and things.)*

But, again, back when Charliene was almost a teenager *(about 11 or 12)*, she had passed her 11 plus with honours, and I knew I had done an alright kind of job up to then, so I decided that I should further my own computer studies, and help out with Eds business as much as I could, *(which wasn't necessarily all that much, I might add!)* But I got stuck into all the clerical and computer work, and did any necessary photo copying for his business. Because I grew to positively love using the computer, and it was going to simplify my life in so many ways, late in 2006, I had called in a young gentleman from Geek Computers - Brent.

Basically, firstly I just asked him to help me put the VHS videos of my performing days, onto DVD's. Had to stay 'with it', now didn't I? *(Not really - I just wanted to make sure the memories would be safely saved. They ran the risk of disintegrating! Some of them were nearly 40 years old!)*

On seeing the videos, and on hearing the story, Brent said that it was a story that should be told - 'Triumph over adversity', 'inspirational and motivational', and all that 'kind of' promotion type stuff. So we have spent a day a week, since the middle of 2007, barring holidays, Christmas, personal things etc., putting together a documentary about my life. It is taking time, over a year and a bit so far, nearly two, because we are both working in a semi dark world. Although Brent knows a lot more about the computer side of things than me, it is a case of learning on the job with this documentary, and things still keep going awry, but we were almost there in the middle of 2009! Now in 2010 we have finally got it finished! What we are going to do with it, still has to be decided. I had actually only started re writing, and editing my autobiography just before he began the documentary, and when we began work on it together, it kind of put a cracker under my 'bum', and impelled me to get on with writing the book.

So I have been kept busy doing that! And if you have read this far, then you are probably among the first to experience the results of my efforts! I kind of keep slowing progress a little, too, which some would again say, is typical of me. One day, back in 2006, around my birthday and anniversary time, I told Ed that I was feeling a bit down.

"Why", says he?

"Well - people come into your studio, not being able to string more than five notes together, and they leave being able to sing a whole song", says me! I think that I can string at least six notes together, maybe not too well, but I want to try.

"Why can't I try", I bawled?

We talked, and talked about it needing a lot of hard work, and that the work might create times of major disappointment for me, if the voice decided not to come back at all. I may not have been prepared for the heartache that trying might cause. *(He really does love me loads, and doesn't want me to be hurt!)* Especially if I achieved a resultant sound that was not what I had expected. *(I'm still not sure if Ed was worried about my heartache if I found that I wasn't able to sing properly again, or his own, for me.)* But he found out, that just as Andy *(remember him?)*, had correctly voiced all that while ago. I was a bit of a stubborn bugger, and I had wanted to give it a go!

So Ed begrudgingly said that if I really wanted to - then we owed it to my 'stubborn bugger' gene, to at least *give it a try*! He told me that if I was prepared to put in the hard yards, then we had best double check with an ears, nose, and throat doctor as to the advisability of it, and that we would take it from there. So an appointment was made!

Dr Brown, the ears nose and throat specialist, he looked at my vocal chords and ummed and aared. His next words made me laugh out loud! He was another really nice, 'with it' kind of doctor. He told me "one chord, the one on the right, is all fit, looking very healthy, with muscles ready for just about anything, and up for whatever I wanted to throw at it within reason. Just needs a little bit of 'weight training'" he said. "The other one though now, well that one is looking a little tired, and possibly a teensy bit 'sick'" he said. "With careful and controlled practise though, it could possibly be realigned with the other one. No real reason why not", he added! Ed smiled!

"Good, that is all we needed to know", said Ed. "We will start with some gentle workouts." So midway in 2006, that is what we started.

A Gym in my throat! *(We worked at realigning the chords, I mean!)*

Well - the whole kafuffle has definitely been more hard work than I ever believed possible, and I am still at it in 2008/9/10. And I had thought that learning to walk again had been hard enough to conquer! This is proving to be the most monumental task that I have ever set for myself. I didn't then, and I don't even now, like to fail and I fortunately, or unfortunately, *still* have my 'not wanting to fail', persistent gremlins!

I guess that there would be just too many people who would hurt, if I failed, so I am not allowed to. *(Fail, that is!)*

My family were making plans for my brother's 60th Birthday, to be held in Noosa (Australia) in the July of 2007. So in about January I figured that I had better get 'down to some even harder work' if I was going to be able to sing Happy Birthday for him. And I did it, I sang Happy Birthday at his party. I am pretty sure that I didn't do it as well as I like to think sometimes, but I think I did alright! You'd probably have to check with them, but then they wouldn't say that it wasn't any good, anyway. Would they? They knew where the voice had come from. Oblivion - to 'not too bad'! Nobody really knew how stoked I was about it, although I think that they subliminally probably guessed how monumental an achievement it was for me. That achievement however, boosted my confidence to do something that I had been secretly training hard for, for a couple of months - Sing at an ALVA luncheon, to my former peers! *(I did it, but it wasn't necessarily mind blowing. They were evidently thrilled at how much I had managed to recover at all! Even if it takes me longer than I initially allowed for though - I am determined to conquer!)* Just where I will get too, is in the hands of the Gods, and just as the results with my walking have not yet reached the point of perfection, *(and probably never will - reach perfection that is),* nor has my singing. Both things will probably always leave room for improvement! But I can walk, and I will sing!

It's the 'properly', that is now the golden ring, and catching that is going to take me a bit of time, if ever! I have a feeling though, that with all the associated problems aside, like overcoming my innate, recently reinstated laziness, I will probably need to continue working on it *(my voice, that is),* for the rest of my life. If for no other reason, than that, as Ed says, "it keeps you fit, and it also keeps your brain alive". *(Or, as it is in my case - it may just keep my half a brain alive! Ha ha!)*

Again, going back a bit when I did all that Granny Kiddles' stuff, the computer that I had done it all on, was a bit like a box from hell, but I have since been diligently endeavouring to master something that I had tentatively begun way back in Australia, some 30 years ago, and it seems that the more I learn how to do, the more extra things that I find I need to learn. I have been working on that with Brent my Computer

Geek, as well as the documentary! With a family of only three, we have somehow managed to have had about five different computers including the original one, that I so lovingly brought with me from Australia, *(unfortunately it has since died and gone to the computer heaven/scrap yard!)*.

What began just as a means of providing an easier way for me to put my thoughts on paper, has turned into a major learning curve for me, and the family, and maybe the start of a whole new business for Ed and I, while Charliene goes to University. Of course Charliene got the hang of it much faster than us, but then I suppose that is probably because she is of the computer generation. I must admit though that for *this oldie* - it is a lot of FUN! - Most of the time anyway!

2008-2010 - NEW FRIENDS - ALISON and LYNNE and a NEW and 'DIFFERENT' third life!

2008 had been a year of achievements for me, thanks to some good fortune, personal acceptance of my state after the accident, as well as determination "not to let the bastards grind me down".. *(Sorry! - A good old Aussie saying?)*

For me it was a good year and a bit!

They may have been small achievements by some peoples standards, but they have been monumental ones for me. I just goes to show what can be achieved b sticking at something long enough.

I sang Happy Birthday to my brother, as well as singing two songs, and giving a speech at an ALVA function, and I am continuing the correct vocal practice so that eventually I will be able to do something more constructive with the singing. One day in the future - not too distant, I hope - I will probably be able to sing properly, and not need to make excuses for any resultant sound.

'This here book' which has taken me a solid year and a half's work to finish, after nearly 22 years of putting my thoughts on bits and scraps of paper and card, is — apart from having been a testament to perseverance and sheer pigheadedness, hopefully also going to provide a way of my paying ALVA back for all it's good and hard work for showbiz's members, and for me over the last 30 years!

As one of the songs I used to sing in my shows says -
"Everything is coming up roses"!

"And it certainly is Ollie", as Stan Laurel used to say to Oliver Hardy!

But -I think that I warned you that this story was a bit of a maze - so here we are again, in this final chapter, going right back to where this half of the story began - when I first came to England, and when my daughter was at St Mary's Primary school. There were lots of other mothers for me to be friendly with. The trick was to find people who didn't mind if you were 'different'. I was fortunate enough to have one friendship that lasted right up to Charliene's high school days, and fortunate enough to have made another good mate when Charliene was at High school. Alison *(Ali)* has a daughter with whom Charliene was best friends all through Primary School – Laurie, and when Charliene went to High worth Grammar for Girls, which was very near where we lived, Laurie went to Tenterden School *(a Co-ed school)*, which was near where she lived. Both are excellent schools, providing the best in education, leading to both girls coming through their A levels with marks good enough to give them both a really good start in life. The world is now at their feet!

Laurie went to Canterbury College, studying to be a teacher, as well as doing childhood studies. Charliene who was accepted at London School of Economics, but then decided to take a gap year, and work for a while to save some money before seriously thinking about going to UNI. When she gets to see Emma, she is still busy cementing what is probably her strongest friendship overall. So Emma's mother Lynne, is my other best friend!

That one gap year that Charliene took has turned into two, and as a mother, I am gutted, but it *is* her life we are talking about here, and now thankfully, she has just in **2009**, reapplied and been re accepted to LSE. So this time - LSE is where she has gone to. She leaves this Sunday, and when she goes she will have done something that I sometimes regret never having done. But then, I suppose that I went to the University of life, travelled, and had FUN! And as you no doubt know by now – **I do like FUN!**

For me, my talents, and my time in Australia, I think it was the right decision!

I was fortunate enough to have an abundance of acquaintances when singing, and a few really good friends, from before I became disabled, and some of them have remained good friends ever since, I obviously though, don't actually see a lot of them these days, and I have not necessarily been as good a friend as I maybe should have been. Not as far as keeping in touch is concerned, anyway. Although if they are on skype, it is easier!

I am though, just so super lucky to have found two ladies here in England, who having lived with my disability in evidence; have either never noticed, or if they have, were not affected by it. *(Probably the second, because it would be just a bit difficult to not notice my funny walk, and my still, 'different' voice).* Some people cope better with disability than others do!

Oh how I do wish though, that *I* wasn't! - *(effected by it I mean!)* Not other people's either! - Just mine!

I continually make excuses for what I see as my deficiencies.

But still - I would have to say that although the last nearly 30 years have been a time of loss *(of a career, and lifestyle);* a time of acceptance and adaptation, along with the associated sadness; they have also been years of incredible joy and happiness.

If you are open to change, which I have been forced to become, and eager to 'muck in', then life in your own sometimes 'different' Corner of the Sky', generally has a compensatory UP for each dismal DOWN.

THE GRANTING OF A CHILDHOOD WISH!

I now feel good, and you can too!

I know that it sometimes seems difficult to do, but try to put your personal angst to one side! Everyone should know that life plods along, sometimes ecstatically happily, sometimes not, and I guess that after all this time, and after everything that has happened in each of our worlds, we are back to the 'half full - half empty', scenario of life.

Do I hear you ask again - "and that is"?

Well now – from a personal point of view, I think now, that I can most definitely look upon my life as definitely being a half full glass, and not, as some would have me look on it as - a half empty one.

Oh sure – things are often there to be won or lost, but again if I may, talking personally I have also found some other elements of life that I would never have known about if it hadn't been for my vocal loss, and my disability. I am not saying that all disabled people feel this way, but most that I have met, *(and I must admit that I have met me quite a few in my 30 years of disability)* feel the same way!

Have you ever noticed the happy faces of so many of them, even when they sometimes suffer far more severely than you or I may!

So make the most out of your life!

Take your 'half full glass' and fill it right up to the brim with friendship, happiness and compassion for others! This world is abundantly full of interesting facets, and I feel that having been miraculously given back my chance to experience them, it is now up to me to truly *fill up the other half* of my half full glass.

I need to fill it up with an equally challenging *('cause I have always liked bit of a challenge!)*, interesting, and enjoyably fun life. One that offers encouragement and hope to those who may need it!

Aw, come on now! You don't need to be a Sister Angelica, or a Mother Superior.

Just be kind, thoughtful, and considerate of other people's feelings!

Nowadays, in ***2009/2010***, I feel that I am an everyday, 'normal' kind of 'wobbly' woman, and I would have to cheerfully say now though, that I have well and truly had my childhood wish granted!

Popular thought says that you are only live once, and then you 'quark' it! - finished - 'kaput'! But there is also a 'Bond' song that says that you - 'only live twice'.

I feel though *(and this may rile the more traditional of you)*, that it is almost as if I have actually lived three lives. Three lives? But how can that be?

Alright - let's do my 'thing' one last time, and have a look back at the wonders of 'My own Corner of the Sky' shall we? Let's have a good look at the **UPS AND DOWNS OF LIFE!**

My **1st life** - Was a wonderful *(if traumatic)* childhood, with amazingly 'different' parents, and young 'up for a great time' street mate friends.

That was the first definite **UP**

I also very fortunately had a very 'different' **2nd life** as an entertainer, travelling the world, seeing fantastic sights, performing in the Sydney Opera House, Australia and enjoying the spreading of pleasure all about me, through my lovely *(so they tell me)* singing voice. As I said before - **UP, UP**

Then came the catastrophic accident, the termination of life for a while, the hospitalisation, and personal adaptation to a new kind of existence. **DOWN/UP!**

And then I have come to my **3rd** life at the ripe old age 56! *(Technically, I'm not even supposed to be here am I?)* And fortunately, it too still *(at nearly 60)* looks like it is going to be an **UP!**

My Corner of the Sky may not always have been nice maybe, but it has definitely been 'different', and with lots of **UPS and DOWNS!**

(Hopefully again in this **3**rd **life** though, there will also be more **Ups** than **Downs, and my Corner of the sky** will be full of rainbows and sunshine!!)

My wonderful husband took an ex-singer *(true - one that he already knew inside out),* but one who suddenly could no longer string two 'in tune' notes together, and he has enabled me to actually SING! Maybe not all that well yet! But you know how you can feel when something is happening inside your head and body? Well that's where I am at at the moment! *(I can at least string half a song and some 'in tune' notes together, anyway! Ha ha!)*

No joking though, it may be nothing like I sang before, but as it should be with anyone that really wants something, "I am not finished yet"! And having an 'in tune' voice, has shown itself to no longer be such an 'impossible dream!

Smile! Grin BIG! And - Snaffle life, full of verve and zest, and with that special love of life!

Come on people! Why don't you grab life by the throat, and shake it in the same way that I shook that cheeky, flea ridden monkey, on my trip of a lifetime, and shake, and shake 'till it spits out the 'different' life you want.

The life that you that you feel that you want, and deserve!

Remember - It may not always seem like it, but life really is there for the taking!

Your own life deserves to be faced, full of confidence, and determination!

Cheers to you all, and may life treat you as well as it has eventually treated me.

Don't panic! - I really am through now - so let's all sing at the top of our voices - **Gotta find My Corner of the Sky!!!!!!**

LOVE CONQUERS ALL!

Twenty years of Magic! Ages 59 and 76 - Young love?

SPARE PHOTOS

**The Monterey lounge room made for a great Christening party –
lots of friends!**

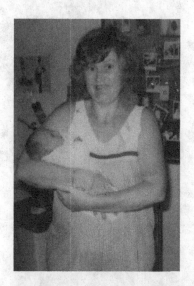

not long out of hospital

learning to stand and walk

my little pickle playing princess

Me receiving my founder member certificate on ALVA's 30th **Birthday 2009!**